ARISTOTLE'S
RHETORIC

ARISTOTLE'S
RHETORIC

AN ART OF CHARACTER

EUGENE GARVER

THE UNIVERSITY OF CHICAGO PRESS
CHICAGO AND LONDON

EUGENE GARVER holds the McNeely Chair in Thinking at Saint John's University and is the author of *Machiavelli and the History of Prudence*.

The University of Chicago Press, Chicago 60637
The University of Chicago Press, Ltd., London
© 1994 by The University of Chicago
All rights reserved. Published 1994
Printed in the United States of America
03 02 01 00 99 98 97 96 95 94   1 2 3 4 5
ISBN: 0-226-28424-7   (cloth)
       0-226-28425-5   (paper)

Library of Congress Cataloging-in-Publication Data

Garver, Eugene.
    Aristotle's Rhetoric : an art of character / Eugene Garver.
       p.   cm.
    Includes bibliographical references and index.
    (paper : alk. paper)
       1. Aristotle. Rhetoric.   I. Title.
    PN173.G37 1994
    808.2—dc20   94-25989
                                                                    CIP

⊗ The paper used in this publication meets the minimum requirements of the American National Standard for Information Sciences—Permanence of Paper for Printed Library Materials, ANSI Z39.48-1984.

To Charles Wegener

πίστεις γάρ τοι ὁμῶς καὶ ἀπιστίαι ὤλεσαν ἄνδρας
—Hesiod, *Works and Days*

CONTENTS

ACKNOWLEDGMENTS

One of the many pleasures of completing a long-term project like this comes from the chance to thank in public the many people who helped along the way. I began worrying about and discussing the *Rhetoric* when I was a graduate student at the University of Chicago's Committee for the Analysis of Ideas and the Study of Methods. Those conversations from long ago with Wayne Booth, Richard McKeon, David Smigelskis, Charles Wegener, and Warner Wick showed me what I was interested in.

Some of the preliminary work that became this book was carried out with the help of a National Endowment for the Humanities summer stipend, and some more grew out of two NEH summer seminars that I directed, one for high school teachers on the *Rhetoric* and Kenneth Burke's *Grammar of Motives* and the other for college teachers on Aristotle for the nonspecialist. I am grateful to those audiences and to NEH. Much more recently, the Classics and Speech Communication Departments at the University of Washington gave me the opportunity to teach a draft of this book as a graduate seminar on Aristotle's *Rhetoric*. The students and faculty, especially Michael Halleran, John Campbell, and Mary Whitlock Blundell, helped a great deal. Alasdair MacIntyre, Jon Moline, Amélie Rorty, and Michael Stocker were persistent writers of letters of recommendation. I hope that it is evident that I learned from their work as well.

Some preliminary results of my investigations were published in "Aristotle's *Rhetoric* As a Work of Philosophy," *Philosophy and Rhetoric* 19 (1986): 1–22; "The Human Function and Aristotle's Art of Rhetoric," *History of Philosophy Quarterly* 6 (1989): 133–46; and "Aristotle's *Rhetoric* on Unintentionally Hitting the Principles of the Sciences," *Rhetorica* 6 (1989): 381-93. Only the most careful reader could find traces of those papers in the first three chapters of this book. Different parts of the first two chapters were also read at Drake University, Stanford University, and the University of Toledo.

Earlier versions of "Deliberative Rationality and the Emotions" (here Chapter 4) were delivered at Boston College, Brooklyn College, the University of Chicago, the University of Nevada, Las Vegas, the University of

Washington, and at the American Philosophical Association. I profited from criticisms by Jonathan Adler, Mary Whitlock Blundell, Alasdair MacIntyre, Wendy Olmsted, Henry Richardson, Amélie Rorty, David Smigelskis, Michael Stocker, and Charles Wegener.

"Making Discourse Ethical" (Chapter 6) has a similarly checkered history. One version was read at the 1988 meeting of the International Association for Philosophy and Literature at the University of Notre Dame, at which Don Bialostosky and Don Marshall had particularly provocative things to say in response. Participants in my 1988 NEH summer institute on Aristotle for the nonspecialist suffered through a further revision. A third draft was delivered at Boston College, and eventually published as "Making Discourse Ethical: The Lessons of Aristotle's *Rhetoric*," in John Cleary, ed., *Proceedings of the Boston Area Colloquium in Ancient Philosophy*, vol. 5 (University Press of America, 1990). Betty Belfiore, Ken Casey, John Cleary, Charles Griswold, Michael Leff, Deborah Modrak, Wendy Olmsted, Amélie Rorty, Charles Young, and an anonymous reader for the Boston Area Colloquium all offered comments that improved the argument and clarity of this paper.

"How to Tell the Rhetorician from the Sophist, and Which One to Bet On" (Chapter 7) was delivered twice, for the Speech Communication Association and for the Society for Ancient Greek Philosophy, meeting jointly with the American Philological Association. Audiences at the University of Iowa and Ohio State University got to hear versions of "Why Reasoning Persuades" (Chapter 5). Don McCloskey, Don Ochs, Michael Stocker, and Laurence Thomas gave useful comments on that chapter.

Many colleagues read many drafts of the different chapters of the book with patience and helpfulness. In addition to those already cited, Tom Conley, Ed Halper, David Keyt, and anonymous reviewers for this press and several journals made especially useful and detailed comments. But I need to single out Jonathan Adler, David Depew, and Charles Young for their persistence and energy in working through various versions over the years. I feel very lucky to have had such diverse and complementary readers and friends.

Back when I was a graduate student I realized how much I owed to Charles Wegener. Looking back on my career thus far, I am still aware of the magnitude of my debt. He is truly one to whom nothing human is alien. I deferred acknowledging him before, because I wished to dedicate my first book to my wife, Jane Bennett. I here resist the temptation to dedicate this one to my son, Leo, for letting me take time out from batting practice to finish the manuscript, or to my parents, to whom I owe everything. I am happy to be able to dedicate this book to my teacher, Charles Wegener.

ARISTOTLE'S
RHETORIC

INTRODUCTION

ARISTOTLE'S *RHETORIC* AND THE PROFESSIONALIZATION OF VIRTUE

This work is the first book-length philosophic treatment of Aristotle's *Rhetoric* in English in this century. I know that the claim sounds immodest, but I mean something quite precise by it. To call it philosophic is to insist, first of all, that the *Rhetoric* be read as a piece of philosophic inquiry, and judged by philosophic standards. Certainly, many others have used the *Rhetoric* to illuminate the *Ethics, Poetics,* or his logical writings, but no one has yet presented a reading of the *Rhetoric* as a philosophic work with its own integrity, and its own philosophic interest.[1] To call my reading philosophic is to say that I read the *Rhetoric* in the hopes of learning something about contemporary philosophic issues. I hope that by the end of the book the reader will be persuaded that my claim is not over blown.

Calling this the first book-length philosophic treatment of the *Rhetoric* is also to insist on reading the *Rhetoric* as a work of Aristotle's, in the light of the rest of his work. My method is the opposite of the one Gerald Else recommends for the *Poetics,* when he says that the reader has to "interpret it on its own terms, without reference to other Aristotelian writings" and the one that Jakob Wisse similarly has recently applied to the *Rhetoric* when he "emphatically refrain[s] from using the rest of the Aristotelian Corpus in interpreting the *Rhetoric.*"[2] Unlike the rest of Aristotle's works, the *Rhetoric* and the *Poetics* have often been treated in isolation in this way. They were first published, for example, not with the rest of Aristotle's corpus, but in the collection *Rhetores Graeci.* These two books have histories of their own, apart from the history of the rest of Aristotle. I would like to make that methodological tradition less appealing by offering an alternative.

If Aristotle's *Rhetoric* did not exist, it would be hard to argue that the history of philosophy would be any different, since it has not figured in that history. The subject is outside the scope of my project, but it is worth noting that the history of rhetoric would not have been much different without

3

Aristotle's *Rhetoric* either, since its influence even there has been marginal—though if a classic can be considered an object of worship, the *Rhetoric* certainly has a place in the pantheon. Its impact, however, has been negligible. While "rhetoric" has recently become a more respectable and even popular subject, Aristotle's *Rhetoric* remains relatively untouched, despite its potential value to discussions concerning such subjects as hermeneutics, *phronesis,* and practical reason. The *Rhetoric* offers a rich articulation of the complexities of practical reason, one whose concrete, practical focus offers complications and insights beyond the brief remarks in the *Ethics* on which so much current discussion is based.

Consequently, I offer this book not as a contribution to a flourishing debate about a central work of philosophy, but as an argumentative presentation of an untapped resource. It is my hope that the study of the *Rhetoric* can transform the future career of discussions of *phronesis,* character, and argument.

Such a philosophic examination of the *Rhetoric* seems to me so timely that I am surprised it has not been done before. There has been a remarkable revival of interest in rhetoric recently and an equally significant revival of interest in Aristotle's practical philosophy as found in the *Ethics* and the *Politics.* But there has been little contact between those two movements. The revivals of rhetoric have come from a variety of sources: from hermeneutics, from the study of scientific revolutions, from arguments against epistemology and "foundationalism." The revivals of Aristotle's ethical and political philosophy, under names like "virtue-ethics" and "communitarianism," have attempted to tie together individual and community, reason and desire, reason and history.

Central to both revivals is the goal of articulating modes and standards of rationality not modeled automatically on a hypothetico–deductive picture of scientific reasoning. Reason, we are told, has to be connected with its purposes as well as its norms. Reason has to be tied to the actual, concrete thinking person, conceived as part of the speech situation or as the situated deliberating agent. Rhetoric in Aristotle has ties to, and is independent of, both logic and the virtues, and so one might think that it would be at the center of many contemporary projects: it offers a model of reasoning that is purposive and concrete, yet remains reasoning.

For some contemporary projects, the *Rhetoric* offers highly useful and provocative resources; for others, I think it might supply some timely cautions against too quick use of rhetoric to get what cannot be found in either logic or politics alone. Aristotle says that rhetoric is composed of analytical knowledge and of the ethical side of political knowledge (I.4.1359b9). The relation of rhetoric to its parents offers an opportunity for noticing useful and neglected connections. It affords the opportunity to ask whether practical reasoning has its own logic and whether logical relations can be transferred *tout court* into rhetorical situations. Similarly, it presents an opportunity to wonder whether the politician knows something other than what the rhetorician knows, or whether he or she does something different with the same knowledge. These relations between rhetoric, logic, and politics also provide grounds for refusing to assimilate rhetoric to either of its parents.

For just one example of Aristotle's *Rhetoric* as the missing connection between the rediscovery of rhetoric and the recovery of Aristotelian practical science, consider Hannah Arendt's emphasis in *The Human Condition* on the role of "speech" in the political life: "rhetoric" and Aristotle's *Rhetoric* are not mentioned. A similar absence characterizes Alasdair MacIntyre's exploration of an Aristotelian conception of "practices," and of the relation between practices and virtues, an exploration which I will use frequently in this book to help place my own investigations within the context of a better-known current project. Since rhetoric is a paradigm case of a practice that is not an ethical virtue, an analysis of the *Rhetoric* should deepen our understanding of what is involved in calling something a practice, and thus the relation between practices, arts, and virtues. Fuller consideration of the *Rhetoric* should put us in a better position either to advance or to criticize the projects in which Arendt and MacIntyre are engaged.

Everyone has to read the *Rhetoric,* or any classic text, against a background, implicit or explicit, of motivating problems. I find the *Rhetoric* of compelling interest not only because I think it enriches current discussions of rhetoric, practical reason, and the revived Aristotelian practical philosophy, but also because I want to develop more fully a project I call the "history of prudence." The good practical use of reason has a history. The Greek word for the power of good practical thinking is *phronēsis;* its Latin translation was *prudentia.* There is no simple and accurate English synonym, so I prefer just to use the word *prudence* and define it as the good practical use of reason. When I wrote *Machiavelli and the History of Prudence,* I chose for my epigraph Aristotle's remark (to which I will revert in the first chapter), at *Politics* I.7.1255b18–23, that "the term 'master' indicates not knowledge but a certain kind of person, and similarly also the terms 'slave' and 'freeman'."[3] That distinction, between being a certain kind of person and possessing knowledge, will be central to this study as well, because the *Rhetoric,* like Machiavelli's *The Prince,* is concerned with the prospect of taking a central political activity and seeing the extent to which it can be made into a craft or *technē.* I will try in the Conclusion, "Aristotle's *Rhetoric* and the History of Prudence," to situate these current discussions as part of the history of prudence.

This history of prudence is a history of ideas. It is possible to write other histories in which the actors are not ideas but the exemplary achievements of a Pericles or a Cesare Borgia, or causal forces such as the expulsion of Sicilian tyrants, the rise of Athenian democracy, or the corruption of the papacy and the rise of nation-states. But the history of prudence I want to trace is the development of ideas of practical reason. Much of that history is a story of shifting relations between practical reason and other forms of reason, especially technical reasoning or *technē*, and between practical reason and other desirable moral and political personal powers. Through time, the meanings of all these central terms—reason, craft, and character—shift. Current worries about the relation, for example, between craft values and moral values in discussions of professional ethics are one aspect of the history of prudence, as is Machiavelli's attempt to teach techniques for being a stable and glorious ruler. Aristotle's *Rhetoric* is another.

At several stages in the history of prudence, including Aristotle's *Rhetoric* and Machiavelli's *The Prince,* the relation between prudence and rhetoric has been a central concern, and it is my hope that it can be so again. Aristotle's formulation of the intellectual virtue called *phronēsis* is one especially important event in the history of prudence, important both for its own intellectual richness and for the ways it helped set a direction for the subsequent history of prudence. While the influence of the *Rhetoric* on subsequent understandings of *phronēsis* has been negligible, I offer it here as a resource for better understanding Aristotle's conception of *phronēsis,* the history of prudence, and what practical wisdom for today could look like. It will consequently be important to bear in mind both the specific meanings Aristotle gives to his key terms, such as *technē, phronēsis, aretē, logos,* and *ēthos,* and to the connections between those technical senses and the same things prior to their technical specification—art or craft, prudence or practical wisdom, virtue, reason, and character.

My title, *Aristotle's "Rhetoric": An Art of Character,* is meant to signal the way his practical, civic art of rhetoric lies between the activities of practical reason, for which moral character is enough, and instrumental activities that can be bought, sold, and taught. Such location makes an examination of rhetoric important for understanding practical reason, and for understanding the relations of the virtues of character to arts and to practical success. In the *Ethics* Aristotle defines *phronēsis* through its relations to the virtues of character and through its contrasts to art; the *Rhetoric* looks at that triangulation between *phronēsis, technē,* and the moral virtues with different preoccupations in mind.

The central question that makes the *Rhetoric* of compelling interest is whether there can be a civic art of rhetoric, and, if so, how such a civic art can negotiate a place for itself alongside professional arts, on the one hand,

and ethical and political activities that are matters of virtue, not art, on the other. Making policy decisions and legal judgments, giving advice, persuading others about matters of policy and law, these are all essential political activities. To perform them is to be a citizen; someone who does not engage in these things is not a citizen, and no one but a citizen does them. Aristotle wants to show how the activities that are central to citizenship and human well-being can be subject to rational analysis and to presentation as an art. A civic art of rhetoric combines the almost incompatible properties of craft and appropriateness to citizens. Reading the *Rhetoric* against the background of the rest of Aristotle's work makes these questions difficult and urgent.

It is easy to see what a professional rhetorical art would be. It is hard to see how something can be an art without becoming a specialty for experts and therefore being for sale, exchange, or rent. A professional art of rhetoric, like any power, proves opposites, while civic activities are oriented toward the good. If civic activities are oriented toward good ends, then must not their artful treatment necessarily be a debasing? Civic activities seem too noble to be subject to artistic standards. How can Aristotle's admonition—"the orator should have the power to convince about *(peithein)* opposites, as in syllogisms . . . not that we should do both (for one ought not to convince people to do wrong), but that we will not miss the way things really are" (I.1.1355a29-32)—be any more than the wishful thinking it is in most rhetorics?

This book is almost entirely an analysis of Aristotle's own arguments. It contains virtually no examination of the *Rhetoric's* historical context. I think it could help at this point in posing the question of a civic art to imagine a narrative in which combining artful intelligence with civic activities becomes a problem with practical political urgency. Picture, then, a supposedly traditional society, in which all individuals know their station and its duties, in which it is clear without argument who is good and what goodness requires in particular situations. The right performance of central civic activities is a matter of birth, of habit, and of education through imitating one's elders or betters. Imagine the shock felt when some outsider, either a foreigner or someone from a lower class, claims to be able to do as well or better than someone with a traditional education and family history at just those activities the society most values. Art—*technē*, teachable techniques for success—is a threat to the established order because it offers equal opportunity, focusing on performance instead of provenance.

Something like that story has often been told, starting with Plato, to describe the political history of the sophists and their introduction of rhetoric. Rhetoric is a liberating force in the hands of democratic politicians, fighting against the irrationalities of entrenched privilege. I tell the story in abstract terms because I want to make it clear that there is no necessary correlation between the partisans of the rhetorical art and the insurgent democrats. Anti-intellectualism, to state the obvious, has just as frequently been deployed as a democratic force to overthrow an existing order based on professional qualifications in the name of the right values or inner voices. There can be "establishments" of intelligence as well as character. Art and knowledge can be the grounds for excluding outsiders, as well as grounds outsiders may use for getting inside.

Aristotle tells neither of these stories, and I find no such narrative, or any competing narrative, implicit in his account either. I think he has no background narrative because he takes seriously the idea that rhetoric proves opposites, and that any art lacks an end of its own and must be deployed for purposes outside itself. If so, then there is no necessary connection between technological advance and any particular political consequences. It is for this reason that I think my analysis of the *Rhetoric* can afford to ignore its historical context. The relation between civic activities and artistic methods can take many forms, but the relation between intelligence and character is at the heart of all of them. It is that relation that is the focus of my analysis. I will argue in the first chapter that the relation Aristotle develops between intelligence and character is fully intelligible only in the specific political context of the polis.

The *Rhetoric* shows how persuasive speech and good practical reasoning integrate intelligence and character, and it does not pursue the background assumptions that make such integration possible. The relations between intelligence, especially as formulated in art, and character, in its various manifestations, are the subject of this book, and so I set aside those further questions about the relation between intelligence, character, and an additional factor, eloquence, that become central in Book III of the *Rhetoric*.

Everybody wants thought and character to go together. After all, good intentions often can cause trouble through lack of foresight. And the purely intellectual bureaucratic rationality that tries to eliminate ethical and emotional considerations is equally frightening. The idea that individual judgment, experience, and wisdom could be replaced by an impersonal decision procedure horrifies most people. We find comfort instead in an ethical ideal that makes intelligence and character coexist. People like to think that in a fair fight truth will win over lies and falsehoods, and that intelligence enriches rather than corrupts our moral lives. Aristotle is on the side of the angels on all these issues. But the integration of thought and character in an art of practical reason is difficult to achieve. Aristotle earns the right to say that they can be integrated. The rest of us usually say so without the right.

My examination of the *Rhetoric* looks very different from the *Rhetoric* itself. I find the *Rhetoric* a strikingly unreflective work. It offers material for reflection, but is itself silent on what I find critical questions. What John

Burnet alleges for Aristotle's work in general is nowhere more true than it is for the *Rhetoric*: "There is hardly any philosopher but Aristotle of whom it is so true to say that he is hard to interpret just because he insists on discussing all the side issues of not very fundamental points, while what strike us as the real problems are dismissed in an oracular sentence."[4]

I think that there is a simple substantive explanation for the frustration all of us feel with Aristotle and which Burnet captures, beyond such obvious causes as the nature of Aristotle's texts as lecture notes not intended for publication, and the subsequent history of their editing, transmission, and corruption. Where we want Aristotle to produce a measured, careful case he is casual, and he labors points contemporary readers are willing to grant easily. Aristotle is confident that when nature produces a problem, she also provides the materials for a solution, and in particular he has confidence in the naturalness of the polis. This confidence masks what from the outside— where we stand—looks like a series of terrible contingencies concerning, in this case, the virtues and crafts, and rhetoric in particular. Aristotle does not need to reflect on things that are critical philosophic questions to us. In the exposition that follows I want to stress these elements of contingency in questioning the claims and inferences that Aristotle seems to think we should accept easily.

The *Rhetoric* thus raises crucial philosophical questions for us that Aristotle himself thought simple. Alasdair MacIntyre expresses the basic problem for rhetoric and the history of prudence this way: "Both kinds of achievement, that of excellence and that of victory, will require effective practical reasoning; and it will be important to learn whether and, if so, how the kind of practical reasoning necessary for the achievement of excellence differs from that necessary for the achievement of victory."[5]

From our point of view Aristotle may look naive and superficial because he fails to recognize the force of skeptical challenges to questions about rhetoric: whether truth will win out over falsehood, whether truth is itself something that can be recognized, whether acting virtuously or artfully usually leads to success, whether the practical reason embodied in the laws of a good state has anything to do with the practical thinking required to effect our own individual purposes.[6] He confidently assumes, as in the *Ethics,* that there is a single human function, human good, a best life, and so can easily bridge the gulf between ethics and rhetoric. There is no great gap between my deliberating on what is best for me and my persuading you about what is best for you, because the human good is best for both of us.

Aristotle may have been in that sense naive, but he wasn't blind. The optimism expressed after the Persian War by Herodotus and Aeschylus was not available to Aristotle. He was certainly aware of particular outrages such as the success of demagogues in Athens, and of theoretical challenges such as those leveled by Socrates. In discussing the vice of boasting, he says that those who boast for profit "pretend to accomplishments that are useful and which can be counterfeited without detection, for instance, prophecy, philosophy *(sophia)* and medicine" (*Ethics* IV.7.1127b19–21), hardly the observation of someone who blithely thinks that audiences will reliably see truth and error for what they are.

Aristotle looks naive, however, because these obvious phenomena are not at the center of his attention when he talks about rhetoric. Once one is converted to a modern, skeptical point of view, such particular outrages become part of a larger pattern in which the various connections between good action and good results are severed. A conception of practical reason in which reason is inherently motivating then seems either false or unintelligible. The idea of a human ergon which we all share, and which means that the better you and I are, the more what is good for me is good for you, looks like metaphysical special pleading. To us, Aristotle might look naive. To Aristotle, we would look not sophisticated but unnatural.[7]

But I think that the difference between what he regards as critical issues and what we take as central is so great that, no matter how much we might admire Aristotle's arguments and results, we cannot adopt them. We can't just take his answers to his questions, since he has no direct answers to ours. Just what value the *Rhetoric* can have for us is a question I will turn to in the last chapter. To take just one oversimplified schematic example, Aristotle's approach invites us to direct attention to rhetoric as an activity, instead of looking at the motives that might inspire a rhetorician or the effects these practices cause. Rhetoric as an activity has its own values, criteria for success and failure, and intriguing internal complexity, and so to consider it as an activity, as Aristotle does, offers clear gains.

But this is an approach worth pursuing only if one thinks that motives and consequences can usually be neglected, either because they are irrelevant or because they pose no serious practical or intellectual problems. In other contexts, where motives do not line up well with practices, Aristotle's work will distort our attempts to deal with real problems. There are contexts, that is, where Kant's dismissive opinion of rhetoric is appropriate.

> Rhetorical power and excellence of speech (which together constitute rhetoric) belong to fine art; but oratory (*ars oratoria*), the art of using people's weaknesses for one's own aims (no matter how good these may be in intention or even in fact), is unworthy of any *respect* whatsoever. Moreover, both in Athens and in Rome, it came to its peak only at a time when the state was hastening to its ruin, and any true patriotic way of thinking was extinct.[8]

In contexts where the consequences of activities, direct or indirect, intended or unintended, dominate attention, then considering the intrinsic values of the activities themselves might be an irresponsible narrowing of vision. In such cases John Dewey's search for the great community might be the appropriate rhetorical inquiry for the time.[9]

The overriding question of Aristotle's *Rhetoric* is whether there can be a civic art of rhetoric, whether activities essential to citizenship can be made subject to rational analysis. If the kind of citizenship that Aristotle has in mind is not an option today, his central question might seem to have no meaning for us. I will return to this objection in the conclusion, but I think the conception of the hermeneutic circle on which it depends is too strong. Aristotle formulates as a question of civic art a worry about rhetoric that we can all share. Rhetoric, he tells us, is a faculty that proves opposites, that allows us to argue on both sides of a question. There is nothing peculiarly Aristotelian about that as a starting point. Yet we all—ancients and moderns—act as though there must be more to rhetoric than that. The question is, how much more. We all often infer that because someone can speak forcefully about an issue, he or she must be capable of intelligent and trustworthy decisions. We entrust America's destiny to masters of self-presentation. We think that advocates who speak so confidently and unflinchingly about their clients' innocence must really believe it, and probably believe it with good reason. Students are attracted by teachers who give the impression that they care about them, and they feel they are learning a lot from such teachers. Also, because we are all familiar with cases where these inferences turn out wrong, we wonder how best to think beyond the fact of eloquence.

My examples might suggest that someone's rhetorical abilities indicate *nothing* further about the person, the way someone's talents as a poet or physician say almost nothing about the person's abilities to make practical ethical decisions. Aristotle, however, does not endorse that debunking attitude; rather, he is on the side of the equally common opinion that, especially when it is a question of rhetorical ability concerning practical matters, that ability seems to be *some* sign, albeit highly fallible, of valuable moral qualities. After all, the ability to formulate alternative recommendations for actions, to foresee possible consequences, to organize data to bear on an issue, to explore the probabilities of different sorts of evidence—these are abilities that both the able rhetorician and the person of practical wisdom seem to display. There is far less overlap between other technicians and practical wisdom, and so less temptation to infer from artistic ability to *phronēsis* in the case of other arts. We would like to know about the proper standard of scrutiny and mistrust for practitioners of the art of rhetoric. I think there is nothing at all Aristotelian in any of that. These are concerns that we can all share. Different people will formulate the issue differently, which is why I think it important to stress both the technical and nontechnical meanings of Aristotle's key terms. Different people can, in different circumstances and for different purposes, come up with different levels of scrutiny and trust toward inferences from rhetorical skill to actual prudential ability. But all should find the richness of Aristotle's approach helpful.

On the other hand, I don't think Aristotle can answer these questions for us. In fact, I don't think that there are any principled answers to these questions in our circumstances. I think that Aristotle can offer answers to the questions but that his answers apply only within the restricted circumstances of his own inquiry. He is able to relate rhetoric to its near neighbors, especially to *phronēsis* itself, because of the political context in which he raises these questions. But seeing the connection between his solutions and his background assumptions can help us to do the best we can do in our circumstances.

My book is not a commentary on the *Rhetoric,* but an ordered series of explorations of related themes. Since the order of my argument does not follow the order of the *Rhetoric* itself, I want to offer a quick overview of what is to come. In this overview, I want to introduce two dimensions of Aristotle's approach to these problems concerning rhetoric and practical reasons, dimensions that will dominate my argument. First, he offers a picture of practical reasoning and rhetoric that bears intimate and complicated relations to character. The history of prudence is a history of changing relations between practical intelligence and character, as those are variously defined. Aristotle's integration of character and intelligence is an achievement. Sometimes, we will see, reason and character are at odds, and so their integration is a significant achievement, not a given. If this art of rhetoric is a civic art, it has to integrate the apparently opposed properties of citizenship and artfulness; within the art, that integration translates into a harmony between reason and character, *logos* and *ēthos.*

Similarly with the second dimension. To talk about rationality is to talk about standards, and therefore about form. As reason is tied to character, so form in rhetoric is tied to purpose and matter. As reason and character are occasionally at odds, so logical form sometimes becomes independent of purpose and matter. At one place in the *De Anima* Aristotle talks about the soul as an "enmattered form," *logos enhylos* (I.1403a25), and I will use that expression throughout to capture Aristotle's unique contribution to understanding practical rationality, an understanding of form as the form appropriate to matter and form that is purposive. I think that out of the complications of these two dimensions of the problem emerge quite rich conceptions of reason, character, and form. The first theme, then, is an exploration of what reason and character, *logos* and *ēthos,* would have to be for Aristotle's integration to succeed. This theme runs throughout the book, and is the principal subject of the first two chapters.

There is a second theme that I will trace throughout the book. Rhetoric, we see from the beginning, has to articulate a kind of reasoning that is suitably flexible and responsive to varying particulars, a kind of reasoning appropriate to a domain beyond the reach of art and method. Aristotle's rhetoric subjects this variability to art, making it intelligible without eliminating this irreducible particularity. The *Rhetoric,* consequently, provides resources for arguing in situations of incommensurability and of conflicting goods. There are four sorts of such resources: the three kinds of rhetoric; the method of topical reasoning, which can argue toward opposites and from opposed principles; the emotions, which permit singular exceptions; and a second set of common topics and other features common to practical reasoning. Together these comprise a diverse panoply of resources for respecting the particularity and variability of practical circumstances. Chapters 3 to 5 examine the theme of arguing in practically variable situations.

At the same time, the flexibility inherent in the power of rhetoric poses the problem of whether there is any ethical control over such apparently irresponsible power. To be an art at all is, for Aristotle, to be both a power of making and an intellectual virtue, a good functioning of the thinking part of the soul. What is the relation between rhetoric as power and rhetoric and *phronēsis* as virtues? How can these two sides of rhetoric coexist? Chapters 6 and 7 explore the dimensions of those questions.

My book, then, has three parts. The first two chapters are designed to create a picture of the *Rhetoric* as a philosophic work with its own integrity and its own deep philosophic problem, that of rhetoric as a political art, with complex relations to art on the one hand and politics on the other. Chapter 1, "Aristotle's *Rhetoric:* Between Craft and Practical Wisdom," can be read as an extended reflection on the problems raised in *Rhetoric* I.1–3, in which Aristotle shows just how rhetoric can be an art, and why the artful side of rhetoric is restricted to argument, what he calls the enthymeme. The remainder of *Rhetoric* I is about the three kinds of rhetoric: political, judicial, and epideictic. My Chapter 2, "The Kinds of Rhetoric," argues that these three kinds of rhetoric together exhaust the practical, civic side of rhetoric because only within those three species are the internal ends of rhetorical practice truly constitutive of the practice. Rhetorical practice is truly art and truly practice only when it has a *function* in a narrow, Aristotelian sense of the term. Only in rhetoric in this restricted, political sense are form and function one. Together, these two chapters show that rhetoric as art and practice has an autonomy and integrity that earn for it its own philosophic and political consideration.

The next set of four chapters articulates a series of aspects of the rhetorical power for proving opposites. They consider in turn the resources I mentioned above for negotiating a practical world of incommensurable goods and conflicting choices. The three kinds of rhetoric themselves, first, permit a certain kind of plural and incommensurable argument: an argument that some action is just and fair might conflict, both in its conclusion and in its mode of argument, with arguments that something else is most useful. Therefore Chapter 3, "Rhetorical Topics and Practical Reason," explores Aristotle's use of the topics peculiar to the three kinds of rhetoric. These topics allow him, in Book I, chapters 4–15, to articulate a kind of *logos* with the requisite flexibility.

But *logos* is only one of three sources of conviction, alongside *ēthos* and *pathos*. Chapter 4, "Deliberative Rationality and the Emotions," examines the first eleven chapters of Book II, where Aristotle explicitly discusses the place of the passions in rhetorical argument. At the beginning of the *Rhetoric,* Aristotle excludes passion from the art of rhetoric, yet without explanation returns to devote extended consideration to the emotions. They are a further resource for grasping and doing justice to the shifting particularities of practice, and I show how he subjects the emotions to argument, and so to art, without dissolving the distinction between *logos* and *pathos*.

The final chapters of Book II return to *logos* and topical reasoning in a different sense from I.4–15, which I covered in Chapter 3. The interesting question for those later chapters of the *Rhetoric,* and for my Chapter 5, "Why Reasoning Persuades," is whether the power of rhetoric is not so great that reasoning takes on a life, and persuasive power, of its own and breaks free from the tie between rational form and political function that made rhetoric a civic art in the first place. The more powerful the art of rhetoric becomes through Aristotle's articulation, and the more autonomous the values internal to the practice of rhetoric appear through his treatment, the more acute the ethical problems with rhetoric become.

There are three sources of conviction, *logos, pathos,* and *ēthos. Logos* has two large sections of the *Rhetoric* devoted to it, I.4–14 and II.18–26, the subjects of my Chapters 3 and 5. *Pathos* gets one large section, II.2–11, which I cover in Chapter 4. But there is no parallel section that treats *ēthos* on its own. The absence within the *Rhetoric* of explicit consideration of rhetoric's ethical problems, that is, has its counterpart in an absence of explicit consideration of rhetorical *ēthos*. These two absences are the subject of the third set of chapters of my book. Because of these absences, I have to abandon at this point the correlation between my order of exposition and that of Aristotle, which I followed in my middle chapters. First, in Chapter 6, "Making Discourse Ethical: Can I Be Too Rational?" I show the place of artful, rhetorical, *ēthos* within Aristotle's art of rhetoric. The power of rhetoric to prove opposites and argue about plural and conflicting values is a dangerous power unless *ēthos* can rein it in.

The final two chapters, "How to Tell the Rhetorician from the Sophist, and Which One to Bet On," and the conclusion, "Aristotle's *Rhetoric* and the History of Prudence" look at the overall problems raised by reading the *Rhetoric* today. Here the subject is not *ēthos* as one of the three sources of proof but *ēthos,* and ethics, in the broader sense of moral and political evaluation of rhetoric overall. My question will be whether an *ēthos* internal to rhetoric is sufficient to keep rhetoric's power to prove opposites from threatening all moral and political values.

The last section of the book, then, moves from an internal analysis of the *Rhetoric,* where I try to present and understand Aristotle's own conception of a civic art, to seeing how the *Rhetoric* can help us understand the philosophical problems that might send someone to the *Rhetoric* in the first place. It is very appropriate that such a movement takes place through a consideration of *ēthos.* This is, however, at the same time one of the three sources of proof, and so a concept internal to Aristotle's own analysis of rhetoric, and an overall term for approaching the relation between craft and virtue. We have to wonder whether those two senses of *ēthos* have anything in common. But notice that, at least prior to refinements introduced by Aristotle's own analysis, there are no parallel problems for the other two sources of proof, *logos* and *pathos.* There is good reason, then, to think that these questions about *ēthos* lie at the heart of the rhetorical enterprise, and at the heart of the history of prudence.

The first time Aristotle introduces the idea that *ēthos* is a source of conviction, he stresses the fact that it must be *ēthos* that comes from the argument itself, not some preexisting reputation of the speaker (I.2.1356a5–13). He does not have to make any parallel qualification for *pathos* or for *logos.* Artificially induced emotions might be undesirable in all kinds of ways, as the involuntary and unconscious result of manipulation against one's better judgment, but all the condemnation one could offer does not make them any less real as emotions. Art and reality are not incompatible when it comes to the emotions. Similarly, a skillfully constructed argument is no less an argument because it is the result of calculation. But the relation between art and reality comes to a head in the consideration of *ēthos*—what does *ēthos* as a product of art have to do with *ēthos* that leads to good action? How are discursive and practical *ēthos* connected?

As my inquiry proceeds, the relation between the *Rhetoric* and the rest of Aristotle's work shifts. Initially, I place the *Rhetoric* in the context of his other works, following his own alignment of rhetoric with dialectic and politics. I try to bring to bear arguments and considerations from his other works in order to clarify the *Rhetoric.* As I have said, I think the *Rhetoric* becomes a much more interesting work when seen in this context. Once I can show the *Rhetoric's* own argument and integrity, the point of my analysis shifts and I try to show what the *Rhetoric* has to say about the rest of the corpus, instead of the other way around. For example, the consideration of *phronēsis* in *Ethics* VI ends with some very brief arguments, gnomic dicta really, concerning the interrelations between *phronēsis* and ethical virtue. Anyone who looks there for a definitive presentation of the relation between good action and good reasoning will be disappointed. The *Rhetoric* helps us to get further. Rhetoric is both a power of proving opposites and an intellectual virtue oriented toward good ends. Confronting the relation between those two sides of rhetoric offers an opportunity to consider in far greater detail than the *Ethics* provides the dependence of *phronēsis* on moral virtue, as well as its independence, and the relation between *phronēsis* and the amoral power of cleverness.

Overall, I want to argue that Aristotle's original conception of artful rhetoric as argument makes possible a new conception of the ethical, and of the relation of *logos* and *ēthos*, as well. I will show that it is this new conception of the ethical that makes Aristotle's *Rhetoric* deserve our attention today.

I need, finally, to say something about the footnotes and references in the text to works other than Aristotle's *Rhetoric*. Reading the *Rhetoric* as an integral part of Aristotle's work means resisting reading it as part of the history of rhetoric, since that history has almost entirely considered it apart from the rest of his corpus. I consequently do not find helpful, and do not use, most of the work on the *Rhetoric* in the tradition of speech communication, which neglects the rest of Aristotle as an interpretive tool. For the same reason, I have rarely drawn on those studies that place the *Rhetoric* in Aristotle's own historical context. That enterprise has tended to separate the *Rhetoric*, as well as the *Poetics*, from the rest of Aristotle's works.

The reader will find instead references that are designed to place the *Rhetoric* in the context of Aristotle's other works, in the context of explorations of the philosophic problems characteristic of the history of prudence, and in the context of contemporary problems concerning the relation of rhetoric to practical reason. I include these references to complementary inquiries in order to help orient the reader: they are designed to place my inquiry in the context of others and show why the *Rhetoric* should be of interest today. All of them are, I think, dispensable. The reader interested in the *Rhetoric* for other reasons, or who already believes that the *Rhetoric* is of intrinsic interest, should be able to ignore them all. In fact, I have been tempted, at several stages in the writing of this book, to eliminate all footnotes altogether. I found no colleague or reader who supported me in this plan. (I have also been tempted to write this as an inquiry into practical reason and to eliminate all references to the *Rhetoric*. But no one else liked that idea either.)

Since I began this Introduction with the seemingly arrogant claim that my book is the first book-length philosophic treatment of Aristotle's *Rhetoric* in English in this century, I want to end on a note of humility, not to back away from my claim, but to indicate that it is not a boast but a wish. I intend this work as the beginning of a line of research into the *Rhetoric* and its relevance for contemporary investigations of practical reason and its history. If I claim that it is the first word, I devoutly hope that it is not the last.

ARISTOTLE'S *RHETORIC:*
BETWEEN CRAFT AND
PRACTICAL WISDOM

Politics arranges which sciences there will be in states, and which kinds of learning will be for which classes of citizen, and up to what point; we see that even the most highly reputed [entimotatas] *of the powers, such as strategy, economy, and rhetoric are subordinate to politics.*

— *Nicomachean Ethics* I.2.1094a29–1094b4

Aristotle's Project: A Civic, Practical Art of Rhetoric

Doesn't it seem base, and a great sign of lack of education [apaideusias], *to be compelled—because of a shortage at home—to use a justice imported from others who are thus [your] masters and umpires?*

— *Republic* III.405b

Aristotle's *Rhetoric* articulates a civic art of rhetoric, combining the almost incompatible properties of *technē* and appropriateness to citizens. It is easy to see what a professional rhetorical art would be, and hard to see how something can be an art without therefore being for sale, exchange, or rent. Civic activities seem too noble to be subject to an art. A professional art of rhetoric, like any power, proves opposites, while civic activities are oriented toward the good. It is hard to see how rhetoric can be a power which proves opposites and yet be oriented toward the good. How can Aristotle's admonition,

> one should be able to argue persuasively [*peithein*] on either side of
> a question, just as in the use of syllogisms, not that we actually do
> both (for one should not persuade what is debased) but in order
> that it may not escape our notice what the real state of the case is
> (I.1.1355a31–33),

be any more than the pious hope it is in most rhetorics?

The idea of a civic art of rhetoric creates problems that extend beyond this tension between the professional and the civic. Aristotle's assertions about his art seem to make rhetoric into an art and a power which operates by articulating rules for a domain beyond rules. His rhetoric is an art of praxis, but praxis is too bound up with particulars to be fully rule-bound. Activities which qualify as fully practical seem too particular, as well as too noble, to be subject to an art. "We call people intelligent [*phronimous*] about some [restricted area] whenever they calculate well to promote some excellent end, in an area where there is no *technē*" (*Ethics* VI.5.1140a28–30). If precision is impossible for general formulations, "the accounts *(logoi)* of particular cases are all the more inexact. For these fall under no craft [*technē*] or profession [*parangelian*], and the agents themselves must consider [*skopein*] in each case what the opportune action [*to kairon*] is" (II.2.1104a7–10).[1]

Aristotle's *Rhetoric* is a political inquiry, and not the first example of rhetorical theory or "applied philosophy." It is a political inquiry of the sort this chapter's epigraph demands. Through the *Rhetoric,* the politician can intelligently rule on the place of rhetoric in the polis. Such an inquiry tells citizens and lawmakers what they need to know about an art for a variety of political purposes, from legislation about rules of evidence to questions about education and discursive proficiency. It will be useful for politicians to know about the relations of one art to another, so that they can know which problems are unique to rhetoric and which shared by other arts. They might value the products of some art without wanting to be practitioners or experts themselves, in which case a professional art at most, not a civic one, will be possible.

Hippocrates at the beginning of the *Protagoras* is a paradigm. He is troubled by Socrates' suggestion that learning from a sophist will make him into one too, and Socrates lets him off the hook by distinguishing learning *epi technei,* in order to become a professional like his teacher, and studying *epi paideiai,* which is suitable for free and wealthy young men *(hos ton idioten kai ton eleutheron)* (312b). If something is a civic art, then it will be valued for more than its results. We would not, like Hippocrates, have to be ashamed of practicing it.

By frequently developing both *phronēsis* and the moral virtues in the *Ethics* through contrast to art, Aristotle at the very least *implies* that praxis and *technē* are incompatible, and an art of praxis consequently impossible. There can be a civic art of rhetoric only if there is an art of praxis. Since an art of praxis is thus the central question of my inquiry, I need to look at its possibility in great detail below. Here I want simply to raise the issue by pointing to one place where Aristotle relies on just such an implication from praxis to the impossibility of art. Once he can establish that slave management is a matter of character, he needs no further argument to assert that there is no art or science of slave management.

> The master is so called not according to a science [he possesses] but through being a certain sort, and similarly with the slave and the free person [*ho men oun despotes ou legetai kat' epistēmēn alla to toisd' einai*] (*Politics* I.7.1255b20–27).

In this case the fact that mastery and slavery refer to kinds of people seems a ground for denying that there are arts of mastery and slavery, along the lines suggested in my earlier citation from *Ethics* VI.5.1140a28–30 that we call people practically wise only if there is no *technē* governing the subject. As I will observe below, he goes on to soften the distinction between character and *technē* in this discussion of slaves, masters, and freemen, and to admit that there are arts of these things. But one must still wonder at this point why deliberative ability and *phronesis* are not subject to the same argument: since these are matters of character, are they not therefore outside the reach of *technē*? Being a good speaker seems in many ways to depend on being a certain kind of person, rather than possessing a body of knowledge. If it can be subject to an art, then its connection to character should vanish. If deliberating and judging are activities essential to free citizens, then they are, like freedom itself, matters of being a kind of person, and therefore *not* of possessing an art.

I chose the passage from the *Politics* quoted above instead of any of several others in the *Ethics* where he makes strict separations of art and character, making and doing, because these lines show that the apparent oxymoron of an art of praxis is not simply generated by idiosyncratic demands of Aristotelian theoretical vocabulary but by ordinary experience, in which some things depend on art and others on the sort of person one is. My purpose is not to impose some set of theses from the *Ethics* or the *Politics* on the *Rhetoric,* but to illustrate the continuities between the problems encountered in ethics and politics and those encountered in the statesman's examination of rhetoric.

The civic art of rhetoric will combine the properties of *technē* and citizenship. It will therefore be centered on those political activities that are indefinite (*Politics* III.1.1275a22–33, b15–16) and for which there can be no specialization: deliberating about the military budget as opposed to designing a test for a new missile. Expertise and specialization are incompatible with citizenship, in that specialized arts depend on knowledge, not on being a certain kind of person. "While the slave belongs among those [persons or things that are] by nature, no shoemaker does, nor any of the other artisans" (*Politics* I.13.1260b2). If there can be arts of the indefinite, there might be arts of praxis, arts that somehow do not exclude character, because they are about the ultimate particulars of praxis.

The *Rhetoric* is about those aspects of human affairs for which there are no experts and for which everyone is assumed to have an opinion. As Protagoras notes in his reply to Socrates, the realm of rhetoric is the realm of politics and justice (*Protagoras* 318–19; see also *Laches* 184–85, *Meno* 89–96, *Republic* I.332–3, *Gorgias* 449–50.) If rhetoric is a practical and civic art, it will not be a specialized one. Yet, it seems, arts are by definition specialized—each has a determinate object to aim at. Praxeis seem to aim at an indefinite, unspecialized end. Whether there can be an art for indefinite ends will be one of the questions facing an attempt to formulate an art of rhetoric.[2]

The example I pointed to earlier, slave management, is relevant again. Slave management is contrasted to definite or finite arts *(horismenois technais)* at *Politics* I.2.1253b25. Since he argues that being a despot is a function of the sort of person one is and therefore not an art, making rhetoric into a practical and civic art will not be a trivial task. Specialized arts are not part of citizenship. The indefinite tasks of citizenship are not artful.

I have said what I think the project of the *Rhetoric* is. The *Rhetoric* is a political inquiry designed to understand rhetoric as an art which can be a civic practice. Before going on I need to say one thing about what it is *not*.[3]

I have by now lost track of the number of things I have read that claim or assume that the *Rhetoric* is a defense of rhetoric against Plato's attacks. It is easy to construct the histories of our disciplines as a series of debates between giants—Plato vs. Aristotle, Newton vs. Leibniz, Kant vs. Mill, Weber vs. Durkheim. There certainly are arguments against Plato at many places in Aristotle's corpus, but the general thrust of Aristotle's works is not polemical. The attacks on Plato come only at certain points, for strategic reasons.[4]

The *Rhetoric* itself, like the *Poetics,* has *no* explicit attacks on Plato or Socrates whatever, no explicit mention of Plato's or Socrates' doctrines or arguments about rhetoric. One can explain this silence in a variety of ways—it is not actually silence but indirection and secret messages; Plato's doctrines were so well known that there was no need to refer to their author by name; the context makes it obvious that Aristotle's affirmations are meant to deny things Plato and Socrates said—but none of these explanations is compelled by the text. It is certainly true that Aristotle denies many things Socrates affirms in Plato's dialogues, but that fact by itself is very weak evidence for thinking that the *Rhetoric* is one half of a disputation. No one writing on rhetoric can avoid saying something on certain matters, and the fact that Aristotle contradicts Socrates is by itself no more evidence that he is arguing against Socrates or defending rhetoric against Socrates' attacks than the fact that Aristotle contradicts Cicero is evidence that he is attacking him! Are similarities and differences in the treatment of communism proof that Plato's *Republic* is a response to Aristophanes' *Ecclesiazusae*? How much stronger is the case that Aristotle is attacking Socrates or Plato than that they are attacking him? I stress my denial that the *Rhetoric* is an argument against Plato not only because I think the contrary a distorting assumption, but also because I think the nonpolemical character of the *Rhetoric* is itself worth noting. I will propose an explanation for this feature of the *Rhetoric* below.

While I think it wrong to say that the *Rhetoric* is a reply to Plato, or a defense of rhetoric against Socratic attacks, there is no question that the intellectual world of Aristotle is in many important ways a legacy of Plato. Aristotle says that Socrates was the first to be concerned about proper definitions and so inaugurated logic, and was also the first to ask philosophical questions about ethics and not just physics. It is only a slight oversimplification to say that Plato invented the word "rhetoric"; the use of "passion" to refer to emotions, sense experiences, and feelings is no older. If philosophy existed before Socrates and Plato, it was a very different thing from what it was afterward, and Aristotle's thought is impossible without the context of their work. Still, the *Rhetoric* is *not* an argument against Plato's thoughts on rhetoric.[5]

Guiding vs. Given Ends

Aristotle begins the *Rhetoric* by saying that since we all persuade by luck or experience, there must be an art of persuasion as well:

> A result is that all people, in some way, share in both [rhetoric and dialectic]; for all, to some extent, try both to test and maintain an argument [as in dialectic] and to defend themselves and attack [others], as in rhetoric. Now among the general public, some do these things randomly and others through an ability acquired by habit, but since both ways are possible, it is clear that it would also be possible to do the same by [following] a path; for it is possible to observe the cause why some succeed by habit and others accidentally, and all would at once agree that such observation is the activity of an art [*technē*] (1354a3–11).

In other circumstances it might be that such an inference is easy, and that such a loose conception of art does no harm. Hippocrates' *On Ancient Medicine* opens with a similar proof of the existence of an art of medicine: "Some practitioners are poor, others are excellent; this would not be the case if an

art of medicine did not exist at all . . . but all would be equally inexperi-
enced and unlearned, and the treatment of the sick would be in all respects
haphazard." Aristotle himself offers a similarly liberal definition of art as an
intellectual virtue in the *Ethics:*

> There is no craft that is not a state involving reason concerned with
> production, and no such state that is not a craft. Hence a craft is
> the same as a state involving true reason concerned with produc-
> tion . . . and the exercise of the craft is the study [*theorein*] of how
> something that admits of being and not being comes to be
> (VI.4.1140a9–13).[6]

But there are many human activities for which Aristotle's first inference in
the *Rhetoric* fails, things that we do by luck and experience but never by art.
There are many human activities that seem to be carried on as they are by
chance and habit, without admitting in any obvious way to treatment by
art. I think that we can see what is at stake in making rhetoric into an art
by contrasting it with a variety of near neighbors that are important both
for the philosophical problems raised by the *Rhetoric* and for the subsequent
history of rhetoric.[7]

We make moral decisions by chance and habit, and Aristotle denies that
there can be an art for them. There is no art of virtue; virtue and *technē*
are often contraries for Aristotle. The sophists, Isocrates, and many later
rhetoricians will claim that virtue can be taught just as rhetoric can, and
taught by teaching rhetoric, but Aristotle never comes close to making such
a claim.

Next, we make judgments about speakers, and are persuaded by them,
by chance and habit, but there is no suggestion in the *Rhetoric* that there is
not only an art for the speaker, but for the audience as well. Later theorists
who will make rhetoric into an art of judgment or of hermeneutics will see
an art which judges whose advice is best and which meanings to impute to
a text, but Aristotle's art of finding available resources for persuasion does
not have a role in helping the audience to judge rhetorical appeals. There
is no art of political judgment. Good audiences are not made through studying a *technē*; good audiences are good citizens. But somehow, on the production side, as opposed to the reception side, there is more to be said.

Finally, Aristotle himself gives several examples of practices for which
there is no art; metaphor is the most famous (*Poetics* 22.1459a6–7). Along
similar lines, rhetors and poets might be able to please their audiences, but
there is no art of pleasure. In what seems to be an allusion to Socrates' attack
on rhetoric in the *Gorgias,* Aristotle says: "The fact that pleasure is not the
product of a craft is quite reasonable; for a craft does not belong to any
other activity [*energeia*] either, but to a capacity [*dynamis*]" (*Ethics*

VII.12.1153a23–25). Many later rhetorics will make the invention of metaphors fundamental, but for Aristotle, the less art there is to a facet of rhetoric, the more tangential that aspect of rhetoric is.[8]

These, then, are three diverse examples close to rhetoric itself in which Aristotle's initial causal inference does not succeed: moral virtue, political judgment, and metaphor. I think, moreover, that the inference fails for a different reason in each of these three cases. Under what conditions can a common human activity become subject to systematic study and practice?

As the counterexamples just listed suggest, I want to concern myself far more than Aristotle himself seems to do with what is at stake in calling rhetoric an art. He seems to regard the inference from rhetorical activity to art as an easy one. The opening inference is echoed in later, in III.10: "It is possible to create [urbanities and well-liked expressions] by natural talent or practice, but to show what they are belongs to this study" (1410b7–8). There is no implication there that the present study will be a third source, along with nature and practice, of the ability to create these stylistic virtues. Even if there is an art that uncovers the causes of natural or empirical success, then, its connection to practice is a further question. Knowledge of causes is not by itself empowering. An art of rhetoric will not necessarily make anyone a better speaker.

Moreover, Aristotle himself criticizes people who infer too easily from practice to art. The so-called arts of rhetoric he attacks in the first chapter failed precisely by making this inference too casually. The sophists neglected, he says, the most important thing of all, proofs (pisteis), which he calls the only part of rhetoric subject to an art [hai gar pisteis entechnon esti monon] (1.1.1354a13).[9] By saying that, Aristotle must be deploying stricter criteria for art than his opening inference, and the official definition of technē in the Ethics, would suggest. Proofs are not the only part of rhetoric whose mastery leads a speaker to success, so his grounds for limiting an art of rhetoric to proof must be other than successfully achieving that external end, and the Rhetoric must be aiming at something other than improving practice. (I will defend the narrow translation here of pistis as proof below, and will also point to other facets of meaning for this fundamental term as the book proceeds.)

For an art to be possible, there has to be what can variously be called either an internal good, an internal end, a guiding end, or a constitutive end for the practice as well as its external, given end.[10] I will explicate this distinction in detail in the rest of this chapter, but here it is enough to refer to Aristotle's definition of Rhetoric and the analogies he draws to two other arts and powers, dialectic and medicine.

> The function [ergon] of rhetoric is not to persuade [ou to peisai] but
> to see the available means of persuasion in each case [to idein ta

huparchonta pithana peri hekaston], as is true also in all the other arts
(I.1.1355b10–12).

Let [*esto*] rhetoric be [defined as] an ability [*dynamis*], in each case
[*peri hekaston*], to see the available means of persuasion [*theopesai to
endechmoneon pithanon*]. This is the function [*ergon*] of no other art
(I.2.1355b26–28).

In each art, one can distinguish between successfully achieving some external goal—persuading, arguing or healing—and doing everything in one's
power to accomplish that end. This latter is the function of the art. Where
success is the only value, there can be no art.

"Doctors deliberate, but scribes do not. Since error occurs in two ways
(for we err either in calculating, or in perception when actually doing the
thing), in medicine it is possible to err in both ways, but in grammar error
only occurs in our perception and action" (*Eudemian Ethics* II.10.1226a33–
37; see also *Nicomachean Ethics* II.2.1104a2–10, III.3.1112a33–b6).[11] The
doctor does not always succeed in healing, but he must, to be a doctor,
succeed in finding in each case the available means of healing, and similarly
the rhetorician might not persuade his audience, but he will exercise his
rhetorical power and fulfill his rhetorical function if he discovers the possible
means of persuasion in a given case.

I find that limitation to "available" or "possible" means *(ta huparchonta,
to endechomenon)* arresting. If we charitably assume that Aristotle is trying to
tell us something more than the not very useful advice to avoid using non-
existent, unavailable, or impossible means, or the tautology that doing one's
best is the best that one can do, it is far from clear what message to ascribe
to him. Aristotle himself does not consider his talk about available means,
to endechomenon, as pleonastic, since he distinguishes between such means
and just any means at all *(ek pantos tropou).* How to draw such a line is
puzzling, and crucial.[12]

One can be a successful practitioner without ever thinking about these
problems. The good rhetorician does not have to worry about the conditions under which art is possible, or the distinction between given and guiding ends. If, however, the *Rhetoric* is not addressed to rhetoricians but to
legislators who need to understand the place of rhetoric in the polis, then
that distinction between given and guiding ends is crucial. The distinction
between civic and professional rhetoric, critical to the decisions of the lawmaker, depends on the distinction between given and guiding ends.

The first part of the puzzle about delimiting the guiding end, to my
mind, is the fact that Aristotle does not seem to find this question difficult
or troublesome at all, in spite of the fact that, as I noted, the sophists go

wrong by having a too casual conception of art determined simply by what is effective. This is a good place to show why Aristotle should be generally untroubled by the issues that I think call for the highest philosophic attention. Some arts exist. Some purposeful human activities can be effected artistically. Tragedy, for one example, is a natural art form, but it only exists because of a series of developments that depend on the innovations of particular people. The state is natural, and "accordingly, there is in everyone by nature an impulse [*hormē*] toward this sort of partnership. And yet the one who first constituted [a city] is responsible for the greatest goods" (*Politics* I.1.1253a29–31).

Therefore, it is a contingent fact that any particular internal ends are reliable means to some given external ends; it is contingent because no matter how natural and important those ends are, the development of arts to achieve them is contingent. The distinction between internal and external ends is characteristic of the human world. Natural objects have powers that can be expected to achieve their ends in the right circumstances, and the artificial human world contains a series of attempts to match such regularity. In later chapters I will recall the distinction from the *Metaphysics* between rational and irrational *dynameis,* in which rational *dynameis* cause opposites and so lack the necessary connection between power and actuality found in irrational *dynameis.* Important external ends may have only contingently associated with them constitutive ends that can become the goals of art. Medicine might be able to treat only unimportant ailments. Dermatologists confidently clear up acne, but psychiatrists are helpless in the face of severe depression. My methods of self-control work only when it doesn't matter much whether I'm in control or not. I can think logically about games and puzzles but not about life.

It is a contingent fact that the instrumental rationality required for achieving external ends and the fuller sense of practical rationality I will associate both with *technē* and with the virtues line up as they do. It is a contingent fact that nobility lines up with activities that are the most fully satisfying for the doers and with activities that have essential political functions. Playing the violin well and running world-class triathlons take such single-minded dedication that the practitioner becomes unfit for anything else, and so Aristotle would call them vulgar. The ethical and political life makes no such demands.[13]

If the polis is as natural as Aristotle says it is, then all such contingencies are satisfied in the polis. In the polis, they are not contingent at all. That is what it means to call the polis natural. They are contingent outside the polis, and their contingency is a mark of the unnaturalness of our lives. In the context of Aristotle's presentation, all these things are natural, but in the context of understanding Aristotle's presentation today, they are not. That is why Aristotle is direct and unreflective in answering these questions about the art of rhetoric that I see as difficult, profound philosophical questions. Consequently, I devote care and attention to premises and inferences that are unproblematic for Aristotle, and I further think the *Rhetoric* is now more interesting theoretically than it was for Aristotle's first readers. Not for the first time, the gain in theoretical interest accompanies a loss of practical application.

Aristotle's definition of the power of rhetoric raises for us, then, the problem of determining the conditions under which it is reasonable to talk about a power or art for performing some action. The inference from activity to art is not as obvious as Aristotle seems to regard it. Nor is the centrality of argument and the enthymeme to rhetoric obvious. Neither conclusion is discernible by inspecting existing practice, let alone existing teaching.

Argument has no privileged status in rhetoric even for Aristotle when when he is discussing argument as a resource for some other inquiry or art. In the *Poetics* he tells the reader to consult the *Rhetoric* for more information about thought (*dianoia*). Thought, he says, includes "all the effects to be produced by language (*hupo tou logou*), including proof and refutation, arousing feelings, such as pity, fear, anger, etc., and for maximization and minimization" (19.1456b2–7). Nothing here singles out "argument" for a special place in the *Rhetoric*.

Yet he identifies artificial proof with persuasion rooted in discourse and in argument at I.2.1356a1, where artificial proofs are called proofs *dia tou logou*. There has to be a tacit premise at work to allow Aristotle to narrow artful rhetoric to argument. Only the idea that arts have internal objects and internal ends could justify this identification of art and argument.

Aristotle claims originality for this isolation of argument. He makes the same claim for originality through isolating the syllogism in the logic too, at the end of the *De Sophisticis Elenchis*. Nowhere else in the corpus does he present himself as an innovator. He sees his scientific contributions as additions to a cumulative enterprise. It is only in the nonscientific powers (*dynameis*) of rhetoric and logic that he sees himself as a revolutionary. Aristotle's originality consists in taking the idea of an internal principle of motion, from the *Physics,* and an internal end of action, from the *Ethics* and *Politics,* and generating the novel idea of argument.

Consequently, his distinction between the artistic and the inartistic is not simply a report of obvious observations. How to draw the line between what is artful and what is not shifts as the argument of the *Rhetoric* proceeds, just as in the *Politics* the line between citizens and others in the state, between parts of the state and mere necessary conditions, and between purpose and necessity, shifts as the argument there goes on. I will return to this point in the last chapter. At every point, however, the distinction will be between those ways of achieving an end that have to be invented and those that only have to be used. Producing a contract or a statement by a witness in court might persuade the jury. It will directly achieve the given end. It cannot aim at or achieve the guiding end of the practice of rhetoric. The resources we invent can. In later rhetorics invention is opposed to judgment; here the contrary of invention is use.

Every art, like every virtue, has two ends. Activities for which there is no corresponding art have only one end, achieving the external, given good. The definition of rhetoric, with its comparisons to dialectic and medicine, highlights this distinction of ends. Some activities, those with only an external end, are *kinēseis,* complete only when they are over and successful. Other activities, those with guiding ends, aim at goods outside themselves but also answer to internal standards of completion and perfection. These fulfillments and enactments of an *ergon* Aristotle calls *energeiai.*[14] Unless achieving the external end were desirable, no one would ever develop an art. Arts do not lose their given ends when they develop their own autonomous ends in addition. Rhetoric begins with the given end of persuasion, but the *art* of rhetoric has its own internal, guiding or constitutive end, finding in each case the available means of persuasion. The external end is the end of rhetoric *qua kinesis,* the internal end the end of rhetoric *qua energeia.*[15] He tells us that "among the products of thought [and *technē*], some never occur spontaneously, e.g., a house or a statue . . . but only with some purpose; but others occur by chance too, e.g., health and safety" (*Posterior Analytics* II.1195a3–6). Internal ends are never achieved spontaneously, but only by thought. I can be convinced by accident; I cannot understand, or produce, an argument by chance.

It should be a surprise that arts like rhetoric and medicine, and not just the virtues, can have internal ends and so be *energeiai,* because Aristotle contrasts the virtues with the arts on just this basis. An enormous amount of effort has gone into applying to his ethical writings the distinction from *Metaphysics* IX between the kinds of *energeiai—kinēseis* and *energeiai* proper.[16] In spite of the fact that Aristotle himself does not explicitly use the *kinēseis/energeia* distinction to organize the *Ethics,* once its relevance is pointed out, its application has been irresistible. I want here to extend that research program to the *Rhetoric.*

The external end of medicine, which sets its problems, is the ordinary picture of health that we use in choosing to go to a doctor rather than an architect. The guiding or constitutive end is the one that the doctor has in mind when prescribing drugs to restore us to health. In the light of the given end shared by expert and patient, the doctor defines the guiding end of his craft. Knowing what that end is and seeing it as desirable are both possible only to the doctor, not the layman. The doctor's possessing an internal end allows him or her to overrule the patient: you might think you're healthy but you're not. We will have to see whether there can be a parallel for rhetoric: can the rhetorician tell the audience that they are not in fact persuaded?[17]

Parallel to his criticism of the other treatises on rhetoric for neglecting the internal end is a criticism Aristotle makes of other studies of politics and constitutions, and I think the analogy will help. Every polis, like every art and virtue, has both a given end and an internal, constitutive end. Like the internal end of rhetoric, the internal end of politics is not obvious by inspection, and most people go wrong in the two cases in the same way, by trying only to achieve the external end. States come into existence simply for the sake of life, but they exist for the good life. Life is the external end of politics: if people could defend themselves and reproduce without the state, it never would have been invented. The good life is the constitutive end. States are rated good and bad not by the size and growth of their population, as Rousseau suggests, or by their wealth, as many, even in Aristotle's time thought, but by how virtuous its citizens are (*Politics* III.9.1280b9–11). Ignorance of the internal end may not make states any worse at procuring security or wealth, but it makes them worse *qua* states. I will argue, similarly, that Aristotle does not claim that practitioners of his art will be more persuasive than devotees of the competition. But they will be worse rhetoricians, because they will not be civic rhetoricians.

The guiding end is the end constitutive of the practices of the art. The guiding, internal, or constitutive end is then a *means* to the given end. By attaining the internal end, the doctor also achieves the given end. More precisely, as Aristotle puts it in the definitions of rhetoric and dialectic, the doctor does not necessarily achieve the given end, but he does do everything possible to achieve it. In acting medically or rhetorically, the doctor or speaker achieves the guiding end, but that is not a guarantee that he achieves the given end as well. There are no such guarantees, regardless of whether one aims at the given or the guiding end. The guiding end, then, is the first actuality, or *energeia,* of the practice, and it is the power for achieving, or doing the best one can do to achieve, the second actuality, the given end of actual success.

The example of politics, however, looks different, and my analogy helps to create a more penetrating understanding of the relation between the guiding and the given ends of rhetoric. If life is the external end of politics, and the good life its internal end, it seems to follow that the good life is a means to the end of life. And that looks like a *reductio ad absurdum* of this line of reasoning.

But in fact the good life is, in a certain respect, a means to life. (I also think this is the only defensible interpretation of Socrates' claim in the *Apology* that from virtue follows prosperity.) To people who are not participating in the activities of politics—its "consumers," for example, such as the citizens of a modern nation-state who pay taxes and occasionally vote but otherwise are not participants in politics but only the beneficiaries of political action—political activity will be evaluated as mere means to life, that is, to wealth and security (III.6.1278b23–30). In the same way, when I hire a lawyer, I want success as the external end of rhetoric. I want victory. From the point of view of the client, the internal end, acting artfully, is nothing but a means to such an external end. Such an external point of view is not automatically reprehensible. If there were no clients, lawyers would have nothing to argue about. If morally virtuous actions did not frequently bring about desirable results, their attractiveness would be much smaller. From such an external point of view, the guiding end is a means toward the given end. But that point of view is not the point of view of the politician.

Since I realize that this distinction of given vs. constitutive ends is not a familiar one for the *Rhetoric,* I want to follow that analogy to the *Politics* with one from the *Poetics.* That the enthymeme is the body of *pistis,* that the artful is coextensive with the argumentative—these are philosophical, not empirical, claims, of just the same status as the claim that the plot is the soul of the tragedy.

> Spectacle, while highly effective [*psychagonikon*] is most unartful [*atechnotaton*] and has nothing to do with making [*poietikes*]. Indeed, the power [*dynamis*] of tragedy exists without actors and performers. Again, to achieve the effects of spectacle, the art [*technē*] of the constumier is more authoritative [*kuriotera*] than that of the poet (*Poetics* 6.1450b16–20).

Spectacle can be more effective than plot in achieving the given end of impressing, moving, and winning the audience. But only plot can achieve the constitutive end of tragedy, the *katharsis* of pity and fear by those emotions.[18]

In the terms I have been using, Socrates in the *Gorgias* accuses the sophists of having no guiding end at all, but only the vulgar given end, which is not sufficiently determinate to be the end of an art. The sophist has a knack, an *empeiria,* for bringing about the given end, persuasion. There is no *a priori* reason to reject the possibility that the sophist, like the good archer, might be a good coach and help his pupils become more successful. Socrates' sophist, however, lacks a guiding end for his art. Socrates, at least in the *Gorgias,* thinks there is no such guiding end. (In the *Phaedrus,* all arts have the same guiding end, the human good.)

Some "crafts" have no guiding or constitutive end. Take, for an example outside rhetoric that I know something about, the skill of the cook preparing a meal, the skill that Socrates compares to rhetoric. It might be that for teaching purposes, someone might erect intermediate ends for parts of that overall skill. There are heuristic and mnemonic rules which good cooks use and which can be taught: decide what can be prepared or cooked in advance and what has to be done right before serving, always preheat the oven, and always remember to turn the oven from preheat to bake or broil before putting the food in, try to balance different tastes, colors, and textures in a meal. There can be teaching and guidance. Cookbooks and cooking schools make people better cooks. But if there is no constitutive end, then there is no art, and I see no reason to think that there is a guiding end for cooking. If you don't enjoy the meal I've prepared, I can't tell you that you're wrong. According to Aristotle, arts are practices for which something analogous to "the operation was a success, but the patient died," is apposite; practices that are not artful are ruled instead by the maxim that "the customer is always right."

Aristotle recognizes that there are such arts. There are kinds of productive powers that are amenable to rational treatment but which have no guiding end. They need not for that reason receive the negative connotations Socrates imputes to rhetoric. I have already mentioned metaphor, which he says cannot be learned. There is, therefore, no art of metaphor regardless of its dignity and importance. Here is another example from the *Poetics* of something that could be efficacious in rhetoric, but is not artful:

> If their natural powers are equal, those who are actually in the emotions are the most convincing; he who is agitated blusters and the angry man rages with the maximum of conviction [*alethinotata*]. And that is why poetry needs either a sympathetic nature or a madman, the former being impressionable and the latter inspired (17.1455a30–36; cf. *Rhetoric* III.1.1404a12–19).

It is a contingent feature of the world that the objects of the most important productive powers have constitutive, guiding ends, so that their production can be rationalized. There are many valuable features of persuasion that do not fall under art in this way, and many of these features become central values in later histories of rhetoric, art, and poetry—genius, grace, naturalness, style, etc. If these are central aspects of the given end, there would be no reason to think that art in Aristotle's sense would regularly, reliably, and efficiently bring about the given end.

Even if I regularly produce dazzling metaphors on demand, or always strike just the right tone to bring the audience along with me, I would still in Aristotle's eyes be acting according to chance, not art. Regularity is a *sign* of art and nature, and the lack of regularity a sign of chance (*Physics* II.5.196b21–30). But I have argued that an internal end is the fundamental necessary property for an art. For the same reasons, chance is best characterized not by lack of regularity but by reproduction that does not work by transmission of form, a central concept that I will have to explicate in detail. In biology, Aristotle can give reasons why those two properties—transmission of form and regularity—necessarily go together.[20] Nature is regular because natural reproduction transmits the form of the parent to its offspring. Nature breeds true.

In art and praxis, however, the connection of these two properties is contingent. The genius, madman, or person of experience might have a great success rate in court, but still not be operating by art. The essence of the rhetorical art is not winning, but arguing. Aristotle places argument at the center of the art of rhetoric because it is the only means of achieving persuasion in which a form, the enthymeme, is transmitted from speaker to hearer. I have to return to the idea of transmission of form, but first I want to concentrate on the relation between external and internal end.

Once there is a distinction between given and guiding end, there can be conflict. The doctor can tell me that, although my body fits the vulgar definition of health, I am in fact ill, or the other way around. The wealthy polis might also be sick. Similarly, the artful rhetorician can claim that he achieved the guiding end of his art, finding the available means, while the audience gave the verdict to his opponent, who achieved the given end, persuasion. Even though the given end is not the end of the art, it is still an end that motivates the speaker. As I said before, Aristotle offers no guarantees that the guiding end will always be the best way to achieve the given end: if it was, all statesmen would aim at virtue, since from virtue wealth and security would follow. Art is different from nature, and in human affairs first and second actuality are not always neatly aligned, even in the best of circumstances. And the worse the circumstances, the less they will be aligned.

It would be silly, consequently, to demand that the artful rhetorician avoid all techniques that are not part of an art. I would be even sillier to claim that aiming at the internal end is always the most efficacious way of achieving the external end. Consequently, there are times in the *Rhetoric* when the speaker should aim directly at the given end of success, and here the speaker is at his least artful and most stochastic (e.g., II.21.1395b10–11: "The speaker should try to guess [*stochazesthai*] how his hearers formed their preconceived opinions and what they are, and then express himself in general terms in regard to them." Cf. *Republic* 493a–b, *Gorgias* 464b–465a; but see *Ethics* II.6.1106b27–28.)[21] A lawyer might hire a consultant for help in deciding how to choose jurors who will give the desired verdict. Aristotle is not foolish enough to decide in advance whether the consultant is worth the fee. Clarence Darrow used to stick a straight pin in his cigar so that the ash wouldn't fall off. The ash would get longer and longer as his opponent was making his summation, and the jury would watch the cigar and not the opponent. That would effect the external end, persuasion, but not artfully—he would not have found and deployed any available means of persuasion.[22]

In the Introduction I quoted MacIntyre: "Both kinds of achievement, that of excellence and that of victory, will require effective practical reasoning; and it will be important to learn whether and, if so, how the kind of practical reasoning necessary for the achievement of excellence differs from that necessary for the achievement of victory."[23] I said at the time that that sentence posed the central problem for rhetoric and the history of prudence. In Aristotle those two kinds of excellence may be far better aligned than they can be for us, but even for Aristotle the two kinds of success remain distinct.

The more subject to art a practice is, the less room there is for chance; *technē* and *tychē* are enemies: "The most artful of these works are those which involve chance the least" (*Politics* I.11.1258b36; see also *Posterior Analytics* I.30.87b19, *Nicomachean Ethics* 1140a17-20; but cf. *Eudemian Ethics* VIII.2.1247a5-7, 21–22). Medicine rather than tightrope walking or archery or metaphor making is Aristotle's model for art. In cases where there is an art, practitioners do better because their eye is on the guiding, not the given, end, and the guiding end is more determinate—easier to aim at, easier to tell when you have hit it—and more practicable—easier to posit as an end toward which to calculate means. But, as my last examples suggest, sometimes the artful rhetorician will in fact be at a disadvantage. If art did not drive out chance, then there would be no reason to think that the artist guided by the internal end would be able to compete successfully against the lucky man of experience who aimed directly at the given end. Whether, and how much, art does drive out chance is a contingent feature of the world.

Nature and art, unlike chance and fortune, work by transmission of form. Whatever regularity there is between cause and effect follows from transmission of form.[24] The connection between regularity and art is weaker than the connection between regularity and nature, since art is only an external cause of motion. Nature will reach her ends more reliably than an art will reach its given ends. These conflicts between given and guiding end come from the fact that art is an external, not an internal, principle of movement, as he has it in the *Physics,* and a rational *dynamis,* as he says in the *Metaphysics.* Still, within rhetoric, arguments, and only arguments, persuade by transmission of form.

Since arts cannot offer guarantees that they will reach their given ends, they had better have something else going for them. Arts are intellectual virtues. For something to be an art, its practice, and not just its results, must be desirable.

Were there not an internal, guiding end for each real *technē,* art could not be an intellectual virtue. Virtues are noble and part of the good life. A craft might be a desirable thing to possess even if the craft were a stochastic one without an internal end, but in that case it would be desired only for its results. If I could have my slave do it for me, I would be better off. Its results would be desirable, but it would not be a desirable state of character.

That is Hippocrates' attitude towards sophistic in the *Protagoras.* He wants its fruits, thinks that they are so valuable that he is willing to learn to procure them himself, but wants only enough knowledge to produce the results. He recoils at Socrates' suggestion that he become a sophist. He wants political skill for purposes he already has. If rhetoric has ends of its own, he wants no part of them. Therefore such an art would not be a virtue, and having it would not be part of the good life. Although all "arts" are valuable because of their results, arts with internal ends are themselves valuable and count as intellectual virtues. The politician has to ask separate questions about the values of the products of an art and about its practice, and Aristotle's *Rhetoric* provides guidance for making that distinction.

The connection between what it takes to achieve given and to achieve constitutive ends is a fundamental reason to read the *Rhetoric* today. What is the relation between the kind of intelligence embodied in the art of rhetoric and the civic intelligence of *phronēsis*? (How loaded is the term "virtue" when art is called an "intellectual virtue"?) Within rhetoric, what is the relation between acting artfully and trying to win?

From Internal/External Ends
to *Energeia/Kinesis*

The internal, constitutive end is the artistic equivalent of the internal purpose of the moral virtues, which aim at the noble and so are their own end. Both constitutive ends are first actualities which are their own ends, and which then lead to desirable second actualities. But it is important not to assimilate rhetoric to virtue. Rhetorical persuasion is not its own end in the way morally virtuous activity is. There is a parallel structure in the discovery of internal ends in the moral virtues and in the art of rhetoric, but that analogy does not permit us to assimilate rhetoric to the virtues of character. That would be much too easy. Persuasion, unlike justice or temperance, is not worth choosing and pursuing for its own sake. Persuasion would not be a worthwhile activity even if, as Aristotle puts it, nothing more resulted from it. But artful persuasion is an activity which is its own end in that its successful achievement is fully contained in its performance, just as Aristotle says in the definition of rhetoric. To say that rhetorical argument is an *energeia* is to recognize a standard for completeness other than success. Something is complete if it "in respect of excellence and goodness cannot be excelled in its kind; e.g., we have a complete doctor or a complete flute-player, when they lack nothing in respect of the form of their proper excellence" (*Metaphysics* V.16.1021a15-18). Speakers achieve the given end when the audience has been persuaded; a *kinēsis* is complete when it is over, as my walking home is complete when I get home. Speakers achieve the guiding end when they have found the available means of persuasion and have made an argument; an *energeia* is complete when it achieves its form. I am successfully and completely engaged in bird watching even when I'm not watching any birds. That is the difference between *kinēsis* and *energeia*. To be complete is then to fulfill some form. Arts are productive activities; they create changes in material and result in products. Productive activities fulfill some form when they create their products through transmission of form.

A civic art of rhetoric will explicate persuasion as something that happens *in* a speech, not simply *by means of* the speech. Seeing rhetorical persuasion as an *energeia* is not looking through some strange Aristotelian perspective or lens. Artful persuasion is something accomplished *in* the act of arguing, while other modes of persuasion are achieved *by* the speech. In the language of speech act theory, all persuasion aims at a perlocutionary *effect*, while Aristotle makes rhetorical argument into an illocutionary *act*. Perlocutionary effects are the given end of rhetoric; illocutionary acts are its guiding and constitutive end.[25]

In the *Physics* the builder's engaging in the act of building and the building's being built are identical. In rhetoric, the speaker persuading and the audience being persuaded will be identical (*Physics* III.3.202b5; *Metaphysics* IX.8.1049b24–26). In both cases, instead of a contrast between *kinēsis* and *energeia*, we see that *kinēseis* are *energeiai*, too: recall that *kinēsis* is defined in *Physics* III.1 as the *energeia* of the potential *qua* potential. If artful activities succeed through the transmission of form and the identity of agent acting and material being acted upon, then it is perfectly plausible for Aristotle to say that the sophists neglected the most important thing of all, proofs *(pisteis)*, the only part of rhetoric that can be treated by an art (*hai gar pisteis entechnon esti monon*) (1354a13). A proof is an *energeia*.

I need to amplify and defend that surprising thesis. Using an Aristotelian conception of causality which depends on distinctions between potency and act, identity of actual cause and actual effect, and the distinction between *kinēsis* and *energeia*, removes apparent ambiguities and inconsistencies from

Aristotle's account. For example, *pistis* does double duty as one of three modes of proof alongside *ēthos* and *pathos,* but these three, only one of which is called *pistis,* are also collectively called *pisteis.* That "logical" source of proof is also called *logos* and *ta pragmata.* As a source of proof, *pistis* is a potentiality; as proof, it is actuality. The enthymeme is called the body of proof, but commentators have frequently wound up talking, for good reason, about the enthymeme as form, which is the opposite of body.[26] Attention to the potency/act distinction, the distinction between first and second actualities, and the coordinate insistence that actual effect and actual cause are identical, will allow us to sort through these difficulties.

Argument is the only kind of rhetorical speech act which can be complete in the doing, and not in a terminus outside itself. It is, therefore, the only kind of rhetorical speech act for which there is an internal, guiding end, and therefore it alone can be subject to art. Argument has form, and it therefore is complete in the doing, because to possess a form fully is to be complete. The builder who puts bricks and timbers together according to plan is a different entity from the building going up. But the act of the builder building a house *is* the change described as the house being built (*Physics* II.3.195b17–21; cf. *Generation of Animals* II.1.734a30). I accomplish the external end of saving my comrade in battle; that achievement is distinct, *qua kinēsis,* from my conquering and despising my fear of death. But that act can, when it is done virtuously, also be seen as an *energeia,* in which choosing to do all I can to save my comrade is the same act as mastering my fear and choosing the mean with respect to fear and confidence. The *Ethics* shows that there are some instrumental actions that can also be lived as *energeiai.* Those are the moral virtues.[27]

The *Rhetoric* shows something analogous for the instrumental act of persuasion. Conviction or belief (*pistis*) is an effect, sometimes of language and sometimes of other things, contingently connected to a variety of possible causes, just as my saving my friend can be an effect of virtue, professionalism, shame, anger, ignorance, or other things. Aristotle's question for the *Rhetoric* is, How much, and which aspects, of that effect can be made into an actual effect identical to an actual cause of someone speaking persuasively? There are many things the speaker can do to effect the external end, persuasion. Why should the side of persuasion for which cause and effect are identical be limited to argument?

A successful argument is something accomplished in the speech, and it is shared by speaker and audience. It is hard to say just where a proof exists, whether in the mind of the teacher or student, or in a book or on a blackboard. Passions are much easier to locate, and I think the difficulty of knowing where to place proofs is a sign that they are *energeiai.* Aristotle would say that in the case of a proof the same thing—the same form—exists in all those places. (Earlier I made an analogy between argument as the form and internal end of rhetoric and the plot as form and catharsis as internal end of tragedy. Given this analysis, it is no surprise that there has been an endless debate about whether catharsis is located in the audience or in the plot.) The acts of building, teaching, and persuading transmit a form from agent to patient. That is how even *kinēseis* are *energeiai,* albeit imperfect ones. When speaker and listener have an identical *energeia,* persuasion takes place through transmission of form. Argument is the only kind of persuasion that works through transmission of form. Therefore, if the art of rhetoric has an internal end, and can be an *energeia,* it is limited to argument.

If any part of the job of persuading can be done in speaking, if any kind of persuasion could contain an identity between the activity of the speaker persuading and the audience's process of being persuaded, proof is the obvious candidate. When I offer you a geometrical proof, you don't have to like it, remember it, act on it; all that is necessary for my successfully performing the act of proving is that you recognize that that is what I'm doing. Proof is something I do in discourse. My doing the act does not guarantee that you will see and understand the proof, but there is nothing further I can do to prove it. "By demonstration I mean a syllogism which produces scientific knowledge, in other words one which enables us to know by the mere fact that we grasp it [*kath' hon to echein auton episteametha*]" (*Posterior Analytics* I.2.71b19). There are things I could do to make you more receptive to my proof, or more attentive, but these things are clearly distinct from the proof itself. Proving a theorem is something I can achieve in discourse, while making you attentive is not; it can only be accomplished *by* the speech, not in it. There is no transmission of form in getting your attention. Aristotle will use just such a distinction to separate what is part of the art from what is merely necessary.

In contrast, an emotional appeal is a *kinēsis.* (To avoid confusion, I want to insert a reminder here that Aristotle on the one hand frequently contrasts *kinēsis* with *energeia,* and on the other he defines *kinēsis* as a species of *energeia.*) An emotional appeal exists fully only in the mind of the hearer. It also exists fully only when it is over. When I am angry, I am no longer being angered, or being induced to become angry. It is the nature of a *kinēsis* to be complete only when it is finished. But the opposite holds for *energeiai.* The teacher is fully proving something and the student understanding throughout the proof, although the student is also engaging in the *kinēsis* of acquiring knowledge, and the teacher in the *kinēsis* of getting some point across. The proof is all over the blackboard, unlike the anger, which is only present at the end. Becoming enraged and being enraged are distinct. I can tell if I have successfully proved a theorem by looking at the proof on the blackboard, while I can tell if I have succeeded in angering you only by seeing whether you are angry. That is what it means for argument to be something accomplished *in* the doing and *in* the speech. One of the standard tests for *energeiai* is that it is simultaneously an attempt and an achievement. Proofs are like that, arousals to anger are not.

Aristotle marks this distinction when he observes:

> The most necessary and specific function [*anagkaiotaton kai idion ergon*] of the prooemion is this: to make clear what is the "end" [*ta telos ou henekatelos*] for which the speech [is being given]. As a result, if the subject is clear or short, there is no need of a prooemion. The other kinds that are used are remedies [*iatreumata*] and [are] common [to all species of rhetoric] (III.14.1415a21–25).

Proof is an *energeia*, achieving a guiding end, where strictly emotional appeals are *kinēseis*, aiming at given ends. There follows a second contrast: proof depends on the hearer recognizing what the speaker is doing. I cannot prove something to you unless you realize that that is what I am doing. Such recognition is neither necessary nor sufficient for emotional appeals to succeed: if I recognize that you are trying to frighten me, it does not follow that I am thereby frightened, and you can frighten me without my realizing that that is what you are trying to do. At the extreme, whereas rational appeals depend on being seen as such, emotional appeals often—not always—depend on being concealed: if I try to appear humble as a means of provoking your sympathy, and you realize it, my actions cannot have their intended effect. Argument is an *intentional* action. It depends for its success on a shared intention. It is shared because it is not identified or individuated by its location. That is what it means for cause and effect to be identical, as odd as this sense of identity may seem to modern ears.[28]

The identification of art with argument is not obvious by inspection. External ends and success are knowable by experience without theory. They are, in Aristotle's terms, better known to us. Internal ends are better known by nature, comprehensible only as part of a theoretical network. That is why the sophists failed to see that the artful and the argumentative were the same, and so neglected argument.[29] In the *Ethics* and the *Politics*, it is only the man who knows what the good life is who can see that the money-making life is incomplete and a *kinēsis*, not a true activity. Similarly, once Aristotle shows that there is a rhetorical *energeia*, and that that activity is limited to argument, only then does the condemnation of emotion deserve to be treated as more than the expression of a preference, or a moral ideal.

The *Rhetoric* is not an anticipation of speech act theory. Aristotle does not isolate the artistic side of rhetoric by looking at a variety of linguistic phenomena and finding those in which an effect is achieved in the act itself.

Rhetorical argument may *be* an illocutionary act, but Aristotle does not locate it by such discrimination. He instead looks at which rhetoric is *about* and finds a subject matter in which the argument proffered by a speaker can be identical to the persuasive argument in the audience. The question of a rhetorical *energeia* is not a linguistic question, but a political one. Aristotle's *Rhetoric* is about a *civic* art of rhetoric.

Aristotle begins, in the first chapter, to identify the constitutive end of rhetoric with argument by a distinction between reason and emotion. But identifying rhetorical argument simply by a contrast to emotion is not fully adequate. That distinction, like the distinction between chance and art with which he started the *Rhetoric,* looks clear initially but turns out to be highly problematic. Reason vs. emotion is too easily turned into a topos for polemics and abuse to constitute the differentia of artful rhetoric. It would take an Archimedian point, which is not available for praxis, to distinguish reason from emotion in a principled way.[30] "In many places, the law prohibits speaking outside the subject [in court cases]; in deliberative assemblies the judges themselves adequately guard against this" (I.1.1355a1–3). In deliberative rhetoric, such external regulation is not necessary. It is fortunate that such regulation is unnecessary, because it is also impossible. What is "outside the subject" is a judgment only the audience can make. Aristotle identifies that part of persuasion subject to art by determining what a speaker should do—he should argue—and what he should argue about, the subject of deliberation. There is no secure point outside the art of rhetoric from which to draw the line between the artistic and the inartistic; similarly, there can be no prescriptions for staying on the point within a speech. One of the central lessons the *Rhetoric* can have for a legislator is to learn how to discriminate those aspects of rhetoric that can be addressed by external legislation, and those problems whose only solution is better practice. It is for this reason, I think, that a work addressed to statesmen contains so much practical detail and technical advice.

The argumentative and the artful are both identified with the subject matter of praxis and deliberation. This is the side of persuading and being persuaded which can be an activity of the speaker. Earlier I showed that Aristotle isolated the guiding end of rhetoric by discriminating the "available means" (*ek ton endechomenon*) from other ways of attaining the external end. The *ek ton endechomenon* are also the subject of deliberation itself (I.2.1357a5; *De anima* III.10.433a29). Therefore the subjects of rhetoric and deliberation are the same. Other arts, such as medicine, are also defined by their use of available means to accomplish a given end. The difference is that in the other arts, those given ends are limited and therefore can be specified. Rhetoric has an indefinite given end—persuasion—because it is about the indefinite ends and indefinite particulars of praxis.[31] Plato forces his rhetorical interlocuters into paradoxes, discomfort, and shame by trying to get them to define the end or object of rhetoric; Aristotle avoids these problems by making rhetoric an indefinite art. The end of rhetoric is general, as the subject of rhetoric is the subject of deliberation, namely those ultimate individuals about which there can be no art: "the assemblyman and the juryman are actually judging present and specific cases (*peri parontōn kai aphorismenōn*)" (I.1.1354b7–8).

Maximizing the active side of rhetoric civilizes and domesticates the activity of influencing beliefs and judgments and minimizes the role played by disreputable tactics such as playing on irrelevant emotions in the hearers. It would be a different story—and a different polis—if only minor aspects of persuasion could be subject to art or practiced by citizens. Earlier I mentioned a series of contingencies that infect the project of a civic art of rhetoric: it is a contingent fact that any particular internal ends are reliable means to some given external ends, and equally contingent that important external ends have associated with them constitutive ends that can become the goals of art. It is a contingent fact that nobility lines up with activities that are the most fully satisfying for the doers and with activities that have essential political functions. I pointed out that it is a contingent fact that the instrumental rationality required for achieving external ends and the fuller sense of practical rationality associated with both *technē* and with the virtues line up as they do. That these are not treated as contingent in the *Rhetoric* is a sign, as I also noted above, of the naturalness of the polis.

Aristotle's political project is to maximize the active—*energeia*—side of rhetoric and so civilize the activity of influencing beliefs and judgments and convert into a minor irritant the role played by disreputable tactics such as playing on irrelevant emotions in the hearers, which so scandalized both Socrates and the conservative opponents of the sophists. Aristotle conducts this maximizing strategy by first finding such a best case, where cause and effect are identical, and then extending his account to deal with cases of persuasion in which the whole effect cannot be constituted by the act of persuasion alone. Thus, he will first restrict the art of rhetoric to argument, as opposed to other inducements to action or assent, and then expand the idea of argument beyond our initial expectations, maximizing how much of persuasive activity can be regarded as argumentative by including ethical and emotional appeals. He will first restrict the subject of rhetoric to things that can be otherwise, and then show how it can, in a secondary sense, be about anything at all. He focuses on deliberation as a best case, and then shows how his account can lead to artistic treatments of judicial and epideictic rhetoric as well.

Since a speech is a substance made of form and matter, one must consider the matter as well. Matter is a necessary cause and condition: it is as necessity that one must deal artistically with style and delivery (e.g., III.1.1404a3). Matters of necessity are, in a secondary sense, subject to deliberation and art because they are, in a secondary sense, good: in terms that I will rely on in the next two chapters, they are not good *haplōs*, but they are good *tini*, not absolutely but relatively. *Topics* III.1.116b8–10: "That which is good *haplos* is more worthy of choice than that which is good *tini*, e.g., the enjoyment of health than a surgical operation, for the former is good *haplōs*, the latter is good only *tini*, namely for the man who requires an operation." Even Book III, then, which is notoriously hard to integrate with the first two books, can fall within the scope of rhetoric, although that treatment falls outside the scope of my inquiry.[32] Aristotle's strategy is to begin with narrowly formal considerations and then use the union of form and matter to derive more expansive rhetorical powers.

Rhetoric and *Phronēsis*

Do you come to a philosopher as to a cunning *man, to learn something by magic or witchcraft, beyond what can be known by common prudence and discretion?*

—David Hume, *Political Essays,* 163

Boasters who aim at profit claim the qualities that gratify other people and that allow someone to avoid detection when he claims to be what he is not, e.g. a wise man [sophia] *or doctor.*

—*Ethics* IV.7.1127b19–21

I have been developing an analogy between rhetoric and the virtues, because both have guiding ends and therefore are *energeiai*. But Aristotle's primary analogon to rhetoric is not virtue but medicine. The analogies from rhetoric to medicine are a reminder that so far there is nothing unique to rhetoric in most of this. *All* arts have internal ends. In all the arts, there is an identity between the *energeia* of artist and of thing acted upon. Rhetoric is a method for dealing with a domain apparently beyond method. But even that is no different for medicine— "the type of accounts we demand should reflect the subject-matter; and questions about action and expediency, *like questions about health,* have no fixed [and invariable answers]" (*Ethics* II.2.1104a3–5). Medicine and rhetoric both seem to be arts whose subject lies beyond the reach of rationality.

But there are differences, albeit differences of degree. Rhetoric, being more noble and rational *(entimotatas)* than medicine (I.2.1094b2-3), is even more dominated by the internal, guiding end. It is a contingent fact about the practical world that the more noble and authoritative the art, the more dominant is the internal, guiding, end. An art of rhetoric is exercised by people in their civic capacities, while medicine is not. Because of this nobility and rationality, the constitutive end has value beyond just being a reliable and efficacious means toward the given end. The more rational the art, the more authority the artist has over the user of the art: "a pilot judges rudders better than a carpenter, and the diner, not the cook, is the better judge of a banquet" (*Politics* III.1.1282a22–24),[33] but, as I mentioned, my doctor can tell me that, although I feel healthy, I am not. It would make no sense for the saddlemaker to say that the girths were fine though the rider kept falling off, but doctors—and rhetoricians—can say that the operation was a success though the patient died. When people, beginning with Socrates, say that the true politician does more than tell people what they want to hear, they are pointing to the dominance of an internal good. Rhetoric is more noble, and more dangerous, than medicine, because the internal end is more dominant. At the beginning I noted that politics has indefinite ends, and that rhetoric was an art of speaking about those indefinite ends. These ends are indefinite because they cannot be determined externally. They are internal ends, they are defined and judged in the doing and by the doers. Productive arts are judged by consumers, and no parallel problems come up.

Problems of political judgment come from the fact that external and internal ends—life and the good life for politics overall, winning and arguing for rhetoric—do not line up smoothly, even in the natural polis. There is no reason to expect, moreover, that the internal ends of lesser arts will simply be subordinate to those of *phronēsis* and politics without remainder. In saying something equivalent to "the operation was a success but the patient died," the artist is appealing to standards internal to the practice of medicine and not to the given ends shared by doctor and patient. Praxis gives authority, so that the practitioner of a practical, but not an instrumental, art can make judgments that are not simply subordinate to the user. The interconnections between judgments by maker and user, speaker and audience, will be complicated here beyond what is the case for any art where the external end is dominant and the constitutive end nothing but a means of achieving it.

Aristotle signals that difference in the *Politics:*

> It might be held that it belongs to the same person to judge whether someone has healed in correct fashion and to heal and make healthy one who is suffering from a particular disease, this being the doctor; and similarly with respect to other kinds of experience and art [*empeirias kai technas*]. Just as a doctor must submit to audit by doctors, then, so must the others submit to audit by those similar to them. But "doctor" [is the term that can be applied to] the [ordinary] craftsman, the master craftsman, and thirdly, the person who is educated [*pepaidumenos*] with respect to the art; for there

are some of this [latter] sort in the case of nearly all the arts, and we assign the task of judging to the educated [*pepaidumenos*] no less than to those who know [the art] (III.11.1281b40–1282a8).

Here it is enough to note that internal goods can only be judged by practitioners, and so the judgments of consumers can be disputed, modified, and even overridden when those internal goods are dominant. Many great examples in the history of political oratory are failed speeches, the equivalent to successful operations whose patients didn't survive. The internal end opens up the possibility for criticizing the external ends.

If Aristotle had not shown that rhetoric was a noble enough art for its internal ends to be dominant, the only problems for the legislator would be regulating the effects of rhetoric. Because of the dominance of the internal end, the legislator has to worry about rhetoric *qua* practice as well as its products. In the *Ethics* Aristotle makes a sharp contrast between *phronēsis* and *technē,* doing and making. Art and *ēthos* are incompatible. Arts and powers are, as he says in *Metaphysics* IX, rational *dynameis*. Rational *dynameis* are powers of producing opposites, and so one cannot infer from the power to its products, or from product to agent (2.1046b22–24, b8–9). Good artistic products do not tell me that their maker is also good. Rational *dynameis* are capacities for contraries. Hence their exercise, Aristotle says, takes nothing but knowledge. Virtuous actions take character. The moral virtues allow such inference from act to agent, and therefore they are not capacities for opposites. We do not infer that because someone is a doctor, that person is therefore healthy, but we make the equivalent inference constantly for rhetoric and *phronēsis*. We assume that if someone can give good advice, he or she must be a good person. That distinction between rhetoric and the other arts sets unique problems for a civic understanding of rhetoric.

One response to that typical human inference from rhetorical skill to virtue is to debunk it and lower our expectations. It is naive to believe the lawyer who declaims that her client is innocent: one needs rather to understand the conventions of forensic argument. Similarly, Homer must not be taken as an expert on military strategy. And the viewer who falls in love with an actor because of the role he plays on television needs such increased sophistication to resist a like fallacy. More generally, experience affords ample evidence that skill at practical argument is no guarantee of virtue.

Aristotle does not simply debunk inferences from speech to character, but provides restrictions under which it can be valid. The limited conditions of validity for these inferences will be the central subject of my later chapters. Here, I think, it is enough to note first that when rhetoric is regarded as a practical art, it is not treated as an imitation. Imitations are valued *qua*

products. Praxeis do not have internal principles of motion, as natural objects, but they do have internal principles of value. Therefore they are not
productive or mimetic.[34]

Secondly, we think that people who give sound advice are themselves
virtuous because we know from the *Ethics* that *phronēsis* and goodness are
more than knowledge:

> For the products of a craft determine by their own character
> whether they have been produced well; and so it suffices that they
> are in the right state when they have been produced. But for ac-
> tions expressing virtue to be done temperately or justly [and hence
> well] it does not suffice that they are themselves in the right state.
> Rather, the agent must also be in the right state when he does them
> (II.4.1105a27–32; see also V.8.1135a15).

Aristotle notes this difference between the poetic and practical arts in a way
that casts doubt on the possibility of practical arts for this very reason:

> But is the case of political science perhaps apparently different from
> the other sciences and capacities? For evidently in others the same
> people, e.g. doctors or painters, who transmit the capacity to others
> actively practise it themselves. By contrast, it is the sophists who
> advertise that they teach politics but none of them practises it. In-
> stead, those who practise it are the political activists, and they seem
> to act on some sort of capacity and experience rather than thought
> (X.9.1180b33–1181a3).

To make it even less likely that praxis can be subject to art, we can hire
doctors to heal us, but—as the quotation from the *Republic* at the head of
this chapter puts it—we cannot defer to a *phronimos* to decide for us (*Ethics*
VI.12.1143b30–35). Civic rhetoric cannot be delegated. Recall the warning
that Socrates gives Hippocrates at the beginning of the *Protagoras* about the
difference between buying food and buying wisdom: you can carry food
away from a market in a bag and have someone taste and test it, but it is in
your soul that you carry thoughts away from the marketplace of ideas. We
do not need to possess knowledge ourselves to be healed, beyond what is
involved in picking a good doctor, but we need more active and continuing
judgment for practical decisions. Medicine has two ends, a good internal to
the practice of healing, and an external good of health. Rhetoric has two
ends, the internal good of finding in each case the available means of persuasion, and the external good of successfully persuading. We infer that someone who gives good advice must be prudent because it takes prudence to

formulate good advice. The audience has to judge the guiding as well as given ends of the rhetorician.

Here is the crucial difference between rhetoric and the other arts. Rhetoric is the most noble art, and the most dangerous to the polis. It is the most rational of the arts. All arts and powers have capacities for opposites, but only rhetoric *proves* opposites. All arts are rational capacities for making. Rhetoric is the art of arts in that rationality fully dominates the art. Just as politics is the architectonic art, so rhetoric is the most artistic of arts. Politics is the ethical perfection of all art; rhetoric is the artistic perfection. When audiences infer that good speakers must be intelligent or virtuous, they are expressing their own perception of the subordination of rhetoric to politics, and of the nobility of rhetoric. All the arts are subordinate; only for rhetoric is the subordination problematic. The legislator making intelligent constitutional decisions about the arts has to know a lot more about rhetoric than about medicine. I said earlier that ethical and artistic *energeiai* can diverge. They do here, and therefore rhetoric is always likely to appear to be politics.

Civic vs. Professional Arts

I claim that the purpose of the *Rhetoric* is to articulate a civic art rather than a professional one. If Aristotle can bring it off, it will be an impressive achievement, because the idea of a civic art is almost a contradiction in terms. How a civic art of rhetoric relates to both its artistic and its civic sides will tell us a lot about the role of reason in action, and about the interrelations between thought and character, *logos* and *ēthos*. Thinking of the purpose of the *Rhetoric* as articulating a civic art has important advantages: it makes Aristotle's purpose philosophical rather than polemical and it helps to integrate the *Rhetoric* with the rest of the corpus.

But there is one obvious difficulty with my thesis. Aristotle never explicitly says anything resembling it in the *Rhetoric*. My epigraph from *Ethics* I.2 mentions rhetoric as one of the more honored powers regulated by the politician. But that is not very strong evidence to build an interpretation on. There is one place within the *Rhetoric* itself, however, where Aristotle gives direct evidence for my interpretation of his project as one of constructing a civic rhetoric. He says that the center of this art is deliberative, not judicial, rhetoric, because deliberation is more noble and appropriate for a citizen (*kallionos kai politikoteras tes demegorikes pragmateias ouses*), and more universal and less specialized (*koinoteron*) (I.1.1354b24–25, b31). I said earlier that Aristotle claims originality for his rhetoric's emphasis on argument. It is deliberative rhetoric that can make argument its center. Aristotle's originality in the *Rhetoric* extends to making deliberation the center, and therefore to the idea of rhetoric as *civic* activity. Still, this is scant evidence. I think there is more, but need to get to it by a Platonic detour.

It might seem odd to formulate the idea of a civic art as opposed to a professional one by analogy to a civil war as opposed to a foreign one, but that is where I want to go for my first non-Aristotelian precedent to explicate the idea of a civic art. In the first book of Plato's *Laws,* the Stranger distinguishes between civil and foreign wars, civil the most bitter *(chalepotatos)* and foreign the milder *(polu praoteron)* (629d). Against external opponents, professional courage itself is enough, but "a man could never prove himself loyal and sound [*pistos kai hugies*] in a civil war if devoid of goodness in its entirety" (630b). For foreign wars, mercenaries will do. On my analogy, for professional rhetoric a professional skill analogous to the courage of a professional warrior is all that is needed, and so one can hire someone else to do the fighting, or pleading. There is a clear goal, and successfully achieving that external goal is the only measure of value. In those situations, there will be no inferences from rhetoric to virtue. The internal end of rhetoric plays no role. In contrast, the Stranger thinks that civil war requires virtue in the fullest sense.

Is there a kind of rhetoric that similarly requires virtue? If not virtue, at least attention to the constitutive ends and not only the given ends of persuasion? Are there rhetorical situations where hiring a professional to do the job just won't work? A civic rhetoric is one in which more than the external goal is at stake.[35] The audience is not an enemy, and the civic rhetorician must construct a civic relation between himself and his audience. The analogy to this difference between civil and foreign war distinguishes civic from professional rhetoric by their purposes. Elsewhere in the *Laws,* Plato distinguishes a civic art from its banausic and professional counterparts by who the speaker and audience for the civic art is. This time the analogy is not to war but to medicine:

As there are slaves as well as free men among the patients of our communities, the slaves, to speak generally, are treated by slaves, who pay them a hurried visit, or receive them in dispensaries. A physician of this kind never gives a servant any account of his complaint, nor asks him for any; he gives him some empirical injunction with an air of finished knowledge, in the brusque fashion of a dictator, and then is off in hot haste to the next ailing servant— that is how he lightens his master's medical labors for him. The free practitioner, who, for the most part, attends free men, treats their diseases by going into things thoroughly from the beginning in a scientific way, and takes the patient and his family into his confidence. Thus he learns something from the sufferers, and at the same time instructs the invalid to the best of his powers. He does not give his prescriptions until he has won the patient's support, and when he has done so, he steadily aims at producing compliance (*Laws* IV.720c–e).

And so Aristotle in the *Politics:* "It makes a difference, too, for the sake of what one does or learns something. What is for one's own sake or for the sake of friends or on account of virtue [*di' aretēn*] is not unfree, while the person who does the same thing on account of others would often be held to do something characteristic of the laborer or the slave" (VIII.2.1337b17–21).[36] Here the crux is whether study and pursuit are determined by internal or external, practical or technical, ends.

Civic rhetoric aims at an identity between the speaker making arguments and the audience receiving them. Such a civic relation between speaker and hearer is not always possible or necessary. According to the passage I quoted from the *Laws,* there is no reason to limit oneself to true, civic courage in fighting foreign wars. Similarly, in the *Rhetoric,* there are occasions in which rhetoric should only look to the external end. That is the rhetoric I want to call universal as opposed to the rhetoric restricted to political subjects and purposes. "Even if we have the most exact knowledge, it would not be very easy for us in speaking to use it to persuade some audiences" (I.1.1355a24–27). If the purpose of the *Rhetoric* is to articulate a civic art rather than a professional one, then such professional uses, while licit, are derivative from rhetoric in the restricted, political sense in the same way professional courage is secondary to fully virtuous courage. (Even the inartistic proofs of rhetoric are derivative in this way. At I.15.1376a29–32 Aristotle says that arguments about witnesses "should be chosen from the same topics from which we derive enthymemes.") Sometimes rhetoric will be only necessary, not noble; there is no reason not to hire an expert to persuade one's child to take his or her medicine. But we would only judge that expert by the measure of external success, by whether or not the child took the medicine. Only restricted rhetoric has an internal end. Only restricted rhetoric is limited to argument. Only restricted rhetoric depends on virtue and citizenship and is thus a political activity.

At the beginning I stressed the contingencies that determine whether or not the project of the *Rhetoric* makes sense. A further contingency is that restricted rhetoric, which is truly a practical art and is actualized into an *energeia,* should be dominant over universal rhetoric. In the next chapter I will argue that the three kinds of rhetoric—deliberative, judicial, and epideictic—are species whose forms are identical to their functions, while the rest of rhetoric consists of instances that are in that sense not members of a kind at all. That the artistically central kinds of rhetoric should also be the most noble, and most central to a practical, political life, does not follow from the nature of *technē* in general or rhetoric in particular. It could well be that today civic rhetoric is of such marginal importance that it cannot be central to other forms of rhetoric.

In the history of rhetoric, when that happens, rhetoric becomes a universal art instead of a civic and practical one. Persuasion is no longer an *energeia* but a *kinēsis* which aims at a goal outside itself. Deciding what is best to do and getting others to do it become separate functions: it is the doctor *qua* doctor who decides what medicine I need, and the doctor *qua* rhetor who gets me to take it. Under such circumstances, considerations that are marginal for Aristotle become central to rhetoric: *to prepon, kairos,* decorum, genius, *sprezzatura*. In civic rhetoric, Aristotle can say, as he does at the beginning of Book II, that "there are three reasons why speakers themselves are persuasive; for there are three things we trust other than logical demonstrations. These are practical wisdom and virtue and good will" (II.1.1378a6–9). In universal rhetoric, these virtues are replaced by minimal honesty and competence. For such arts, Aristotle's claim about *technē* in *Ethics* II.4 holds good: knowledge is enough to arrive at the right result. When accomplishing the external end becomes the only value, then rhetoric needs additional moral restraints distinct from the activity of argument itself to keep it from inaugurating a new state of nature.

The more noble and honorable an activity, the less it can be turned over to experts or slaves. Masters have to know how to manage slaves, but, because such knowledge "has nothing great and dignified [*ouden mega, ouden semnon*] about it . . . for those to whom it is open not to be bothered with such things, an overseer assumes this prerogative, while they themselves engage in politics or philosophy" (*Politics* I.7.1255b32–37; cf. I.2.1253a11–18). If rhetoric is a civic art, then the good citizen, even if he can afford it, will not delegate its practice. There is nothing wrong with hiring mercenaries for foreign wars, but this does not make sense in a civil war. It's like the busy parent telling a child, "Here's some money; buy yourself a birthday present."[37]

I find these analogies from the *Laws* illuminating. But there is also an Aristotelian analogue to my idea of civic rhetoric. The discussion of music in *Politics* VIII, incomplete as it is, is fairly close in its concerns to the ones I want to raise for rhetoric. This treatment of music examines music to determine its place in the polis. It intentionally leaves unanswered many questions that are important only to the professional and asks instead what sorts of musical studies and musical practices are suited for citizens rather than professionals.

The *Rhetoric* offers a larger and more complete examination of the same kind. If there is a single power which requires such extensive treatment, it is rhetoric, the noblest art and the one most easily confused with politics itself. Aristotle does not treat it in the *Politics,* because rhetoric is complex enough to need its own full treatment in the *Rhetoric.* He cannot refer as many technical questions to professionals for rhetoric as he can for music, because rhetoric is more noble and dangerous.

In *Politics* VIII Aristotle begins by noting that music is useful for relaxation, and once again, denies that utility is a bar to civic status.

> Yet we must investigate whether this result is not accidental and its nature [*physis*] is not more honorable [*timiotera*] than [just giving pleasure] . . . [we must] see whether in some way it contributes to the character and the soul. This would be clear if we acquire a certain quality in our characters on account of it (VIII.5.1339b42–1340a7).

Music is not simply useful. It has intrinsic value, and for a citizen it is worth pursuing therefore, because it affects the character and the soul. Those effects—whatever they are—are proof that music cannot be regarded as pure technique.[38] The test of whether an activity is political is whether it affects the souls of those engaged in it. Then the judgment of success and achievement is a judgment on the agent and not just the product, the internal end and not simply the external one.

The analogy to the discussion of music in *Politics* VIII has more power still. Aristotle there asks whether and how citizens will learn music. There is a danger in specialization. Becoming too good a musician is vulgar. A lot of learning, it seems, is a dangerous thing. We can reserve some competitions for amateurs alone, as the modern Olympic games tried to do, or prevent professionals from learning some skill: for example, by making it too expensive, like playing polo or mastering Greek composition. In this way, the civic, professional distinction becomes a division by social class.[39] I think Aristotle's own response is more interesting. The only motive for specialization is an extrinsic motive, not the development of the artful power itself.

> It is evident that the learning of it should neither be an impediment with a view to later activities, nor make the body vulgar and useless with a view to military and political training. . . . This would result in connection with the learning [of music] if they did not exert themselves to learn either what contributes to contests involving expertise in the art or those works that are difficult and extraordinary (which have now come into the contests, and from the contests into education) (VIII.6.1341a6–14).

In rhetoric, Aristotle notes that excessive precision is not persuasive (II.22.1395b28–1396a1). Rather than putting this down to a fault in audiences, he shows that unpersuasive rhetoric is rhetoric perceived as professional rather than civic. When Aristotle declares some conclusion in the

Rhetoric adequate and says that it requires no more precision, he is signaling this distinction between a civic and a professional art. Specialization and precision are not natural developments in the history of an art (*Politics* I.11.1258b37–38; but see II.10.1271b24–5). In later chapters I will offer an interpretation, from the point of view of a civic art, of Aristotle's warnings about excessive precision. I will show that in a civic art being overexact does not just make speakers less persuasive; it is a failure in *ēthos*, a fault in character.

Civic rhetoric aims at the internal end, and is therefore governed by internal standards and values, while professional rhetoric, as a purely technical and rational *dynamis*, aims at an external end and so is ruled by ulterior motives. The *only* reason to become exact is an ulterior motive. Again, the treatment of music in the *Politics* is apposite and worth quoting extensively:

> Both in regard to the instruments used, and the degree of profi-
> ciency sought, we reject any professional system of instruction. By
> that we mean any system intended to prepare pupils for competi-
> tions. On such a system the player, instead of treating music as a
> means to his own improvement, makes it serve the pleasure—and
> that a vulgar pleasure—of the audience to which he is playing.
> That is why we regard his performance as something improper in
> a citizen, and more befitting a hireling. The players themselves may
> also become vulgar in the process. The standard by which they fix
> their aim [i.e., the pleasure of their audience] is a bad standard; the
> commonness of the audience tends to debase the quality of
> the music; and the artists themselves, with their eyes on the audi-
> ence, are affected by it—affected not only in mind, but also even
> in body, as they move and swing to suit the taste of their hear-
> ers (VIII.6.1341b9–19, Barker translation).

The inferential sequence here illustrates my claims about civic vs. professional arts. Professional arts aim only at external ends: the vulgar pleasure
of the audience rather than the education of the practitioner. Therefore
professional arts are not worthy of citizens and degrade their practitioners.
In the *Rhetoric* judicial rhetoric is especially prone to precision because its
speeches can have a more finished (*akribestera*) character (III.12.1414a7–18,
17.1418a2–4); so the opportunity and danger of specialist expertise is largest
in judicial rhetoric. With good laws and good audiences, the technical vir-
tuoso will not be persuasive. Professionalization is a danger only in restricted
rhetoric and only in corrupt conditions.

If my overall thesis about the *Rhetoric* is right, this book is a political inquiry which determines the place of rhetoric in the polis. If so, it is surprising that Aristotle thinks such an inquiry requires the kind of detailed, practical knowledge of rhetoric presented in his text. In the *Politics* Aristotle does present a discussion about whether civic musicians should learn to play the flute, but the whole of the *Rhetoric* is marked by such details. It will itself present the right amount of precision.

Let me briefly summarize the results of this chapter. Aristotle's *Rhetoric* articulates a civic art of rhetoric, combining the almost incompatible properties of *technē* and appropriateness to citizens. How a civic art of rhetoric relates to both its artistic and its civic sides will tell us a great deal about the role of reason in action and about the interrelations between thought and character, *logos* and *ēthos*.

What is at stake in claiming that there is an art of rhetoric? If there is an art of rhetoric, what does that tell us about the relation between civic activities and artistic performances?

When I put the questions this way, it seems as though Aristotle has nothing to say about them. But I have argued that he does speak to them by the particular definition of the art of rhetoric he gives, which identifies the artful with an internal end to the practice: finding in each case the available means of persuasion. The internal, constitutive, end is an artistic equivalent of the internal purpose of the moral virtues, which aim at the noble and so are their own end. Once Aristotle discovers such an internal end, then art has values and standards of excellence of its own, which are not reducible to successfully persuading an audience. Aristotle not only determines that rhetoric has an internal end, but shows that that end consists in arguing. Aristotle's great innovation in the *Rhetoric* is the discovery that argument is the center of the art of persuasion.

Like the virtues, the art of rhetoric has internal standards and values. But, I have argued, it is important not to assimilate rhetoric to virtue, although both have internal ends. In fact, the discovery of internal ends might make things worse and drive rhetoric and virtue even further apart, because if rhetoric has its own proper values, it then becomes more of a competitor to virtue than a rhetoric with purely instrumental worth. The more firmly Aristotle has established rhetoric as a *technē* according to his particular criteria, the more crucial it is to specify the relations between rhetoric and politics, a pursuit that will occupy us in the next two chapters.

THE KINDS OF RHETORIC

One of the surprising lessons of the *Rhetoric* is that the legislator for whom it is written needs to know so many of the technical details of rhetorical practice. The legislator has to see what rhetoric looks like from a formal-technical point of view, even if that is a viewpoint he himself does not share. The legislator has to understand the rhetorician's strategic thinking, while subordinating those strategic considerations to higher ends. A statesman could regulate the *effects* of rhetoric without knowing much about its internal workings, but to legislate intelligently about rhetoric as an activity, an *energeia,* takes more detailed understanding.

Since my purposes are different from Aristotle's, I ignore many of the details that Aristotle presents and spend a lot of time on parts of the argument through which he moves quickly. Aristotle finds the existence of the three kinds of rhetoric as unproblematic as he finds most of his conclusions, whereas I think the determination of these species is a large achievement. I noted in the last chapter that his *Rhetoric* places deliberative rhetoric at the center of rhetorical activity, while for his competitors and most other people judicial debate is the first kind of rhetoric that comes to mind. Deliberation puts form and function together in particularly powerful ways, and invites, consequently, questions about the precise sense in which rhetoric has species. In this chapter I ask why there are three kinds of rhetoric, and focus on these kinds, or *eidē,* in detail. Looking at how species are constituted will help to explicate further the ideas of *ergon* and *energeia* central to Aristotle's conception of rhetorical argument, and to clarify the relations between argument and political context, argument and purpose.

Similarly, he seems to regard the relations among the faculties of dialectic and rhetoric and the science of politics as equally unproblematic. In the next chapter I shall look at the topics, the *eidē* in that sense, to discuss the relations between rhetoric and politics and rhetoric and dialectic. Plato seemed to pose the following dilemma: either there is a "true rhetoric" identical with political wisdom, or rhetoric is so far from grasping truth that it is not fit to be part of a state at all. Aristotle has to make rhetoric subordinate to politics while keeping it an art with its own internal ends and integrity.

Aristotle's great innovation in the *Rhetoric* is the discovery that argument is the center of the art of persuasion. If there are three sources of proof, *logos, ēthos,* and *pathos,* then *logos* is found in two radically different guises in the *Rhetoric.* In I.4–14, *logos* is found in enthymemes, the body of proof; form and function are inseparable. In II.18–26 reasoning has force of its own. I.4–14 is hard for modern readers because it treats persuasion as logical, rather than emotional or ethical, but it is not in any easily recognizable sense formal. How can reasoning, or a source of reasoning, be logical yet not formal?

Rhetorical arguments are so related to their purposes—that is the key to Aristotle's success—that it is hard to see how they can be formal. When form is tied to function, what can "form" mean? The institutional context offered by the kinds of rhetoric will be part of the solution. The topics, as forms of argument in quite a different sense, will be another part. The *eidē,* both as kinds of rhetoric in this chapter and as topics of reasoning in the next, show how the enthymeme can lie at the center of a civic art of rhetoric. We will see that to tie form to function, argument must eventually be tied to character so as to constitute a civic art of rhetoric. Later, in Chapter 5, I will return to the second treatment of enthymeme and *logos,* where the ties between logical form and rhetorical function are removed.

The Plurality of Practical Discourse and the Diversity of Goods

It makes an immense difference with respect to pleasure to consider a thing one's own. It is surely not to no purpose that everyone has affection for himself; this is something natural.

—*Politics* II.5.1263a40–b1

Up and down are not the same for all individuals as for the universe.

—*De Anima* II.4.416b3–4

Why are there three kinds of rhetoric? The answer might seem so obvious that the question is not worth raising. Simple observation, pure induction, shows that we all, as Aristotle says in the opening of the *Rhetoric,* "try both to test and maintain an argument [as in dialectic] and to defend themselves and attack" (I.1.1354a3–5). When he introduces the three kinds of rhetoric at the beginning of I.3, he sees nothing problematic in them:

> The species [*eidē*] of rhetoric are three in number; for such is the number [of classes] to which the hearers of speeches belong, to whom the end or object [*telos*] of the speech refers. . . . A member of a democratic assembly is an example of one judging about future happenings, a juryman an example of one judging the past. A spectator is concerned with the ability [of the speaker]. Thus, there would necessarily [*host' ex anagkes*] be three genera of rhetorics, *symbouleutikon* ["deliberative"], *dikanikon* ["judicial"], *epideiktikon* ["demonstrative"]. . . . The "end" of each of these is different, and there are three ends for three [species] [*telos de hekastois touton heteron esti, kai trisin ousi tria*] (I.3.1358a36–b21).

In the lines following he identifies those ends: "The end of the deliberative speaker is the expedient or harmful. . . . the end of the forensic speaker is the just or the unjust. . . . the end of those who praise and blame is the honourable and disgraceful" (b22–28). As the *Rhetoric* proceeds, we learn that each, moreover, has its own characteristic method: deliberation relies mostly on example, judicial rhetoric on the enthymeme, and epideixis on the more and the less (I.9.1368a23–35).

I reject any empirical answer to the question, Why are there three species of rhetoric? These sets of practices may be given and beyond question, but their definition and their interrelations are not. The more Aristotle enumerates their properties, the less could he be drawing his conclusions simply from observation. As the *Rhetoric* goes, Aristotle turns, as he says we should, from things better known to us to things better known *haplōs,* things as they really are (e.g., *Posterior Analytics* I.2.71b33–72a5; *Ethics* I.3.1095a31–b4, I.7.1098a34–b8, VII.1.1145b1–7). The species of rhetoric are given as data known to us at the beginning. Those same species become the conclusion of the inquiry, known in their nature, their relation to rhetoric in general, and to each other. The status of the three kinds of rhetoric as species, their differentiae and interrelations, cannot be known by simple inspection. Are they, for example, jointly exhaustive of some field? Are they mutually exclusive? By purely empirical means, there is no way to tell whether the kinds of rhetoric are not simply classes of speeches grouped together by similarity, or whether there is a stronger kind of species identity here, as in his biology.

In this case, moreover, Aristotle cannot even be moving from the given fact that there are three kinds to a reasoned explanation for the phenomenon. No such fact is given. There are obviously many instances of rhetorical practice that do not fall under his three species.[1] Aristotle mentions, thus, the extrapolitical uses of rhetoric, as when a math teacher has to explain the mean value theorem to resistant students. The rhetoric that is unconfined by subject matter does not fall under the three species. I will argue that such rhetoric has no internal end, and consequently no form that can be identified with function.

The species of rhetoric, I will show, are essential kinds of practical activity, while the instances of rhetorical practice that fall outside these kinds, such as my math teacher, have no such central place in our practical life. To anticipate, it is the species, not rhetoric in general or great individual acts of persuasion, that best exhibit the *forms* and function of persuasion, and hence the *ends* of rhetorical activity. Other examples of rhetoric that fall outside the three species might be needed because of the weaknesses or exigencies of audiences, but the three kinds of rhetoric are instances of practical rationality functioning well, because in the precise sense they are instances of practical rationality *functioning*. This thesis is all the more peculiar because there is no correspondence, as I will show below, between the three kinds of rhetoric and the three parts of government.

In the first chapter I emphasized the way this *Rhetoric* is embedded in the particular circumstances of the polis, and so simultaneously demonstrates the naturalness of the polis and the unnaturalness of our own lives. Aristotle's isolation of the three kinds of rhetoric and his making them central to the art and his lack of interest in the more universal aspects of the art will be a further sign of the distance between his world and ours.

In part, my puzzle about why there are three kinds of rhetoric is just a symptom of a much more general perplexity Aristotle causes. I think that this trinity has the same status as the four causes and the ten categories. There is no transcendental deduction and proof of their necessity. But they are not merely empirical either. That disjunction does not capture the status of these things. If the polis is natural, and if the natural world is not wildly different in science than it is in ordinary understanding, then these lists fall somewhere between the transcendental and the empirical. It is hard to think back from the world we live in into such a world.[2]

Kant complained that Aristotle's categories were arbitrary, because they could not be systematically deduced. The same charge could apply here. I want to show why rhetoric has to have kinds or species, in which practical reason exercises its plural functions. To move from such plurality to these three kinds of rhetoric cannot be accomplished by philosophical deduction, but by examining the institutions of the polis which define human functioning and human flourishing.

The kinds of rhetoric are defined by their purposes and ends, by their practical and conventional contexts, and by the methods they usually employ to accomplish those ends. The kinds of rhetoric are conventional, but not therefore arbitrary or unreal. That is how these kinds, like the ten categories, four causes, and the rest, can have a status that is neither purely empirical nor purely transcendental. The fact that there are plural kinds of rhetoric, instead of a single system of practical discourse, follows from the nature of the practical world as Aristotle describes it. The plurality of practical languages is a consequence of the plurality of practical goods, and of the precise kind of plurality of goods that he finds.

He sees a practical distinction between what is good for me and what is good simply, and that is the ultimate source of plurality of both practical goods and of practical languages: "What is fine and what is just, the topics of the inquiry in political science, differ and vary so much that they seem to rest on convention only, not on nature. Goods, however, also vary in the same sort of way, since they cause harm to many people" (*Ethics* I.3.1094b14–19). "'The good' has two meanings: it means both that which is good unconditionally [*haplōs*], and that which is good for some thing or person, or relatively [*tini*]" (VII.12.1152b29; see also *Topics* I.5.102a26, II.12.115b11, 22–30).[3] Only people, among all the animals and among all the substances in the world, can have such a distinction between what is best for an individual and what is best for a species.[4] That distinction between what is good *haplōs* or in the abstract and what is good for me here and now is the first step towards praxis and toward the plurality of kinds of rhetoric. Sometimes people wrongly choose the apparent good over the real one, but sometimes they *should* choose what is good for them, and not what is simply good. Beings who live by reason and deliberation—even citizens of good states—*must* encounter a diversity of goods. The more unnatural our political circumstances, the more divergence will there be between what is good *haplōs* and what is good in the circumstances, and the greater the diversity of goods. The discovery of unlimited accumulation and the autonomy of the economy enlarges the scope of people who aim at life, not the good life. Under such conditions, there should be no reason to think that there would be a single best life, let alone a common good. Once what is best for me diverges too much from what is best *haplōs,* an analysis in terms of the human good loses its point.[5]

Without a distinction between good and goods, between what is good and what is good for me, there could be a general practical reason that would simultaneously say what we should do, what is right, and what is good. The diversity of goods, however, requires a diversity of the kinds of practical discourse. The diversity of goods is organized practically, and not theoretically. In a natural polis, the kinds of rhetoric will be conventional without being arbitrary. Attempts to make the diversity of goods into a theoretical problem, from Plato on, make diversity incoherent or irrational. (The only issue then is whether the diversity is illusory, and should be eradicated, or whether it shows that ethics is in fact irrational. That is the issue between Plato and the sophists.)

Aristotle not only thinks that such reduction is intellectually mistaken, he further thinks that assimilating what is good and what we should do is the cause of *injustice*. Injustice results from someone inferring from the fact that something is good to the conclusion that it is therefore good for him. Instead, he says, we should *choose* what is in fact good for us and *wish* that what is good for us be good *haplōs* (*Ethics* V.1.1129b1–17; cf. *Rhetoric* I.7.1365a35, *Metaphysics* VII.3.1029b5f). Similarly, the *akolastos* of *Ethics* III.10 thinks that because pleasure is good, he should aim at it.[6]

These reductions are wrong not just intellectually, but ethically. Something can be good *haplōs* but not desirable in some given circumstances. If contemplating the bust and poems of Homer is an intrinsically good activity, it does not follow that I should engage in it now. Intrinsic value and unconditional value are not the same.[7] Because of such complications, practice cannot be reduced to theory. Therefore, there is a need for deliberation, choice, and rhetoric.

Later, in Book II, Aristotle will say that the sophists' art was really an elaboration of a single supposed insight, the fallacy of *secundum quid*, the idea that if something is true overall it is true in a particular case and conversely (II.24.1401a23–24). In Chapters 5 and 6 I will use the example of this argument for "creation science": since evolution falls short of some unstated standards of certainty, it follows that both evolutionary biology and "creation science" are each only probable, hence equally probable, and hence they deserve equal standing. Injustice is based on such a fallacy, the thought that because something is good *haplōs* or *simpliciter*, it is good *pros ti,* and so desirable now, and accordingly, the thing I now should do. We might not call injustice, even on this etiology, a fallacy today, but if we don't, that will be because we presuppose a logic with distinctions of form and content that I will question in those later chapters. Aristotle thinks that such an error is better diagnosed as ethical than logical.

The distinction between what is good *haplōs* and what is good for me, the first datum that leads to the plurality of kinds of rhetoric, entails a further complication in the relation of goods to good, a potential bidirectionality between good and desire. Because there is a difference between what is good and what is good for me, I have to decide what to do. The privileged position of agency is connected to the purposiveness of practical discourse, which will, in turn, generate the plurality of kinds of rhetoric and of moral languages. As soon as it is not the case that because something is good, I should choose it, it then becomes possible that my desires be a means of choosing among goods, and so to that extent a source of goodness in itself.

That privileged position of the agent, as I will show, must force a modification for purposes of practical argument of such ontological claims as "We desire an object because it seems good, rather than it seems good because we desire it" (*Metaphysics* XII.6.1072a29–30). In *Rhetoric* I.6 we find instead topics of argument like: "Things that are deliberately chosen [are good]" (1363a19); "And [things are good if they turn out] as people want" (1363a25); "And [people value] things they think they are lacking in, even if small; for nonetheless, they choose to get these things" (1363a29–30); "And [people value] things they happen to long for; for this seems not only pleasant but also rather good" (1363a37–38); "And most of all, each category of people [values as a good] that to which their character is disposed" (1363b1). Arguments in the *Rhetoric* are responsive to the fact that my valuing something gives me a reason for action, and that my thinking something good gives me a reason to value it. As he puts it in the *Politics,* "there are two things above all which make human beings cherish [*philein*] and feel affection [*agapeton*], what is one's own and what is dear" (II.4.1262b22–23; cf. *Nicomachean Ethics* IX.7.1167b32–1168a9, IX.9.1169b30–1170a4; *Eudemian Ethics* VII.12.1244b28–34; *Rhetoric* I.11.1371a31–b12). The *Ethics,* the *Politics,* and the *Rhetoric* all in different ways show that to live beyond rules in the world of praxis is not to be blown about by passion but to act through character. Similarly it need not open doors to subjectivity to say that something is desirable and worth choosing because I want it. (Note that it isn't *good* because I want it. Instead, of the things that are good, some are good for me, and of those good for me, the ones for me to do are the ones I want to do.)

Rhetoric has to be flexible enough to be a responsible, obedient offspring of a politics whose subjects—justice and utility—exemplify a similar variability. What is just is determined relative to a constitution. But those constitutional conceptions of justice can still be criticized by an absolute justice. That absolute standard of justice, however, cannot itself be directly instantiated (except perhaps in the best state *haplōs* in *Politics* VII and VIII). Utility, similarly, is relative to a person and also relative to the fixed standards of the good man. I want to show that the kinds of rhetoric are conventional without being arbitrary. What is good and what is practicable are similarly conventional without being arbitrary, variable without being capricious.

While the *Rhetoric* follows the *Ethics* and *Politics* in emphasizing the need for perception and judgment of the particular, the *Rhetoric* has a stronger thesis. In the *Ethics* and *Politics,* the plurality of goods and of loci of goods, types, and tokens, looks for the most part unsystematic because they are beyond the reach of formulae. The individual *phronimos* measures what is to be done here and now; where rules leave off, there the work of the *phronimos* begins, and nothing further, it seems in the *Ethics* and *Politics,* needs to be said. The indefinite plurality of goods in the *Ethics* and *Politics* generates the *systematic* plurality of kinds of rhetoric. That such plurality can be systematic is one of the outstanding achievements of the *Rhetoric*. If the diversity of goods comes from the fact that what is good for me is not defined fully by what is simply good, it is surprising that such a diversity could issue in a systematic plurality. Aristotle has found an orderly plurality.

The diversity of goods and variety of goodness generate the idea of deliberation about things that are up to us, and things in which our actions make a difference in the world. But the diversity of goods and the varieties of goodness are not enough to lead to plural species of rhetoric, let alone to the particular interrelations Aristotle's kinds of rhetoric have to each other. That conclusion only follows from a far more precise conception of practical reason, one informed by Aristotle's distinctions between abstract and concrete good, and by his conception of the relation between something being good and my desiring it, and so between first and third person understandings of the good. I need to explore more closely the relations among the kinds of rhetoric.

Plurality, Function, and the Three Kinds of Rhetoric

The producer is fond of the product, because he loves his own being. And this is natural, since what he is potentially is what the product indicates in actualization
—*Ethics* IX.7.1168a7–9

In many respects, the kinds of rhetoric resemble biological species. Each is the unit of analysis; each possesses an integrity missing in more general phenomena, like persuasion or life, and in the concrete individual, a speech, or an animal. Resembling Aristotle's biological species, the kinds of rhetoric are unlike what genres become in the more literary context of most later rhetorics.[8] The kinds of rhetoric are not only the terms of analysis for Aristotle's *Rhetoric,* they are the *forms* that persuasion takes. Individuals are members of species when they have functions, and the possession of a function requires a peculiar relation of form and matter, based on a relation of form to end. Earlier I argued that the art of rhetoric was limited to argument because only in arguing was the cause identical with the effect. The three kinds of rhetoric, deliberative, judicial, and epideictic, are cases in which persuasion is something that can be accomplished *in* as well as *by* the speech, and hence are situations in which the actual cause and actual effect can be identical, while other instances of persuasion consist in a gap between what the speaker accomplishes and what happens to an audience.[9]

There is an ambiguity about *telos* in the *Rhetoric,* the same ambiguity that has to be found in any practical *energeia,* which is its own end, and which still has an external goal as well. Aristotle says that we deliberate not about ends but about things that lead to the end. The telos of each particular choice is the end about which we do not deliberate but towards which we deliberate. In choosing to act liberally now, I am hoping to give financial help to some particular person for some specific reason in a particular set of circumstances. At the same time, if I am acting liberally and as the liberal person acts, and not just doing a liberal act, my telos is to be a certain kind of person. Similarly in rhetoric: I am always aiming at persuading someone. At the same time, if I am arguing artfully, I have another, internal, end, which means measuring up to some artistic standards not exhausted by success.

In the *Ethics* Aristotle shows that individual acts of virtue do indeed fall into species. There are kinds of virtuous actions which, *qua eidē,* are my internal ends. There is no guarantee prior to his analysis that that has to be true. It could have turned out that each individual act has its external telos, and that in addition I aim at being good *simpliciter,* or being a good person. Then there would be nothing intermediate between individual acts and an overall goal of goodness. In the same way Aristotle discovers species in the *Rhetoric.* He finds that the central set of individual instances of persuasion fall into kinds. Therefore telos can have the same pair of meanings in rhetoric. In each case I try to persuade someone. Also, in each artful case, I have an end of persuading, limited by the species of argument—I am persuading about the useful, the just, or the noble.

The existence of rhetorical species, therefore, pushes Aristotle's argument one stage beyond the discovery of internal ends. These internal ends are species.

The three kinds of rhetoric represent rhetorical activity at its best, as it exercises most directly essential human political functions. In these species, there is a rhetorical form which matches the argumentative function: that is what it means for them to be *energeiai.* In persuasion in general, there is no such form. I showed before that argument is the only kind of rhetorical act that can be accomplished in the speech itself. Here I am pointing to the limited conditions under which such identity of cause and effect is possible. If practices are identified by internal goods and internal ends, only the rhetorical acts that fall under the three species qualify as practices.

It follows from the dependence of rhetorical species on their practical ends that there are many individual members of the genus rhetoric which are not instances of a kind. Aristotle's criterion for being part of the *art* of rhetoric is narrowed by the same functional criterion as that for membership in a species. Aristotle also notes that rhetoric is employed outside these species, for example, by the lawyer explaining the kinds of liability to a client in a hurry, or the doctor convincing a patient to take medicine, but such rhetoric lacks the full sense of form and function exhibited only in rhetoric's species. The art of rhetoric is only about the kinds of rhetoric, because it is only there that rhetoric can be practical and not poetic, an illocutionary act and not a perlocutionary effect, an *energeia* and not a *kinēsis*.

In the practical sciences and arts, there is no guarantee that individuals within a genus must fall within some species of that genus. Most biological individuals fall within species because they are generated naturally, but no practical individual—no individual instance of persuasion, for example, and no polis or citizen either—comes into being by nature, and so the reason— the internal principle of motion—which guarantees that biological individuals will generally be members of species does not obtain in rhetoric or other arts. Natural individual substances exist in kinds: this is one of the crucial, central, facts about nature and substance articulated in the *Physics* and the *Metaphysics*. Just because art imitates nature, there is no reason to expect, and some reason not to expect, that the human world will resemble the natural world in this respect. How much of the world of praxis and art will similarly sort itself out into species is a fundamental question for Aristotle in the *Ethics,* the *Politics,* and the *Rhetoric.*

In the first chapter I noted that the transmission of form and regularity are more tightly connected in nature than in art. For that reason, there will be more made objects that are not members of kinds than there will be anomalous natural objects. That is the reason I maintain that the species of rhetoric are rhetoric at its best: they are functional kinds of rhetoric. Other instances of rhetorical practice might be necessary: a doctor explaining oncology to an frightened and ignorant patient needs rhetorical skill, in addition to medical knowledge, for success. In that case, though, there is no identity between the doctor persuading and the patient being persuaded. It is necessary, but not good; it would be better in cases like that if rhetoric were unnecessary. Rhetoric in general, Aristotle tells us in a metaphor that will be central to the next chapter, is the offspring (*paraphues,* I.2.1356a25, cf. I.4.1359b10) of dialectic and of politics. On my analysis, nature breeds true only in these species, and often has progeny which are not members of a kind. The conventions of the kinds of rhetoric not only supply continuities that substitute for natural inheritance, they provide places in which rhetorical activity has political functions, and consequently the proper relation to both its parents, dialectic and politics. These species are not just instances grouped together by similarity.

Like biological species, rhetorical kinds are the primary locus of existence and of form. But in other respects, the kinds of rhetoric differ in important ways from biological species. These kinds of rhetoric, unlike biological species, are interdependent, since they are parts of a single art and a single polis. Biological species are all part of a single cosmos, but plants and animals are primary among things that have a nature, while the cosmos as a whole has none. In politics, it is the other way around: particular activities have functions, and their own good, only by being parts of the whole of the polis.[10]

This difference between the natural and the human world is already anticipated in Protagoras's myth. According to his story, there is a single picture into which all animal species fit, and they are interrelated by predator/prey relationships. There is a single polis into which different men fit, interrelated first by the division of labor and exchange and then by justice and piety, the gifts of Hephaestus and Prometheus.

While not accepting Protagoras's myth as such, Aristotle points to a number of interrelations among the kinds of rhetoric that would make no sense for fully natural, biological, species. Striking the right balance between independence and interdependence for the three kinds of rhetoric is a critical ethical project, much as striking an analogous balance between personal independence and interdependence is a critical ethical project for understanding the self-sufficiency of good lives, friendship, and the *polis*. There is no equivalent in biology to the problem of the unity of the virtues, because that is a problem of interdependency. So too for the kinds of rhetoric. It is clear that they are not jointly exhaustive, but we can still wonder whether they are mutually exclusive, and how they are interrelated.

The simplest and most direct answer to the question, How are the kinds of rhetoric related to each other? comes in a passage from I.3 that I quoted in part at the beginning: "For the deliberative speaker [the end] is the advantageous and the harmful . . . and he includes other factors as incidental [*symparalambanounti*]: whether it is just or unjust, or honorable or disgraceful . . . and they make other considerations incidental to these" and similarly for the other two kinds of rhetoric (1358b21–27). What is the end of one kind of rhetoric is an accessory in another.[11] Here are three ends, the useful, the just, and the noble. Each can be an accessory consideration in a persuasive discourse about the other.

It is easy enough to see what he means in practical terms, but not simple at all to understand what this interrelation means about how the species of rhetoric are species. Sometimes I begin, in deliberative rhetoric, with a legitimate policy goal. To take an example that I will return to periodically in the next four chapters, I take as my end the useful result of a unified American commonwealth, and calculate how educational institutions can further that goal. Sometimes there are considerations of rights, more the field of judicial rhetoric, that constrain my deliberations. I may not, for example, promote a more perfect union by requiring all children to attend public schools, since that violates their right to free exercise of religion.

In that case the considerations of judicial rhetoric are accessory to deliberation, even if a significant enough accessory to make me reject a given line of deliberation. But the relations between deliberative and judicial rhetoric can be different. I can face a judicial situation in which I have to decide what punishment is right for this criminal. Policy considerations, about how to make this particular punishment serve as an example to deter others, are accessory to the determination of desert, fairness, and proportionality.[12]

But these examples do not speak to the theoretical question: What must the relations among these three ends be if each can also occupy a subordinate position in arguments about the other? In the *Politics* and the *Poetics,* where he also talks about some things being accessories, no such reciprocal priority is possible: spectacle is an accessory, and often a distraction, to the proper pleasures caused by plot, and that is a hierarchy that is not subject to reversal. Slaves are accessories and necessary conditions of the state, while citizens are essential to it, and no reversal is countenanced. Similarly, at the beginning of the *Rhetoric* (I.1.1354a13–15), Aristotle says that "only *pisteis* are artistic (other things are supplementary [*prosthekai*]), and these writers say nothing about enthymemes, which is the 'body' of persuasion" (see also III.1.1404a1–7; III.14.1415a21–25). He immediately goes on to identify those accessories with appeals to irrelevant emotions. There is no other art in which those emotional appeals are central, and the enthymeme an accessory.

Clearly, one essential difference between the kinds of rhetoric and biological species will be this strange fact that what is essential to one kind will be an accidental accessory to another. This odd possibility can come about only because the ultimate unity here is not the species, but the art as a whole, and, even more, the polis itself as a whole.

Aristotle does not face the problem by wondering about reciprocal priority, but instead notices a series of functional interrelations. First, each can check the other, and either correct or fortify judgments. Both deliberative and forensic rhetoric talk about the expedient, at I.10.1369b32, and deliberation and epideixis are even more tightly connected: "Praise and deliberations are part of a common species [*koinon eidos*] in that what one might propose in deliberation becomes encomia when the form of expression is changed." (I.9.1367b36–1368a; cf. II.23.1399b32–1400a4). Some of the interconnections among the useful, the good, and the just are articulated and employed in the *Ethics* and the *Politics.* Justice is often defined by the useful in the *Politics,* and throughout the *Rhetoric* (e.g., III.6.1279a17,

III.7.1279a28–29, III.12.1282b17; cf. *Ethics* V.1.1129b14–16, IX.9.1160a13; *Rhetoric* I.15.1373b19). When justice is defined in the *Ethics* in terms of what is good for the individual, there are interrelations among good for me, good for others, and good as such; the *Politics* revolves around problems connecting living, living together, and living well.[13] (Similarly, to mention a point I will return to in later chapters, *phronēsis* and the virtues of giving and taking advice, *synesis, eubolia,* and *gnōmē,* are all functions of the same character in the *Ethics.*) The causes of injustice for forensic rhetoric in I.10 can be known partly from the epideictic discussion of the virtues in I.9, and partly from the subsequent discussion of the emotions, he says (I.10.1368b24–26).

Those cross-references and that reciprocal priority make for complications. If a just act looks even more attractive to a jury because it will also set a useful precedent, it becomes equally possible for justice and utility to be at odds. Once there is plurality, conflict is always a possibility. That possibility for conflict emerges as soon as Aristotle defines the ends of rhetoric's kinds and, consequently, the subordination of accessory considerations. A sign of this subordination, he says immediately after the lines I quoted above, is "and these speakers bring up other considerations in reference to these qualities" (I.3.1358b29). In the first two examples of lack of dispute, the opposite of argument is concession:

> A judicial speaker [might not deny] that he has done something or done harm, but he would never agree that he has [intentionally] done wrong. . . . Similarly, deliberative speakers often grant other factors, but they would never admit that they are advising things that are not advantageous [to the audience] (1358b30–37).

But his third example is different:

> And similarly, those who praise or blame do not consider whether someone has done actions that are advantageous or harmful [to himself] but often they include it even as a source of praise that he did what was honorable without regard to the cost to himself (1359a1–3; cf. I.9.1366b35–1367a1).

Here the lack of utility is evidence for honor. Because utility is an accessory, its neglect is proof that the man rightly disregards (*ouden phrontizousin* at b39) it in the name of honor. From plurality come not concessions, which signal irrelevance, but conflict.[14]

Each of the three kinds of rhetoric can be prior to the other two. This potential for reciprocal priority and multiple relations of subordination makes each kind of rhetoric, and each purpose, serve double duty, first as an organizing, or second-order, principle, and then as a preference, exception, counterweight, etc. Justice is tempered by concerns of utility, so that we wonder about the deterrent value of different sentences for the guilty; considerations of utility leave room for further interstitial determination by considerations of fairness. Moreover, sometimes it is tactically useful to insist on the purity of one kind of rhetoric, rejecting contamination of a determination of justice by considerations of utility. The interrelations among the kinds of rhetoric can itself thus become the subject of rhetorical argument. To recall two arguments I quoted above, in deliberative rhetoric one should prefer what is useful to oneself to what is useful *haplōs,* while in epideixis it is a sign of nobility to do what is good *haplōs* over what is good for the individual (I.7.1365a35, I.9.1366b35–1367a1).

The useful, the just, and the good are all mutually translatable. None of them, therefore, admits of or requires univocal definition. I can choose one thing over another because it is more useful, without being able—without needing—to define the useful further. Earlier I noted that it is the error of the unjust man to reduce deliberation to knowledge of the good. Here there would be a similar error in attempts to define the *summa genera.* In the *Ethics* it is the man whose goal is honor who would give the noble independent definition, and the *Politics* argues against those who try to define the just without thinking about the useful. The *Rhetoric* stops being *practical* discourse, and becomes applied theory instead, if practical deliberation and judgment presupposes definitions of utility, justice, and the good.

However, as *summa genera,* that trio can be converted one into each of the others. They are not independent variables, like color, weight, and shape. Unlike the transcendentals, which are also mutually convertible, the ends of rhetoric can also conflict and compete with each other. It might sound strange to affirm both that the ends of rhetorical kinds define each other and that they can also conflict with each other. But that double relationship follows from the difference with which I began between goods *haplōs* and what is good for me. Considered abstractly, what is just, useful, and noble define one another; in particular cases, the demands of justice, utility, and nobility can conflict. What is good for me is not necessarily what is good *haplōs,* but what is good for me must always be understood relative to what is good *haplōs.* The end of deliberative rhetoric, the useful, is defined relative to happiness; the end of forensic rhetoric, the just, is defined through a long discussion of the principal cause of injustice, pleasure. The end of epideixis, the noble, requires an understanding of virtue, and these three are interdependent enough sometimes to conflict. Biological species are defined by differences within a genus, but rhetorical species are defined in terms of each other. What is essential in one kind is an accessory in another.

Plurality, Diversity, and
Incommensurability

Most people wish for what is fine, but decide to do what is beneficial; and while it is fine to do someone a good turn without the aim of receiving one in return, it is beneficial to receive a good turn.

—*Ethics* VIII.14.1162b34–1163a1

The benefactor's action is fine for him, so that he finds enjoyment in the person he acts on; but the person acted on finds nothing fine in the agent, but only, at most, some advantage, which is less pleasant and lovable.

—*Ethics* IX.7.1168a10–12

Knowing what is good does not by itself tell us what to do. There is a further reason, apart from conflict, that translation without remainder is impossible. There is a further respect in which the *Rhetoric* points to a complexity in the diversity of goods. This additional reason leads not to conflict but to incommensurability. Because of the difference between what is good and what I should do, a given rhetorical *argument* and plea within one kind cannot be translated automatically into another genre. Overall, what is just, noble, and useful coincide, but each has its own kind of surplus that resists translation.

The necessary, the lawful, and the conventional are the characteristic forms taken by the surplus of deliberation, judicial rhetoric, and epideixis respectively. Because each resists translation, each is a way of placing a proposed action or judgment beyond argument: to say that it is necessary to do something means that I do not have to defend it any further. To say that someone needs to be punished because the law says so is designed to put that verdict beyond argument. And the same for the conventional in epideixis: this is good because this is the way we have always done things. Moreover, the autonomy of each provides for specific kinds of abuses. Corrupt pleading, legalism, and emotional appeals are abuses naturally at home in forensic rhetoric. The impractical moralizing of epideixis can make morality purely arbitrary and conventional. The narrowly utilitarian topics of deliberation pleading necessity make necessity into a convenient excuse. But these three forms of surplus offer more than new avenues for abuse. They are the sorts of situations in which translation fails because the useful, the just, and the honorable do not coincide. For that reason, these are cases which fall short of the central and best kind of praxis: they are the mixed cases in which we must do something although we do not fully choose to do it, and in which things, because conventional, could be otherwise, but not through our efforts. That is why they generate their own forms of abuse and corruption.

Owing to the interconnections of the kinds of rhetoric, each can modify the other, and so particulars can exert their practical authority in a rational, indeed articulable, way. Considerations of justice and goodness can intervene in otherwise instrumental policy decisions, and utility can modify, or fortify, judgments of criminal liability. Sometimes it is not so much the act itself, or its results, that are chosen. We choose to be, and act like, a certain kind of person. But there are also times when it is better to follow rules than display one's character, and the connected variety of purposive discourse permits both.[15]

Having plural, often redundant, and therefore sometimes conflicting, practical languages, in this way furthers practical decision making. As I will show in much greater detail in later chapters, rules of logic authorize and justify their conclusions, but rules of practical reason do not: their conclusions receive multiple and sometimes conflicting authorization from their antecedents, their consequents, from similar judgments, from the need to harmonize one conclusion with established judgments in related areas, and from a variety of other sources.

The useful is not automatically just or honorable: there is a surplus, usually marked off by *necessity,* for what it is best to do, although unjust, or at least not just. Deliberative rhetoric is especially concerned with the possible and the impossible (II.18.1392a6–7), and so necessity becomes its special plea. The characteristic method of deliberation is reasoning from example, and so a concern with consequences and success dominates. It is easy for pleas of necessity to get a hearing. Apart from that surplus, in the area where translation is successful, the intertranslation between utility and justice assures that deliberative reason not be reduced to instrumental reason. If the useful is generally just, then it is not useful in the amoral sense that arguments from necessity bring with them.

The just is not automatically useful or noble. Its surplus is the lawful. Its reliance on the enthymeme can make it relatively immune to claims of utility and nobility. Apart from that surplus, we can generally tell whether something is just by seeing whether it is useful, and useful for what. Deliberative stands to forensic rhetoric here as the other moral virtues stand to justice. Justice is reason without passion, and so justice includes, although it is not exhausted by, the intelligent application of rules. That is the sense in which the lawful is the surplus of forensic rhetoric. The other moral virtues include some advice and rules of thumb, but nothing that binds the agent more fully, as laws do for the just man. There are no rules that could be used in forensic rhetoric to exclude emotional appeals completely, and the convertibility between justice and the other moral virtues, and so between forensic and deliberative rhetoric, shows that the division between reason and the passions cannot be a permanent one, or some deep psychological claim.

What is praiseworthy, finally, is sometimes neither useful nor just. I have earlier pointed out instances in which the fact that something is harmful is a sign of nobility. There the useful and the noble conflict. Here I want to look at the incommensurable surplus in which considerations of justice and utility simply do not apply. I want to spend more time on this surplus, because it indicates something about the unusual status of epideixis among the kinds of rhetoric. We can praise "not only a man or a god . . . but inanimate objects and any random one of the other animals" (I.9.1366a28). Praise extends further than deliberation, exactly as wish in *Ethics* III.2 and 4 extends further than deliberation: e.g., "we wish [not only for results we can achieve], but also for results that are [possible, but] not achievable through our own agency, e.g., victory for some actor or athlete. But what we decide to do is never anything of that sort, but what we think would come about through our own agency" (III.2.1111b24–6).[16] This excess of the epideictic over the deliberative comprises the aspects of the noble that resist translation into the useful. "Most men pursue what is fine (*to kalon*) only when they have a good margin in hand (*periousia*)" (*Eudemian Ethics* VII.10.1243a38–39). "And possessions that bring no fruit [are more honorable]; for [they are] more characteristic of a free man" (*Rhetoric* I.9.1367a27). These goods are not only not useful, they are useless, and their nobility consists in their lack of utility (cf. *Nicomachean Ethics* IV.3.1125a11–12; *Eudemian Ethics* III.5.1233a7). Once again, incommensurability and plurality can lead to conflict.

There are also lines of argument that are simply irrelevant to choice, such as the one that follows immediately on those I just quoted from *Rhetoric* I.9:

> Things peculiar to each nation are honorable [among them]. And whatever are signs of the things praised among them [are honorable]; for example, in Lacedaimon it is honorable to have long hair, a sign of a free man (1367a28–32).

If epideixis extends further than deliberation, and yet "praise and counsels have a common idea," then there is a part of the noble that is not reducible to the useful, although they are in another respect inseparable. The surplus of wish over choice allows evaluations of things ouside an agent's control.[17] Without getting distracted by the current debates about incommensurability, I think that these three kinds of surplus that resist translation, and so are incommensurable values, show that incommensurability does not imply unintelligibility.[18]

Before leaving this discussion of the strange status of epideixis, I want to explore briefly a problem that we will see increasingly as the central problem of the *Rhetoric,* the relation between *ēthos* and *logos*. Each of the three kinds of surplus highlights one aspect of the complex and crucial relation between *ēthos* and *logos*. Each of the three kinds of rhetoric has its own way of being simultaneously ethical and logical, and each, consequently, has its own characteristic danger and vice. The three kinds of surplus reappear as three opportunities for abuse as the logical and ethical sides of rhetorical argument fall apart.

Deliberation is both ethical and logical because it is reasoning that requires knowledge of ends as well as means. Deliberation is always in danger of becoming merely instrumental reasoning, since, as chapter 8 shows, it simply takes for granted whatever end is desired by the audience; we deliberate about means, not ends. Pleas of necessity, the deliberative surplus, separate the demands of *logos* from the end-grasping side of *ēthos*.

Because epideictic argument reasons without commitment to truth, Chapter 9 emphasizes and advocates paralogisms justified by success more than the other kinds of rhetoric. There are no external criteria for success, as there are in speech that aims at a truly useful policy or at deciding who is really guilty of what. Epideixis is the most purely conventional of the kinds of rhetoric, and the sense in which its argument is ethical is similarly conventional. The lack of commitment by a speaker, which is the form that *ēthos* takes here, allows *logos* to degenerate into the display rhetoric that makes cleverness into virtuosity.

Judicial rhetoric is, when it functions well, simultaneously ethical and logical because its practical conclusions are essentially ethical and political decisions concerning guilt and desert and not just causation in some neutral sense. Judicial rhetoric lends itself to the abuse of relying on the lawful, having for its ideal a judgment that is trustworthy precisely because it excludes character as an intrusion of the "subjective."

Each of these kinds of abuse results from the separation of the logical from the ethical. Each of these forms of abuse could be read by contemporary eyes as a variety of relativism, and each ethical form of rhetoric consequently as a practical overcoming of relativism. Although I cannot pursue the point here, the whole problem of relativism is a problem of trying to make purely logical arguments where only ethical arguments can fit. In deliberative rhetoric, without the scientific unification of the things people include under happiness, there is the possibility that different people will have different ends, and so Aristotle shows in chapter 8 how ends vary with constitutions. What is *good for* one person and one polis will not be good for another. Similarly, in chapter 9 we learn that what is *good according to* one person or polis will not be good according to another.[19] In chapter 11 we will find similar variations among the causes and varieties of pleasures, and in chapter 13 among the differences in justice defined by the lawful. To argue ethically does not, we now see, mean actually being a good man outside the activity of making this particular speech (I.2.1356a5–13). All these sources of relativism come from the distinction between things that are absolutely good and those that are relatively good. As he puts it in the *Topics,*

> It is honorable in some places to sacrifice one's father . . . but *haplōs* it is not honorable. . . . Again, it is expedient at certain times to take drugs, for example, when one is ill; but it is not expedient *haplōs.* . . . Now the honorable *haplōs,* or its contrary, is that which you will say is honorable or its contrary without any additional qualification. For example, you will not say that to sacrifice one's father is honorable, but that "in the eyes of certain people" it is honorable; it is not, therefore, honorable *haplōs.* But you will say that to honor the gods is honorable without adding any qualification; for it is honorable *haplōs.* So whatever is generally regarded as honorable or disgraceful, or anything else of the kind, without any additional qualification, will be called so *haplōs* (II.12.115b22–35).

It is worth noting that what could be for other purposes quite different forms of relativism are, for the argumentative purposes of the *Topics,* thrown together—something which is relatively good because it is thought good within a specific community, and something which is relatively good because it is in fact good for someone in particular circumstances.

Each of these descriptions of the three kinds of rhetoric as ethically subordinate yet still ethical, unifying goods in argument, is an Aristotelian—and not a Platonic—form of imitation, in which a nonsubstantial form is incorporated in nonnatural matter. Each has a *hoti* without a *dioti;* each uses reasons which are not its own. That is what it means to have an external principle of motion. These are, to anticipate a term I will use in Chapter 5, external reasons. Therefore, in Aristotle's sense, but not in Plato's, rhetoric is an imitation of politics. In lieu of the systematic interest of science, whether theoretical or practical, each kind of rhetoric constructs its own kind of unity, a unity in the end of a determinate judgment of the useful, the noble, or the just. In deliberation, instead of system, we find a collection of examples, in epideixis, a catalog of virtues, and only in forensic rhetoric, the need for systematic justification. Consequently, just as the example is dominant in deliberation, it makes sense for amplification to do the principal work of epideixis and for the enthymeme to be fundamental in judicial rhetoric (I.9.1368a26–33).

Aristotle declares the three kinds of rhetoric to be coequal, despite devoting only one chapter to epideixis, compared with five to deliberative and six to forensic. While Aristotle downplays it, I want to emphasize the strange status of epideixis. While of course it can have political *effects*—

consider Pericles' funeral oration—epideictic rhetoric is not tied to a fundamental political *function* or office, as the other two kinds are. Political effect
or importance is not enough to make a practice into an *eidos*, a kind, of
rhetoric. After all, tragedies and epics have political effects too, and participation in tragedy at least was limited to citizens; Aristotle uses literary examples throughout the *Rhetoric*. But tragedy and epic, unlike epideixis, are
not therefore kinds of rhetoric. Deliberation and judgment qualify as kinds
of rhetoric because of a tie to political function; if a looser standard of political effect is to let in epideixis, the doors will have to open much more
widely. The place of epideixis is an anomaly.

There is no correspondence between the three branches of government
in the *Politics* and the three kinds of rhetoric. It would be easy to erect such
a connection, by asserting an affinity between administration and epideixis.
For example, the general motivating his troops seems a prime example of
epideixis. But Aristotle posits no such connection. Man is distinguished
from the animals by possessing *logos,* which expresses opinions about the
useful and therefore the just, the subjects of deliberation and judicial rhetoric (*Politics* I.2.1253a12–15). The noble, the subject of epideixis, seems to
have no such direct function. The assembly and the law courts are essential,
functional parts of the polis: citizenship is defined as the ability (*exousia*) to
share in judicial and deliberative functioning (1275b18–20); panegyrics have
no such special place. (My guess is that generals do not practice epideictic
oratory for the same reason that medical and pedagogic rhetoric are excluded: these are fields in which practitioners actually have to know something beyond what the citizen as such knows. Generals have specialized
knowledge, while civic rhetoric is about the indefinite.)

Epideixis differs from the other kinds of rhetoric in that it is the genus
made into a species. The genus, rhetoric, has no particular practical role,
while deliberation and forensic rhetoric do. Epideixis, like the genus rhetoric, has that lack of function. Therefore it is impractical, does not issue in a
decision. It is not tensed, but concerns an indefinite present, and it is not
personal. When Aristotle introduces the three kinds of rhetoric in I.3, he
says that deliberation concerns the future, judicial rhetoric the past, but he
does not say that epideixis is about the present, rather that epideictic spectators judge "the ability of the speaker" (1358b5). Later in the chapter, he
does claim that each kind of rhetoric has a specially appropriate time, but
again makes an exception for epideixis: deliberation is about the future,
forensic the past, and

> to epideixis most appropriately [*kuriotatos*] [belongs] the present,
> for it is the existing condition of things that all those who praise or
> blame have in view. It is not uncommon, however, for epideictic

speakers to avail themselves of other times, of the past by way of recalling it, or of the future by way of anticipating it (1358b17–20).

The characteristic method of epideictic rhetoric is the method of the genus as a whole—arguments concerning the more and the less, maximizing and minimizing. (That it is the method of all rhetoric is noted at I.3.1359a16–24: "All, whether they praise or blame, exhort or dissuade, accuse or defend . . . endeavour to prove that the same things . . . are great or small. . . . it is clear that it will be necessary for the orator to be ready with propositions dealing with greatness and smallness and the greater and the less.") The existence of epideixis provides a mooring in goods independent of particular desires and particular situations. So it is important to our understanding of rhetoric and of its role in ethical life, even though epideictic practice is itself not very interesting from the point of view of practical rhetoric.

That epideixis is one of the three kinds of rhetoric could not be known by inspection. It is one of those truths better known *haplōs,* not better known to us. It is its place in the whole art that makes epideixis a species, because it has no specific constitutional role, as the other two kinds do. Each of the three kinds of rhetoric is subordinate to ethics and politics, and to analytics and dialectic, in different ways. The species of rhetoric, unlike the genus, connect to reality. The genus is practically indeterminate. Its general purpose, persuasion, is not connected to a political function as deliberation and judicial rhetoric are. Without a political function, epideixis has no extradiscursive criterion for success. All this is not true for the genus of rhetoric, but only for one of its species, epideixis. There the general telos, persuasion, becomes praise and blame. For that reason, epideixis really is a species, not just a series of similar-looking monsters that instantiate the genus without any specific articulation.

Epideixis, therefore, unlike the other species, can be "serious [*spoudes*] or not" (a27). Mock epideixis is still epideixis, while a mock debate might employ forensic rhetoric without being an instance of it. The convertibility between deliberation and epideixis looks in some respects like the mutual translatability between use and mention, since deliberative rhetoric uses opinions about the good to advocate a policy while epideixis displays those opinions to win applause for the speaker. For that reason, epideixis will become central in rhetorical treatments of literature, which display or teach values instead of employing them in decisions. In epideictic rhetoric, there is not only a mutual translation between practical and impractical goods, between the objects of choice and things we can admire and value without necessarily doing anything about them, there is also a mutual translation between the values in what is talked about and the values in the act of speaking. Epideixis therefore makes the art of rhetoric complete.

From Guiding Ends to Species

I began by asking why there are three kinds of rhetoric. The answer, we now can see, is that civic rhetoric requires this differentiation because there is no immediate inference from the good to what is to be done, from evaluation to deliberation. But that answer is not specific enough to say why there are these three kinds of rhetoric. The situation for the moral virtues is parallel. In both cases, the kind of general argument I am making is enough to establish what is functional about plurality, but is not strong enough to derive the specific series Aristotle presents us with. There can be no deduction of kinds from the nature of the genus. To continue my biological parallel, one has to specify the environments in which the genus differentiates itself into species as well. In both the cases of the kinds of rhetoric and of the moral virtues, this exhibition of the limits of argument and the dependence on changing experience is not, in my judgment, a weakness, but an indication of the proper places for abstract and concrete considerations to coexist in the rational articulation of a practical art.

Because of the institutional side of the definition of the kinds of rhetoric, Aristotle is in fact making an even stronger claim for the kinds of rhetoric than he does for the plural moral virtues. He thinks that the three kinds of rhetoric form a single, unified, complete art, not simply a complete life made up by the moral virtues. Both a complete art and a complete life are subject to revision because their nature is relative to the conditions in which arts and lives flourish. The *Rhetoric,* like the *Ethics* and the *Politics,* is historically bound. Even so, what it takes to claim that an art is complete involves stricter criteria than a complete life. That the kinds of rhetoric are conventional and contingent phenomena does not make them arbitrary. The conventional aspects of the kinds of rhetoric are not accidental or peripheral properties, but are central to the definition of these species. Conventions and well-defined political roles allow the kinds of rhetoric to have a stability that is possessed otherwise only by naturally generated objects.

To summarize: I have been building a case for civic rhetoric. I have been trying to show that citizens must practice rhetoric, and that Aristotle shows how their practice can be understood as a craft, that is, as a rational productive capacity. Artful rhetoric is argumentative. It has internal ends. The existence of rhetorical species pushes Aristotle's argument one stage beyond the discovery of internal ends. Just as in nature, things with internal ends and functions fall into species. The species offer an orderly plurality of modes of practical discourse. The plurality is generated by the nature of practical reason and its context in a political world in which the good does not simply determine what is to be done.

I have been trying to show how impressive Aristotle's achievement is. But at the same time my argument up to here leaves us with a problem. The more intelligible and attractive Aristotle makes the art of rhetoric, the harder it is to keep it subordinate to politics, as he insists it is. Indeed, by redescribing the kinds of rhetoric as kinds of practical discourse and practical reason I may have myself contributed to this insubordination by abstracting the kinds of rhetoric from the institutional setting in which they function. Consequently, in the next chapter I want to focus attention on the relations between rhetoric, logic, and politics. Aristotle will somehow show that an art of rhetoric is a power without being a kind of knowledge, and will have to show that that result is not as threatening as it might sound.

In the following four chapters, I will look, as I indicated in the Introduction, at a series of aspects of the rhetorical power for proving opposites. These are the resources I mentioned above for negotiating a practical world of incommensurable goods and conflicting choices. Now I don't think that Aristotle is a pluralist *avant la lettre,*[20] nor is the *Rhetoric* a charter for pluralism in the contemporary sense, because this rhetoric is subordinate to politics. But the *Rhetoric* offers resources to pluralists, that is, to those who live outside the polis and so have no political activity, in Aristotle's sense, for constituting a good life.

Before looking at the details of Aristotle's presentation, I want to offer an example of a contemporary dispute that seems to involve plural values and conflicting arguments. From time to time I will recall this example when talking about some of the particular resources for argument Aristotle offers, to see what help he can give. There are today many people who strongly oppose bilingual education on the grounds that the purpose of the American school system is to unify the population by providing a common experience. There is a set of things that every American needs to know, it is the business of the schools to provide them, and the more that children are separated on the basis of language or anything else, the more the common culture of America is threatened. So the argument goes.

Most of the people who oppose bilingual education on those grounds at the same time, however, support public aid to parochial schools, which would seem to further division and insularity, not unity. The purpose of many parochial schools is explicitly to provide an alternative to a dominant culture from which parents want to protect their children. Roman Catholic schools were founded to provide an alternative to the explicitly Protestant foundation of the American public school system, and today religious schools of all kinds are attractive to parents who want to avoid the explicit secular foundation of the public schools today. (Similarly, most people who support bilingual education also seem to oppose public aid to parochial schools.)

How should we evaluate these arguments, both by themselves and especially in conjunction with each other? Is there hypocrisy here? Inconsistency? I think that the answer is that on the evidence so far we can't tell. Can Aristotle help?[21]

Someone could appeal to the three kinds of rhetoric for support. What is useful is not necessarily what is just. Beyond deliberative and judicial rhetoric, the public schools have powerful value in an epideictic rhetoric that uses them to display what America stands for. We can also reason in deliberative fashion that there are many examples of past success in English-only schools. The public schools are part of a great American success story of assimilating immigrants. People who want bilingual education are rejecting that story and those values. Even if nonnative speakers more quickly learn through bilingual education, such utility would not be enough to overcome the symbolic value of English as the unifying language of America.

On the other hand, there are both epideictic and judicial arguments in favor of public aid to parochial schools: it is a powerful symbol showing that religion is a fundamental part of what it is to be American, and it is only fair that parents, who pay taxes and have some legal interest in their own children, be allowed to decide what is best for those children. Judicial rhetoric can also say that religious grounds deserve deference in a way that other preferences and practices, such as speaking a language other than English, do not.

(People who disagree on both issues have a somewhat easier time. They can argue that deliberative considerations of utility apply to support bilingual education but that the Establishment clause of the First Amendment to the Constitution prevents us from even thinking about utility when it comes to public support for religious institutions. What might otherwise be good policy cannot be considered.)

Classifying these arguments as deliberative, judicial, and epideictic helps to show why people often misunderstand each other. It also helps to show how people can easily be inconsistent without being aware of it. It does not, however, say anything about how to tell whether, at least in this case, people, or their arguments, *are* being inconsistent. Over the next four chapters, the challenge will be to see whether Aristotle's detailed consideration of the resources rhetoric offers for proving opposites can help in making these further political judgments.

RHETORICAL TOPICS AND PRACTICAL REASON

How can an art of rhetoric be a power without being a kind of knowledge? Rhetorical power, Aristotle says, makes no one any wiser (I.2.1356a32–34). Isn't the possession of power without knowledge just what Plato warned against? How can Aristotle proclaim such a thing without being similarly troubled? Arts have autonomy because in order to qualify as true arts, they must have internal ends and proper standards of excellence and perfection. The difficulty is seeing how such internal ends do not prevent the subordination of rhetoric to politics that Aristotle also demands. Internal ends would seem to liberate an activity from any external subordination. Because rhetoric is a practical, not a productive, art, the mode of its subordination to politics will differ from the easier subordination of producer to user.

As I noted at the beginning of the last chapter, one of the surprising lessons of the *Rhetoric* is that the legislator for whom it is written needs to know many of the technical details of rhetorical practice. The general does not have to know anything about how a saddle is made in order to use it for his own purposes. Saddles have no internal ends or intrinsic values; their goodness is purely instrumental toward purposes that the general has and the saddlemaker does not. The subordination of rhetoric to politics cannot be like that. As I showed in the first chapter, the more rational and noble the art, the more authority the artist has over the user of the art. Internal ends are defined and judged in the doing and by the doers. Productive arts are judged by consumers, and no parallel problems come up. If rhetoric is subordinate to politics, it is not subordinated by being silenced.

Instead, Aristotle finds that rhetoric is by its own nature subordinate— internally subordinate, if the expression makes sense—to politics, and not because politics exercises external control over it. In this chapter, I want to explore in detail Aristotle's principal resource for insuring subordination. It is a technical resource, a resource within the art of rhetoric, namely the use of topical argument. Rhetoric is not subordinate to politics by being subject to an external control, as a productive art must be, but by its very nature as a practical art.

Topics and the Marriage of Politics and Dialectic

The history of rhetoric, and of Aristotle's *Rhetoric* in particular, is a wildly diverse set of answers to a series of related questions: What is a topic? What is an enthymeme? What is invention? What is practical reason? In spite of that varied history, I have a simple thesis about what topics, enthymemes, and invention are, a thesis that I think is not only true, but which can account for this history of divergent interpretations.

Rhetorical argument differs from argument in general in that rhetorical argument is essentially ethical. With rhetorical argument the criteria for success and failure are ethical, as are the essential properties that make it what it is. Ultimately, the project of the *Rhetoric* is to construct a civic relation between argument and *ēthos,* and so between *technē* and *phronēsis.* His account of topics offers material to help show just what that civic relation between argument and *ēthos* is. The definitions of topics, enthymemes, and rhetorical invention must be consonant with the ethical nature of rhetorical argument. I will fill in what I mean in saying that rhetorical argument is essentially ethical, but already it is clear that if rhetorical argument can be seen as essentially ethical, then its subordination to politics can indeed be accomplished by the art of rhetoric itself, and not by external political regulation.

In explicating the idea of topics, I want to take as seriously as possible Aristotle's locating rhetoric as the offspring of dialetic and politics. Rhetorical argument will be simultaneously dialectical and political, and will be responsive simultaneously to two sets of standards. Aristotle's great insight, which makes his *Rhetoric* so complex, is that these two are not *independent* standards. Argument must be in the service of *ēthos,* but on the other hand, *ēthos* is revealed and manifested primarily through the articulation of argument. The enthymeme is the body of proof, and *ēthos* is its soul. Enthymeme is the center of the art, but *ēthos* is the most persuasive source of proof.

For *ēthos* and *logos,* the political and dialectical inheritance within rhetoric, to be related as soul to body, ethics cannot be a matter of having the right sentiments, nor can ethics or reasoning admit other, non–Aristotelian, interpretations. In the *Ethics,* choice is deliberate desire, *phronēsis* is the *orthos logos* of the moral virtues: it is only with those connections between character and thought that topical argument is possible. Only under these conditions could a power not grounded in knowledge have a place in civic life.

Only under Aristotle's own conception of the relation of thought and character can argument be ethical: under a different moral psychology of the virtues, the relation of rhetoric to politics would have to be different. Practical reason is practical through being ethical.[1]

Whatever topics are, they are the rhetorical substitute for principles, doing the job that principles do in scientific argument. The universal faculties of dialectic and rhetoric use topics where specialized sciences use principles. Facility at rhetoric and dialectic will make no one wiser, as knowing the principles of the various sciences does. More precisely, the *idia* or "special topics" which comprise my subject here organize the three *eidē* or kinds of rhetoric of the last chapter. The *koinoi topoi,* which I will look at in Chapter 5, organize practical discourse in a more general sense. In the last chapter, I said that the kinds of rhetoric are kinds because in them form and function are identical. The *idia* or special topics have the same property. They are formal, but formal in a way tied to their purposes. In Book II, chapters 18–26, Aristotle will discover that there are other topics, the *koinoi topoi,* which are formal in quite a different way, because they organize practical argument without being tied to function and end.

Topics have been given a wildly diverse series of meanings in the history of rhetoric, and in the interpretation of the *Rhetoric.* Not only do I give my own alternative meaning for topics, but on my reading, this proliferation of meanings itself has a simple explanation. The relation between character and argument is different in the different kinds of rhetoric, and even within each kind as the problems treated in successive chapters of the *Rhetoric* shift. If the function of practical discourse is to make the practically determinable determinate, then the roles of *logos* and *ēthos,* and the relation between them, will differ in deliberative, judicial, and epideictic rhetoric. Without a picture of how the *Rhetoric* works as a sustained inquiry and argument, the particular remarks Aristotle makes about topics will look like an incoherent series of dicta.

Topics substitute for principles in¹ rhetoric by being the domain-organizing instrument appropriate for an activity whose connections to extradiscursive reality are problematic.

One of Aristotle's most remarkable achievements in the *Rhetoric* is not only to preserve but to systematize the ambiguities between discourse and reality inherent in political argument. Living with the ambiguities allows Aristotle to ignore the oversimplified summary judgment that rhetoric is simply an imitation of true discourse about politics, and that the subject of rhetoric is itself an imitation of the real good. Facility at rhetoric will make no one wiser, but it isn't empty or phony on that account.

The strangeness and complexity of the rhetorical relation between discourse and reality is signaled initially by Aristotle's brief descriptions of the relations between rhetoric and its two parents, politics and dialectic. Rhetoric is, in the very first line of the *Rhetoric*, the counterpart of dialectic (*antistrophos*, I.1.1354a1). But it is soon described as the offspring (*paraphues*, I.2.1356a25) both of dialectic and of politics or ethics.[2] Two chapters later he expands on that description by saying that rhetoric is

> composed of analytical knowledge and of the ethical side of political knowledge, and that on the one hand it is like dialectic, on the other like sophistic discourses [*rhetorikē sugkeitai men ek te tēs analutikes epistēmes kai tēs peri ta ethē politikēs, homoia d' esti ta men te dialektikē ta de tois sophistikois logois*] (I.4.1359b9–12).

As gnomic as those sentences are, I think that ultimately they will turn out to be a more useful way of framing the multiple connections between discourse and reality than either a Platonic conception of discourse as an image or mirror of nature or contemporary speech act theory's distinctions of constantives and performatives, or of word-to-world vs. world-to-word fit. Those other modes of analysis presuppose, as Aristotle's rhetorical analysis wisely does not, a preexistent world to which language can fit itself, with some gaps in that world that can be filled in by the actions of authorized speakers. Instead of an ontology of hard facts moving in a void, Aristotle places rhetorical argument within a practically indeterminate world which praxis makes determinate. Practical situations become determinate when they reach their end. "The 'end' of each of these is different, and there are three ends for three [species] [*telos de hekastois touton heteron esti, kai trisin ousi tria*]" (I.3.1358b20–21). Each kind of rhetoric moves from the indeterminate to the determinate in a characteristically different way, and each differently uses and is bounded by preexisting determinacies. If topics substitute for principles by being argumentative means of organizing practical domains, topical argument negotiates the relation between *logos* and reality by making reality determinate through argument.

Rhetoric is a *faculty* which, like its dialectical parent, can prove opposites. Rhetoric as a civic *activity*—the *energeia* of that *dynamis*—aims at proving the truth and advocating the better cause. Only reasoning which is ethical can do that. The subordination of rhetoric to its two parents allows Aristotle to have it both ways, as neutral faculty and ethical activity. Aristotle's understanding is quite different from a conception which sees rhetoric as a pure technique which consequently needs extrinsic moral restraints. If he can integrate the ethical and the logical *within* the art of rhetoric, instead of seeing rhetoric as an unstable compromise, he will have succeeded in giving positive determinacy to praxis.

If rhetoric is going to be a logic for praxis, then the relation between word and world and between assertion and truth will have to be complex enough to do justice to the interrelations of the two sources of value I referred to in the last chapter: "there are two things above all which make human beings cherish and feel affection, what is one's own [*to idion*] and what is dear [*to agapeton*]" (*Politics* II.4.1262b22–23; cf. II.5.1263a40–b1). I prize some things because they are mine; I want to possess other things because I think they are good. The two sources of value make for complicated relations between word and world: sometimes saying makes it so, and sometimes I need to match my statements to the world.

The meaning of Aristotle's configuration of rhetoric, dialectic, and politics will be the answer to the following questions: If an aspiring speaker is adept at logic, and knows what people think about practical matters, what more is there to know that the *Rhetoric* can teach? Does the art of rhetoric have any emergent properties that cannot simply be deduced from its parents? Moreover, are there differences between the logic inherent in rhetoric and its logical parent? Between the *ēthos* inherent in rhetoric and its ethical parent? So, rhetoric makes it possible for the clever speaker alternately to denounce bilingual education and to advocate public aid to religious schools. Is such a speaker consistent? If logic or dialectic gives one answer and ethics or politics another, rhetoric will be such a monstrous offspring that it won't be able to survive for long. The question at issue is whether the determination of consistency—and the other terms that go with it, such as integrity, hypocrisy, special pleading, sincerity—belongs to logic, to rhetoric itself, or to an ethics or politics outside rhetoric.

When Aristotle says that rhetoric is made up partly of logic and partly of politics, he is saying something stronger than the simple claim that the speaker must reason cogently and must, in addition, know what he is talking about. The physicist has to do both of those too, but physics is not an offshoot of logic and knowledge of nature. Unlike physics but like its dialectical parent, rhetoric deals with mere *logoi*, not facts (I.4.1359b17; cf. II.25.1402a34). That is why possession of the faculty will not lead to wisdom. Rhetoric is, as I suggested at the end of the last chapter, a practical power without being a form of practical knowledge.

Rhetoric is about *logoi*, while those *logoi* are in turn about something outside themselves. But what it means for rhetoric to have as its subject *logoi* which themselves are about political facts is far from self-evident. For Plato, a true rhetoric would be transparent enough to allow inferences from rhetoric to the reality those *logoi* were about, so that true rhetoric would be indifferently about political language and political truth. The rhetoric that concerns mere opinions about political goods would then be twice removed from reality. The relations between rhetoric and its two parents in the *Rhetoric* make Aristotle's account more complex.[3]

The enthymeme is a rhetorical syllogism. The question is how that modifier, "rhetorical," works. My thesis is that the overall difference between rhetorical reasoning and reasoning in general is that the enthymeme and example, unlike syllogism and induction, must be ethical throughout. One of the consequences of the effect on reasoning of the political and ethical parent is that rhetorical argument, unlike its dialectical counterpart, is conservative and nonampliative. Aristotle encourages innovation in the sciences, but not in politics (*Politics* II.8.1269a15–25); similarly, rhetoric *should* not teach us anything new. It is no flaw that rhetorical argument allows speakers to affirm what we all know anyway. Dialectic can test the principles of the sciences. Even if possessing the dialectical faculty makes no one wiser, it can make that indirect contribution to wisdom. But even such an indirect role for rhetoric would deny its subordination to its political parent. The picture of argument that Mill champions, in which truth emerges from the clash of ideas, has no place in a rhetoric subordinate to politics.

Rhetoric shares with its logical parent the property that facility in the art does not make one wise about anything in particular. But there is also a resemblance to the other parent that makes rhetoric, but not dialectic, a civic art. Dialectic, like rhetoric, is a faculty, not a kind of wisdom. But while rhetorical argument sometimes chances on a scientific principle, dialectic is designed to test the principles of the sciences. In both places where he gives the genealogy of rhetoric, at I.2.1358a1–28 and at I.4.1359b12–17, Aristotle recognizes that rhetoric is at least occasionally and in some respects a second-best method, sharing with dialectic the property of being a faculty, and so falling short of the higher standards for calling something a science. On the other hand, he says in both those passages, the speaker who hits on a principle finds himself or herself suddenly doing science and talking about reality rather than just using words. Unintentionally and temporarily, rhetoric can inherit the behavior of its other, political, parent, and lose its logical provenance.[4] Aristotle's assessment of this achievement is morally, and technically, neutral; hitting on a principle is by itself an object neither of aspiration nor of aversion. Dialectic might test principles, but when rhetoric hits on a principle, it stops being rhetoric. Dialectic makes no one wise either, but it can lead to knowledge. Rhetoric does not even lead to knowledge, except when it accidentally hits on a principle and stops being rhetoric.

Where science, including political science, is about things out there in the world, rhetoric is, as I mentioned, about mere *logoi*. The *pragmata/logoi* distinction is not an ontological one; it is a distinction made at different times for different practical purposes. Because of the shifting relations in rhetoric between discourse and reality, the definitive method of rhetoric, the use of topics, is neither purely formal nor purely substantive. Rhetorical reasoning speaks to both logical and ethical standards and hence is neither purely formal nor fully substantive. It is formal without being indifferent, as formal logic is, to the matter it organizes. Because of these peculiarities, people often get the false impression that practical reason has its own logic. (Maybe my advocate of religious schools but not of bilingual education is not logically inconsistent because he or she marches to a different drummer whose rhythms have their own rhetorical logic.) If one performs the kind of formal abstraction appropriate to science but not to rhetoric, it will look as though rhetoric has its own logic, and that that logic is a bad one, admitting all sorts of contradictions and inconsistencies. But that abstraction is not a productive procedure in rhetoric. Neither the understanding of practical discourse nor its successful practice is advanced by that kind of abstraction. Where deliberative rhetoric, at least, can fairly be called a second-best, inexact, ethics and politics for the masses, it would be wrong to describe the relation of rhetoric to its dialectical parent in the same way, as a second-best, or vulgar, logic.[5] There will be no distinctions between the logic which rhetoric manifests and the logic of its logical parent.

The topics used in rhetorical argument range over that entire domain, and so are unlikely to admit of a univocal definition. While scientific principles hook up to reality throughout a demonstration, the topics in rhetoric function in situations where such a possibility is rare, and not in every respect desirable. The diversity of answers given by commentators to the question, "What is a topic in Aristotle's *Rhetoric?*" suggests not confusion but the possibility that what topics are and how they function vary with the purpose for which they are employed and the manifold on which they are used. If these forms are tied to their function, then what "form" means will have to vary. The diversity of meanings of such expressions in the secondary literature as "prephilosophical," "second-rate," "vulgar," or "applied," *is* a confusion, which I will try to dispel. How to make the indeterminate determinate will vary with the particular nature of the indeterminacy; as that varies, so will the means of making argument ethical. As the argument of Book I proceeds, the topics will be sometimes more, sometimes less formal, sometimes will point outside themselves and sometimes be more self-sufficient, sometimes be given as premises, sometimes as imperatives. There is no corresponding range for the topics in the *Topics*.

While there is no single definition for the topics, the result is not confusion. There is an argument and a development to Aristotle's treatment. In each of the three kinds of rhetoric, Aristotle will begin with the political or ethical parent of rhetoric, and move toward its logical progenitor. Each kind starts with the need for the orator to know what he is talking about, to be responsible to, and reflective of, the nature of the *polis* and its laws; as the treatment of each kind of rhetoric proceeds toward the audience's judgment of particulars, the speaker will uncover increasing freedom to his arguments as they can be flexibly arranged on both sides of questions and adapted to fit the needs of his case.

That order is not reversible: Aristotle gives us no reason to think that starting from the free competition of ideas, one can eventually hit up against truth and reality; as I suggested above, such a picture, which conflates dialectical and rhetorical reasoning, produces a different relation between rhetoric and politics. Such rhetorical competition works in a good polis; it does not produce a good polis. Given a grounding in a knowledge of the state's aspirations, needs, resources, and laws, an advocate can argue for policies and judgments too specific to be laid down in advance by the laws, but there is no corresponding license to begin with advocacy and end with truth. There is no marketplace of ideas in Aristotle. The latter picture would release rhetoric from its political subordination; then rhetoric could become a means of discovering new truths in a way completely alien to Aristotle.

Dialectic has two functions relative to the sciences: it both tests first principles and, through its mental gymnastics, puts the mind in a condition to receive those principles (*Topics* I.2.101a27–29). The same art, and *dynamis,* that moves the person from first potency to second potency through mental training, moves from first act to second act through testing principles. These two functions are *both* lacking in rhetoric: rhetorical argument neither leads to testing the principles of conduct (as, for example, in a debate between the partisans of pleasure and of honor), nor does it lead to a strengthening of the moral principles of any individual. Once freed from political subordination, rhetoric may well have these more exciting functions. But then it isn't Aristotle's *Rhetoric* any longer.

Deliberative Rhetoric:
Rhetoric I.4–8

Deliberative rhetoric differs from political science as words or *logoi* differ from facts or *pragmata,* but deliberative rhetoric still takes knowledge and not just an ability to manipulate discourse. As I have said, rhetoric is a faculty whose possession makes no one wiser; yet is not purely a formal art of words. The different kinds of rhetoric, and the different kinds of resources Aristotle supplies for each kind, are means of evading that false choice between rhetoric as pseudopolitics and rhetoric as empty manipulation.

There is a consequent difference between the way I.4 is "formal" and invites filling in with details and the formal character of other materials offered in the rest of Book I. Chapter 4 is about the *peri hōn* of deliberation (I.4.1359a30), which is limited to the field of praxis, things that can be otherwise through our choices (a32–b2). It is here, with respect to the subjects of deliberation, that Aristotle subordinates rhetoric to politics by making rhetoric a rougher and less exact kind of knowledge. It is only for deliberation, then, that Aristotle mentions the possibility of inadvertently hitting on a principle. Typically, he gives no indication of a reason for this limitation, but we should try to figure out what it means.

Because of the connection of deliberative rhetoric to deliberation, he tells us that precision is unnecessary here: "It is not necessary at the present moment to enumerate these subjects accurately [*aletheian*] . . . or to say what would be a true definition of them, since that is not a matter for the rhetorical art but for a more profound and true [*emphronesteras kai mallong alethines*] [discipline]" (1359b2–7). Throughout the *Rhetoric* Aristotle will remind the reader that excessive precision drives out character; as he puts it later, in the section on style, "it is more fitting that a virtuous man should show himself good than that his speech should be painfully exact" (III.17.1418b1–3). I.4 gives us the first example of the progeny of politics and dialectic. While deliberative rhetoric is no less logical than its analytical parent, it is less exact than its political parent. It is less precise not in order to be more logical, or more persuasive, but to be more ethical.

The orator must know what he is talking about, and so chapter 4 consists in Aristotle's giving organized directions about what must be known and where the speaker can find out about it.[6] This is the sense of topic Aristotle has in mind in II.22 when he says that the speaker must have "on each subject a selection of premises about probabilities and what is most suitable [*peri ton endechomenon kai ton epikairotaton*]" (II.22.1396b5–6), and then calls this method (*tropos*) the topical method of selection and proof (b20–21). Topics are grand headings for substantive premises.

Rhetoric here is a rough and popular politics, concentrating on knowledge of resources and means that are meant to bring about ends that are themselves presupposed and unproblematic. Some means are useful toward a rather restricted range of ends; some tools are so precisely designed that they can be used for a single end. The latter would call for more accurate reasoning, not rhetoric. But the resources and instrumentalities for deliberative rhetoric discussed in chapter 4 are indifferent to the purposes for which they are employed. Therefore it is only for such unlimited means that topical reasoning is apposite. "The important subjects on which people deliberate and on which deliberative orators give advice in public are mostly five in number, and these are finances [*peri to poron*], war and peace, national defense, imports and exports, and the framing of laws" (1359b19–22). The subjects of deliberation and of deliberative rhetoric are the same. The good speaker is someone who knows what he is talking about: "It is not only possible to get an overall view of matters from experience in the affairs of one's own city [*peri ta idia empeirias*], but it is necessary also to be willing to do research about what has been discovered elsewhere in regard to deliberation about these things" (b26–27). Thus, my orator who opposes bilingual education and supports public aid to religious schools can show how language has in other nations been a divisive force, and can point to American history to show that we are exempt from the general rule that religion has usually divided people too.

Concerning the last of these five subjects, legislation, the boundary between politics and rhetoric is unclear, however. Of the five, Aristotle says that legislation is the most important, "for the safety of the city is in its laws" (1360a20). Aristotle explains what the orator must know in the following lines, and it sounds like a program for the *Politics*: "So it is necessary to know how many forms of constitution there are and what is conductive to each and by what each is naturally prone to be corrupted, both characteristic of that constitution and those that are opposed to it" (a20–23).[7] He ends the chapter, however, by seeming to take it all back: "But all these subjects belong to the function (*ergon*) of politics, not to rhetoric" (a38). At this stage, topics and deliberative argument are ethical because it takes character and perception, not just following rules, to notice and assess probabilities and signs.

Chapter 4, like the chapters to follow, offers a *technē,* but it shows that the orator needs more than an art. The logical side of rhetoric is a self-sufficient art, but the political side is not. Attempts to make deliberative rhetoric apprehend too precisely the *peri hōn* of deliberation will make it politically self-contained. It will then be a form of knowledge which makes *ēthos* otiose. Practical intelligence is needed in addition to make the determinable determinate; character prevents that act of determination from being capricious.

Chapter 5 concerns the *ex hōn,* the "sources from which arguments of exhortation or dissuasion about these and other matters should be derived" (1360b2), and there too the speaker must have knowledge. But in this case the speaker must possess knowledge of the audience's beliefs, and needs knowledge of logic to investigate these beliefs and their connections to each other. The topics of chapter 5 are the commonly held opinions that corroborate Kenneth Burke's preferred translation, in *The Rhetoric of Motives,*[8] of *topoi* as *values,* except that these values and beliefs are assumed to be universal and noncontroversial; the beliefs and values that vary from one audience to another will appear in chapter 7. The subjects about which we deliberate in chapter 4 are means; the sources of arguments in chapter 5 are the ends of action. The chapter begins, therefore: "Both to an individual privately and to all people generally there is one goal [*skopos*] at which they aim in what they choose to do and in what they avoid. Summarily stated [*en kephalaio*], this is happiness and its parts" (1360b4–7). All of deliberative rhetoric is the offspring of politics and dialectic by being rough and vulgar. There is this difference between the rhetorical knowledge of the ends and of the means of action: whereas in chapter 4 Aristotle had to point to what the speaker needed to know—knowledge that the art of rhetoric itself could not supply—in chapter 5 he simply states what happiness is. That is why the topics of chapter 4 look like pigeonholes: Aristotle can say that the speaker should know about the city's defenses, but an art of rhetoric cannot itself supply that knowledge. But in chapter 5 he can say that "a good reputation is a matter of achieving the respect of all people, or of having something of the sort that all or the general public or the good or the prudent desire" (1361a25–27). In that way chapter 5 itself supplies the knowledge the speaker needs. Argument is ethical because it is based on agreed-upon values held by the audience. This part of the rhetorical art can be self-sufficient without ceasing to be ethical, because it is about *logoi*. Arts about *logoi* do not have to face the danger of being too exact to be ethical.

One difference between a rhetorical and a scientific—ethical and political—account of happiness is the lack of organization of chapter 5. The scientific equivalent of chapter 4 would exhibit some connections between means and ends, show how some means are limited to certain ends, how means need to be proportioned to ends, etc. The scientific equivalent to chapter 5 would make happiness into a unity in a stronger sense, suitable for understanding the good life instead of arguing about what to do. The components and means of happiness are simply additive in the *Rhetoric*, while in a practical science, their interrelations must be systematic. Deliberative rhetoric will use examples. Chapter 4 tells the speaker to collect particulars that can be used as examples in argument. No one would claim that the collections of military history and of different constitutions had to be consistent, and Aristotle calls such research *historiae* (I.4.1359b27 and 1360a38). History, at least in Aristotle's eyes, is not systematic or coherent.

What is interesting and less obvious is that the same obtains for the description of happiness in I.5. He introduces it by saying, in Kennedy's translation, "Let us, then, for the sake of giving an example [*hōste paradeigmatos*] [of what might be more fully explored], grasp what happiness is, simply stated" (I.5.1360b7–8; see also I.9.1366a32). (The Loeb translation has "for the sake of illustration.") But "for the sake of giving an example" cannot be the right translation of *hōste paradeigmatos* here; instead it must mean that speakers should take this account of happiness as an example in argument.[9] Where chapter 4 talks about things that one needs to know, chapter 5 gives a series of definitions: "The meaning of many friendships and good friendships is not unclear if friend is defined" (I.5.1361b30). "If happiness is something of this sort, it is necessary for its 'parts' to be . . ." (1360b15). (Where chapter 4 was full of verbs indicating knowledge, here they are replaced by *lego*, or declarations of a definition.) The movement from chapter 4 to 5 is from the first to the second of the four *organa* listed in *Topics* I.13.105a22–26, from the provision of propositions (*to protaseis labein*) to the power to distinguish in how many senses a particular expression is used (*posachos hekaston legetai dynasthai dielein*). The last two *organa*, the discovery of differences and the investigation of similarities will also figure in 6 and 7. Just as increased precision was unnecessary in chapter 4 because we were dealing with unrestricted means, about which topical argument is appropriate, so here in chapter 5 increased precision about happiness would not help the orator, because happiness is the final, and unrestricted, end.[10]

Thomas Cole argues that the typical "art" of rhetoric prior to Aristotle's "is itself a text set down in writing rather than a set of rules by means of which other texts are generated."[11] If that is the case, then Aristotle's presentation of the topics in I.4–14, and especially in the five chapters that deal with deliberation, begins with this earlier notion of the presentation of information, and advances to a similar presentation of more formal, dialectical, materials. That is why I stress the way "for the sake of giving an example" must not be the translation of *hōste paradeigmatos*.

Where the earlier handbooks on rhetoric presumably supplied model discourses for copying and imitation, Aristotle offers an articulated art. There is an ordered development in the *Rhetoric* which takes the place of such a model. It is not just the individual materials and forms of argument that the student learns from the *Rhetoric,* but the argument of the *Rhetoric* itself. Topic and argument are essentially ethical in each chapter of Book I, but the real ethical nature of rhetoric argument is exhibited most clearly in the argument and overall development of each kind of rhetoric. As the section on deliberative rhetoric develops, he presents a structure of increasing determination, moving from resources that can be used toward any end, through the ultimate end of happiness, presented in the most ecumenical and eclectic fashion. I.6 structures its subject much more fully, because we are approaching more closely the actual act of persuasion and its structure. So here we are given explicitly things that look more like argument forms, modes of inference. Topics here function much as Toulmin's inference warrants.[12] Throughout the chapter, he gives reasons for his premises: the term *gar* appears constantly. Reasons or warrants are required to talk about goods, whereas they were not necessary either for the resources of 4 or for happiness in 5.

Within deliberative rhetoric, it is only chapters 6 and 7 that clearly fit the common understanding of topics as resources for arguing both sides of a question. If rhetoricians answered to the description of amoral advocates who can advocate any position without endorsing or believing any, if practical reasoning consisted in developing a facility that has no truth value and is agnostic toward the opinions it presents and examines, only this section of Aristotle's treatment of deliberative rhetoric would be relevant.

Chapters 6 and 7 are really a single sustained presentation of another, more practical, facet of deliberative argument. The presentation has four sections. First, chapter 6 begins presenting modes of argument by starting from good in itself, and moves to predicates that can be securely associated with it. Second, starting with 1362b11, Aristotle enumerates things generally recognized as goods (1362b29), speaking of them one by one. The third section starts at I.6.1362b22 and is a consideration of doubtful goods; for each doubtful good Aristotle tells the reader how to argue for it. This transition from generally recognized goods to doubtful (*amphibetesimoi*) ones shows that the topoi Aristotle lists are premises for argument: "In the case of doubtful goods, the syllogisms are out of these [*ek tonde hoi syllogismoi*]"; some require nothing but subsumption—useful friends are good; he is a useful friend—and some require more arguments I.6.1363a20. This section ends by moving as near as possible to the form a determinate decision takes, by giving the ultimate grounds of choice, ultimate here in the sense of last, nearest to the decision itself; from the individual goods enumerated, he ends with a generalization. Thus, one could argue for tax revenues supporting religious schools on the grounds that adherents have already proved that they value religious education by paying and sacrificing in other ways for their religion, and that this desire therefore deserves special respect.[13] Native speakers of languages other than English have not had to pay such a price. They therefore would be getting from the government support they would not themselves pay for.

The fourth section, which occupies all of chapter 7, stands to the second as the third to the first. Both the enumerated goods and the good in general have a secure part and a debatable part: 1362b22 covers doubtful goods, and I.7.1363b5 begins to discuss comparative goods. The word for doubtful, *amphibetesimoi*, reappears at the beginning of chapter 7: "Both sides in a debate often agree about what is advantageous but disagree about which is more advantageous [*peri tou mallon amphisbetousin*] [among possible courses of action]" (1363b5–6).

In each of these last two parts of the discussion of goods we encounter for the first time topoi that allow for contradictory arguments. The first argument form for doubtful goods is the opposition of good and evil, e.g., what is useful to our enemies is harmful to us, and on that kind of argument Aristotle observes that it is not true always, but only for the most part (I.6.1362b33–34). Later, at I.7.1364a16, for example, a thing may be greater in two competing ways (*amphoteros*), and (a20), the scarcer is both more and less preferable than the abundant, from different "points of view" (*allon tropon*) (a26). (Similarly, I.7.1364b3, *antikeimenos*).

Because of their proximity to facts of the case, the resources for action discussed in I.4 and the argumentative materials supplied through the account of happiness is I.5 seemed to ignore Aristotle's earlier reminder that rhetoric resembled dialectic and differed from politics by proving opposites. Chapters 4 and 5 explore arguments that appear to reflect only the political and not the logical parent of rhetoric. In chapters 6 and 7 the notion that rhetoric proves opposites describes something much more intrinsic to rhetorical activity. Rhetoric proves opposite conclusions, starting from at least potentially contradictory data, by means of *contrary argument forms.*

The topoi presented in the latter part of I.6 and throughout I.7 present speakers with means for arguing reasonably in both directions on a variety of practical subjects. But chapter 7 introduces a further sense of contrariety by reminding the speaker that there may be competing proposals among which an audience can decide. It does not follow that the speaker must be prepared to refute or discredit his opponent. A civic art of rhetoric, one whose activities are *energeiai,* is not a polemical art. (Similarly, the *Ethics* does not picture choice as a decision among alternatives but as the calculation of means to an end.) In fact, the more practical the argument, the less competitive: epideixis is the most competitive of the kinds of rhetoric, because it is impractical, and for the most part the techniques emphasized in *Topics* VIII fall outside the art of rhetoric.

Instead, the fact that there are competing proposals means the speaker must be prepared to dispute matters of degree, arguing that a given policy is not only good and choiceworthy but better and more choiceworthy than the competition.[14] People desire exemptions from the general principle that American education should promote unity on grounds of both linguistic and religious difference, but my hypothetical speaker can provide arguments to show that in America desires based on religious motivations deserve special attention and deference, compared to desires based on linguistic or cultural factors. Their opponents can argue that in America desires based on religious motivations deserve special scrutiny and suspicion.[15]

Aristotle again begins making his case about how rhetorical argument works from the institutional setting of persuasion, but the value of comparative arguments about greater good and greater utility extend beyond the situations in which there are competing hypotheses about what to do. Even the speaker who does not have an opponent, even a speaker who maintains that his recommended course of action is the only one a reasonable person could ever pursue, must, to make a complete and concrete case, show awareness of possible and rejected alternatives, as serious alternatives—as serious as called for by the case.[16] Awareness of alternatives is evidence of *ēthos* and *phronēsis.*

Chapter 8 seems to represent an anomaly in the order for which I am arguing, and its authenticity or placement has therefore been doubted. It returns to the subject of chapter 4, the kinds of government, the most persuasive and authoritative of rhetorical appeals. The difference between chapter 8 and chapter 4 is that in chapter 4 the kinds of government are data to be studied, matched with values to arrive at a course of action.

Instead, in chapter 8 the form of government becomes a formal, almost stylistic consideration of how the speaker can sound most authoritative. Chapter 8, though it is about forms of government, is really about what people believe rather than what is true, about the conventional as opposed to the real.

As we move through the topics of deliberative rhetoric, they become less political and more logical. Here the apparent return to politics is in fact logical, but perhaps the better translation of *logikōs* would be "verbal," rather than "argumentative," inasmuch as Aristotle shows how to construct arguments out of things like grammatical inflexions. If the progress of chapters 4 to 8 is one of increasing determination, the final step in deliberative rhetoric and of determining an action is establishing an identity between a proposed action and the authority the speaker derives from the audience. A policy concerning education, whether it is bilingual education or public aid to religious schools, had better look as if it is advancing the ideals of the Constitution, as well as satisfying the requirements of the individual clauses of the document. "A distinctive feature of American republicanism is hospitality toward heterogeneity, rather than fear of it." [17] Religious pluralism, free exercise and nonestablishment, might in this way be part of the American constitution, and public aid to religious schools then furthers its ideals. In the last chapter I said that the characteristic surplus of judicial rhetoric was the merely lawful as opposed to the just, which was translatable into the noble and the useful; a satisfying constitutional argument should not be about the merely lawful but the just, and that means, in America, the spirit of the Constitution. A deliberative argument that appeals to the laws must similarly embody their spirit and *ēthos* and not just their *logos,* as in Aristotle's observation that law is reason (*nous*) without desire.

Although this chapter appears to concern logic rather than politics, the political parentage of rhetoric does return in chapter 8. The forms of government as here detailed provide not a demonstrative argument but the exhibition of a character in an ethical argument (*ou monon hai pisteis ginontai di' apodeiktikou logou alla kai di' ēthikou*) (1366a9–10). If these forms of government offered a demonstrative argument, then they would be merely verbal, and unreal. The difference between ethical and demonstrative argument would be an opposition: being logical would be morally and politically subversive, and being ethical would be illogical. Arguments have to be ethical to be persuasive.

Rhetorical argument can be ethical without the speaker being ethical. Aristotle thinks it makes rhetoric worse, not better, to try to depend on, and so infer to, the actual character of the speaker apart from the particular speech (I.2.1356a5–13). He often says that the character of the speaker is the most authoritative means of persuasion: e.g., "*ēthos* constitutes the most effective [*kuriotaton*] means of proof" (I.2.1356a13; see also I.9.1366a28); here he maintains that "the greatest and most important [*megiston kai kuriotaton*]" of all things in an ability to persuade and give good advice is to grasp an understanding of all forms of constitution and to distinguish the customs and legal usages and advantages of each" (I.8.1365b22–25). Such knowledge is knowledge of character, the most powerful means of proof. It is knowledge of the end and purpose of deliberative speech, because character is in accordance with *prohairesis,* and *prohairesis* is toward an end. Argument is ethical when it is rooted in this knowledge of the diverse forms and purposes of *politeai.*

This seems a very weak meaning to attach to my thesis that it is the essence of rhetorical argument to be ethical. It seems to mean nothing more than that rhetorical argument has to take as its premises values held by the audience. But the point is that the knowledge the rhetorician has, especially the knowledge indicated in chapter 8, will not be confined to the premises of argument, but will penetrate all aspects of the argument. For rhetorical argument, "all aspects" means not only premises and modes of inference (although it certainly includes both these), but also ethical and logical decisions about relevance, application, assertability conditions, and all the other pragmatic aspects of argument that must be a part of the practical uses of discourse.

Earlier I noted that the closer a topic is to science, the more remote it is from the choice that is the end, *telos,* of deliberative rhetoric. Similarly, the more logical and less political rhetoric becomes, the better it is equipped to argue both sides, to become a neutral *dynamis* rather than a part of politics inherently oriented to the good. That process of becoming more logical and more neutral, and hence at least potentially manipulative, is stopped here by Aristotle reminding his readers that persuasiveness is persuasiveness to someone, and so choice too is relative to the characters of the speaker and hearer; the section on deliberative rhetoric ends by moving from rhetoric as political to rhetoric as logical and back again to the ethical side of politics. What is in fact expedient (the subject of chapters 6 and 7) varies with different governments; in addition (1366a3), the ends that govern choices vary with different constitutions. Given the variety of kinds of government, each with an appropriate kind of character that will correspond to the things that such a constitution values, the orator must take an external view of these plural audiences. To the extent that the different constitutions have different ends, the orator must be agnostic about which end is in fact the best end, and so will try to shape his character accordingly (1366a15).

The combination of logic and politics indicates the necessity for combining the facets of argument that are and are not audience independent. Whether an argument is valid has nothing to do with what an audience thinks; whether an argument is persuasive has everything to do with the audience's judgment. Socrates interpreted this difference as the difference between a science which knows what is best and a knack of flattering the audience and telling it what it wants to hear. Aristotle is showing how to study argument *as argument,* albeit with some of the criteria for its success practical, and so dependent on how it makes its way in a world it helps to make determinate. Chapter 8 closes the section on deliberative rhetoric as it opened in chapter 4, with a reference to the subordination of rhetoric to more accurate political discussion (*diekribotai en tois politikois*) (I.8.1366a21–22), and hence a subordination of rhetorical to practical success.

That ending is a reminder that all of deliberative rhetoric has a more exact form in political science. Nevertheless, it is only for the subject of chapter 4, the resources of action, that unintentionally hitting on a principle is a possibility. That is, there can be no program designed to separate off the economic from the political, questions of resources that can be answered by science from questions of choice that are the subject of permanent debate. And for the same reason, as chapter 8 illustrates, there is a difference between rhetorical discourse, which is about *logoi,* and political science, which is about real things, *pragmata,* but there is no method—and certainly no method within rhetoric—for keeping that distinction in mind, no method for separating discourse from reality in practical argument. The difference between *logoi* and *pragmata* is a rhetorical, and therefore an ethical, not an ontological, distinction. The difference between *logoi* and *pragmata* can itself become a topos.

As the argument of chapters 4–8 proceeds, Aristotle shows the shifting role and value of contradiction, dispute, and hence, consistency, in practical argument. Terms like these—contradiction, consistency, harmony, and dispute—can sometimes take purely logical meanings, and sometimes must be viewed as practical, political, or ethical terms.[18] Logical consistency, natural predictability, and ethical reliability do not always coincide, but each has its place in argument. Sometimes one, sometimes another is the relevant value. To each corresponds a different meaning of authority, and a different function for authority in argument. Aristotle exemplifies what it means for practical affairs not to admit of complete accuracy, and for accuracy to become even less attainable as things become more concrete. There is agreement on happiness and goods, but such agreement is easy, based on agglomeration. The closer one comes to actual choice, as I.4–8 proceeds, the more does conflict emerge. Logical consistency recedes as an ideal, to be replaced by personal dependability. Only because character can go where logic itself cannot is rhetoric able to argue from the practically indeterminate to the practically determinate.

There is a different inferential relation from a *hexis,* such as virtue, to and from a chosen act and from a *dynamis,* including rational *dynamis,* such as a *technē*. That difference will be the theme of the last third of my book, especially of chapter 6.[19] Even if character here means something not existing antecedent to argument, so that there is a difference betweeen an argument being ethical and a speaker being ethical, it is not trivial to claim that rhetorical argument must be ethical. Making discourse ethical puts together rhetoric's two parents, and makes it possible to hold together the ways in which rhetorical argument has some standards different from those in logic or dialectic but is still argument. The more doubtful a subject, the more we depend not on demonstration but on character (I.2.1356a8), so that the section on deliberation must end with its emphasis on character as rhetorical proof. The sort of dependability appropriate to the field of rhetoric, things that can be otherwise, is ethical reliability rather than logical validity, and so argument need not beome more indeterminate as it becomes less exact and approaches the actual decision.

Aristotle tells us in the *Ethics* that the god man aims at doing things for the sake of the noble, and that this is equivalent to choosing an action in conformity with his character. That ethical ideal has its rhetorical parallel: the most persuasive of proofs is the speaker's character, because the direction of inference runs parallel to that of the good person deliberating—the most persuasive of proofs allows the audience to infer that since the speaker is trustworthy, we should do as he recommends. The way in which the speaker's character is the most persuasive of proofs will be the subject of chapter 6.

Epideictic Rhetoric: *Rhetoric* I.9

"The function [*ergon*] [of rhetoric] is concerned with the sort of things we debate and for which we do not have [other] arts [*technas me echomen*]" (I.2.1357a1–2). What replaces the other arts and science in the *Rhetoric* differs from one of the three kinds of rhetoric to the next; the topics which substitute for principles have a different nature and function in each of the three kinds of rhetoric, and, as I have shown for deliberation, within each kind. This is something like the *Politics,* in which there are six forms of constitutions and forms of each form. There are three rhetorical situations and so three kinds of rhetoric, and then there are more specific argumentative situations and more specific *eidē* or special topics corresponding to problems the speaker confronts.[20]

As I showed in detail in the last chapter, epideixis always seems the odd genre in Aristotle's presentation. Pure induction observing Athenian rhetorical practice would never come up with precisely these three kinds. A further clue to the place of epideixis in Aristotle's inquiry comes from a parallel between chapters 8 and 9.

There were two reasons for knowing the forms of government in chapter

8. First, one does a better job at arguing for expediency if one is aware of the ends to which different policies are means (I.8.1365b24). And second, knowledge of different forms of governments allows us to know what character we should appear to have. The same doubling, offering first a logical structure of choice and deliberative argument, and then an ethical one, also occurs in I.9. Aristotle is there more explicit about the doubling, but expounds the two simultaneously. Speaking of the subjects of epideixis, virtue and vice, noble and disgraceful, he says: "Moreover, as we speak of these, we shall incidentally [symbesetai] also make clear those things from which we [as speakers] shall be regarded as persons of a certain quality in character, which was the second form of pistis [deutera pistis]; for from the same sources we shall be able to make both ourselves and any other person worthy of credence in regard to virtue" (I.9.1366a23–28).

Looked at strictly logically, it might be possible to separate discourse that is merely logical from language that is about actual facts, but when discourse is organized and structured ethically, such separation is impossible. Purely logically, truth is transmitted by valid inference forms from premises to conclusions. Desirability and motive force are transmitted by enthymemes. The transmission of desirability and value makes these *ethical arguments*. This transmission will be the subject of my chapter 5.

There is no equivalent in epideixis to the sense of topics in chapter 4, where the good speaker has to know what he is talking about. There is nothing that the epideictic orator has to know, and so, like the treatment of happiness in chapter 5, the topics for the noble in chapter 9 are self-contained; the orator needs to know what the audience believes, and, at a certain level of generality, the art of rhetoric itself can supply that knowledge. Chapter 9, like chapter 5, is full of definitions and assertions about the nature of nobility, its causes, parts and consequences. As the chapter progresses, though, Aristotle moves to topics that more closely resemble the tactical topics of chapters 6 and 7. This section begins at 1367a32–34: "One should assume that qualities that are close to actual ones are much the same as regards both praise and blame." Here, as in chapters 6 and 7, Aristotle shifts his attention to the external end of rhetoric, successfully persuading an audience, and so his tactical advice includes using fallacies that are likely to succeed. Such arguments from similarity are justified by the fact that "most people will think so" (1367b3). He goes on to recommend the paralogism drawn from the motive (paralogistikon ek tēn aitias): "for if a person meets danger unnecessarily, he would be much more likely to do so where the danger is honorable" (b5–6). In the same vein, we should "consider also the audience before whom the praise [is spoken]."

As he moves through epideixis in chapter 9, the shifts in meaning of "topics" seems to reflect the development in chapters 5–8. As virtue and

happiness are interrelated, so are deliberation and epideixis: "Praise and deliberation are part of a common species [*eidos*] in that what one might propose in deliberation becomes encomia when the form of expression is
changed" (I.9.1367b36–1368a1). How, then, do the topics function differently in epideixis from the way they work in deliberation?

The science of politics and ethics is systematic, and, in a different way,
the *phronimos* leads a systematic life, one understood and seen as a unified
whole. An art of rhetoric is not systematic, but each of the kinds of rhetoric
needs a different sort of substitute for system. Chapter 9 begins by claiming
that acquaintance with the topics of praise and blame will also show the
means of appearing to have a desired character. But it ends by asserting that
each kind of rhetoric has its own preferred method of proof:

> In general, among the classes of things common to all speeches,
> amplification is most at home in those that are epideictic; for these
> take up actions that are agreed upon, so that what remains is to
> clothe the actions with greatness and beauty. But paradigms are
> best in deliberative speeches; for we judge future things by pre-
> dicting them from past ones; and enthymemes are best in judi-
> cial speeches, for what has happened in some unclear way is best
> given a cause and demonstration [by enthymematic argument]
> (I.9.1368a26–33).

This parceling out of preferred methods to the kinds of rhetoric shows
something further about how topics work. Although in the sciences we
reason both from causes to effects and from effects to causes, and although
Aristotle insists on the distinction of inferring to and from principles, the
same rational structure can be discerned in all theoretical uses of reason.
Rational structure and form, then, is independent of the purposes of reasoning.

That seems not to be the case in practical reason. To impute liability to
someone's acts is not necessarily to blame the person himself, nor to make
any predictions about future actions. Punishment may deter, but judgments
about punishment are distinct from decisions about the deterring effects of
such punishment. Calculating means to ends in deliberation, inferring from
effects to causes in judicial rhetoric, and constructing a picture of a whole
out of parts, as in epideixis, are not identical activities.[21] It often looks as
though practical reason and rhetoric are either illogical or have a logic of
their own. The reason for this appearance is the multiple functions of reason
in action, and the ties between function and form.

In chapter 5 I will return to some of the problems that this difference
between theoretical and practical reasoning—and so between logic and
rhetoric, syllogism and the enthymeme—presents. Just what a rhetorical

"form" is will be questionable, and how to individuate forms of enthymemes will not just be derivative from a classification of moods and
figures in the *Prior Analytics*. Moreover, I will try to show why these formal
aspects of rhetorical reasoning have persuasive value of their own, apart from
those ties to function that I think Aristotle stresses in his presentation of the
idia. That is in fact the difference between proper and common places,
between *idia* and *koinoi topoi*.

Here, however, I want to look at the special topics, the *idia*, and show
how their connections between form and function allow them to do the
job I ascribed to topics: topics substitute for principles in rhetoric by being
the domain-organizing instrument appropriate for an activity whose connections to extradiscursive reality are problematic. Each of the three kinds
of rhetoric has a distinct relation of subordination to politics that substitutes,
for Plato's single postulated relation of imitation, a new form of imitation
according to Aristotle's definition: an external principle of motion, art, produces an artificial object in which some nonsubstantial form is taken from
a natural object and incorporated into different material.[22] Deliberative rhetoric is second-best, politics in a hurry. Forensic, as I will show in the next
section, is applied political and ethical theory. Epideixis is politics bracketed
or suspended, said but not asserted.

Forensic Rhetoric: *Rhetoric* I.10–15

The section on forensic rhetoric looks more like applied or popular ethics
than do the parts on deliberation or epideixis because forensic rhetoric is
related to the laws as particular to general, and proceeds by subsumption
and enthymeme. Where deliberative and epideictic rhetoric take for granted
the ends of their audience, forensic speech accepts as given the laws of the
polis. While the enthymeme is central throughout rhetoric, it also makes
sense to claim it as the special method of judicial rhetoric, because subsumption is less useful than appeals to examples in deliberation, and because the
only enthymematic operations in epideixis concern things on which everyone agreed; it is the use of amplification that sets one speaker apart from
another. Where deliberation adjusts means to ends, forensic rhetoric adjusts
particular cases to general laws. In this section, as in the treatment of the
emotions in II.2–11, Aristotle will frequently put the speaker in a position
of being able to construct an argument through subsumption; e.g., "If, then,
fairness is what has been described, it is clear what kind of actions are fair
and what are not fair and what kind of human beings are fair" (I.13.1374b2–
3). Forensic rhetoric consists in arguments about the causes of injustice, and

causal analysis is suited to enthymeme. Legal rhetoric is the only kind which has a theory, because it is the only place where reasoning from rule to case, i.e., the enthymeme, is central. The laws to which forensic rhetoric is subordinate are generalizations, and, consequently forensic rhetoric itself consists in a general theory of justice, its causes, motives, and typical agents and victims. The section on forensic rhetoric opens:

> Holding to our plan, we should [next] speak of accusation and defense: from how many and what sort of sources should their syllogisms be derived? One should grasp three things: first, for what, and how many, purposes [heneka] people do wrong; second, how these persons are [mentally] disposed; third, what kind of persons they wrong and what these persons are like. Let us discuss these questions in order after defining wrongdoing (1368b1–6).[23]

The fact that forensic rhetoric offers *applied* theory, theory which it must adopt from outside itself, makes this rhetoric subordinate to politics. In particular, this section offers a causal analysis that is by design superficial in its consideration of motives and consequences. Such superficiality makes it look as if it can in ideal circumstances be replaced by a better, more accurate, theory, but Aristotle makes no suggestion of hitting on a principle here. That remains a possibility confined to deliberative rhetoric. While forensic rhetoric uses a superficial causal analysis, there is no scientific concept of cause available to replace the more complicated disputes about causality that characterize forensic rhetoric, where we have to rely on the "usual consequences of different conditions" (1369a24–25). Such reliance insures that the reasoning in forensic rhetoric will be ethical rather than scientific.

Of the three subjects of argument in judicial rhetoric, the first, motives of injustice, is the subject of chapters 10 and 11, and the last two are treated in 12, the state of mind up to 1372b23, and the persons and circumstances that are objects of injustice through the rest of the chapter. Voluntary action comes from desire, and "through longing is done whatever seems pleasurable" (1369b15), and so chapter 11 turns to the definition of pleasure, supplying material for arguing about the motives of injustice.

Here too something like the paralogisms I mentioned earlier can occur. Among elements in the frame of mind of injustice is the likelihood of getting away with the crime. "[Wrongdoers] are likely to be unsuspected if [their appearance and condition in life is] inconsistent with the charges" (I.12.1372a20). The more improbable it is that one commits a crime, the easier it will be to escape. In other words, any set of rules, whether formal rules of justice or informal rules of probability, creates opportunities for abuse. Ultimately, those opportunities lead to the sophistic art.[24]

Injustice is defined, at the opening of chapter 10, as voluntarily causing injury contrary to the law (1368b6–7)—the stipulative nature of the definition is signaled by *estō*. From a quick analysis of the voluntary, he concludes that "similarly each of the others [is unjust] in regard to each of their underlying vices" (b24). Nothing more is needed here, he says, because it can be filled in partly from the prior analysis of the virtues, and partly from the impending treatment of the emotions.

He then, as promised, turns to "for what reason people do wrong and in what state of mind and against whom" (b28). He runs through a series of superficial dichotomies:

> All people do all things either not on their own initiative or on their own initiative. Of those things not done on their own initiative they do some by chance, some by necessity; and of those by necessity, some by compulsion, some by nature. . . . But whatever they do on their own initiative and of which they are the cause, these [things] are done by habit or by desire, sometimes rational desire, sometimes irrational (1368b32–1369a7).

From this rapid classification, Aristotle concludes that there are seven causes (*aitiai*) of action—chance, nature, compulsion, habit, reason, anger, and desire—and he then remarks that it is superfluous (*periergon*) to make further distinctions based on age, habits (*hexeis*), or anything else (1369a7). Further specification would not be helpful because age, wealth, character, or anything else still operate through the seven he lists, and not by themselves: "But these, too, will act not because of wealth or poverty but because of longing" (1369a14–15). The other things that make men's characters different (*poeie diapherein ta ēthē tōn anthropōn*) (a28–29), which turn out to coincide with the other causes Aristotle postpones here, will be taken up in II.12–17.

Consequently, chapter 13 points to a gap between proof or admission of a fact (*homologountes peprachenai*) and proof of its descriptive name (*epigram*) or definition, so that argument purely through subsumption can only go so far, and there is a further matter that requires rhetorical argument even in the best managed states. What lies between a neutral and agreed-upon description of what happened and the disputed names for the event is purpose and character:

> In all such cases the question at issue [*amphisbetesis*] relates to whether a person is unjust and wicked or not unjust; for wickedness and being unjust involve deliberative choice, and all such terms as violent assault and theft signify deliberative choice (I.13.1374a9–12).

These lines are parallel to those at *Ethics* V.8.1135b27–a1:

> Moreover [in these cases] the dispute is not about whether [the action caused by anger] happened or not [*peri tou genesthai*], but about whether it was just [*peri tou dikaiou*]. . . . For they do not dispute about whether it happened or not, as they do in commercial transactions, where one party or the other must be vicious, unless forgetfulness is the cause of the dispute. Rather [in cases of anger] they agree about the fact and dispute about which action was just.[25]

There is a gap between law and case, and argument about purpose is the only way of bridging that distance. Purpose and character, in other words, are not additional causes to be added to Aristotle's list of seven; they have a different status: they are always part of the conclusion, not the data. In practical reason both the inferential activity and the grasping of principles are ethical acts. So here: arguing about causes, and inferring finally to judgments of character are both ethical activities. That is the reason, as I said above, that although rhetorical causal analysis is superficial, it cannot be usefully improved. If our objective were to develop a more accurate assessment of the voluntary, and, further, to tie punishment and liability to the voluntary, then increased accuracy could be useful for that purpose.[26] But if the ultimate end in judicial rhetoric is justice, and if justice requires decisions about character, then no such progress is possible. Increased precision cannot remove the need for ethical judgment, for the same reason that good laws cannot determine everything. That is why the equitable decisions of chapter 13 and the other comparative judgments of that chapter and chapter 14 cannot be generalized.

The difference between questions of fact and of definition is not an ontological distinction between kinds of entities, real ones vs. mental ones or something similar, or between empirical questions and questions of value. For Aristotle the distinction between fact and definition in rhetoric is always a contextually and tactically defined one, based on the ways speech hooks up with the world through its purposes. Laws can set up classifications within which questions become questions of fact, but there are limits to the power of even the best laws. In Aristotle's first example, someone can admit that he took something, but deny that he stole it (*ou, klepsai*); in his third example, someone admits that he stole something (*klepsai*), but denies that he was guilty of sacrilege (1374a2–4). The difference between taking and theft, *and* the difference between theft and sacrilege, is parallel to the distinction in the *Ethics* between doing something unjust and acting as the unjust person would act. There might be arts, and there certainly are laws, for doing what is just, but there can be neither for acting justly. That is why Aristotle can say that

> People think it takes no wisdom to know the things that are just and unjust, because it is hard to comprehend what the laws speak of. But these are not the things that are just, except coincidentally. Knowing how actions must be done, and how distributions must be made, if they are to be just, takes more work than it takes to know about healthy things (*Ethics* V.9.1137a9–14).

After discussing the causes of injustice in chapters 10–12, Aristotle turns in chapter 13 to a classification of the kinds of injustice and justice. I.13–14 is about the disputatious part of forensic rhetoric. There are three dimensions of controversy. Chapter 13 covers the arguments I just mentioned concerning names (epigrams) and definitions, and it then moves on to equity, and chapter 14 deals with comparative judgments. Equity is thereby placed in the context of other controversies over particulars as Aristotle juxtaposes arguments over the ultimates, pointing to the gap between a complete statement of the facts and the imputation of a crime, based on the agent's purpose.[27] While the ideal in forensic rhetoric is to present arguments that succeed through subsumptions, there are limits to how closely that ideal can be approached. There are no debate-closing facts about purposes, and so guilt and innocence must be determined by argument. Once again, just as in deliberative rhetoric, the more disputable, the more opportunity for fallacious arguments (I.14.1375a8); in both cases the movement is from the ethical and political parent of rhetoric to the logical. It is a mistake to think of the equitable as equivalent to a realm of discretion or caprice; that is to conflate the practically rational with the rule-bound, so that once we leave the world of rules, anything we decide is equally legitimate. Once we leave the world of rules, a verdict cannot be appealed, but that does not mean that it was not arrived at rationally, or that there are not better and worse ways of making the decision.[28]

The arguments for clemency in I.13 are followed at the beginning of I.14 by arguments for degree that go in the other direction. The chapter begins: "A wrong is greater in so far as it is caused by greater injustice" (I.14.1374b24).[29] The chapter ends by offering the speaker a pair of arguments on opposite sides of a question, arguing first that violating unwritten laws does a greater wrong, and then that violating written laws does.

Topics and Practical Reason

Rhetorical argument differs from argument in general in that rhetorical argument is essentially ethical, and that rhetorical topics are the means of making argument ethical. I want to close by showing how this conception of rhetorical art and rhetorical argument prevents an assimilation of the faculty of rhetoric to the virtue of *phronēsis*, and instead insures that rhetoric remain subordinate to politics. Faculties, such as dialectic and rhetoric, do not make anyone wiser about anything. Topics insure that rhetoric show proper deference to its political parent and not usurp the function of politics.

The topics are a brilliant solution to a difficult problem about practical discourse. I have repeated Aristotle's dictum that rhetorical arguments are about *logoi*, not *pragmata*, and have insisted that we give the distinction a rhetorical, not an ontological, intepretation. If rhetoric were about the facts of politics, it would be a substitute for politics, and facility at rhetoric could be a substitute for political wisdom and *phronēsis*. To say that rhetoric is about *logoi* suggests instead that it is merely a verbal art—recall Gorgias's first definition of rhetoric as an art of words (449d)—and learning rhetoric is learning a language. That is an obvious interpretation of the fact that rhetoric will not make anyone wiser. But on that reading, rhetoric would not be any more subordinate to and a part of politics than it would to medicine or anything else that gave the verbal art something to talk about. The rhetorician would accept a political or ethical position from his client and uphold it, just as he would persuade the doctor's patient to drink her medicine. The posited relation between rhetoric and politics requires a different relationship between *logoi* and *pragmata*, one that could adequately capture rhetoric's, and practical discourse's, world-making, as well as world-representing, nature.

Parallel to the interpretation of the words/deeds distinction that makes *logoi* into "mere words" is the interpretation of values as "mere preferences," things that are good because we hold them, not the other way around. We could only hold such goods and values as principles by believing, wrongly and even irrationally, that we have rational grounds for adopting them.[30] Justice is really whatever settles disputes and allows people to get on with the business of life; there is nothing more, such as fairness or rightness, involved. Unfortunately, people have to believe that there is more to justice than that, or else they will not hold to it firmly enough. So they have to believe, falsely, that the gods like them because they are good in some fuller sense. On that reading, Aristotle's claim that rhetoric is about *logoi*, not *pragmata*, requires the rhetorician to be either cynical or self-deceiving. The rhetorician has to act as though he is talking about facts, while he really is only arguing about words.

In the last chapter, however, I argued that the world-making function of rhetoric, and of deliberation, did not reduce values to preferences. I want to quote again my favorite sentence from the *Politics:* "For there are two things above all which make human beings cherish and feel affection, what is one's own and what is dear" (II.4.1262b22–23). There is a need for rhetoric only in practically indeterminate situations, in which knowing what is good is not by itself completely dispositive of questions of what should be done. Rhetoric and practical reason overall have to be open to the way in which my desiring something is a reason to act—not that something is good because I want it but something should be done because I want to do it—without allowing the inference that my wanting it is what makes it good. At the beginning I claimed that for rhetoric to be a logic for praxis, the relation between word and world and between assertion and truth would have to be subtle enough to do justice to the interrelations of those two sources of value, that something is good and that something is mine. Some things are good because they are mine; I want some things because they are good. Sometimes saying makes it so, and sometimes I need to speak of things as they actually are. The two sources of value are not easy to disentangle, and we would be in a lot of trouble if they were. Recent thinkers have used ideas like "strong evaluation" and "metapreferences" to stress the inseparability of the two sources of value.[31]

Parallel to induction and deduction, rhetoric relies on example and enthymeme. If facility at rhetoric makes no one wiser, then neither rhetorical examples nor enthymemes can make someone a *phronimos*. "*Phronēsis* is concerned with particulars as well as universals, and particulars become known from experience, but a young person lacks experience, since some length of time is needed to produce it" (*Ethics* VI.8.1142a14–16; see also VI.11.1143b12–17). History is no substitute teacher that can replace actual ethical experience. We should already doubt the possibility of learning from history, not only because of the famous line in *Poetics* 9 that tells us that poetry is more philosophical and serious than history, but from the fact that history has no privileged status over the other forms of example listed in II.21. Actual examples are no more authoritative, although they are sometimes easier to find, than fables and parables. Knowing that the lesson of Munich is never to appease aggressors will make someone a better speaker, but not a better deliberator. Rhetoric has a use in exhorting and encouraging the young to virtue (X.9.1179b4–11), but not in offering lessons of history.

There is a parallel limitation on the enthymeme. Enthymemes fall short of rigorous deductive inferences because they have no reliably universal major premises. We can give reasons for action without those reasons being themselves justified by further reasons or rules. For example, I helped him because he is a friend. But I have no such rule as: Friends are always to be helped. That I prefer x to y does not mean that things like x are always preferable to things like y.[32] If I oppose bilingual education because I see it as a barrier to cultural and social unity, I don't have to oppose public aid to religious schools for the same reason. "Surely it is not easy to define all these matters exactly. For they include many differences of all sorts—in importance and unimportance and in what is fine and what is necessary" (IX.2.1164b27–29). Premises derived from the topics can have no universal scope.

But such falling short is no weakness for rhetoric. It is a way of assuring that methods of rhetorical argument, while mirroring the methods of ethical deliberation, do not provide a substitute for *phronēsis*. There is still work for the *phronimos* to do in deciding whether a principled distinction can be made between bilingual education and publicly supported religious education, or whether the difference can only be special pleading. It is tempting to think that this lack of universal scope for topical premises is a weakness, and that practical reasoning would be better if its premises were more reliable. In fact, universal premises would substitute one sort of reliability, that of theoretical predictivenss, for another, ethical dependability and trust. That distinction between prediction and trust will become central later, in chapters 5 and 6, as I explore further the way rhetorical argument is essentially ethical.

Today, we accept without difficulty the fact that aesthetic arguments lack universal premises, but that is because aesthetic arguments do not concern anything serious.[33] In Aristotle, practical arguments have the property we attribute to aesthetic arguments, and it is worth seeing how the topics allow practical argument to have this flexibility without being trivialized. Without this lack of universality, topical argument could not be ethical.

Ultimate scientific principles are grasped by a nondiscursive *nous* because no *logos* can be given for them; that is what it means for them to be ultimate. Topics share a function with principles, that of supplying reasons without themselves following from prior reasons. That is how topics can substitute for principles, how dialectical topics can test principles, and how rhetorical argument can sometimes accidentally hit on a principle. Topics, however, unlike principles, do not have to be mutually consistent; arts organized by topics can prove opposites. It looks as though that ability to prove opposites should license immorality, the notorious rhetorical ability to make the weaker cause the stronger. My point is that on the contrary, the fact that topics prove opposites makes them no threat to politics, and insures their moral subordination. Topics prove opposites because their principles make no universal claims, and consequently leave untouched the principles of morals and politics.[34]

I end with a surprising and, I think, gratifying discovery about how topics work. It is because rhetoric is a mere faculty, and so able to prove opposites, that it can be subordinate to politics. It is properly ethical by not being autonomous. When it is autonomous, it is not ethical but skeptical.

IV

DELIBERATIVE RATIONALITY
AND THE EMOTIONS

I have been arguing all along that one of the surprising lessons of the *Rhetoric* is that the legislator has to see what rhetoric looks like from a formal-technical point of view, even if that is a viewpoint he himself does not share. Nowhere is that more true than it is for the treatment of the emotions. In my first chapter I showed how Aristotle limits, in *Rhetoric* I.1, the artful side of rhetoric to argument. His distinction between his own art of rhetoric, where argument allowed the shared *energeia* between speaker and hearer, and the existing works on rhetoric, which relied on emotion, seemed fundamental. The first eleven chapters of Book II, however, teach the speaker how to evoke emotions in the audience. Others apparently create a bad kind of rhetoric by relying on emotional appeals, but Aristotle allows the speakers who follow his art to use those same appeals.

Detached from the argument of the *Rhetoric* that I have been developing, the reason why Aristotle, or anyone else, should want to understand the place of the emotions in practical argument is easy to see. First of all, they are powerful, and for that reason alone cannot be overlooked. For me they also obviously continue the project I have been following through the last two chapters, that of offering resources for arguing about incommensurable ends and conflicting values. The question is whether these resources can be offered responsibly.

Corrupting and Enabling Emotions

ATHENA: *It is my task to render final judgment:*
this vote which I possess
I will give on Orestes' side.

For no mother had a part in my birth;
I am entirely for the male, with all my heart.
                                    —*Eumenides*, 734–39, trans. Grene and O'Flaherty

The framers operated within a political and moral universe that had experienced arbi-
trary passion as the greatest affront to the dignity of the citizen. . . . In our own
time, attention to experience may signal that the greatest threat is formal reason sev-
ered from the insights of passion.
                —William Brennan, "Reason, Passion, and 'The Progress of the Law,'" 17

Problems with squaring Aristotle's opening remarks condemning rhetoricians who rely on appeals to the passions with his detailed practical instructions in Book II for appealing to those same passions confront every reader
of the *Rhetoric*. The problem is not unique to my analysis of rhetoric as a
civic art. Anyone reading the *Rhetoric*, regardless of overall view of how the
Rhetoric works, has to face this problem. There is nothing unique to the
emotions in this apparent contradiction: he offers instructions in the *Rhetoric*
about many techniques he also condemns. Nor is there anything unique to
the *Rhetoric* in this denigration of the emotions. After all, both the *Ethics*
and *Politics* tell us that all animals have passions, and only man has reason
(e.g., *Ethics* VII.3.1147b4; *Politics* I.5.1254b23), and that the law which organizes communities is reason without desire (*nous aneu orexeos*), because
"spiritedness [*thymos*] perverts [*diastrephei*] rulers and the best of men" (*Politics* III.16.1287a31–32; cf. *Ethics* V.4.1132a2–7). The *Rhetoric* simply echoes
those lines from the *Politics* when it says that all the passions do is "make
a straightedge rule crooked [*diastrephein*] before using it" (I.1.1354a24; cf.
III.1.1415b5–8).[1]

But at other times, in the *Rhetoric* and elsewhere, the emotions receive
more favorable valuation. The crookedness and flexibility of the measuring
stick that makes the emotions suspect is the very property that makes them
sometimes appear desirable, and so he praises the Lesbian rule, "which does
not remain rigid but adapts to the shape of the stone" and its practical equivalent, equitable decrees and decisions (*Ethics* V.10.1137b28). It is part of
virtuous decision making to take the particularities of persons and circumstances into account (II.9.1109b20–23; see also II.6.1106b16–23, VIII.
1.1155a22–30, VIII.9.1160a5–8; *Politics* VII.7.1328a1; *Rhetoric* I.4.1360a23–
30, II.1.1377b30–1378a2; *Poetics* 11.1452a30–32). Crooked rules and flexible rules may be different, but is there any principled difference, or is it just
that I call adaptations I like flexibility and the ones I don't like, corrupt
warping? To appeal again to my running example, is the apparent inconsistency of someone who opposes bilingual education but supports public aid

to religious schools sensitive flexibility in the light of complex particularity, or is it an instance of spirit-warping judgment?

In an abstract, schematic sense there is a ready answer for this apparent contradiction between Aristotle's barring the emotions at the start and then devoting such attention to them. *Kinēsis* and *energeia* are sometimes contrasting terms, and sometimes Aristotle reminds us that *kinēsis* is a form of *energeia,* inferior because an incomplete *energeia,* but an *energeia* nonetheless. When he narrows artful rhetoric to argument in contrast to emotion, he means *energeia* as opposed to *kinēsis.* When he shows that there is an artful treatment of the emotions, he shows that even in the emotions there are *energeiai.* When he subordinates the emotions to reason, he recalls that *kinēseis* are incomplete and inferior *energeiai.*

I do not think that anyone should regard that explanation as satisfactory. It shows why Aristotle's overall metaphysical scheme generates what looks like a contradiction, and why within that scheme it is not a contradiction. The price is a complete removal from the concerns about argument, emotion, and praxis that generated the question—and the *Rhetoric*—in the first place. In what follows I will try to supply a substantive explanation, one that will fit that abstract model, but not be led by it.

The emotions sometimes make practical judgment wise and determinate by considering the particularity of a case, and they sometimes corrupt judgment by making it partial, using those same particularities to override justice. The emotions are the form in which we perceive practical particulars (*De Anima* I.1.403a5–8). In any but the easiest cases, it is not simple to determine whether the emotional coloring of an issue is enabling or corrupting. It is characteristic of the realm of praxis that there be no theoretical standpoint, outside the practical situation itself, for making such decisions.

Consider, for example, my epigraph from the *Eumenides,* where Athena announces, prior to the vote, the grounds for her decision for Orestes and Apollo against the Furies. It would be hard to find more corrupt grounds for the decision. Athena's reason, that she was herself born without female aid, is however, an improvement over Apollo's sophism that "she that is called the mother of the child is not its parent" (658–59), because it states her own interest in one party, and does not try to rationalize it. *Pathos,* Athena's interested preference, does a job well which Apollo's *logos* does badly. Because she does not offer her preference as an argument, she is able, once the vote is counted, to turn immediately from forensic to deliberative rhetoric and decide how to institute justice for the future. The *ad hoc* nature of this decision helps to end the cycle of outrage and revenge.

Both the initial condemnation and the subsequent elaboration of the emotions are central to the *Rhetoric,* and to Aristotle's practical philosophy as a whole. There are times when he affirms both simultaneously, which I take to be sufficient evidence that the contrary quotations from the *Rhetoric* with which I began cannot be explained away as signs that the work was composed over time, or contains interpolations by later editors. Both attitudes, that we should treat friends and enemies differently, and that we should not, are found together in the single nameless virtue of friendliness in *Ethics* IV.6. The amiable man

> will behave this way to new and old acquaintances, to familiar companions and strangers without distinction, except that he will also do what is suitable for each; for the proper ways to spare or to hurt the feelings of familiar companions are not the proper ways to treat strangers (1126b25–8).

The law is reason without desire, according to the *Politics*, but Aristotle's judgment there is more balanced than that commonly quoted line would indicate:

> What is unaccompanied by the passionate element generally is superior to that in which it is innate. Now this is not present in the law, but every human soul necessarily has it. But one might perhaps assert that this is made up for by the fact that he will deliberate in finer fashion concerning particulars (*Politics* III.15.1286a18–21).

In the *Politics* the solution to these opposed arguments is to make the law sovereign, except in particular cases where it leads to injustice. It does not help much to say that the law should be followed except when it should not be, but Aristotle has nothing more to say because that is where philosophy ends and *phronēsis* takes over.

I think that the *Rhetoric* does better. In the *Rhetoric* the solution is to exclude irrelevant passions, and to incorporate emotions into the art of rhetoric by connecting them to argument. The role of the passions in the *Rhetoric* greatly expands the often schematic formulae from the *Ethics* and *Politics* on the relation between receptivity and activity. In what follows I will emphasize the following points on which the *Rhetoric* goes beyond and fills in what we know from the *Ethics* and *Politics*.

1. The ambivalent attitude toward the emotions comes from the paradox of an art of praxis. That paradox has animated our inquiry from the beginning. Rhetoric is necessary because not everything can be settled by laws and rules, and rhetoric consequently presents itself as a method for dealing with a domain beyond method. In the *Ethics* Aristotle reminds the reader of the need for *aisthēsis*, the habits of good character, and for *nous*, in order to complete the practical virtue of thought, *phronēsis*. It is sufficient for Aristotle's purposes in the *Politics* to insist on the need for these same things to make the laws fully determinate. Neither the *Ethics* nor the *Politics* contains

an argument which shows why such perception is encountered in the form of the emotions. Is the reason metaphysical, psychological, or political? The *archai* from which our practical choices are inferred are apprehended by the several passions enumerated in those chapters of the *Rhetoric*. The sense that praxis and *phronēsis* require a judgment that goes beyond rules will look different when that judgment depends not simply on perception but on a series of discrete passions. These emotions provide a methodical way for the *Rhetoric*, and for the *phronimos*, to apprehend the practical particular.

2. The *Rhetoric* follows the *Ethics* and the *Politics* in saying that as much as possible should be determined by reason and law, and that rhetoric should be limited to those things which reason and law leave indeterminate. The *Ethics* and the *Politics* can give the impression that the role of perception and emotion is interstitial, that only on those occasions when argument and rules are incomplete do we have to turn to the emotions to make judgment determinate. (On that reading, justice and equity are distinct virtues.) The *Rhetoric* shows, instead, that the emotions are continually at work in good decisions. (On that reading, equity is already at work in true justice.)

On the other side, reading the *Rhetoric* apart from the *Ethics* and the *Politics* might suggest that emotional appeals are necessary only because audiences are weak and corrupt. If that were the case, there would be no emotional proofs in an ideal state with good laws and good judges. But the *Rhetoric* will instead exhibit a constitutive role for the emotions that derives from its constitutive role in good praxis and good character.

3. The emotions Aristotle discusses in *Rhetoric* II.2–11 are the emotions of citizens. They are manifestations of the *thymos*, and they show how the *thymos* is essential to personal and political identity. They show the essential connections between *thymos* and *eunoia*, aggression and friendliness. Where the *Ethics* might seem to be founded on a metaphysical biology or anthropology that is somehow independent of and prior to the practical sciences, the *Rhetoric* helps us to see that in fact the picture of human beings presupposed in the *Ethics* and developed in the *Politics* is a picture of citizens. The *Rhetoric* is about civic emotions.

4. The *Politics* differentiates political rule from other kinds of rule, especially the despotic, by saying that we come to rule politically by being ruled politically. The *Ethics* shows how we choose and act by being affected, through passion and desire. The *Rhetoric* fills in the picture further by showing that we become ethical and political agents by experiencing the appropriate emotions, and that we perform our ethical and political functions emotionally as well as rationally. Our acts should not only be responsive to circumstances, and passive in that sense, but should be responsive via the emotions. We should be beings with not only thought but emotions. Practical character is responsive; a practical agent is defined by what he has done

and what he feels as well as by what he does. Therefore, what is true for a good agent should also be true for a good action. It should be, and should evidently be, the product of emotion as well as thought.

The Place of the Emotions in Rhetorical Argument

Guardians must be intelligent [phronimous] *and capable* [dynatous], *and further-more careful of the interests of the state* [kedemonas tēs poleōs]. . . . *One would be most likely to be careful of that which he loved . . . and most likely to love that whose interests he supposed to coincide with his own.*

—*Republic* III.412c-d

The role of the emotions in rhetoric follows from their role in practical decisions, that of making judging determinate. Where there is no need for the emotions to effect this particular function, then good laws should exclude emotional appeals from rhetoric. But where the emotions have a function, legislation cannot discriminate between their good and bad uses. The same emotions singled out in the first chapter of the *Rhetoric* for exclusion—"prejudice, compassion, anger, and similar emotions [*diabolē kai eleos kai orgē kai ta toiauta pathē*]" (I.1.1354a16–17)—form the subject of II.2–11. Similarly, the same *thymos* that corrupted the judgment of even the best men in *Politics* III will be central to that treatment of the emotions.

Where reason points in a single direction, there is no need for either character or emotion, no need for rhetoric. Where reason alone is not sufficient, practical argument requires consideration of the source and target of argument, the character of the speaker and the emotions of the hearers, generating the trio canonized in the history of rhetoric as *ēthos, pathos,* and *logos*:

> Since rhetoric is concerned with making a judgment . . . it is necessary not only to look to the argument, that it may be demonstrative and persuasive [*apodeiktikos kai pistos*], but also [for the speaker] to construct a view of himself as a certain kind of person and to prepare the judge (II.1.1377b20–24; cf. I.2.1356a1–20, III.1.1403b7).

Passion enters the *Rhetoric*, then, at the same place as rhetoric enters practical reason. Any place where argument alone is incomplete, and needs the supplements of *ēthos* and *pathos*, there the emotions will have a constitutive role. By constitutive, I mean that the need for rhetoric comes not from the weakness of audiences but from the complexity and indeterminacy of the world. The emotions can be constitutive of particular judgments because they are constitutive of the enterprise of judging and deliberating. I noted in chapter 2 that rhetorical argument has a different sense of form, and therefore, individuation, from logical argument, and that the circumstances of an argument, including speaker, hearer, and purpose, were among an argument's identity conditions. *Pathos* is not an accessory to argument, but a part of it.

Distinctions between *ēthos* and *pathos* and between *logos* and *pathos* were quite common before Aristotle, but the construction of this trio is original with him. The three sources of proof, *ēthos, pathos,* and *logos,* are not co-equal. In I.2, where the trio first appears, Aristotle condemns earlier hand-books for ignoring argument and concentrating only on *pathē*. But he then says that when *logos* alone cannot compel a conclusion, *ēthos* comes into play (I.2.1356a1–11; cf. I.8.1366a11–12, III.17.1418b1–3). *Ethos* is missing from the first formulation; *pathē* from the second. When there is certainty, the need for trust in the speaker's character is minimal—an accountant's skill is one thing, his character another, but we cannot make a clean separation of skill from character for an economist, and still less for a politician. But what of the passions? Although Aristotle frequently writes as though reason and passion were contraries, that distinction cannot be self-interpreting if he also places them as two entries in a list of three.

The reintroduction of the trio in II.1 is even stranger. As soon as he reintroduces *ēthos* and *pathos,* he seems to abandon the distinction between *logos, ēthos,* and *pathos* and instead makes a different cut, and the eventual detailed treatment of the emotions only emerges after a detour.[2] After saying that in addition to demonstration, consideration must be given to both the character of the speaker and the emotions of the audience, he goes on to say that, independent of demonstration, there are three qualities *in the speaker* that cause belief: *phronēsis,* virtue (*aretē*) and goodwill (*eunoia*). The orator produces *eunoia* through his practical knowledge of the emotions. It is for that reason that the passions form part of the art of rhetoric. The quality of *eunoia* in the speaker is generated through producing emotions in the audience. That move is the ultimate explanation for the puzzling interconnection of *logos, ēthos,* and *pathos* in I.2. Stimulating the appropriate emotions in an audience is a necessary part of displaying the desired character in a speaker. *Pathos* is, in the art of rhetoric, subordinate to *ēthos*.

He generates and justifies this new trio of *phronēsis, aretē,* and *eunoia* by finding three ways the speaker can go wrong (*diapseudontai*). Leaving aside the difference between *phronēsis* and *aretē,* Aristotle says that through lack of goodwill, a speaker might not give good advice, although knowing what it is (II.1.1378a10–14).[3] The parallels to my epigraph from the *Republic* should be clear.

The person who has *aretē* and *phronēsis* is not necessarily friendly toward everyone, nor should he be. The ability to persuade an audience that one possesses both qualities follows, he says, from being able to make arguments about *phronēsis* and *aretē* in others (e.g., II.1.1378a16, I.9.1366a27), but the speaker establishes *eunoia* by *causing* emotions in the audience. *Aretē* and *phronēsis* are properties of the speaker as such, and so knowing how to argue about them tells the speaker all he needs to know about appearing virtuous and wise himself. *Eunoia* is essentially a relational property of the speaker relative to an audience. To instill *eunoia* the speaker has to know not only about *philia* and *charis* but a whole range of allied emotions as well, creating what Socrates calls a "community of pleasure and pain" (*Republic* V.462b, 464a). "A friend [is] one who spends his time with his friend, and makes the same choices; or one who shares his friend's distress and enjoyment" (*Ethics* IX.4.1166a7–9); "we feel anger at friends . . . if they do not perceive our needs . . . for this want of perception shows that they are slighting us— we do not fail to perceive the needs of those for whom we care" (*Rhetoric* II.3.1379b13–18; cf. *Ethics* 1167a26–b4, *Politics* VII.10.1330a16–20, *Poetics* 14.1453b14–26).[4] Therefore, despite the importance of *eunoia* in Aristotle's scheme, the term itself occurs only in this introductory section, II.1. Thereafter, the problem is explored strictly in terms of particular emotions.

The role of passion might be a subordinate one in rhetoric, but it is not restricted to certain cases of praxis. Those quotations suggest, on the contrary, that the range of *eunoia* is coextensive with the entire realm of the practical. If he only occasionally needed to show *eunoia,* the emotions would be needed only intermittently. *Eunoia* is always at work, and therefore the emotions are always appropriate. Athena suggests, following the lines I quoted above from the *Eumenides,* that her emotional preference is merely a tiebreaker: "So if the votes are but equal, Orestes wins" (740), and the use of the emotions consequently merely interstitial. But Athena's actual verdict so completely overturns the moral world of Orestes, Apollo and the Furies that those emotions are constitutive of the verdict, even though it appears to be only a tiebreaker. That is, the verdict cannot be explained or understood apart from her emotion. Her preference therefore does much more than just fill the gap left by an incomplete law or a conflict of laws.

Aristotle bases his account of rhetorical persuasion on the correct empirical observation that a speaker makes the audience think he is on their side through a range of emotions that extends beyond *eunoia* itself, by, for example, evoking anger as well as goodwill. *Eunoia* is defined in the *Ethics* as inoperative (*argen*) friendship, the potentiality without the activity (IX.5.1167a12; cf. VIII.2.1155b32–34); the speaker will be successful who exploits the full width of this potency. The speaker shows himself to be trustworthy, *axiopiston,* when he shares pleasures and pains, and so expectations and evaluations, with his audience. The emotions, then, are part of the art of rhetoric because understanding them provides the speaker with ways of exhibiting *eunoia,* in that they enable him, and deliberators and judges in the audience, to apprehend the relevant particulars for sound ethical decision and *phronēsis.*

Instead of positing a single feeling such as benevolence, sympathy, or pity to bridge gaps (1) between self-interest and the goods of others, (2) between our evaluation of actions, of agents, and of consequences, (3) between judgments of the past and of the future, and (4) between agents' and spectators' judgments and valuations, Aristotle will display a variety of emotional connections, all of which lead to *eunoia.* Direct argument is a dangerous strategy for developing *eunoia,* since "those who have many friends and treat everyone as close to them seem to be friends to no one, except in a fellow-citizens way. These people are regarded as ingratiating" (IX.10.1171a15–18). The politician who says, "I am not a crook" is not trusted.

In the *De Anima,* the plurality of sense faculties allows us eventually to build a single, consistent, objective world (*De Anima* III.1.425b4–10). The plurality of emotions does more, and less, than that.[5] The plural senses help us to see and understand a unified world; the plural emotions lead to the perception not of a unified world but of a unified character and a unified life. The multiple senses provide access to a unified world of scientific universals. Relative to those universals, the particulars of sense are either instances of those universals or accidents. The multiple emotions provide data for a unified character responsive to the authoritative particulars of praxis. The interconnections of the emotions show the ways in which those unities of character and life exceed and fall short of the unity of nature. The multiple senses yield redundant and mutually correcting data for judgment by the understanding, but the multiple emotions go further and persist as a redundant set of sources for decisions alongside the understanding, as considerations of the particular compete with general reasons and an integrated vision of the good life. Their continuing authority makes them more than instances or accidents. That is the difference between practical and theoretical particulars. If the emotions are not, like the senses, modes of involvement with a neutral, external, world but instead with a practical world constituted by relations with other people, then it makes sense for them to have the irreducible plurality they do have. Because these emotions are practical and interpersonal, they will turn out to be political emotions.

Love and Anger, *Eunoia* and *Thymos*

Eunoia and *thymos* work together in constituting these political emotions. *Eunoia* is their collective name in the *Rhetoric,* but the first emotion considered is anger, the feeling most strongly associated with *thymos. Thymos* and *eunoia* each have a broad and a narrower sense. Just as there is a broad sense of *eunoia* that includes all the emotions which Aristotle treats in *Rhetoric* II.2–11, and a narrow sense where it could be identified with *charis* (and is certainly closer to *philia* than it is to indignation), so there is a broad sense of *thymos*, which equally inspires friendliness and aggression, and a narrow sense tied to reactions to insults. In the broad sense, *thymos* both makes us angry toward enemies and makes us show good will toward friends: "For as to what some assert should be present in guardians, to be affectionate toward familiar persons but savage toward those who are unknown, it is spiritedness [*thymos*] that creates affectionateness; for this is the capacity of soul by which we feel affection [*dynamis hē philoumen*]. . . . It is from this faculty that power to command and love of freedom are in all cases derived" [*Politics* VII.7.1327b39–1328a7). *Thymos* is the faculty which makes *eunoia* possible. Without *thymos*, one cannot participate in a political community because the *thymos* makes possible the distinction between mine and thine. And, just as centrally, without membership in a *polis*, one cannot have a properly developed *thymos*: it is an emotion which leads to desires fully possible only to a person who stands in certain kinds of relationships to other people:

Let them give joy for joy in harmony, a community united.
Let them hate, too, with one mind—for among mankind, this, too, cures much.

Eumenides, 984–86

In the *Politics* Aristotle explains why the *thymos* is necessary for citizenship. The same explanation accounts for the place of *eunoia* and the emotions in the *ēthos* of the good speaker:

The nations in cold locations, particularly in Europe, are filled with spiritedness, but relatively lacking in thought and art; hence they remain freer, but lack [political] governance and are incapable of ruling their neighbors. Those in Asia, on the other hand, have souls endowed with thought and art, but are lacking in spiritedness; hence they remain ruled and enslaved. But the stock of the Greeks shares in both—just as it holds the middle in terms of location. For it is both spirited and endowed with thought, and hence both remains free and governs itself in the best manner and at the same time is capable of ruling all (VII.7.1327b24–33).[6]

Thymos, then, is not simply will, the will to put one's judgments into action. The European and Asiatic character flaws show that without the *thymos*, and, on my reading, without *eunoia*, certain *cognitive* capacities would be incomplete, and *phronēsis* impossible. *Phronēsis* is incomplete without citizenship, and citizenship impossible without *thymos*.[7] The laws may be reason without desire, but someone who has intelligence without spirit makes the ideal slave. The good speaker exhibits all three qualities, *phronēsis, aretē,* and *eunoia.* Analytically separable, to possess any one fully requires possessing the others.

Our understanding of how practical knowledge works is incomplete except when reason is seen as one among several interrelated practical psychic capacities defined politically. Reason and passion ought to be distinct, not for psychological or metaphysical reasons but for political reasons. There are occasions when *ēthos* is the appropriate source of proof, occasions which call for *logos,* and times when *pathos* is appropriate. Thus I claimed that Athena's emotional verdict is an advance over Apollo's special pleading, because her passion does well a job his reason does badly. When *ēthos, pathos,* and *logos* are not distinct, as they are not in animals, slaves, or children, then there is some faculty, whether *epithymia, thymos,* or even *logos,* which is doing double duty, and people consequently cannot live well. The separation of reason and emotion is part of a full articulation of the soul, in which different parts perform different functions. In *Ethics* VI Aristotle says that "there are three [capacities] in the soul—perception, understanding, desire [*aisthēsis nous orexis*]—that control action and truth [*ta kuria praxeus kai aletheias*]. Of these three perception clearly originates no action, since beasts have perception, but no share in action" (VI.2.1139a17–22). Animal sensations do not lead to praxis, while the whole point of the discussion of emotions in the *Rhetoric* and the *Ethics* is to show that human praxis requires it. But praxis needs a kind of sensation defined by its connection to the other two psychic rulers, *nous* and desire.

The same passions which make practical judgment determinate also motivate action, so they are not independent of the other two ruling elements in the soul, *nous* and desire. "The [part] with appetites and in general desires [*thymetikon kai holos orektikon*] shares in reason [*logos*] in a way, in so far as it listens to [*katekoon*] reason and obeys [*peitharchikon*] it (in the sense in fact in which we speak of 'paying heed' to one's father and friends, not in the sense of the term 'rational' in mathematics)" *Ethics* (I.13.1102b31–33). Practical reason is reason appropriate to a being who also has *thymos.* The emotions discussed in *Rhetoric* II are civic emotions, oriented toward practice. If our political and moral lives today are governed by a very different moral psychology, then this alignment of *aretē, phronēsis,* and *eunoia,* and this relation between *logos* and *thymos,* and so between *logos* and *ēthos,* will be almost unintelligible.

The justice shown through *phronēsis* and *aretē* and the friendship exhibited through *eunoia* are therefore allies in the process of fitting judgments to individual cases. Friendship is not a concession that stern justice pays to weak humanity; friendship is what makes possible true justice, as opposed to the mere letter of the law operative in commercial justice or international law. Justice as a *techne* would be sufficient for the latter kinds of just arrangements and results; only the justice that characterizes communities requires justice as a virtue. The law might be reason without desire, but legal and political activity require emotion to modify the dicates of law. He explicitly allies justice and friendship by finding their point of contact in partiality! "What is just also naturally increases with friendship, since it involves the same people and extends over an equal area" (*Ethics* VIII.9.1160a7–8).

Discussions of the relation of reason and passion usually begin from the assumption that we know what reason is and what it is for, and simply have to ask the same for the passions. That assumption is a source of the tempting idea that the function of the emotions is interstitial and something to fall back on only when reason cannot do the job by itself. That assumption itself comes from an apolitical conception of reason and, consequently, of emotion. I used the quotation from former Justice Brennan as an epigraph to suggest that we should not automatically think that reason should be championed and the burden of proof fall on passion. Passion is not called before the bar of reason and asked to show that it continues to have a practical role and is not merely an evolutionary survival. Brennan's remark seems very Aristotelian to me in its sensitivity to the varying virtues, and vices, of different psychic functions, and the way different political circumstances have different characteristic ethical problems. Today, it could be that we should worry less about the tyrant ruling arbitrarily so as to satisfy his passions than about the sentimentalist or the bureaucrat.

Aristotle's Definition of Emotion: How Emotions Modify Judgment

I want to force some more precision here than Aristotle himself seems to think necessary. He defines the passions in II.1 this way:

> The emotions are those things through which, by undergoing *change*, people come to differ in their judgments (*metaballontes diapherousi pros tas kriseis*) and which are accompanied by pain and pleasure (1378a19–22).

This definition seems so different from the accounts of emotion offered in the *Ethics,* the *Metaphysics,* and the *De Anima* that it must be a definition of the passions especially relevant to the problems at hand.[8] The definition is *consistent* with those offered elsewhere, but the idea of a decision is absent elsewhere.[9] There must be some modification in any passion, because only differences are perceptible: "We have no sensation of what is as hot as we are" (*De Anima* II.11.424a2–4). What is surprising is that Aristotle should see those changes as the defining feature of *pathē*. It clearly will not do to explain the discrepancy away by saying that the *Rhetoric* is about *logoi* and what people believe, while the *Ethics, De Anima,* and other scientific works aim at truth. For the speaker successfully to cause emotions in an audience, he or she must know what the emotions are, not just what people think about them. This definition does not have to be scientific, but at minimum the definition must be true, and precise enough to provide the speaker with a rational capacity for production—in other words, with an art.

Passions change judgments. Without emotion, Aristotle tells us, judgment is incomplete. The emotions make judgment complete. But the term "complete" is ambiguous. An argument, like anything else, can be completed as an *energeia* or as a *kinēsis*. Emotion completes judgment in both ways. As *kinēsis*, emotion completes reasoning by bringing it to a close, telling the thinker when it is over. Emotions make arguments conclusive and put an end to argument. Emotions make judgment decisive. They decide when the thought is finished and action can begin. As *energeia,* emotion completes reasoning by making it particular enough to have something definite to do, making it into this judgment rather than another. We should retaliate or shrugg off an insult, we should see the death as premeditated or as an accident. Emotion makes reasoning decisive by helping to choose a particular alternative. The emotions allow reasoning to become decisive Forcing a decisiveness on our reasoning focuses attention and transforms reasoning into something practical. It is not surprising, then, that the same emotions that make reasoning decisive also carry information to the reason, changing the judgment. The same passions that make reasoning decisive also lead the thinker to draw this conclusion rather than that one.

Modifying or changing a judgment can mean overriding a decision in favor of doing something else, as in judgments of equity and mercy. But the idea of modification is broad enough to include fortifying the judgment with additional pleasures and pains, or "colorings," that can further motivate the chosen action or further determine our judgment of the act and person on trial. Our emotions can modify a decision by demonstrating that we take the decision seriously: even if choosing among alternatives is easy, we sometimes agonize over the decision, not because we are unsure of what to do, but to show we realize it is a decision with heavy consequences. Through intensifying or weakening our feelings toward someone, a single guilty verdict can change from "Off with his head!" to "Poor lamb!" "Instead of saying: What horrible things I did to people! [They would say] What horrible things I had to watch in the pursuance of my duties, how heavily the task weighed upon my shoulders."[10]

By allowing for that whole range of emotions and of various kinds of modifications of judgments, Aristotle wisely does not single out the one kind of change—tempering justice with equity or mercy—that seems to dominate contemporary discussions of hermeneutics and *phronēsis*. Only in forensic rhetoric is the relation of reason and passion one of general rule vs. particular application, because forensic rhetoric revolves around the enthymeme. There, consequently, the emotions have their greatest role, and greatest possibilities for abuse. Deliberative rhetoric principally uses reasoning from example, and consequently allows more pervasive, though less systematic, relations between reason and emotion. Reason and emotion have to separated in forensic rhetoric, but not elsewhere: it is only the law, not *phronēsis* in general, that he calls reason without desire.

One of Aristotle's innovations in the *Rhetoric* is to make deliberation, not judicial rhetoric, the center of his art. When he puts forensic rhetoric in the wider context dominated by deliberative rhetoric, he is able to transform the judicial distinction between reason and passion into the political trio of *logos, pathē,* and *ēthos.* That development is one of the fundamental achievements of the *Rhetoric.*

To the extent that deliberative rhetoric is the model throughout the *Rhetoric,* the relation of rule to case is secondary to the deliberative relation of ends to the things that lead to the end. There is no deliberative equivalent to the distinction between justice and equity, or between spirit and letter. The apprehension of particulars via the passions can make practical and particular one's general commitments in a variety of ways besides finding exceptions to rules. *Phronēsis* is more than interstitial, necessary only where rules leave off. The perception of particulars does more than qualify some general precept in light of a recalcitrant case.[11] The emotions situate the action in relation to one's character, when one does something with relish, with regret, or out of following the rules. Someone who grows up in a monolingual but religiously pluralist society will likely have different attitudes towards linguistic and religious differences than someone raised in a society of one religion and many languages. These unities and pluralities will partly define those people's *thymos* and *eunoia.*

Agamemnon and Orestes both kill because the gods tell them to, but their character and their guilt are revealed by their emotions as well as those acts. Similarly, as Aristotle is about to point out, we judge the actions of others differently when colored by shame, benevolence, pity, or envy (*Ethics* III.1.1110a19–26). In the *Politics,* he advises tyrants who want to seize young boys to make it appear that they are acting from lust rather than the insolence generated by absolute power (V.5.1315a22–24). Feelings such as regret, guilt, vindication, and others, are used in practical argument to produce a single judgment from ambivalent material and from a character that contains conflicting desires, values, and opinions.[12]

The person of practical wisdom does not simply reach the right decision about what to do, or even reach the right decision for the right reasons alone; such a person also holds that decision with the right emotions.[13] Bilingual education might be a terrible thing, but isn't there something wrong with someone whose only reason for opposing it is: "My grandparents had to learn English; why can't *they*?" While the resultant action might be the same, there should be a difference between marrying for money and marrying where money is. Jefferson, Lincoln, and Reagan all acted *ultra vires;* is it irrelevant that the first two did so conscious of the gravity of their actions and the other with contempt for the law? (Justifying the latter's actions by saying that earlier presidents did so too is itself a form of contempt.) The moral emotions represent ways in which opposing reasons, and contributing and fortifying reasons, are not lost once a conclusion is drawn. Only then can those emotions provide connections between complex characters and decisive practical judgments. The same passions make judgment complete as *kinēsis* and as *energeia.*

Analytically separating *phronēsis, aretē* and *eunoia* creates a relative independence of thought, action, and emotion. This independence in turn permits the ⁓gent to act decisively in the light of conflicting evidence and conflicting opinions. Otherwise, the more balanced the reasons for and against a given choice, the more moderately and the less aggressively one should act. On such reasoning, balanced arguments dampen the *thymos;* since the best slaves have the Asiatic combination of *logos* with a lack of *thymos,* it follows that training in arguing both sides of the question produces a slavish temper. That is not Aristotle's reasoning but Thucydides' account of words losing their meaning: "any idea of moderation was just an attempt to disguise one's unmanly character; ability to understand a question from all sides meant that one was totally unfitted for action" (3.82). Aristotle's development of the deliberative faculty does not dampen the emotions, it directs them to appropriate objects.

Instead, the relative independence of thought, action, and passion allows the emotional coloring of a decision to place a proposed course of action in a context of a wider or narrower range of possibilities, so that it looks like the only thing to do, the best of a bad lot, or the better as opposed to the good. These further ways in which the emotions can "change" a judgment make all the difference. Without them, it is only weakness that allows us to modify judgments in the light of our feelings, and only efficacy that makes it necessary for the art of rhetoric to include treatments of the emotions.

The emotions are part of the *Rhetoric,* however, because they provide accessible evidence for *eunoia.* The orator learns how to appear virtuous and practically wise as a sideeffect of learning what people think about *aretē* and *phronēsis* in Book I. But if the speaker is to arouse emotions in the audience, the definitions and expositions of the passions in Book II must be more than reports of what people believe—they must be true. The asymmetry is crucial: the speaker must instantiate commonly held conceptions of virtue and *phronēsis,* but he must *cause* emotions.[14]

Nevertheless, the discussion of the emotions, like that of *phronēsis* and virtue, serves two functions: Aristotle will show both how the emotions, like *phronēsis* and virtue, can be generated in an audience, and how to argue from the emotions present in the situation to be discussed, as from *phronēsis* and virute, to a judgment about the people and actions at issue.[15] As resources for the orator, the abilities to appear good, wise, and benevolent are used in parallel ways. We know how to make ourselves appear virtuous and practically wise through knowing how to argue about them. Similarly, we know how to produce emotions by knowing how to use arguments about them.

This convertibility is critical because it bars all sorts of ways of producing effects that fall outside an *art* of rhetoric, from making you think I am courageous by wearing my combat uniform to disposing you to become angry by nervously tapping my pencil. If all the artful means of presenting oneself can be converted into *arguments* about the relevant qualities, then those other methods are not available to the orator *qua* practitioner of the art. The emotions are themselves persuaded by reasoned argument, and so are generated, destroyed, deflected, intensified and minimized by argument. To that extent, they modify judgment rather than replace it with something irrational.[16]

My first chapter established the thesis that art, argument, and *energeia* were interconvertible terms in the *Rhetoric.* The mutual convertibility can be used to show what it means to subject *pathos* to art. To say that a pathetic appeal, to be artistic, must be argumentative does not mean that it has to be presented syllogistically, or that deviations from syllogistic form are to be counted as deceptive. By my convertibility thesis, artful pathetic appeals must be *energeiai.*

But what does that mean? A frightening appeal is in *energeia* if it not only results in fear in the audience, but if the connection between that fear in the audience and the speech which caused it is the relation of actual effect to actual cause, that is, if the fear in the audience and the fear in the speech are identical.[17] The power of Aristotle's analysis extends this far: even motions are not affairs of external efficient causality but of transmission of form. The causal analysis Aristotle offers comprises directions for constructing such actual causes and effects.

The fact that these causes are *reasons* makes persuading, including emotional persuading, an intentional act. It means that if someone asks me why a certain speech frightened me, I can reply by talking about these causal, argumentative factors in the speech. I don't give a personal history to explain my fear, and I don't point to things the speaker has done apart from those factors. The argumentative nature of artful pathetic proofs is revealed not syllogistically but causally in the activity, the *energeia*, of persuasion. Because even *kinēseis* are *energeiai*, all persuasion works by transmission of form; even when I am being most imposed upon, it is the material of *my* soul that it is being actualized into the form of being persuaded.

There is one single form, but it exists in different materials. The matter of anger *qua* rhetorical *energeia* isn't boiling blood but frustrated expectation *in the audience*. Artfully produced anger, then, is *real* anger. (In the next chapter I will raise the analogous and much harder question of whether artfully produced *ēthos* in the speaker is real *ēthos*.) Therefore there must, in the audience, be an identity between the anger, *qua* discursive structure and *energeia* shared by the speech and the audience and the anger of the hearer, not just *qua* hearer but *qua* concrete individual.

The building *qua energeia*, the building being built, which is identical to the builder's building, had better be the same as the finished building the builder walks away from. The patient being healed, *qua* patient being healed and identical to the doctor healing, had better also be numerically identical to the patient who then gets up and walks away. The doctor *qua* actual healer has to be identical to the doctor as an entity which persists in time even when not doctoring. Otherwise, there would be no one to send a bill and no one to pay it.

Similarly here. The audience *qua* audience must be the same individual or group that then goes on to vote. Artful anger must be real anger. Persuasion in general in the audience, *qua* artful persuasion, is limited to the argument in the speech. At the same time, the identity of cause and effect means that the speech, *qua* rhetorical persuasion, is limited to the consequent belief or trust in the audience. That is Aristotle's reason for excluding *atechnoi* in general, and for beginning the *Rhetoric* by excluding appeals to the passions. Torture produces conviction in the audience, but there is nothing in the speech for it to be identical to. Exordia which do not present the argumentative structure of the proof might be necessary, but there is nothing in the eventually convinced hearer for it to be identical with. That is why it is necessary rather than artful. Similarly, nonargumentative ways of stimulating the passions might produce a favorable audience, but audience and speech do not then share an *energeia*.

Once Aristotle shows that his causal analysis through transmission of form extends past argument defined in opposition to emotion to the emotions themselves, we have to wonder whether anything is excluded. Everything that is is an *energeia*. Does it not follow the art of rhetoric cannot exclude *any* methods at all? In treating emotional appeals as argumentative, has Aristotle redescribed a practice, or reformed it?

The list that I gave in the last paragraph but one still holds. Torture is an *atechnos*. The introduction in which I charm the audience with tales of my past acts of heroism is outside the case at hand and so outside the art of rhetoric. When I make you hate the accused by drawing attention to his race, I have evoked an emotion outside the rhetorical situation. None of these is simply incorporated into the art of rhetoric. They are at best matters of necessity, not art, although Aristotle will show that even there he can find aspects of art.

But these other methods work too. "Wrong" is not only "increasingly serious in proportion as it is done to a friend" (*Ethics* VIII.9.1160a7–8). In my experience wrong is also increasingly serious in proportion as I have not slept well recently. The latter modification of judgment does not have a place, except as a distraction, in the moral life. "A person is not said to have a particular moral character [*ēthos*] merely for being fond of sweets or savouries" (*Eudemian Ethics* II.10.1227b11–12; cf. *Rhetoric* I.10.1369a25–30, III.16.1417a21), regardless of whether a speaker can capitalize on these preferences. If friendship counts for more than a purely physically based mood, it does so because the same emotions allow for perception of the ultimates in both directions, ultimate particulars and ultimate ends. The surliness that results from my lack of sleep does not fall into this category. Emotions that are translatable into arguments—and only those—can be part of artful rhetoric.

Translatability between emotion and argument about emotion means that the separation of *logos* from emotion can serve a purpose in practical life, and not just be some sort of evolutionary survival of emotion after its work has been replaced by reasoning. In the *Ethics phronēsis* is the analogue of *sophia,* the combination of *nous,* a nondiscursive apprehension of principles, and *epistēmē,* a faculty of reasoning with respect to those principles. *Phronēsis* is not a combination of two independent factors, cleverness and natural virtue, the way *sophia* is the sum of *nous* and *epistēmē.* Instead, Aristotle presents cleverness and natural virtue after *phronēsis* itself, as kinds of falling away from *phronēsis.* Calculation is itself ethical in the *phronimos,* not just ethically directed and oriented, but ethical throughout. Once again, the emotional apprehension of particulars is not merely interstitial, and it does not come into play only when reason gives up in the face of indifferent or incommensurable alternatives. Mutual translatability between emotion and argument expands the role of emotion just as its role in modifying judgments restricts it.

Pleasure, Pain, and Good
Practical Decisions

So far I have looked at only the first half of the definition of the emotions in *Rhetoric* II.2. "The passions are those things that lead to *changes [metaballontes]* in decisions, and are accompanied by pleasure and pain." I have talked thus far about the passions changing decisions. I want now to examine the significance of the second half, the obvious-sounding claim that passions are accompanied by pleasure and pain, and take more seriously the idea I suggested above that *eunoia* creates what Socrates calls a "community of pleasure and pain." What kind of community is that? It is part of Aristotle's genius in the *Rhetoric* to exhibit a variety of ways in which one's pleasures and pains are interdependent with the pleasures and pains of others, instead of bringing all such connections under a single head, be it benevolence, pity, pride, sympathy, or envy. I can be pleased at your pain, when I avenge insults. I can derive pleasure from fulfilling your expectations and so causing you pleasure, as in benevolence. I can be pained at your pleasure, as in envy or indignation, or at your pains, as in pity. I can be pained at your displeasure in a different way in shame, or desire the pleasures of your approbation through emulation. I can want to support public subsidies for religious education through the pleasure I would get at seeing others flourishing. I can set my face against bilingual education as a way of showing my superior power over people who cannot fight back.[18] The general definition of emotion is differentiated into kinds by these different interrelations of my pleasure and pain and yours.

Instead of working out a systematic theory along the lines suggested in the last paragraph, Aristotle seems to abandon his definition of emotion and turn to a causal analysis of particular passions that seems to have nothing to do with that definition. Each particular passion must be carved out from the general definition of passion by three causes, the "disposition of mind" (*pōs*), the persons that are the object of the emotion (*tisin*), and the "occasions that give rise" to the feeling [*poiois*] (II.1.1378a25).[19] The three causal facts are not themselves generated by the definition of passion. This is not a scientific treatment of the emotions but a practical one; the causes are things the speaker can do something about. There is no simple proportion between a passion and any one of those three causal factors. If I envy those who have undeserved good fortune, it does not follow that the greater the undeserved good fortune, the greater my envy. Therefore the passions must be understood in *Rhetoric* II through the coincidence and interference of different kinds of causal factors.

This lack of proportionality between an emotion and any single cause

makes possible many of the abuses of the emotions, and some unacknowl-
edged ethical advantages as well. The examination of the individual emotions reveals differences that stem from these different interrelations of
causes: anger can be appeased but hatred can go on indefinitely
(II.4.1382a14). The rooting of emotion in pleasure and pain allows a freedom to the emotions, and it sets limitations on that freedom. That freedom,
of course, can be used to the rhetor's advantage as it sanctions practical
irrelevance, but it has an essential moral function as well. This emotional
freedom is at the root of the moral function of the emotions, permitting a
flexibility of judgment, making it relatively independent of generalizations
and, moreover, of our interests. (In the next chapter we will also see how
rhetorical reasoning itself can extend further than, and even act against, our
interests.) The emotions permit us to remain committed to our principles
and values even when we cannot act on them directly; we can follow out
their consequences, in our choices and in other desires, in ways that need
not be tied to our own more directly practical interests and to action-
guiding reasons. The emotions relevant for Aristotle's purposes are those of
the *thymos,* as opposed to the more directly purposive but less cognitive
epithymia: "*thymos* follows reason in a manner [*pōs*], but *epithymia* does not"
(*Ethics* VII.6.1149b1–2; but see *Rhetoric* I.11.1370a18–27).[20] *Thymos,* like
bouelsis in *Ethics* III.4, extends beyond what is directly practicable. In the
Ethics Aristotle tells us that *eunoia* does not necessarily involve desire (e.g.,
IX.5.1166b34, 1167a9–11). The essential function for the moral emotions
comes from their connection to *eunoia* as we demonstrate our—speakers'
and hearers'—allegiance to values on which we cannot always act.[21] At the
same time, this freedom is the root of all of the abuses of the emotions that
have made people, including Aristotle in the *Rhetoric*'s first chapter, suspicious of the power found in the emotions. Thus the freedom which allows
us to demonstrate allegiance to values on which we cannot act, and so
permits the sympathetic expressions of regret, also makes possible phenomena such as "the spiteful person [who] is an impediment to [another's]
wishes, not to get anything himself but so that the other does not"
(II.2.1378b18–19). Many people oppose bilingual education out of such
spite; others are against public aid to religious education through a similar
feeling. The freedom from a direct action-guiding function can lead to irre-
sponsibility: I can defend a choice by freely indulging in the contrary emotions—Yes, I stole the money, but I did feel terrible about it. Agamemnon
thinks he can mitigate the hubris of walking on the carpet by announcing
that he feels shame at doing it. Here the freedom to feel leads to sentimentality, according to Oscar Wilde's definition: A sentimentalist is one who
wants to have the luxury of an emotion without paying for it.[22] A community of pleasure and pain makes it possible to have pleasures and pains apart

from their normal practical consequences or their standard objects and occasions.

This freedom of the emotions and the necessity for a multidimensional causal analysis follows from the second part of the definition, their connection to pleasure and pain. While all the emotions are incipient desires, they can also be experienced as complete in themselves, and so as independent of any actions.[23] the moral sentiments explored in *Rhetoric* II.2–11 are all incipient desires as the passions are liberated from their directly practical role and allowed to range more freely. These emotions must be purposive, not simply "expressive," but they need not be tied in each instance to their purposes. Pain is the genus, or material cause of anger, and at II.2.1379a10–13. that material substrate, irascibility, is discussed without any attention to either the lack of desert or the desire for revenge, which jointly constitute its differentia.

Pain, the genus of anger (1378a30–32), is simply defined as the frustration of desire, regardless of its cause; one particular emotion, emulation (*zelos*) is a feeling of pain because we do not possess something we value.[24] More generally, the pleasures and pains that are the material substrate for all the emotions are defined by the fulfilling and frustrating of expectations and the evaluations of desert; these are not the common physical pleasures that figure, for example, in the discussion of *akrasia*. (For two more from the first emotion discussed, 1378b4: "It is pleasant for him to think he will get what he wants"; 1379a26: Someone is angry "if he happened to be expecting the opposite [treatment]; for the quite unexpected hurts more, just as the quite unexpected also delights if what is desired comes to pass.") The emotions discussed have pleasures and pains defined by expectations and by conceptions of desert. (Recall that in the *Poetics* too the specifically tragic emotions and pleasures have desert as part of their definitions.) These emotions are related to what we want and who we think we are. What we think we should get, as well as what has happened, is part of the definition of anger. Anger is a response to a slight or insult, not to a harm, and Thucydides' Athenians say "Men are more passionate for injustice, than for violence. For that, coming as from an equal, seemeth rapine; and the other, because from one stronger, but necessity. Therefore when they suffered worse under the Medes' dominion, they bore it; but think ours to be rigorous" (I.77).

I can illustrate this point about the kind of pleasure and pain relevant here by comparing the definition of anger in the *Rhetoric* (which is very similar to *Topics* IV.6.127b30–31, VI.13.151a15–16, VIII.1.156a32–33), to what he calls the dialectical definition of anger in *De Anima* I.1 403a30–31. The rhetorical and dialectical definitions are not scientific because they do not consider the scientific matter, boiling blood around the heart. The definition of anger in the *Rhetoric* should not include that kind of matter because it is not present in the speaker. The speaker is not angry, or need not be angry. The speaker possesses the form without the matter, possesses the form as a definition. The matter in the audience is not subject to art, only the form. But as subject of the speaker's art, there is a matter to the emotions, just not the matter of science. The material with which he works is the pleasures and pains of expectations.

Emotions carry with them the judgment that the emotion is appropriate: the speaker makes an audience feel ashamed, for example, by showing that they should be ashamed, and when I am convinced that I should not be angry, my anger dissipiates. "To be pleased or pained is to act . . . towards what is good and bad" (*De Anima* III.7.431a10–11); to desire something is to think it good. All the emotions can consequently be translated into judgments and arguments. Appropriate means appropriate to the object, but also to the person feeling them. If I am angry, I am committed to the belief that I should feel insulted. Just as emotions carry with them the judgment that the emotion is appropriate, so, similarly, is *eunoia* aroused by virtue and goodness. Whenever one person thinks another beautiful, brave, etc., he feels *eunoia* toward him (IX.5.1167a19–21).

Pleasure and pain appear in the definition of passion as its genus. The other two causes, objects and circumstances, provide the differentiae for the individual passions. The three qualities of the speaker, *phronēsis, aretē,* and *eunoia,* are abilities to apprehend particular things to be done, not necessarily individual phenomena—this is a practical, not an ontological, sense of particularity. The function of the emotions is to allow practical judgment to grasp particulars, but when we learn, for example, that hate differs from anger because the object of anger is always an individual, "whereas hate applies to classes [or groups of people]" (II.4.1381b18), we see a useful difference between the particularity of individual decisions and the particularity of their objects. Moreover, the emotions, no less than reason, have generalizing powers as well as the ability to place particulars under generalization given by reason: Men "pity those like themselves in age, in character, in habits, in rank, in birth; for in all these cases something seems more to apply also to the self" (II.8.1386a24–26). Just as the meaning of particularity is expanded, so there is a broadening of the idea of ethical perception: "The aim of anger is pain, of hatred evil. . . . painful actions are all perceived by the senses, but the greatest evils—injustice and thoughtlessness—are least perceived; for the presence of evil causes no pain" (II.4.1382a17–19). As is usual in his accounts of practical phenomena, he offers a general description which undergoes modification when it comes to species. In chapter 7, I will show some consequences of the fact that many of the moral virtues do not fit the general qualification of lying in a mean. Something similar is at work here. In the discussion of each particular emotion, only some of the causes are explicitly treated—those causes that can be manipulated.[25] The pleasures and pains that are supposed to be the genus appear in different ways in different emotions; the relation of emotion to action varies.

Thus, there is no discussion of a state of mind for love and hate, since they have no physical substrate and are not connected to hopes and fears concerning the consequences of action (but see *De Anima* I.1.403a18–19). If there is no physical substrate in pleasure and pain for love and hate, then love and hate are the most stable of the emotions, and the hardest to manipulate. Love and hate are the most conservative of emotions, and consequently those that are most apparently *de re:* I love this person and hate that group, rather than some qualities that they possess.[26]

Love (*philia*) is a wish (*boulēsis*) for another's good (II.4.1380b35), but hate, while it has objects and causes, has no desires associated with it. Because of the presence of a material substrate in anger but not in hate, anger can be cured by time, while hate cannot.[27] There is pleasure felt with anger, imagining revenge, but no pleasure with hate. Hate does not have desires connected with it. It is easy to hate someone but still emphatically reject any suggestions that one try to injure the person, but an anger disconnected from the desire for revenge is no longer anger.

Fear, confidence, shame, pity, indignation, envy, and even emulation are defined without any mention of incipient desires. In defining benevolence (*charis*) Aristotle seems to go out of his way to see it from the spectator's point of view precisely to avoid mention of an associated desire: it is the feeling in accordance with which one who has it is said to render a service to one who needs it (II.7.1385a18).[28] There are projected actions here, but no desires.

Just as in many contemporary accounts of emotions, the emotions in the *Rhetoric* are intentional, defined by their objects. But the objects of emotions are people, and not propositions.[29] In the *Ethics*, we fear *for* our own skins, but here we are afraid *of* someone. Aristotle here makes the emotions correspond to the fundamental meaning of belief, *pistis*, in the *Rhetoric*, where the primary object of belief is not a proposition but a person—we believe *in*, put our trust and faith *in*, someone, instead of believing that something is true.[30] As my argument develops, especially in Chapter 6, I will show how the integration of *ēthos* and *logos*, which is the fundamental achievement of the *Rhetoric*, turns on the interrelation between belief and trust in the speaker and belief that his arguments are cogent and reliable. That interrelation between the ethical and the argumentative is crucial in the analysis of the emotions too.

That the object of emotion is a person, not a proposition, does not stop us from giving reasons for our emotions. At the beginning, Aristotle attacks the other writers on rhetoric for concentrating on emotion and ignoring proofs; once he made the enthymeme the center of his art, emotional appeals can become emotional *proofs*. Because we give reasons for emotions, the rhetorician can calculate how to bring emotions about. It is a part of the richness of Aristotle's account that the relations between personal object and propositional structure will vary. I am angry with, or at, someone because she insulted me; when I discover that she did not in fact insult me, anger disappears immediately. But I hate someone because he can't stand listening to jazz, which I enjoy passionately. When I find out that he doesn't mind jazz so much after all, my hatred does not automatically disappear. I may well find another reason to hate him.[31] The fact that emotions have as their objects people, not propositions, does not make them less rational. It does not mean that their relation to judgment can only be causal, not rational. Even though emotions have people as objects, I can make inferences from one emotion to another just as from one proposition to another: if I am afraid of you, I cannot be angry with you.

Not all the causes are relevant in each emotion. There is also a shift in the proportion of discussion devoted to arguing about rather than causing different emotions. The definition of benevolence (*charis*) in terms of the three variables is brief and almost perfunctory, and he quickly turns his attention to how to produce and remove the feeling of benevolence by argument. "Since it is evident to whom and for what reasons kindliness is offered and in what state of mind, it is clear that [speakers] should derive it from these sources" (II.7.1385a30–32). Those arguments consist in nothing more than showing that something or someone does or does not fit under the terms of the definition.

The connection of the relevant emotions to *eunoia* and to *thymos* accounts for their sequence of treatment in *Rhetoric* II. Aristotle exhibits the development of passions from externally caused events such as insults to perceptions tied to habit and character. Anger, the emotion sometimes simply identified with *thymos,* is the first resource for the speaker to develop *eunoia.* Anger, with its privation, calm, is followed in Aristotle's exposition not by hatred but love. Where anger is painful, love is pleasant; where anger is purposive, constituted by a desire for retaliation, love is disinterested. Those emotions that Aristotle treats after benevolence—indignation, pity, envy, and emulation—can be transformed into one another. The discussions of pity, envy, and emulation, by contrast, begin with the genus pain (II.8.1385b16, II.10.1387b24, II.11.1388a38). The same pain underlies each of these, allowing such transformation. If I envy someone because I think she has acquired a great good, and then I find out that what she obtained isn't a good after all, I pity her. Conversely, "if the speech puts the judges into this [hostile or indifferent] frame of mind [toward the opponent] and shows that those who think they deserve to be pitied are unworthy to attain it . . . it is impossible for pity to be felt" (II.9.1387b17–21).

Those later emotions are more closely tied to character (9.1387b32) because they are part of that network of transformations. Anger is the passion least tied to character because it is the most passive of the emotions. Therefore its removal results not in another emotion but in a mere privation, calm. Anger can cause the loss of self-control and *akrasia,* but none of the other emotions in the *Rhetoric* can. Fear lies between anger and the last four in the order of Aristotle's treatment, and also in its connection to character: pity and fear are not transformed into each other, but we pity in others what we would fear in ourselves. Similarly, and more generally, the *thymos* which makes us friendly and well-disposed toward some is the same *thymos* which rouses us to action against our enemies.

Because of the argumentative nature of the passions, there is an association of emotions as well as an association of ideas. For a few examples, "[Through] regarding [the other's] distress as just retribution, they cease from their anger" (II.3.1380a15); "Men esteem those who admire them and those whom they admire, those by whom they wish to be admired, those whose rivals they are, and whose opinion they do not despise" (II.6.1384a28); "Men feel shame for those whom they themselves respect" (1385a5). Again, fear drives pity out (II.8.1385b33), indignation removes envy (II.9.1386b22–24), but we should fear the mild more than the sharp-hearted and obviously angry (II.5.1382b18). Earlier I said that while the plurality of sense faculties allows us eventually to build a single, consistent, objective world, the plurality of emotions does more, and less, than that. Here we are in a position to spell that out further. Feeling one emotion can either cause a second emotion, as anger causes hatred, or can make it impossible to feel a second emotion, as envy and fear both preclude pity. Part of the task of *Rhetoric* II.2–11 is to exhibit these oppositions and interdependences, a job which has no equivalent in the commonsense integration of distinct proper sensibles in the *De Anima*.[32] The more one person loves, or hates, another, the more the second person will love or hate in return, but the more frightening one person is, the less afraid he should be (II.5.1383a36), and one cannot be angry with someone who is himself angry (II.3.1380b1), nor can one be angry with oneself (1380a13).

The Political Function of Emotion

These emotions are not raw, natural, human emotions, but the emotions of citizens. The warm Asians could be free from anger caused by resentment, but they could not, consequently, act politically. But the Europeans have *thymos,* and they are not political animals either. The example of these Northerners shows that both *thymos* and *eunoia* have prepolitical forms. They are the natural material out of which civic souls are formed. (There can even be *eunoia* between master and slave, where justice is impossible. *Politics* I.7.1255a18). At the start I denied that Aristotle needed some sort of metaphysical biology prior to and authoritative over political psychology. Seeing how reason and *thymos* work in the polis allows him to extend his account to human beings outside the polis, not the other way around. General human psychology is a corollary of the psychology of the polis.

The moral sentiments of *Rhetoric* II occupy the same field as the social emotions that are the material for the moral virtues of *Ethics* IV, as opposed on the one hand to courage and temperance, the virtues of the "irrational part of the soul" (III.10.1117b24), and to justice on the other. The relevant emotions are those passions whose objects are other people, either other individuals (as in anger), or groups (as in hate), or things about us caused by other people (as in shame) (II.6.1383a23–b26).

Connected to *eunoia,* they are variations on political friendship, the emotions that make a polis different from a family, a mere alliance, or exchange arrangement. Even fear is in the *Rhetoric* a social passion; for example, its signs are "the enmity and anger of those able to injure us" (1382a26), and its objects are narrowed to other people.[33]

The material cause of all the emotions is pleasure and pain. In courage and temperance the material cause is identical with the human body in its somatic pleasures and pains. In contrast, the matter of the passions of *Rhetoric* II is the pleasure or pain of fulfilled and frustrated expectations. That is the significance of pleasure and pain in the rhetorical definition of the passions, and these are the emotions that Socrates located in the *thymos* (e.g., *Republic* 439e–440b, 547b–550b).[34] These are the emotions of man the political animal, and things that might fit the definition of passion in II.1 but which are not connected to man's political nature do not come in for consideration.[35] Pleasures and pains tied to expectations generate political emotions, emotions related to *eunoia* and *thymos.* These are the emotions for which translation back and forth between arguing about them and causing them are possible. Translation between argument and cause is possible because every emotion carries with it the implication that the emotion is appropriate to its object and to the person feeling it.

This understanding of the place of pleasure and pain in the emotions and the limitation of the emotions to civic emotions shows another gain in Aristotle's focus on the emotions, instead of perception in general, for making judgment determinate. In the *Ethics* the virtues are about actions and passions. We come to act by being acted upon. Thought by itself moves nothing. Fear, he says here, makes us deliberate. Pleasure and pain give the connection between judgment and desire. It is possible to have judgment, even determinate judgment, without such pleasure and pain. That is judgment based on *logos* alone. It is certainly possible to have pleasure and pain without any consequent desire to act. But those are not the pleasures and pains of expectations; they are the pleasures and pains of sentimentality. For them to make judgment determinate would be corrupt. Advertisements for *Time* magazine make this lack of connection between pleasure and pain and motivating desire a selling point—*Time* cries, and you are there. The magazine quite successfully induces feelings, which are sentimental degradations of *eunoia,* which leave the reader satisfied without having to act.

The emotions that fortify the bonds of goodwill between speaker and hearer are the very emotions that enable the perception of particulars required for wise decisions. That is the connection between the rhetorical use of the passions in exhibiting *eunoia* and their ethical use in apprehending the particular. In other words, you have to be a citizen to make good practical decisions; you have to be a citizen to apprehend the particular.

Because of their civic nature, the emotions in *Rhetoric* II have a range parallel to the moral virtues in *Ethics* IV, but in another respect their treatment is parallel to that of justice in *Ethics* V. The emotions relevant to *eunoia* range beyond the narrower feelings of friendship and benevolence in a way parallel to the treatment of justice in *Ethics* V. Justice there is a virtue of character, not a *technê,* a science, or some other kind of intellectual virtue, but justice seems to stand out from the other moral virtues by its lack of a specific passion. *Injustice,* of course, has a characteristic passion, *pleonexia,* but justice seems *dis*passionate rather than constituted by the right amount of some relevant emotion.

Justice, however, has two forms, general and particular, in the same way that *eunoia* means something limited to inactive *philia* (e.g., *Eudemian Ethics* VII.7.1241a11–17), and also stands for the general condition of trust in the audience, and *thymos* means anger in particular and partiality in general. General justice is moral virtue in general, exercised toward another, while it is particular justice that has as its opposite injustice motivated by *pleonexia.* General and particular justice have more in common than just a name, because general justice is a mean of the desiderative soul towards other people, which is precisely the range of the passions Aristotle explores in the *Rhetoric.* So it makes sense for neither justice in the *Ethics* nor *eunoia* in the *Rhetoric* to be tied to specific passions but instead to the wider range of sociable emotions; general is to particular justice as the whole range of moral sentiments in II.2–11 is to *philia* and *charis* in particular. It is no longer just a curious fact that *eunoia* is engendered through this variety of emotions, and not more narrowly through a display of *eunoia* itself, and no longer is the lack of an emotion corresponding to justice in the *Ethics* a parallel anomaly. Instead, the connection between the individuating faculty of judgment and the emotions tells us something crucial about the relations among passion, character, and *logos*.

Since only individuals feel emotions, but, in the *Rhetoric,* practical decisions are made by audiences acting collectively as legislatures or juries, the emotions picked out must permit and facilitate participation in such collective decision making. And so Aristotle can say: "The individual's judgment is bound to be corrupted when he is overcome by anger or some other such emotion, whereas . . . it is a difficult thing for all the people to be roused to anger and go wrong together" (*Politics* III.15.1286a33–36). Through the connections of the other emotions to *eunoia,* we can feel fear for what threatens someone else, not just sympathize with the person's fear. We can be ashamed for what people we respect do (*Rhetoric* II.6.1385a1–6), as well as for our own mistakes. The particular passions Aristotle picks out, then, serve an additional role necessary for the kind of public, political decision making he assigns to rhetoric. These emotions serve to integrate distinct individuals into a deliberative or judging body, or *demos.* The emotions, Aristotle notes, are especially suspect in judicial rhetoric, but have a constitutive function in deliberation: they aid in the construction of the "community of pleasure and pain." "Just as the multitude becomes a single man with many feet and many hands and many senses, so also it becomes one personality as regards the moral and intellectual faculties [*peri ta ēthē kai tēn dianoian*]" (*Politics* III.11.1281b5–7).[36] The emotions that apprehend ultimate ends and ultimate particular circumstances of action are potentially public, communal emotions.

Aristotle, of course, is aware that these are also the emotions that distort and destroy community. Anger, hate, love, envy, can lead to privatization, faction, and undifferentiated benevolence and so destroy the bonds of community.

> [In a state composed of excessively rich and excessively poor
> . people] the ones do not know how to rule but only how to be
> ruled, and then only in the fashion of rule of a master. What comes
> into being, then, is a city not of free persons but of slaves and
> masters, the ones consumed by envy, the others by contempt.
> Nothing is further removed from affection and from a political
> partnership; for a partnership involves the element of affection (*Politics* IV.11.1295b20–25).

Judges, whether as individuals or organized bodies, come to judgment; practical reason is not automatically something that goes on within individual minds, and only secondarily between them (II.18.1391b10–13; but see

II.23.1399a25). Since, according to *Ethics* VI, *phronēsis* and political wisdom are the same virtue, the means of coming to a decision individually and collectively should be the same. But the place of the emotions in those processes must be different. Practical reasoning, like these emotions, can be directly attributed to audiences collectively.[37]

Therefore, when an audience feels that a speaker shows *eunoia* toward them, they come to feel *homonoia* to each other. While in the *Ethics* Aristotle does not say what the connection is between *eunoia* and *homonoia*—the chapters are connected by *de kai*—in the *Rhetoric* he shows what the connection is. I have been claiming that in the *Rhetoric* the scope of *eunoia* is the same as the range of the practical and political. Aristotle says in the *Ethics* that *homonoia* has just that range:

> *Homonoia* is not merely sharing a belief, since this might happen among people who do not know each other. Nor are people said to be in concord [*homonoia*] when they agree about just anything, e.g., on astronomical questions, since concord on these questions is not a feature of friendship. Rather a city is said to be in concord when [its citizens] agree about what is advantageous, make the same decision, and act on their common resolution (IX.6.1167a22–30).

See also b3–4: "Concord, then, is apparently political friendship [*philia*] . . . for it is concerned with advantage and with what affects life." The community of pleasure and pain is a practical community, a community of deliberating citizens. These emotions are predicated directly of a collective deliberative body: they all feel *eunoia* toward the speaker because they feel *homonoia* to each other. The audience thinks that it has feelings and interests in common, as my quotations from the *Ethics* indicate, because they not only feel the same emotions, but together agree on the appropriateness of those emotions to the events and to themselves. That is, they not only have the same reactions, but recognize that they have them *qua* parts of the community. It is a *community* of pleasure and pain because members of the audience recognize each other as having the same emotions, and that mutual recognition is necessary for *philia*. *Homonoia* is not unanimity on premises: Aristotle is not talking about a credal community, but about agreement on what to do. *Homonoia* and *eunoia*, like virtue and *phronēsis*, are more a matter of knowing *how* than knowing *that*. More than a community of pleasure and pain, it is a deliberative community.

A deliberative, political community is in one respect then not a community simply of pleasure and pain, but of these moral emotions that are rooted in *eunoia* and *thymos*. Political communities are communities of justice and utility, not simply pleasure:

Man alone among animals has speech [*logos*]. The voice indeed indicates the painful or pleasant, and hence is present in other animals as well . . . but speech serves to reveal the advantageous and the harmful, and hence also the just and the unjust. For it is peculiar to man as compared to other animals that he alone has a perception [*aisthēsis*] of good and bad and just and unjust and other things [of this sort]; and partnership in these things is what makes a household and a city (I.2.1253a11–18).

The friendships of utility and pleasure are not engendered by, nor do they in turn produce, *eunoia*, but only perfect friendship. There can be communities of pleasure and pain *simpliciter*, rather than the moral emotions, and therefore communities built around friendships of pleasure. A group of Chicago Bears fans suffers and rejoices together, and a putative political community might be mobilized around a common pleasure in seeing the American flag. There can be communities of pure utility, which do not have *eunoia* or *homonoia*. These are communities whose members have expectations about one another and who can predict and count on one another's fulfilling contracts, but there is no trust, and no *eunoia*. Just as in the *Ethics* it is a sign of the power of Aristotle's analysis that he can show that friendships of utility can exist, that is, that utility and friendship are not incompatible, so here community and *eunoia* can issue from common useful projects (*Nichomachean Ethics* VIII.9.1160a11–12; *Eudemian Ethics* II.8.1242b22–23). *Logos* indicates the useful as well as the just.

A political community might be destroyed when its members start to conceive its functioning in terms of pure utility as a contract, exchanging taxes for services, or of pleasures of patriotism dissociated from any purposes or actions. Rhetoric based on such appeals destroys *eunoia*, although it can be consistent with a purely aggressive *thymos*. The community founded on *eunoia* and *thymos* is a deliberative community.

The passions of the *Rhetoric* stand midway between reason and causes and midway between general reason and individual pleasure and pain events, between *logos* and *epithymia*. Like reason, the emotions are inherently intentional, while pleasures and pains *qua* pleasure and pain are not intentional; unlike reason, persuasion through emotion does not proceed simply by the transmission of form, because when we feel an emotion we "are affected by the matter at the same time as the form" (*De Anima* II.12.424b3); these are *logoi enhuloi*.[38] When he says, in the lines I quoted before, that "to be pleased or pained is to act . . . towards what is good and bad" (III.7.431a10–11), those are experiences of pleasures and pain where we feel them as particular passions, and not just as pleasure or pain, since these are pleasures and pains attendant on perceptions, which is just what an emotion is. We can think about an object whenever we like (II.5.417a27), and even imagine when we like (III.3.427b15–21), but we cannot feel at will (I.1.403a22–23; *Ethics* II.5.1106a2–3).

For that reason, we cannot hypothetically feel a passion, or be angry for the sake of argument.[39] Hume observes that "the moment we perceive the falsehood of any supposition, or the insufficiency of any means, our passions yield to our reason without any opposition,"[40] but we have no trouble reasoning from suppositions we know to be false. Thought by itself moves nothing, we are told, but we can think a thought at will; sensations require the presence of the external object, as well as a receptive organ.

The passions are neither simply informative nor simply desiderative. For this reason, pleasure and pain can destroy ethical knowledge, but not geometric knowledge (*Ethics* VI.5.1140b13–19). (Proofs from *ēthos* and *pathos* are consequently out of place in mathematics.) And for the same reason, being overcome by anger is less disgraceful than being overcome by desire (VII.6.1149a25–26). Ethical knowledge is ineluctably emotional, and, conversely, only perceptions of moral qualities, not pleasure and pain themselves, fall within the domain of deliberation and *phronēsis,* and therefore within the domain of the art of rhetoric.

The emotions are *logoi enhuloi.* When we feel an emotion we "are affected by the matter at the same time as the form." For that reason, all the emotions can be transformed into arguments; all the emotions treated in the *Rhetoric* are caused and destroyed by argument, and yet emotional appeals are not reducible to logical ones. If they were *logoi* but not *logoi enhuloi,* they could be reduced to their associated arguments. But those associated arguments show that I *should* feel those emotions. I can always say equally, "I am angry," and "You are behaving outrageously." When I say that I am afraid of you although you are not frightening, I am saying something equivalent to "I believe in fate, although I know there is no such thing." That latter conjunction has the consequence: "I believe, but know that I should not." There are similar oughts with respect to feeling. In saying "I am afraid of you although you are not frightening," I am saying, "I am afraid, although I should not be."[41] (But see *De Anima* III.3.428b2–4). For example, in the *Phaedo,* Socrates thinks that his interlocutors' fear of death is irrational. If he can get them to admit that it is irrational, that is a useful step toward removing the fear altogether.

Because emotional appeals are intentional and argumentative, they do not rely essentially on deception. How explicit and argumentative-looking their presentation is is a tactical question, not a criterion for whether an appeal is emotional or not. When an emotion is translated into an argument, it becomes defeasible. Often, but not always, when an emotion is translated into the parallel argument, the emotion is diminished or removed: "When you create pathos, do not speak in enthymemes; for the enthymeme either knocks out the pathos or is spoken in vain, for simultaneous movements drive each other out" (III.17.1418a13–15). But sometimes the argumentative structure can, by being made explicit, intensify the emotion: Don't you see she's just doing that to make you angry? Yes, that's what makes me so angry.

Because of these implicit judgments of appropriateness, which accompany all emotions, the emotions carry normative and hence ethical ties between the act of judgment and what is judged. The emotions are modes of receptivity, and so emotional appeals are as little reducible to logical ones as the moral virtues are to *phronēsis*.

The Emotions, Good Action, and the Good Life

Where the plural senses help us to see and understand a unified world, the plural emotions lead to a unified character and a unified life. Sensations which do not lead to knowledge are discounted as nonveridical, but the emotions which do not lead to action are not necessarily abandoned. The perceptions of sense provide access to a world to which thought tries to be adequate, but the emotions are partly constitutive of the practical world, and so are measured by values other than correspondence. In that practical world, purely logical criteria of consistency are replaced by ethical values like dependability and trust. The interconnections of the emotions show the ways in which those unities exceed and fall short of the unity of nature. Socrates in the *Philebus* asks whether pleasure and pains can be good or bad other than by being true or false; Aristotle sees that the emotions can have more than informative value. The emotional apprehension of particulars is practical. It is not as though the trustworthy speaker, the man of *aretē*, *phronēsis*, and *eunoia*, sees some realities to which people with bad habits are blind; rather, the good man perceives particulars because he knows what to do, and how to feel about what to do. In his Second Inaugural Address, Lincoln transforms the triumphal feelings of vindication he sees in his audience into feelings of humility. By seeing the Civil War as an instance of divine judgment, he makes us regard the losing side differently because we now will act differently towards the South. Our emotional perceptions not only have to be true to the world, but to our values, our needs, and ourselves. As Lincoln's example shows, the passions cannot simply be interstitial tie breakers because they have other roles as well: in this case having an emotion predisposes us to see and judge in a certain way.

Ethos, pathos, and *logos* occupy different roles in rhetorical argument.

Moreover, they are not independent of each other. If ethical knowledge is ineluctably emotional, the passions that figure in the *Rhetoric* are not independent of argument and character. The emotions are modifications of judgment accompanied by pleasure and pain. Pleasure is a sign of the smoothness of connection between agent and act, and pain shows that act and agent are at odds. This is the fundamental place of pleasure and pain in the process by which *phronēsis,* via the emotions, apprehends the ultimates in both directions.

The apprehension of particulars is not only not discursive, but must involve emotion, not a form of *nous* or *aisthēsis* that is purely cognitive. Under such conditions the emotions are not intermittent interferences with more reliable modes of coming to judgment. Only those emotions come in for consideration which are connected to the agent's character. (Recall the irascibility which I attribute to having had a bad night's sleep. That permits no inferences to character, and so is not part of the scope of the emotions treated in the *Rhetoric,* unless my insomnia is itself evidence of character.) The ways in which we can infer via the various emotions from act back to character will differ, much as the ways the different emotions lead to action will differ: consider the differences between the desire for the noble and the desire to avoid shame, or the differences between emulation and envy. The emotions are part of the art of rhetoric because they are part of our political and moral life.

Phronēsis in the *Ethics* apprehends *archai* in both directions: it decides what particular actions to undertake, and it sees the ends of action as part of a greater whole, the integrated end of a good life. The emotions figure in practical judgment not only by providing a means for reason to descend to particulars, but also by permitting ascent to an integrated character. *Eunoia* aids in perceiving both these *archai.* One can not only reach the best decision about what to do, but can act as the person of good character would. The ends in those two directions—choosing the best thing to do, and leading the best life—are connected, via *eunoia,* in a single power to make determinate judgments in a unified, practical, political world.

Eunoia is distinct from *phronēsis* and *aretē* in this context because it allows translations between judgments from an agent's and from a judge's point of view. The emotions, centering on *thymos* and *eunoia,* bridge the gap between disinterested and interested. The same is true for politics overall: it too is a combination of the interested and purposeful. The *logos* that Aristotle says makes man a political animal articulates, he says, the useful and therefore the just. The glorious and praiseworthy, located in epideixis, are available, recall, by a change of phrase, in deliberation (I.9.1367b36–1368a1; cf. II.23.1399b32–1400a4).

The interdependent plurality of emotions is parallel to a similar finding about the interdependent plurality of the kinds of rhetoric that I argued for in Chapter 2. In Book I Aristotle takes note of three species of rhetorical discourse, political, judicial, and epideictic. Each is independent: each has its own end and purpose, its own subject matter, and its own set of resources, or *topoi*. But the three kinds of rhetoric are parts of a single art as well, and so translation must be possible—not automatic and often not without further argument—between judgments of past, present, and future, between the useful, the just, and the honorable, between the reasons an agent has for making a choice and the reasons a spectator has for praising an action.

At the beginning of this chapter I noted the apparent contradictions between Aristotle's praising the emotions for giving flexibility to judgment and his condemning the same emotions for corrupting judgments. Recall the example of the amiable man from the *Ethics:* he will act "this way to new and old acquaintances, to familiar companions and strangers without distinction, except that he will also do what is suitable for each; for the proper ways to spare or hurt the feelings of familiar companions are not the proper ways to treat strangers" (1126b25–28). If we judge differently according as whether a friend or enemy is harmed, we have to be prepared to offer an argument justifying the differential treatment. Friendship can be a reason for differential treatment, but I have to be prepared to assert it as such. I cannot simply refer to the passion in justification. I cannot say, "I don't pity her, because I'm indignant about what she did, and the one feeling precludes the other." I can say, "I don't pity her, because she got what she deserved." I do not offer the emotion as reason for my decision[42]—that would be to admit that the emotion corrupts judgment—but the *appropriateness* of the emotion as the reason. When Aristotle says that "wrong is increasingly serious in proportion as it is done to a nearer friend," he immediately follows that claim with examples of *arguments* showing that wrong *should* be increasingly serious in such cases: "It is more shocking, e.g., to rob a companion of money than to rob a fellow-citizen, to fail to help a brother than a stranger, and to strike one's father than anyone else" (*Ethics* VIII.9.1160a5–8). Partiality and justice are not enemies; justice harmonizes the general and the particular.

In many respects the *Rhetoric* is a less philosophically satisfying work than the *Ethics* and *Politics*. Acquiring a facility at rhetoric and dialectic, Aristotle says, does not make one wise about anything in particular, while the *Ethics* and *Politics* are supposed make people wiser and better. On most issues the *Rhetoric* is by design superficial where the *Ethics* and *Politics* are more penetrating. In chapter 3 I tried to make precise the ways in which the *Rhetoric* is by its nature a less exact and penetrating work. The *Ethics* and *Politics* are concerned with the good life overall, while the *Rhetoric* leads the reader to focus attention on particular tactical choices. The plurality and independence of emotions is left without any attempt at reduction or systematization. There is, for example, nothing parallel to the arguments for the unity of the moral virtues in the *Ethics*.

But occasionally that narrowing of attention leads to insights of its own, and the treatment of the emotions is a case in point. The emotions offer a nonsystematic mode of plurality for practical argument and action, but it is not clear that its nonsystematic character is a fault. In the *Ethics* we are told, with frustrating brevity, that *phronēsis* needs *aisthēsis* and *nous* to apprehend the ultimate principles of the good life and the ultimate particulars of concrete decisions. The *Rhetoric* fills out that remark by showing how it is not *aisthēsis* in general but the series of emotions that tie reasoning to these ultimate terms. In the *De Anima* perceptions lead to the grasping of a universal which then has full authority over those perceptions. In the *Rhetoric*, emotional experiences lead to rational and ethical generalizations, but retain authority of their own. The world of the practical is a world that is inherently uncertain, beyond rules, and in such a world it makes sense to have divided authority, redundancy, and a separation of powers. The *Rhetoric* shows how the plurality of emotions allows us to build a moral world with its own appropriate complexity and unity.

V

WHY REASONING PERSUADES

When men are unable to refute an argument they are forced to believe what has been said.

—*Eudemian Ethics* I.6.1217a10

There is nothing I distrust more than my elocution.

—Hobbes, *Leviathan,* 296

If we were to stop here, I would still be willing to claim that the *Rhetoric* is an impressive philosophic achievement. Aristotle has shown how rhetorical persuasion can be artful and still qualify as a civic practice. Artful rhetoric, because of and not in spite of its internal ends and values, is a noble activity, worthy of citizens. Moreover, practical reasoning, as elaborated in an art of rhetoric, can be responsive to the shifting particulars of praxis by showing how rationality does not exclude plurality. It is tempting to declare victory after articulating a picture of practical reasoning that is substantive, not purely procedural and formal.

There are two reasons, which are the subjects of this and the next chapter, why declaring victory would be premature. The picture of practical reasoning that the *Rhetoric* offers is reasoning as a power, or faculty, and we have to wonder what relation that could have to reasoning as an intellectual virtue. Despite their close interrelations, rhetoric is a *dynamis* while *phronēsis* is a virtue. The relation between the craft and virtue sides of practical reasoning will be the subject of the next chapter, and of the remainder of the book. I will look in detail there at what *ēthos* could mean in rhetoric. It has to be a function of the art, and yet it must supply the connection to rhetoric as an intellectual virtue, and the connection to the architectonic practical intellectual virtue of *phronēsis* and political wisdom.

I have been arguing that Aristotle's success came from his tying argumentative form to function. That was how he was able to construct an art of rhetoric that centered on argument. But even in persuasive contexts, reason seems to have a life and persuasive force of its own, as it apparently bursts the bonds that tie it to function. This persuasive force, which exists apart from purpose, will offer yet another resource for arguing about plural ends and conflicting purposes, for proving opposites—but it will be an especially dangerous one. From being a form that is necessarily a form-of-this-matter or form-for-this-purpose, the forms of reasoning seem independent of matter and end: rhetoric looks as if it can be reduced to logic. If making practical reason into a substantive and purposive form of reasoning is an achievement, the end of *Rhetoric* II suggests that the achievement might be short-lived.

The achievement of the *Rhetoric* depends on Aristotle's developing a sense of rhetorical form in which form is intimately tied to matter and function. In the first chapter we saw that rhetorical sense of form emerging with the discovery of internal ends to rhetoric, and in the second with the subordination of rhetorical argument to political purposes in the three kinds of rhetoric. Something is an argument, and is the kind of argument it is, because of its purposes, not because of its form, in the more familiar logical sense. We therefore have to wonder about the connection between this specifically rhetorical sense of form and logical form. One aspect of that connection is the subject of this chapter, but I want first to approach the problem through an analogy.

From the seventeenth century on, scientists had to struggle with the problem of the unreasonable success of mathematics. Mathematics obeys its own laws. Must the universe follow those same laws? Does mathematized physics "work" because mathematics is really an empirical science, albeit a very abstract one, or because the universe is constructed according to mathematical forms, which are then revealed by human mathematical methods?

Someone could raise a similar question about the relation between rhetoric and logic in the *Rhetoric*. To the extent that "form" depends on function, on purpose, and on the material that is being formed, why should one expect any connection at all between rhetorical form, expressed in the kinds of rhetoric and kinds of enthymeme, and logical form, which derives its formal cogency and validity precisely from an independence from purpose and matter? Should we look for the kind of preestablished harmony that so delighted mathematical physicists?

In *Physics* II.2 Aristotle distinguishes the physicist from the mathematician by the different kinds of form they treat. They both have forms as the object of their sciences, but the physicist's form is inseparable from matter and purpose. Similarly here: the rhetorician's form, like the physicist's, is inseparable from matter and purpose, while the mathematician's is independent of matter and end. Aristotle did not have to worry, as we do, about the relation between mathematics and physics, but I think he should worry about the relation between rhetorical and logical forms of argument.

He did have to worry, however, maybe even more than we do, about those two senses of form, one that is tied to matter and purpose and one that is not. Similar tensions are crucial throughout Aristotle's work. The central problem of the *Metaphysics* is whether substance is to be identified with form or with the inseparable composite of form and matter. Similarly, the *Nichomachean Ethics* reaches a climax in questions about the relation between *phronēsis* and the ethical virtues: is *phronēsis* nothing but the form, the *orthos logos,* of the moral virtues, or does it have a life of its own, suggested by the interrelations between it and political knowledge, and between it and the other intellectual virtues, such as *eubolia, gnōmē,* and *synesis?* Similarly here. Can the enthymeme, the body of proof, be understood as nothing but the purposive reasoning that moves from evidence to decision, or does reasoning have power, and value, apart from those purposes?

This chapter looks at what happens when *logos* becomes a power separate from *ēthos.* The next chapter examines what happens when *ēthos* becomes an object of attention, and artful effort, apart from *logos.* Aristotle's procedure in the *Rhetoric,* like that in the *Ethics,* the *Politics,* and the *Poetics,* has been to discover human artifacts that will substitute for the natural substances of the *Metaphysics,* the *Physics,* and *De Anima.* Just as natural things are defined by their *dynamis* and *ergon,* so was the art of rhetoric in my first chapter. Just as natural things are defined as members of kinds, so I showed Aristotle demonstrating the purposive unity, and identity of form and end, in chapter 2.

He follows an analogous procedure in the other practical and productive sciences. The plot is the soul of the tragedy, and it serves as an organizing principle that as far as possible serves as formal and final cause of the tragedy. The state exists by nature, and the constitution is both the formal organizing principle of the polis and its purpose, the good life. Virtuous activity is, in the same way, the rational organizing principle of the desires, and also the *end* of practical action.

In each case, however, there are problems that have no parallel in the natural sciences. There it is true to say that "we can wholly dismiss as unnecessary the question of whether soul and body are one" (*De Anima* II.1.412b7; cf. *Metaphyics* VIII.1.1042a28–29, 6.1045b17–21). But in artificial unities, form and matter are distinct—citizens are not only citizens but are men too, and desires are not just potencies actualized, if at all, in virtuous activities. Similarly here, as we see *logos* and *ēthos* fall apart. In the theoretical sciences, we understand a first actuality by knowing the second actuality (IX.2.1046b22–24). We understand physical and biological powers by seeing what natural bodies do. The faculty of sight, for example, is defined by the act of seeing. But in the practical arts and sciences, which deal with artificial and not natural *energeiai,* the power and its further second *energeiai* are distinct objects of attention. If rational powers are powers for opposites, and the art of rhetoric consequently a power for proving opposites, then the power and what it produces have to be distinct objects of understanding.

Arguing and Persuading

Arguments are effective as weapons only if they are logically cogent, and if they are so they reveal connexions, the disclosure of which is not the less necessary to the discovery of truth for being also handy in the discomfiture of opponents.
                                        —Gilbert Ryle, "Philosophical Arguments," 195

Logic makes but a sorry rhetoric with the multitude. . . . Logicians are more set upon concluding rightly, than on right conclusions. They cannot see the end for the process. . . . For most men argument makes the point in hand only more doubtful, and considerably less impressive.
                                        —John Henry Newman, *Essay*, 90

My title, "Why Reasoning Persuades," is an allusion to Hume's "Why Utility Pleases," the title of chapter 5 in the *Enquiry Concerning the Principles of Morals*. When I first saw Hume's chapter title, I thought the question answered itself. Something has utility if it is useful in bringing pleasure. If something didn't produce pleasure, it wouldn't be useful—that's what "useful" and "utility" mean. But of course that is not the question Hume asks. He notices that I enjoy seeing useful acts, even when they are not useful to me. I admire the courageous heroes of the past, even those whose achievements do not help me. I can even admire the virtues of my enemies. My pleasure is therefore not analytically connected to the utility the action has for me. Nevertheless, there must be a pretty stable and reliable connection, since it has to underlie the progress from a language and set of practices that revolve around pleasure to the language and practice of morality.

Whereas Hume asked why utility pleases, I want to ask, of the *Rhetoric*, why argument and inference persuade. It seems as impossible to ask why reasoning persuades as to question why utility pleases. As I have noted repeatedly, the same word, *pistis*, is correctly translated in different contexts as persuasion, as proof, as trust, and as belief. *Pistis* is used to refer both to the effect aimed at (e.g., I.2.1355a6, I.9.1367b30), and to the process of proof that brings persuasion about (e.g., I.1.1354a14, I.2.1356b6–8, II.20.1393a21–24). What could be a closer connection than that?[1]

There must for Hume be a strong and reliable connection between utility and pleasure, even though the connection is not automatic or necessary. Similarly in this case, there seems to be a reliable and surprisingly strong connection between cogent reasoning and persuasion. The chapters on the formal side of rhetorical argument that end Book II exhibit the persuasiveness of reason independent of interest and desire. Because Agamemnon cannot refute Clytemnestra, he does something he does not want to do and which he thinks is the wrong thing to do. His walking up the carpet shows the power of reasoning to persuade. Or, as the epigraph to this chapter, from the *Eudemian Ethics,* has it, "Now when men are unable to refute an argument they are forced to believe what has been said." If I want something, and come up with some reason for you to give it to me, often, when you refute my reason, my desire decreases. How can that happen?

Sometimes I'd like reasoning to have more effect on my judgment, and sometimes less. Can Aristotle help us to determine the best connection between reasoning and decisions? Can the *Rhetoric* help adjudicate what seems to be a disagreement between my epigraphs, where Ryle claims that we are convinced in proportion to the cogency of argument, and Newman asserts that cogent argument makes a speaker less persuasive?

Aristotle aside, the question, Why does reasoning persuade, is not a trivial one. Frame the question around some of the varieties of reasoning, and its importance is clearer. Why are we moved by precedent? What is the power of example? What is the force of analogy? A full account of the persuasiveness of reason must explain the persuasiveness of *kinds* of reasoning. How metaphorical are the terms "movement," "power," and "force" in those questions? How do appeals like "That would be McCarthyism," "It's better to be feared than loved," and "If I let you do that, I'd have to let everybody," actually work? When reasoning persuades, it seems to do more than simply transmit credibility or probative value from premises to a judgment. Can a cogent argument *increase* one's commitment to a conclusion, making the conclusion *stronger* than the commitment to the premises?[2]

Aristotle's own success in the *Rhetoric* has made the question of why reasoning persuades all the more difficult to answer. In Book I, Aristotle has shown three practical functions of reason in the three kinds of rhetoric—deliberating, judging, and praising. So long as attention stays on those restricted contexts, no question of why reasoning persuades can come up. Reasoning does not need to be persuasive by itself, because the enthymemes of Book I are directly in the service of the special ends of the three kinds of rhetoric. Reasoning leads to a determination of the useful, the just, and the noble. What reasoning is and how it works are derivative from what it is for. Reasoning persuades because reasoning has a function. There is no such thing as reasoning in general; there is deliberation, accusation and defense, praise and blame. Rational *form* and practical *purpose* are inseparable.

The more successful Aristotle is, then, the more questionable become the connections between persuasion and reason under any other definition of reason. Form, he argues in the *Metaphysics,* provides both the principles of classification and the principles of identity (VII.17.1041a10, VIII.6.1045b3–7). At issue in my question, Why does reasoning persuade, is the relation between rhetoric and logic. What is the relation between reasoning tied to its functions and reasoning whose form is independent of purpose? What is the relation between reasoning when it is defined by these practical purposes and reasoning in general?[3]

A lot is at stake in addressing the question of why reasoning persuades. We have to appeal to some sense of form to show what kind of argument a given appeal uses, and to show where one argument ends and another begins. On a purely logical understanding of form, it is easy to tell when two people are presenting the same argument. In rhetoric, what an argument is—its form—will in part depend on who is arguing to whom.

In the sciences, reasoning serves a variety of functions, and it is Aristotle's achievement in the *Organon* to show that there is a single logical structure and a single organon that applies to all those functions. Syllogisms are valid and complete regardless of whether they are employed for discovery, proof, or teaching. As I argued in Chapter 1, Aristotle in the *Rhetoric* shows how rhetorical argument can be an *energeia;* the appropriate sense of completeness here is precisely what distinguishes an activity that is complete in itself from a *kinēsis* or movement that is complete only when it is over. The question we face now is whether we can articulate a sense of form for rhetorical argument that matches that purposive meaning for *energeia.*

Even without Aristotle's own understanding of form and function, it should be surprising that argument forms have standards independent of their purposes, functions, and uses; from within Aristotle's own way of thinking and against the background of the *Organon* it is a remarkable achievement. It is that independence of form from purpose that is in question for rhetorical argument. Like scientific reason, practical reason serves many functions, but in this case their variety prevents the abstraction of an organon.

Where reason has a function, the connection between reason and desire is unproblematic. In deliberative rhetoric, I am aiming at my advantage and calculating what will get there. I already desire an end, and that desire commits me to wanting to achieve the end, and therefore to desiring anything I am convinced is a means to it. I am reasoning in order to know what to do, so reasoning is persuasive because it allows me to move in thought from an end to means, and therefore move in action from means to end (*Ethics* III.3.1112b13–25; *Metaphysics* VII.7.1032b6–14).[4]

Aristotle's psychology is not Hume's, and the question of why reasoning persuades has a different force and meaning for the *Rhetoric* than it would have under other conceptions of the relations of reason and desire. Aristotle's practical reason is intrinsically connected to desire and motivation. Practical reasoning, unlike theoretical reasoning, has motivating and persuading force, and so his frequently quoted claim that "thought by itself moves nothing" continues: "what moves us is thought aiming at some goal and concerned with action [*he heneka tou kai praktike*]" (VI.2.1139a35–36); a few lines further on he will say that choice is indifferently called desiderative reason or rational desire (b4). For Hume, the sentence "thought by itself moves nothing" is categorical; for Aristotle, practical reason is exempt. In the *Ethics* Aristotle shows that the instrumental picture of practical reason he used to define deliberation can extend to acts chosen for their own sake.[5] Practical thought need not, we learn there, be instrumental in order to be effective. The *Rhetoric,* and especially the end of Book II, is going to need a similar broadening from the restricting and functional powers of reason if my question, Why does reasoning persuade, is to have an answer.

In cases of deliberative and instrumental reasoning, reason persuades me because I want it to; otherwise I would not have engaged in reasoning in the first place. Prior to deliberation, I am committed to following reason where it leads, because I am deliberating about means to an end I already have. The reasons involved in deliberative rhetoric are internal, personal reasons, which by themselves necessarily motivate. Deliberation transmits desire.[6]

Judicial rhetoric too has internal reasons, but in a different sense of the term.[7] In judicial rhetoric, when I am acting as a judge, the practice itself demands that reasoning persuade. If the speaker says, "The accused had means, motive, and opportunity," my judicial office requires that I find the conclusion of guilt persuasive. Reasoning persuades because—and to the extent that—I'm doing my job, and my job requires that I judge on these bases, not on prejudice or caprice. The reasons here are internal to the *practice* of judging, although not necessarily to the *person:* I can ask why I should be a judge, but not why a judge should be rational.[8]

The formal aspects of thought whose persuasiveness Aristotle displays in II.20–26 are precisely those aspects which, unlike practical thought, move nothing by themselves because they are not directed to an end and do not in that sense deal with action. And yet they do persuade.

A comparison of reasoning with emotion and *ēthos,* the other two sources of persuasion, raises further questions about why and how reason persuades and should be persuade. Why emotion persuades is clear. Most emotions include some disposition to act as part of their definition. When the rhetorician evokes an emotion, the disposition to act follows. The hearer is persuaded. It is also obvious why character or *ēthos* persuades: the end of rhetoric is belief and trust, and belief and trust attach primarily to people whom we trust, and only derivatively to propositions which we believe.

There is no reason to expect a correlation between degrees of persuasiveness and degrees of validity or coherence, or any other strictly logical value, as there is for *ēthos* and *pathos*. The angrier I am, or the more pity I feel, the more easily I assent to what the speaker wants. The more trustworthy a speaker, the stronger my belief. The parallel assertion for reasoning, however, is false. It is not true that the more logical an argument is, the more believable it is. Sometimes cogency seems to backfire: judged by persuasion, it seems that arguments can fail by being too strong!

It is a good thing that there is no such proportion between cogency and persuasiveness, because such a connection could not coexist with the proportion between character and belief:

> [There is persuasion] through character [*ēthos*] whenever the speech
> is spoken in such a way as to make the speaker worthy of credence
> [*axiopiston*]; for we believe [*pisteuomen*] fair-minded people to a
> greater extent and more quickly [than we do others] on all subjects
> in general and completely [*pantelos*] so in cases where there is not
> exact knowledge [*akribes*] but room for doubt. . . . character is al-
> most, so to speak, the controlling factor in persuasion
> (I.2.1356a5–13; cf. I.9.1366a28, II.6.1384a23).

Argument will persuade to the extent that it makes us believe and trust the speaker. Reason does and should persuade as it serves character and trust. It destroys trust when it tries to produce belief independent of character. It is no consequence of human weakness that reasoning does not always persuade. Reasoning does not always persuade because practical reason and practical truth depend on character, and audiences consequently employ ethical standards in their judgments.

Therefore, not only does reasoning not always persuade, but it should not always be persuasive. In scientific reasoning, once I show that a given argument satisfies formal requirements, that settles disputes about validity. But when I show that a given rhetorical argument exemplifies some topic, I haven't shown anything at all about whether it is or should be persuasive. When I point out that you are using historical arguments, or appeals to consequences, to oppose bilingual education, I have said nothing about the quality of your arguments. Classifying an argument by moods and figures helps me determine its validity. There is no parallel process in rhetoric. Aristotle will classify kinds of argument in II.18–26, but that scheme does not lead to evaluating arguments, because there are no debate-closing values in rhetoric.

Aristotle notes this lack of proportionality in a passage that will become central in the next chapter:

> And do not seek enthymemes about everything; otherwise you do what some of the philosophers do whose syllogisms draw better known and more plausible conclusions than their premises. And when you would create pathos, do not speak in enthymemes; for the enthymeme either knocks out the pathos or is spoken in vain. (Simultaneous movements knock out each other and either fade away or make each other weak.) Nor should you seek an en-thymeme when the speech is being "ethical"; for logical demon-stration [*logos*] has neither *ēthos* nor moral purpose [*prohairesis*]. Maxims should be used both in a narration and in a proof; for they are "ethical" [*ēthikon*]: "I have given [the money] though knowing one should not trust" (III.17.1418a10–21).[9]

If there were a direct proportion between rationality and persuasiveness, then the ethical distinction between *phronēsis* and cleverness would be irrele-vant rhetorically, just as it is out of place in logic or science. *Phronēsis* per-suades, but cleverness should not. People are persuaded by what they think is *phronēsis;* they are not persuaded by what they take to be cleverness.

Even when reasoning is exercising independently persuasive force, as it does in the last chapters of Book II, that force comes from the fact that people are inferring from argumentative cogency to *phronēsis* and *ēthos*. That will be my answer to why reasoning persuades: reasoning persuades because it is evidence of *phronēsis* and character. Aristotle's purpose in these chapters at the end of Book II is to show that even when rhetorical reason looks most logical and most independent of purpose, it is still persuasive only as evidence of *phronēsis* and character.

In the rest of this chapter I want to follow out the consequences of that thesis. I want to end this section with two brief addenda. First, I see an objection that needs to be met. Then I will supply an example that shows the truth of the claim that in matters of praxis, reason does not persuade apart from character.

Someone could object by saying: It is impossible to explain the persua-siveness of reason by saying, as I do, that reason persuades when it is evi-dence of character. After all, there are lots of strong, persuasive arguments offered by vicious people with ulterior motives for offering the arguments. These persuasive reasonings, then, have nothing to do with character.

But in fact persuasiveness by vicious characters is further evidence on my side. Reasoning persuades because *we think* it is a sign of character. No one infers that because someone is a doctor and knows health, that the doctor is therefore healthy. But we make that inference all the time with respect to rhetoric and *phronēsis*. We assume that if someone can give good advice, he or she must be a good person. Such inferences are grounded in the belief that *phronēsis* and goodness are more than knowledge. Reasoning is persuasive to us because it is evidence, fallible and defeasible as all such evidence must be, of *phronēsis* and character.

It is evidence for the character created in the speech. There are, in addition, presumptions concerning the relation between that artful character and some real character standing behind it, and sometimes people make mistaken inferences based on those presumptions. I will argue in the next chapter that those presumptions are more conventionally governed than natural—we don't think that the lawyer pleading that her client is innocent is a liar, just that she's doing her job, and we make those inferences far more frequently in deliberative than in judicial rhetoric—but in any case the arguments derive their persuasiveness from our beliefs that they are signs of *phronēsis* and character.[10]

Finally my example. The following story is designed to show that even when it looks as though reasoning has independent persuasive force, it persuades as evidence for *phronēsis* and *ēthos*. A judgment of character can destroy what looks like a purely rational appeal. And that shows that what looks like a purely rational appeal is in fact an ethical appeal.

I convince you to stop smoking. I pull out the usual considerations. You should want to live, and get enough pleasure from life to avoid self-destructive behavior. I present examples and arguments so that you see smoking as an instance of addiction rather than pleasure. Eventually, I convince you that smoking is bad, it's not attractive to you anymore, and that you don't even want to smoke. Then you stop smoking. Nothing in my arguments has had reference to me: I don't claim to be an ex-smoker who has learned by my mistakes; I don't claim to care about you, or to have any ethical qualities at all. Some of my arguments look logical, some move you emotionally, but none looks like an ethical appeal based on my own character.

You then discover that I smoke. Immediately, my arguments look hollow and unpersuasive. By purely logical criteria, the arguments haven't changed, their persuasiveness has. Our criteria for individuating, classifying, and evaluating arguments cannot be purely logical, but rather, ethical.[11] What looked like arguments that had independent persuasive form and force turn out to persuade ethically.[12] Socrates treats Glaucon's and Adeimantus's arguments for injustice differently because, he says, their actions contradict the arguments. If they really meant it, he would respond differently. Theristes is berated and beaten for making the same arguments as Agamemnon. Is that wrong?

Arguing and Persuading: Ethos and Trust

Honest things, like honest men, do not carry their reasons in their hands like that. It is indecent to show all five fingers. What must first be proved is worth little. . . . One chooses dialectic only when one has no other means. One knows that one arouses mistrust with it, that it is not very persuasive. Nothing is easier to erase than a dialectical effect: the experience of every meeting at which there are speeches proves this. It can only be self-defense for those who no longer have other weapons.
—Friedrich Nietzsche, *Twilight of the Idols,* 476

Reasoning persuades because it is evidence of *phronēsis* and character. That is my thesis, but what kind of guidance can that answer give? If we should not find reasoning persuasive to the extent that it is logically cogent, but should subordinate logic to *ēthos* and trust, what sort of reasoning is and should be persuasive? Can my answer address the complications I listed in the first section?

The enthymeme is a rhetorical syllogism. The question is how that modifier, "rhetorical," works. Is a rhetorical syllogism like military intelligence? Is it more like Jewish cooking or Jewish science? (Cooking is an activity where the modifier makes sense, but I take it that science is not.) Is it something which is trying to be a syllogism, and not quite making it? Or is it doing its best with inferior materials, so that the difference is not in the reasoning at all, but only in the premises? In chapter 3 I have already argued that rhetorical reasoning is inherently ethical; the last section of *Rhetoric* II puts that thesis to the test. In that chapter I looked at how rhetorical argument could be ethical throughout as a way of understanding the subordination of rhetoric to politics and ethics; here I want to show the consequences of that same thesis, that the enthymeme and example must be ethical throughout, for the relation between rhetoric and logic. *Phronēsis,* or practical wisdom and practical reasoning, is ethical throughout; the difference between *phronēsis* and cleverness is not just that the former has morally good ends. As I argued before, if that was the only difference, then the professional rhetorician whose clever skills were in the service of a client with good ends would, if only temporarily, *be a phronimos. Phronēsis* could be a combination of two independent psychic and moral functions, one which obtained god ends and the other good means toward those ends. The two kinds of goodness would then be just as independent.

If the difference between *phronēsis* and cleverness is not just a difference in premises, because *ēthos* permeates practical reasoning, then too the difference between a rhetorical syllogism and a syllogism *per se* will not just be a difference in premises. We cannot define the rhetorical syllogism as syllogism with defective or probable premises, or with a missing premise. As I noted, Aristotle calls choice indifferently desiderative reason or rational desire. Reasoning that is persuasive will give evidence of that integration of reasoning and desiring.

Aristotle is faced with a dilemma. If reasoning persuades *qua* reasoning, we have to show why there is no proportionality between logicality and persuasiveness, and to square the fact that logic is not audience-relative with the fact that persuasion is. On the other hand, if reasoning persuades just like any other cause of persuasion, then there is a purely instrumental relation between reasoning and belief. On the latter interpretation, the fact that logical values are not audience-relative, but rhetorical values are, is no problem. Rhetoric aims at success, so of course its values differ from logic. But then rhetoric is not, as Aristotle says it is, about argument, and there is no good reason to make the enthymeme central. The orator and rhetorical theorist would then be saying, in effect, "If casting a magical spell over the audience works, do it. If appropriate style convinces, use it. If making them feel guilty works, do it. If proving that the accused is guilty works, then you may as well do that." Under such circumstances we might wonder whether "belief" or *pistis* is the right name for the effect of persuasion. (If I give you a love potion, is your resultant emotional state really love? If you trust me so absolutely that I can change my policy from neutrality to intervention in World War II and you follow without discomfort, should your change really be called "changing your *mind*"?)

There is, however, a third option that evades this dilemma, although it will take longer to state than those choices, and will initially sound stranger than the alternatives. Rhetoric has to have argumentative standards which are audience-relative but still argumentative. What counts as a good argument *ought* to be audience-relative, and it therefore cannot be simply reducible to success. Here is the answer to my question about the force of the adjective "rhetorical" in "rhetorical argument." Rhetoric can have argumentative standards which are audience-relative but still argumentative through the connection of argument to *ēthos*.

The enthymeme is the body of proof, Aristotle says. I want to unpack the image a bit. *The enthymeme is the body of rhetoric, and character is its soul.* Soul is defined in the *De Anima* as the first actuality of an organic body, and the use of the word "organic" in that definition shows that body and soul are each defined in terms of the other. Natural bodies have organic structures and parts: Aristotelian body is not matter but power. In the lines I quoted earlier in the chapter, "we can wholly dismiss as unnecessary the question of whether soul and body are one" (*De Anima* II.1.412b7). At its best, a similar relation obtains between reasoning and character. To say, as I have been saying, that reasoning gives evidence for character is too weak; good practical reasoning *is* the discursive embodiment of good character. The character of the speaker *is* what is revealed in the speech, and specifically in the reasoning of the speech. Reasoning *is* what reveals character. Reasoning of course has other functions in rhetoric, roles connected with the speaker's knowing what he is talking about. Those roles are paramount in Book I, but, again, insufficient to produce persuasion.

This identity between the enthymeme as the body of proof and *ēthos* as its soul explains how Aristotle can assert on the one hand that the enthymeme is the body of proof and that "we most believe when we suppose something to have been demonstrated" (I.1.1355a5–6), and on the other, that character is the most persuasive of proofs (I.2.1356a13). It explains how he can accuse his predecessors of concentrating on the passions alone and so by implication ignoring *both* his other sources of proof, argument and character. Their advice was directed only at effect on the audience [*ta pros ton akroatēn*] (III.14.1415a1–2, b7–8, 34–36). The sophists dealt with neither reason nor character because to deal with one is to deal with the other. The terms of my false dilemma make sense only for a psychology in which there are either logical or causal relations, either reason or passion. That is not Aristotle's psychology.

If the character of the speaker *is* what is revealed in the speech, and specifically in the reasoning of the speech, and if reasoning *is* what reveals character, then an art of rhetoric is far less threatening than it would be if character could be shown more directly. If character were independent of reasoning, it would then be much easier to fake, and easier to make into a skill available for sale. He emphasizes the intimate relation between argument and *ēthos*, in which character is what is revealed in the speech, in one of his early polemics against the other writers on rhetoric in which he claims that the sophists neglected *ēthos* and that *ēthos* is the center of persuasion.

I quoted part of this passage above, where Aristotle said that "[There is persuasion] through character [*ēthos*] whenever the speech is spoken in such a way as to make the speaker worthy of credence." But he goes on to insist that

> this confidence must be due to the speech itself, not to any preconceived idea of the speaker's character. For it is not the case, as some writers of rhetorical treatises lay down in their "art," that the worth of the orator in no way contributes to his powers of persuasion; on the contrary, *ēthos* constitutes the most effective [*kuriotaton*] means of proof (I.2.1356a5–13).

When we look at some of Aristotle's explanations for why specific rhetorical tactics persuade, it is hard to classify some of his accounts under a dichotomy of reason vs. passion or reasons vs. causes. Thinking that a tactic must persuade either rationally or causally makes Aristotle's advice look more manipulative and cynical than it really is. His explanations make a different kind of sense if reason persuades when it is oriented to character. Many of his remarks seem difficult to classify as either logical or psychological. Such difficulties should make us pause. When he says that examples persuade, because the future resembles the past (II.20.1394a9), is that an explanation that shows why this kind of reasoning persuades *qua* reasoning, or is he appealing to some general psychological principle of mental inertia? When he says, a few lines later, that examples persuade because they are like witnesses, and witnesses always induce belief (II.20.1394a15), is that a rational explanation for the rationality of persuasion, or an observation about one of the nonrational aspects of human psychological response?

Enthymemes should be short (II.22.1395b28; cf. I.2.1357a21, II.23.1400b31–34, III.10.1410b10–26, III.18.1419a18; *Topics* I.11.105a8– 10) because audiences cannot follow a long series of inferences. Brevity hardly looks like a logical property. On the other hand, whereas accuracy and precision might be thought to be logical, Aristotle nevertheless makes them audience-relative and ethical:

> Some people do not listen to a speaker unless he speaks mathematically, while others expect him to cite a poet as witness. And some want to have everything done accurately, while others are annoyed by accuracy, either because they cannot follow the connection of thought or because they regard it as pettifoggery. For accuracy has something of this character, so that as in trade so in argument some people think it mean (*Metaphysics* II.3.994b32–995a17; cf. *Topics* VI.4.141b36–142a2, *Rhetoric* I.10.1369b31–32, III.12.1414a7–18, 17.1418a2–4).

Is the following advice rational or psychological: "One should also speak maxims. . . . whenever the speaker's character is going to be made to seem better or the maxim is stated with *pathos*" (II.21.1395a21). "Maxims make one great contribution to speeches because of the uncultivated mind of the audience; for people are pleased if someone in a general observation hits upon opinions that they themselves have about a particular instance" (1395b2–4). As rational grounds of belief, we can see these precepts as neither logical nor psychological, but ethical.

As I showed in Chapter 1, persuasion is always an *intentional* act. Recalling that feature of persuasion will help us to evade the reasons-vs.-causes dilemma. It will be reason *qua* reason, and *qua* evidence for *ēthos,* that persuades; nevertheless rhetorical reasoning is not reducible to logic, because of its intentional nature. It is part of enthymematic persuasion that the hearer not only be persuaded but recognize that persuasion, and this kind of persuasion, is occurring.

Persuasion has to be intentional, and require this mutual awareness, because belief, the end of persuasion, is similarly intentional. *Pistis* is best rendered here as trust: You can arouse my indignation without my knowing that that is what you are doing, but I cannot trust you without being aware that I am trusting you.[13] Making the audience do the speaker's bidding because he has made them indignant is in this sense *not* persuasion. Evoking assent through an ambiguity that masks the fact that the speaker has nothing to say is not an intentional act, and consequently not an act of rhetorical persuasion. That does not prevent Aristotle from giving advice on how to succeed in fooling an audience in that way: Do not "use amphiboles— unless [obscurity] is being sought. People do this when they have nothing to say but are pretending to say something. Such are those [philosophers] who speak in poetry, Empedocles, for example. When there is much going around in a circle, it cheats the listeners and they feel the way many do about oracles" (III.5.1407a31–37). So we have not fully resolved the question of the manipulative side of Aristotle's advice, and will have to return to it in later chapters.

In matters outside the sphere of praxis, where there is reliable knowledge, the most persuasive speaker should be the most rational one. There can be no distinction between cleverness and *phronēsis* outside praxis, and consequently in such domains reasoning should persuade. *Phronesis,* however, is, in the language of *De Anima* I.1., a *logos enhulos,* a form that is by definition form *of this matter;* the other intellectual virtues are not. Similarly, the enthymeme is a *logos enhulos;* other kinds of argument are not. (I noted earlier that while Aristotle only uses the term *logos enhulos* once, at *De Anima* 403a25, it captures his notion of form as form of some particular matter, not a Platonic form whose relation to its instances seems more arbitrary and problematic.) The need for conviction and trust—for *pistis*—disappears outside praxis. If the speaker can predict what will happen, trust is beside the point: prediction, unlike the reliance we place on someone we trust, is *not* an intentional relation. Aristotle notes that *eunoia* does not exist in the friendships of utility or pleasure but only in the true friendships based on nobility and virtue for just this reason:

> If one man wishes another prosperity because he is useful, the motive of his wish would not be the other man's interest but his own, whereas it is thought that *eunoia* is not for the sake of the person who feels it himself but for the sake of him for whom he feels kindly . . . so that it is clear that *eunoia* has to do with the kind of friendship that is ethical (*Eudemian Ethics* VII.7.1241a5–10).

Speakers lose our trust when they act as though the problems we face are not practical but theoretical, like those unpersuasive philosophers Aristotle discusses in the lines I quoted earlier from III.17. "If one has logical arguments, one should speak both 'ethically' and logically; if you do not have enthymemes, speak 'ethically.' And to seem virtuous suits a good person more than an exact argument does" (III.17.1418a37–b1). Former Judge Bork caused people to mistrust him through his claims that *logos* is not only sufficient for good decisions, but that anything else, anything that we might call *ēthos* or *pathos,* was an indication of the judge "making things up" or injecting "subjective values" into the process and thereby corrupting the decision.[14] That is how arguments can fail by being too strong. Reason persuades when it is evidence of character.

Logical Forms and Rhetorical Forms

Even when the words remain the same, they mean something very different when they are uttered by a minority struggling against repressive measures, and when expressed by a group that has attained power and then uses ideas that were once weapons of emancipation as instruments for keeping the power and wealth they have obtained. Ideas that at one time are means of producing social change have not the same meaning when they are used as means of preventing social change.
  —John Dewey, "The Future of Liberalism," 291

Logic, as developed in the *Organon,* gives an account of the transmission of necessity, and of the necessary transmission of truth. Here we wonder whether, parallel to the necessary transmission of truth, there is a logic for the transmission of belief and trust.[15] Truth is transmitted from premises to conclusion in a logic of necessity, but it is not clear that trust is, or even should be, transmitted from premises to conclusion in a logic or rhetoric of probability. In science, inference is a relation among propositions. In practical reason and in rhetoric, inference is a relation among intentional acts which have propositions as their objects. Practical logic does not have its own special set of supposedly rational rules; to know logic and dialectic is enough for the rhetorician (I.1.1355a10–15). The same logic governs relations among propositions and among intentional states, such as belief and trust. But just because there is an inferential relation between two propositions, there is not necessarily a corresponding relation between intentions that have them for objects.[16] Reasoning does not automatically persuade; yet, if artful rhetoric is argumentative, nothing but reason persuades.

Even if rhetoric has no special rules of argument, there is a fundamental difference between logical and rhetorical forms. Rules of logic authorize and justify their conclusions, but rules of rhetorical inference do not. My obeying *modus ponens* assures that my argument is valid; if I equivocate, it is invalid. But my using an *a fortiori* argument says nothing about the argument's value, or whether the conclusion is authorized. It is saying nothing about whether the argument is or *should* be persuasive. It says nothing by itself about whether the speaker should be trusted. Therefore these general modes and topics of reasoning provide yet another way in which rhetorical argument permits plural judgment about plural and conflicting values. If topics, premises, and rules of rhetorical inference authorized their conclusions, then the faculty of rhetoric could not prove opposites. But if these forms do not authorize their conclusions, in what ways are they *forms* of thinking?

This section of the *Rhetoric* suggests yet another rhetorical resource for confronting the plural desires and values of praxis. The three kinds of rhetoric generated a systematic set of plural ways of arguing towards plural ends: the useful, the just, and the good. The special topics directed toward those three ends generated an orderly way of arguing from principles without being committed to their universal application. The emotions afford resources for staying loyal to values on which we cannot always act, and negotiating in yet another way between the demands of universal reason and particular circumstances. Here, in addition to all of these, these plural modes for arguing about the common elements in practical argument allow for plurality in argument without leading immediately to irrationality. Each of these, while not automatically irrational, does immediately raise questions about their ethical nature. I claim that rhetorical argument is ethical throughout. It should now be clear that it *had better be* ethical, because if it isn't, then it is a power that should be either reined in or destroyed.

Like persuasion and *pistis,* and unlike theoretical reason, practical reason is intentional. Because of this intentional character, purpose and form cannot be separated, as they can be in theoretical reasoning. Because inference serves several irreducible functions in practical reason, the *phronimos* and not a theory of argument must have ultimate authority, in practice and in practical reflection. The *phronimos* has authority in practical argument, and the authority is of a kind which prevents replacement by theory. Validity can be an overriding value in logic, but not in rhetoric. *Pace* the quotation from Ryle at the beginning of the chapter, cogent reasoning does not always produce persuasion, nor should it.

That reason persuades by being evidence for *phronēsis* and character explains an observation of Hume's about the difference between theoretical and practical reason:

> Whatever speculative errors may be found in the polite writings of
> any age or country. . . . There needs but a certain turn of thought

or imagination to make us enter into all the opinions which then prevailed, and relish the sentiments or conclusions derived from them. . . . [But the] case is not the same with moral principles as with speculative opinions. . . . I cannot, nor is it proper I should, enter into such sentiments . . . and where a man is confident of the rectitude of that moral standard by which he judges, he is justly jealous of it, and will not pervert the sentiments of his heart for a moment, in complaisance to any writer whatsoever (*Essays*, 252–53).

With these problems about the relation between logic and rhetoric in mind, I want to turn to some of the details of Aristotle's presentation. Instead of directly answering the question of how reason persuades, I will look at how examples persuade, and then how enthymemes persuade.

How Examples Persuade

A fox, while crossing a river, was carried up into a hole in the bank. Not being able to get out, she was in misery for some time and many dog-ticks attacked her. A hedgehog came wandering along and, when he saw her, took pity and asked if he could remove the ticks. She would not let him and, when asked why, [said], "These are already full of me and draw little blood, but if you remove these, other hungry ones will come and drink what blood I have left." "In your case too, O Samians," said [Aesop], "this man will no longer harm you; for he is rich. But if you kill him, other poor ones will come who will steal and spend your public funds" (II.20.1393b23–1394a2).

By reading the *Rhetoric* in the light of my overall thesis that reasoning persuades because it is evidence of *phronēsis* and character, I hope to make Aristotle's presentation of the general topics and kinds of reasoning look less like a list or compendium and more like a coherent presentation in which the ethical character of practical reasoning gradually unfolds. Both the suspicion that reason engenders—recall the epigraph from Newman—and its independent persuasive value—as in the quotation from Ryle—have the same source in the independence of form and function. I want now to look at what sort of argumentative form Aristotle is left with apart from that separation of form and function.

The first thing to note is that ethical character is progressively detached from any particular purpose the reasoning might possess, as Aristotle moves from common elements or topics of proof in II.19 to the common forms of reasoning in the succeeding chapters. The first kind of reasoning he looks at is examples, which are the most clearly ethical. Maxims, the subject of II.21, are more obviously ethical than the enthymemes that follow, and refutative enthymemes are more logical and less ethical than demonstrative ones, so the entire presentation moves from cases that are most obviously ethical to those where the ethical nature of the persuasiveness of reason is hardest to make out, because it is obscured by the purely formal and logical side.

My thesis will have to help in answering the question, What is a kind of practical reasoning? Syllogisms are classified by moods and figures, the kinds (*eidē*) of rhetoric by their ends and political purposes, but the differentiation of example, maxim, and enthymeme, and the kinds of each, seem far more complex. If reasoning persuades *qua* reasoning, it must in some sense be formal, but it is hard to see how the kinds of example, maxim, and enthymeme are differentiated by form. A satisfactory answer to the question of why reasoning persuades, will have to show why, and how, examples persuade, and why and how enthymemes persuade. It will have to show how refutations persuade, and the difference between real and apparent enthymemes. It will have to show the connection between this generalized rationality and the embedded reasoning of Book I by relating these common proofs and common topics back to the proper places of Book I that I considered in chapter 3.

Aristotle begins the general treatment of reason in chapter 20 by looking at examples. By starting with examples, he emphasizes that when reason persuades it is never reason to the exclusion of character, but reason as evidence for character. Example is the rhetorical version of induction, and so it has a rational structure—it reasons from particular cases to a general rule.

But it never is just the presentation of instances. All examples have emotional and ethical coloring: "Munich" is not just an instance of appeasement turning out unsuccessfully, but carries with it connotations and associations of what Hitler then did, and even mental pictures of Chamberlain getting off his plane. "Never appease aggressors" is a silly major premise, with many available counterexamples undermining its persuasive force. Willie Horton is not just an instance of a paroled prisoner committing a crime. Munich and Willie Horton are examples of ethical arguments appealing to reasons internal to a community, which are weakened if regarded as purely logical appeals. One's choice of examples cannot help making discourse ethical. When I argue against bilingual education to an audience of English speakers and claim that language is a divisive force that destroys communities, I will point to Quebec instead of Spain or Belgium, because in Quebec it is English speakers who appear to be victims, despite the fact that otherwise that example might be an argument in favor of bilingualism. Syllogisms may be manifestations of either cleverness or *phronēsis,* that is, of detached intelligence or of intelligence as the organization of good habits of practical choices. But *all* examples reveal character, whether intentionally or not.

Because of this necessarily ethical nature of exemplary arguments, the speaker has a freedom in presenting examples not available when the enthymeme is used. Enthymemes must be drawn from premises close at hand (see II.22.1395b28 and III.17.1418a10–21, cited above), but not so for examples. Because the choice of example always reveals character, the speaker can afford to draw them from a wide variety of sources. "There are two species of paradigms; for to speak of things that have happened before is one species of paradigm and to make up [an illustration] is another. Of the latter, comparison is one kind, fables another, for example, the Aesopic and Lybian" (II.20.1393a27–30). Telling a fable or referring to an invented parable does not destroy credibility, as a far-fetched argument does. Examples give a clear answer to the question, Why does reasoning persuade? Examples do not persuade by form alone, but they transmit motive force and trust ethically and intentionally. Examples have form or structure because they are the rhetorical counterpart of induction; the three kinds of examples are differentiated not by logical form but by how they are gathered and to what they are appropriate:

> Fables are suitable in deliberative oratory and have this advantage, that while it is difficult to find similar historical incidents that have actually happened, it is rather easy with fables. . . . Although it is easier to provide illustrations through fables, examples from history are more useful in deliberation; for generally, future events will be like those of the past (1394a2–9).[17]

The only other thing to be said about examples or paradigms is their strategic connection to enthymemes.

> If one does not have a supply of enthymemes, one should use paradigms as demonstration [*apodeixesin*]; for persuasion [*pistis*] [then] depends on them. But if there are enthymemes, paradigms should be used as witnesses, [as] a supplement to enthymemes. When the paradigms are placed first, there is the appearance of induction, but induction is not suitable to rhetorical discourses except in a few cases; when they are put at the end they are witnesses, and a witness is everywhere persuasive (1394a9–14).

It is fair to call these distinctions and interrelations formal if we recall the intentional nature of rhetorical argument and persuasion. The person being persuaded must know that he or she is being persuaded. The person being persuaded by an example must know that it is an example, and know that it is a fable, a parable, or a historical parallel. If I use one of Aesop's fables and you think I am illustrating a general theory of animal behavior from which I will then deduce consequences for human action, you have not grasped my argument, even if you vote my way. The audience does not need a logical or rhetorical theory, or an extensive vocabulary, but it does have to be conscious of these differences. Reasoning persuades *qua* rhetorical reasoning.

From the point of view of logic, the persuasiveness of examples seems tainted by psychological factors. Comparison or parable, Aristotle says, "is illustrated by the sayings of Socrates" (1393b4): when Socrates compares the unjust man who acts with impunity to a pickpocket, the point of the comparison and the conditions for its being understood and being persuasive are ethical. Socrates shows himself to be the kind of person for whom all injustice is the same, regardless of scale. His opponent must try to defend a different classification, in which the size of a crime affects its nobility and therefore its morality. Socrates' argument is not "psychological" in the sense of working strictly as an efficient cause, because it succeeds through the audience's being aware of what is going on. That is, it succeeds through the transmission of form, and the transmission of trust *via* transmission of form.

The audience has to grasp the species of argument form just as they had to grasp the kinds of rhetoric itself. They have to know that this is a deliberative argument, aiming at utility, in order to assess its subordination of justice to advantage. Similarly, it has to know when an example is an argument, and when it is evidence for an enthymeme.

Two important consequences follow from this demand on the audience. First, we can now see that these shared intentions are in a certain respect conventional. The kinds of rhetoric are kinds because of the practical political circumstances that unite form and function. The kinds of argument are kinds because of the expectations and understandings that underlie any particular intentional act. Shared intentions depend on a shared *ēthos*. Second, although conventional, the kinds of argument have to be differentiations that an audience can grasp, and grasp without taking a course in rhetoric. That is, like the differentiation of *ēthos, pathos,* and *logos,* the classification of kinds of argument must be rooted in the civil psychology of the good polis. The analysis of form cannot be too exact. It has to be a classification that is somehow related to the operations of good civic activity.

After showing the ethical nature of rhetorical induction, we should expect Aristotle to go on to show the ethical nature of the enthymeme. He said at the beginning that there are, corresponding to induction and syllogism, two kinds of proofs in rhetoric, example and enthymeme (I.2.1356a37–1356b23). But he inserts a third, the maxim (*gnōmē*), between example and enthymeme in chapter 21. Since these maxims will be subject to detailed examination in my next chapter, I can be brief here. There are four kinds of maxim. Maxims are the premises or conclusions of enthymemes without the syllogism (1394a26–27), either accompanied by an epilogue or not (1394b7). Maxims can be made into enthymemes by adding reason (*aitia kai dia ti*) (1394a31). Maxims are evidence of practical reasoning and character, despite the fact that they do not need to have or to display an illative form, except for tactical purposes: "One should make moral purpose clear by choice of words [*lexis*], but if not, then add the cause [*aitia*]" (1395a26–27).

"Maxims make one great contribution to speeches because of the uncultivated mind of the audience; for people are pleased if someone in a general observation hits upon opinions that they themselves have about a particular instance" (1395b2–4). I quoted these lines earlier and asked whether Aristotle's account was logical or psychological. These hearers who are pleased when speakers formulate in general terms the opinions they already hold are being persuaded of the intelligence and character of the speaker by his ability to formulate in general terms what they believe in particular cases. "The First Amendment guarantees freedom *of* religion, not freedom *from* religion." Aristotle need not be derogating his listeners or appealing to irrational features in their souls in explaining why maxims persuade. Maxims give evidence of *phronēsis* and so grounds for trust. Reasoning persuades *qua* reasoning because its ability to generalize is pleasant and trustworthy. The hearers are simply judging the intelligence of the speaker by the only measure they have, their own beliefs.

But this last quotation from the *Rhetoric* shows something else. The fact that persuasion must be intentional for reasoning to persuade, and that audiences consequently must be aware of the nature of persuasion, does not mean that the speaker must be honest or open or that the audience cannot be deceived. Intentionality leaves room for manipulation.[18]

Dogs and cows cannot be manipulated and deceived to the extent that people can, because they reason less. Aristotle notes something analogous in the discussion of pleasure, and particularly the pleasures of being restored to health. Healing works not on the diseased but the healthy part of the body. The pleasure of being persuaded, and the persuasiveness of rational appeals, is similar to the restorative pleasures of the body discussed in the *Ethics*. The locus of pleasure, he says there, is always in an activity and not in a process or a passion. In rhetoric, the audience cannot take pleasure in being affected by a speaker, but in its own activities. The pleasure of being persuaded, like the pleasure of being led back to health, is a pleasure in "the activity in the appetites belong[ing] to the rest of our state and nature [i.e. the part that is still undisturbed]" (1152b33–1153a2). In the rhetorical case, the pleasure in being persuaded is the pleasure in the activity of judging arguments. For example,

> Refutative enthymemes are better liked [*eudokimei*] than demon-strative ones because the refutative enthymeme is a bringing to-gether of opposites in brief form, and when these are set side by side they are clearer to the hearer. In the case of all syllogistic argu-ment, both refutative and demonstrative, those are most applauded that [hearers] foresee from the beginning, but not because they are superficial (at the same time, too, people are pleased with them-selves when anticipating [the conclusion]) and [they like] those that they are slower to apprehend to the extent that they understand when these have been stated (II.23.1400b25–31; cf. *Poetics* 9.1452a5, quoted in the last chapter).

I said before that one of the reasons the *Rhetoric* seems more manipulative and cynical in its advice than it really is is because readers presuppose the dichotomy that appeals must be either logical or psychological. Seeing the *Rhetoric* as presenting ethical appeals—and logical appeals *qua* ethical—soft-ens the appearance of immorality. Nevertheless the *Rhetoric*, by showing how to make arguments ethical still offers advice about how to win, how to achieve the external end of persuasion instead of keeping all attention on the internal end. It offers a way of thinking about rhetorical tactics that avoids the assumption that an audience must be deceived in order to be manipulated. And I think that that is an important and useful insight. Many voters reported responding to the Willie Horton advertisements by saying, "I know that it's an unfair ad, and that it's wrong to blame Dukakis for a program lots of states use; still, I'm voting for Bush on the strength of that ad." An analysis that does not turn on deception gives the audience more credit, without excusing the immorality of the appeal. Rhetorical manipu-lation is rarely deceptive, and even when it is, it seldom persuades *qua* de-ception. Agamemnon is persuaded while aware that he does not want to be, but he does realize that he is being persuaded. Understanding intention-ality forces us to direct attention and criticism elsewhere.

To call rhetorical persuasion ethical is not to praise it, but to identify the kind of criticism appropriate to it. On the basis of what I have argued so far I would call the *Rhetoric*, in contrast to a hermeneutics of suspicion, a hermeneutics of trust. But even a hermeneutics of trust is not a hermeneu-tics of gullibility. In the *Poetics*, Aristotle notes that people enjoy watching imitations of painful events (4.1448b10–13; cf. *Rhetoric* I.11.1371b4–11, but see *Politics* VIII.5.1340a25–28). Such pleasures are not passive pleasures that come from being deceived—if audiences were deceived they would not think they were watching imitations and would consequently be pained—

but from the delight in imitation that comes from the pleasures of learning and recognition. Deception and imitation are the wrong vocabulary for rhetorical criticism.[19]

Not only is there a false dilemma between reasons and irrational causes, and between the amoral and the fully ethical, there is a similar false dilemma between rhetoric as an appearance (and illusion) and as a manifestation of reality. Instead it exists in a space in which Aristotle denies an antecedent distinction between appearance and reality. As I argue in the next chapter, an apparent argument is an argument. A piece of deliberation presented in aid of persuasion is a piece of deliberation, even though the speaker might be presenting it with some further end in view. We detect the fallaciousness of apparent enthymemes not by finding hidden motives but by looking more closely at the argument *qua* argument. Recall, in this respect, his exclusion from the art of rhetoric of "preconceived ideas of the speaker's character" (I.2.1356a5–13, quoted above). That is how a hermeneutics of trust rather than of suspicion works.

How Enthymemes Persuade

If other professionals are not contemptible, neither are philosophers. And if generals are not contemptible because they are often put to death, neither are sophists.
—*Rhetoric* II.23.1397b25–27

The question, Why does reasoning persuade, has an overall answer: reasoning persuades because it is evidence of character and so gives grounds for trust. The question has more specific answers in the case of the first two sorts of reasoning, example and maxim. Both of these have species, and hence a formal structure that can ground a shared intention. I want now to see if we can give a similarity specific answer to why enthymemes persuade. Chapter 22 should be the payoff of my reading of *Rhetoric* II.18–26 as an exploration of why reasoning persuades. There are two kinds of enthymeme, demonstrative and refutative. Like the kinds of examples, these are differentiated by the source of their premises: "The demonstrative enthymeme draws a conclusion from what is agreed, the refutative draws conclusions that are not agreed to [by the opponent]" (II.22.1396b26–28). But after that, the classification scheme or list of argument forms gets very elaborate. There are twenty-eight kinds, or topics, of demonstrative enthymemes, and by my count, ten topics for apparent enthymemes. There are two kinds of refutation, first, countersyllogism, which uses the same topics as demonstrative enthymemes, and then, objections (*enstatis*), which are of four further kinds (cf. *Topics* I.1.100b23–101a4; *De Sophisticis Elenchis* 2.165b7–8).

The profusion of classification is an indication that enthymeme is, in some sense, more formal than example and maxim. The same topics and tactics seem to appear both in the list of real and of apparent enthymemes. What a topic is, and the difference between real and merely apparent enthymemes, will be harder than the parallel discussions of example and maxim. Instead of trying to give an account of all these textual peculiarities, I want to focus on the distinction between real and apparent enthymemes.

There is no logical criterion that separates enthymemes from apparent enthymemes. Apparent enthymemes are not enthymemes that do their job poorly; "apparent enthymemes . . . are not enthymemes since they are not really syllogisms [*ouk onton enthymematon, epeiper oude syllogismon*]" (II.22.1397a3–4). What then is the difference between real and apparent enthymemes? In earlier chapters I have pointed to a couple of arguments Aristotle calls paralogisms. At I.9.1367a32–34: "one must assume that qualities that are close to actual ones are much the same as regards both praise and blame." Such arguments from similarity are justified by the fact that "this will seem true to most people" (1367b3). He goes on explicitly to recommend the paralogism drawn from the motive (*paralogistikon ek tēn aitias*): "for if a person meets danger unnecessarily, he would be much more likely to do so where the danger is honorable" (b5–6). These arguments are part of the art of rhetoric; presumably therefore they are real, not merely apparent, enthymemes. These paralogisms, and their apparently manipulative nature, are matched in the *Politics*, where constitutional devices that are intended to make citizens satisfied are called *sophismata*. (See e.g., IV.13.1297a14–b1, V.7.1307b40–1308a2, VI.8.1322a21). A contemporary example that fits Aristotle's description is giving eighteen-year-olds the right to vote in order to rebut the claim that the government is sending people off to die who are not considered mature enough to vote. Harder to judge are these lines from Book III: "The proper *lexis* also makes the matter credible [*pithanoi to pragma*]: the mind [of the listener] draws a false inference [*paralogizetai*] of the truth of what the speaker says because they [in the audience] feel the same about such things, so they think the facts to be so, even if they are not as the speaker represents them" (III.7.1408a20–23) But when he says that "another [fallacy] is from a [nonnecessary] sign; for this, too, is nonsyllogistic [*asyllogiston*]" (II.24.1401b11) he seems to be condemning all of rhetoric. Considered purely logically, all rhetorical arguments are invalid; among invalid arguments it is hard to find a further distinction between real and apparent enthymemes.

I do not think this lack of a logical criterion of demarcation between real and apparent enthymemes is a flaw on Aristotle's part. It points to a similar difficulty on the ethical side. On the ethical side, there are no modes of reasoning that only the good man would use. The difference between real and apparent enthymemes is not parallel to the logical distinction between valid and invalid reasoning. The difference between real and apparent enthymemes is parallel to the distinction at the beginning of the *Rhetoric* between the rhetorician and the sophist, a distinction that will be the subject of chapter 7. Here it is sufficient just to note that Aristotle casts that distinction as one between people, not arts.

> It is a function of one and the same art to see the persuasive and [to see] the apparently persuasive, just as [it is] in dialectic [to recognize] a syllogism and [to recognize] an apparent syllogism; for sophistry is not a matter of ability [*dynamis*] but of deliberate choice [*prohairesis*] [of specious arguments]. In the case of rhetoric, however, there is the difference that one person will be [called] *rhētor* on the basis of his knowledge and another on the basis of his deliberative choice, while in dialectic *sophist* refers to deliberative choice [of specious arguments], *dialectician* not to deliberate choice, but to ability [at argument generally] (I.1.1355b15–21).

The difference between real and apparent enthymemes is not one of logical form, or, more broadly, of artistic power, but of purpose: not formal or efficient cause, but final cause. Logic is as incapable of distinguishing the rhetorician from the sophist as it is in telling apart *phronēsis* and cleverness. Only ethical criteria will work. The difference between real and apparent enthymemes is not a metaphysical distinction between appearance and reality, but a rhetorical and ethical distinction between art and external purpose. The sophist aims directly at winning the case, while the rhetorician aims at the internal end of finding in a given case the available means of persuasion.

When talking about the real enthymeme, Aristotle can warn that the topic of relative terms can lead to paralogism (1397a28–b6), and that the topic of considering whether there is a better course of action than the one chosen can be false (*pseudos*) (1400b1–3). There are no topics of real enthymemes that could not be abused. The apparent enthymemes are of use *only* for the external end, while real enthymemes can be used to achieve the internal end of rational persuasion.

The sophist using apparent enthymemes is guided by an ulterior motive (*prohairesis*), while the rhetorician persuading through real enthymemes is acting in accordance with his power (*dynamis*). Apparent enthymemes therefore try to short-circuit the process of achieving the given end of persuasion via the guiding end of artful or rational persuasion; therefore they short-circuit the artful process by which inference proceeds in practical reason by engaging the character of speaker and hearer.

There is no Archimedean point from which one can judge ethical and rhetorical matters in the way a logician can employ neutral standards in evaluating arguments. Rhetoric does not provide some powerful critical tool which I can use as a neutral referee to decide whether my advocate of English-only religious education is a hypocrite or not. That lack of Archimedean point is an overriding theme of the *Rhetoric,* in which such an external point of view is replaced by the statesman's point of view. The statesman has to understand rhetorical argument from the inside, while he can regulate the effects of rhetoric from without. Aristotle here has formulated the distinction between real and apparent enthymemes from the inside.[20]

Rhetorical argument shares with virtuous action the problem of identity and classification. What is from an external point of view the same action is understood and evaluated differently because the act's purpose is part of the definition of the act; what is from a logical point of view the same argument is understood and evaluated differently because form is tied to function. Recall· my earlier example about persuading someone to stop smoking. What is logically the same argument for stopping smoking is a different argument when offered by the smoker, the nonsmoker, the exsmoker, and the closet smoker.

In a similar way, what can be described as the same action—a president nominating a black man to the Supreme Court—is a different action according to the motives of the agent and the purposes of the act. Lyndon Johnson's act was seen as an act of political courage, while George Bush's was considered to be cowardly and cynical. And this example helps us to sort the point out further. I maintain that Johnson's act was courageous. It was also calculated; everything he did was. But it would be wrong to describe it as pure calculation and to ignore its purpose. In that sense it was done for its own sake, but it was virtuous while still aiming at external political success as well. Bush's nomination was seen as pure calculation of advantage, that is, as aiming at nothing but the external end. Undertaking an act for its own sake does not exclude having an external end in mind; arguing does not mean that one does not want to win.

And to return to my running example, I might support public aid for religious schools because I believe that strengthening religion will strengthen my country, or because I pay tuition in a parochial school and would like a tax break. I can believe a policy is right, and still hope that it will succeed because of personal interest. The fact that I may benefit does not mean that I do not sincerely advocate the policy. The fact that I may benefit also does not mean that the policy is wrong. These examples simply show that arguments can be evaluated as arguments and as means to a further purpose, and that sometimes what makes an argument *an* argument partly depends on it purposes.

From these examples I conclude that real and apparent enthymemes cannot be distinguished by purely formal criteria, the way good and bad logical arguments can. All rhetorical arguments aim at an external end, persuading the audience. Real and apparent enthymemes differ because real enthymemes offer themselves as arguments, and so submit themselves to logical evaluation as well as to judgment about whether or not they succeed.

The absence of a sure sign for distinguishing *phronēsis* from cleverness does not lead to an overall skepticism about the uses, and users, of reasoning. The most striking feature of the presentations of topics for both real and apparent enthymemes in II.23–24 is their heterogeneity. They range from the logical to the verbal and tactical; they range as broadly as the word *logos* does. All the topics of real enthymemes are forms of argument that a reasonable person could reasonably use. They are forms that can be intentional objects, shared by speaker and hearer, and so persuade *qua* reasoning.

Even the least logical-looking of the topics of real enthymemes fits this description. For example, the second topic is similar inflections, and, stated as a general logical rule, it looks like an invitation to absurd reasoning: "in like manner the derivatives must either be predicable of the subject or not." But when Aristotle gives an example—"for example, [to say] that the just is not entirely good; for then what is done justly would be a good, but as it is, to be put to death justly is not desirable" (1397a20–22)—one can imagine circumstances in which the good deliberator would appeal to it. (It doesn't take imagination in this instance; all it takes is reading the *Gorgias*.) Similarly, the twenty-third is, in modern terms, "where there's smoke there's fire." "Another, in reference to human beings or actions that have been prejudged or seem to have been, is to state the cause of a false impression; for there is some reason why it seems true" (1400a22–24). It would be hard to extract a logical rule, but it is easy to see how using such a topos would reveal purpose and character. Character is exhibited in whether one chooses to use such an argument in a given case. In that sense, in rhetoric as opposed to dialectic, one never argues merely for the sake of argument.

Even the last topic, which seems to have nothing logical about it at all is a kind of reasoning that a *phronimos* could use. The topic is deriving a conclusion about someone from the meaning of his name, as Socrates does of Polus in the *Gorgias*. Aristotle mitigates the absurdity of such reasoning by noting that the topic is commonly employed in praising the gods, where it has a certain sense and ethical value. Such a piece of reasoning might not have great probative value, and a speaker would forfeit trust by hanging too much on it, but when it persuades me, I am aware of what is going on. I am not persuaded through some vague acquiescence, as in the similar-looking but merely apparent enthymeme of II.24.1401a12–23. These are the forms which a shared intention can take.

I said earlier that it is hard to square Aristotle's initial claim that the sophists neglected rhetorical reasoning with the evident fact that they used these apparent enthymemes. He does nothing with that initial claim until II.24

when he finally returns to the sophists. Now we see an answer that is consistent with my claim that reasoning persuades as evidence of character. The sophists ignored reasoning *because* they ignored character; they ignored character by offering techniques for getting to a judgment that avoided ethical determination by aiming directly at the external end. The sophists proposed to cut out the ethical middleman. Consequently, there is no shared intention in their apparent enthymemes. Argument becomes a means to the external end, and is not constitutive of an internal end. In the sophists and in apparent enthymemes, there is no argument because there is no *ēthos*. Here is the converse. The sophists—whether successful at reaching the external end or not—fail to argue because their intelligence is not connected to *phronēsis* but to an external motive. Therefore there is no shared intention, and therefore no argument.

The simplest way of achieving persuasion directly, instead of through argument and *ēthos,* is to fool the audience into thinking that they have been presented with an argument and conclusion when there is none. So Aristotle begins the chapter on apparent enthymemes with just that, the "topic of diction," which occurs "when the final statement takes the form of a conclusion without constituting a [valid] syllogism ('since such and such [is true], necessarily also this and that follows'), and in the case of enthymemes [i.e., in rhetoric] a statement appears to be an enthymeme whenever it is spoken compactly and antithetically; for verbal style of this sort is the place where an enthymeme is at home" (II.24.1401a3–6). Several of the succeeding topics are similar in only appearing to be arguments: the second is homonymy, the fourth "is constructing or demolishing an argument by exaggeration. This occurs when one amplifies the action without showing that it was performed" (1401b3–4), avoiding the necessary intermediate step of proving that the events happened.

But there are more sophisticated ways of persuading through apparent enthymemes, topics that are harder to see through. Almost all rhetoric works through signs, so why should argument from signs count as one of the topoi for apparent enthymemes? Yet Aristotle says that it is "illogical" (*asyllogiston*). All the topics that follow the sign in Aristotle's presentation seem to hold a similar position: they are used by rhetoricians and so seem part of the art of rhetoric.

There is the topic of accident. Aristotle's example—"if someone were to say that to be invited to dinner is the greatest form of honor; for Achilles' wrath against the Achaeans at Tenedos resulted from not being invited" (1401b17–18)—does not sound different from many admissible arguments. Next come propositions that are not convertible: because the high-minded live by themselves, if Paris lives by himself, he is high-minded. That is followed by *post hoc, ergo propter hoc.*

What makes all these merely apparent enthymemes is the immediate jump to a conclusion. The last topic of apparent enthymeme gives it away: it is the "omission of consideration of when and how" (b34). Aristotle's example helps: The claim is that Paris had a right to carry off Helen because her father had given her the right to choose a husband. She had already exercised that choice once, Aristotle observes, and "the father's authority only lasts till then." And so, in what I think is a generalization that applies to all these apparent enthymemes that do not simply turn on diction, "just as in eristics an apparent syllogism occurs in confusing what is general and what is not general but some particular . . . so also in rhetoric there is an apparent enthymeme in regard to what is not generally probable but probable in a particular case" (1402a2–5), what later is called the fallacy of *secundum quid*.[21]

This, he says, is what it means to make the worse appear the better argument (II.24.1401a23–24). Formally, it is the fallacy of four terms, and what is missing is an argument which adjusts what is probable overall with what is probable in this case. For a contemporary example, consider the fallacy in the popular argument for equal treatment for "creation science." Partisans argue that since evolution falls short of some unstated standards of certainty, it follows that both evolutionary biology and "creation science" are each only probable, hence equally probable, and hence they deserve equal standing. That argument can stand as a paradigm of an argument that is empty because there is no means of weighing probabilities and signs, and so no way of coming to judgment. But for that adjustment to be missing is for the art of rhetoric to be missing.

Here is a clear case in which the lack of *ēthos* is immoral. *Ethos* is revealed in the mutual adjustment of general and particular in our choices. If rhetorical inferences are in general not necessary, then what distinguishes a fallacious immediate inference from a legitimate enthymeme cannot be a middle term that causes a predicate to inhere in a subject, but an ethical middle term that causes the conclusion to be asserted on the basis of the evidence, and so uses arguments *as* arguments. *Ethos* is necessary in order to see and assess probabilities and signs. Without such an ethical middle, the speaker cannot offer an intentional object, and cannot therefore aim at rational persuasion.

Without such an ethical middle, the speaker must be guided, like the sophist, by an external purpose, and not by the rhetorical art. When the speaker is guided by an external purpose, the hearer cannot be persuaded through a shared intentional object: the audience must be the passive object of his designs, and therefore *cannot* be aware of what the speaker is doing. In a real enthymeme, the hearer need not be aware of all that is going on, any more than an individual agent has to be fully conscious of all the premises and modes of inference he or she is employing. That is the same as saying that there are no enthymemes that only the good person would use. But ignorance of the tactical choices still has to coexist with shared intentions. There are enthymemes, namely the apparent enthymemes, that only a sophist could use, because using them is equivalent to being guided by an external purpose and not by art.

Rhetorical Persuasion and Practical Reason

Whether II.18–26 succeeds in opening up the possibility of abstracting practical reason from specific practical purposes and contexts is an important question for us today. We too want to know whether practical reason is just reason, employed on a different kind of materials, or whether there is anything distinctive about practical reason *qua* reason. Aristotle's answer to my question, Why does reasoning persuade, is an answer that applies only in rhetoric, and not to reasoning more broadly. Reasoning persuades because, first, it tracks desire in deliberation, and consequently in judicial and epideictic rhetoric. Form and function are tied in Book I. Reasoning persuades because, second, it tracks trust and is a sign of character in rhetoric in general. That is why Aristotle has to return to *logos* for a second time in II.20–26 after treating it in I.4–14. The enthymeme is not just a syllogism with a premise suppressed or missing, and it is not a syllogism about probabilities. The enthymeme as rhetorical syllogism is essentially rhetorical because it is essentially ethical.

But these explanations extend no further than rhetoric and praxis. Indeed, it is an achievement on Aristotle's part to make them extend as far as they do. Outside rhetoric, we should not even ask why reasoning persuades. Instead, we need to wonder why reasoning leads to truth, which—outside of rhetoric—is another matter altogether.

Within rhetoric itself, however, this result is a culmination of the initial set of overall problems of practical reason. Purely instrumental reason is easy to understand. It is harder to make out how rationality develops purposes and values of its own. It is harder still to see how *practical* rationality can have its own internal ends and standards. On the other hand, as many philosophers have pointed out, there is very good ground for thinking that reason, even practical reason, must not be confined to its instrumental roles alone. If the purpose of reason is to help us satisfy our desires, many have observed, it doesn't do its job very well. Beings without reason are probably more satisfied than rational beings.

I see Aristotle in the *Rhetoric* exploring a smaller and more urgent version of that same problem. Rhetoric, like any practice and art, generates its own ends out of given, external ends. Therefore, from being a means to such an external end, reason—in this case, rhetorical argument and the en-thymeme—becomes its own end. Therefore, there is a pair of problems in this chapter and the following one.

How does the pursuit of this internal end not interfere with the achieve-ment of the external end? Can I not, this is, be too rational, so successful in achieving the internal end that I cause suspicion and so fail to persuade? That is the subject of the next chapter. Here I have been raising the opposite question: How do rhetoric and practical reason, both always directed to an external end, really achieve these internal ends, and so exhibit the automony I have been attributing to them? The most artistic rhetoric still aims at con-vincing an audience—this is not rationality for its own sake in a way that discards the external end. It is still practical rationality. Once again I think Aristotle has made an important discovery and has not trumpeted it as loudly as he should. Reasoning persuades. Reasoning persuades *qua* reasoning. But even reasoning that seems to be persuading simply because it is logically cogent is in fact persuading because it is a sign of *ēthos*. In a flourishing polis, there are no persistent conflicts between reason persuading and reason being reasoning and answering to its own standards.

The problem, in the last chapters of *Rhetoric* II, of why reasoning per-suades is another instance of the *Rhetoric*'s exploring more slowly and in more detail something Aristotle argues more schematically in the *Ethics* and the *Politics*. In this case the question of why argument forms detached from purpose can have persuasive value is equivalent to the question, which Aris-totle seems to think easy, concerning the relation between *phronēsis* and the ability to give good advice (*synesis*) in *Ethics* VI.10. "Comprehension [*syne-sis*] is not the same as intelligence [*phronēsis*]. For *phronēsis* is prescriptive, since its end is what must be done or not done in action, whereas *synesis* only judges" (1143a7–10). The same people, he later says, possess both (VI.11.1143a27). But he has nothing further to say in the *Ethics* about how *synesis* and *phronēsis* are related. We have the same question in front of us now, but with more resources for confronting it.

Our question is, What is the connection between the purposive forms of practical reason explored in *Rhetoric* I and the enthymematic forms explored in II.20–26? *Synesis* and *phronēsis* are both concerned with practical particu-lars, but *phronēsis* is directed toward decisions and *synesis* is not. The formal enthymemes of II.20–26 share with the purposive enthymemes of I.4–15 the property of being concerned with those same practical particulars. *Syne-sis* and *phronēsis* differ in that *phronēsis* is directly practical and purposive, and the same is the case for enthymemes of I.4–15. If we can understand how reasoning persuades, we can better understand the relation between *synesis* and *phronēsis*.

The problem, in the last chapters of *Rhetoric* II, of why reasoning persuades is in this sense the opposite problem from that posed by *akrasia* in the *Ethics*. Because practical reason supplies its own motivation, those occasions in which practical reason does not lead to action are puzzling. One expects practical reason to lead to action, and Aristotle has to explain what happens when it does not. Here one cannot expect reasoning that is not directed to an end to be persuasive. Yet it is.

In a flourishing polis, and in artful rhetoric at its best, *logos* and *ēthos* are aligned. That alignment is reflected in the *Ethics*, the *Politics*, and the *Rhetoric*. In the *Ethics*, *phronēsis* is the *orthos logos* of the moral virtues, and has almost no life independent of the moral virtues. In the *Politics*, we become rulers by being ruled, and rulers differ from other citizens only by the possession of *phronēsis*. In the *Rhetoric*, *ēthos* is the most powerful proof, and the enthymeme is the essence of rhetoric.

In many other circumstances, *ēthos* and *logos* can fall apart. The traditional moral virtues can be inadequate to the ethical demands of reason if the world requires more intelligence, and more detachment, than custom and good habits will allow. Good practical reason then becomes something other than the fulfillment and good orientation of desire. In subsequent political contexts, the ruler needs a form of political intelligence that is not just the culmination of the moral virtues, and he must accept a different set of standards for political success, standards that have nothing to do with exercising the virtues of character. Such rulers do not become rulers by being ruled.

And in such moral and political contexts, it is unlikely that reason and character can be aligned in rhetoric either. Rhetoric then would have to be either the expression of a truly good character, as in the Roman *vir bonus peritus dicendi,* or rhetoric would be a purely manipulative form of rationality, with no ethical ties at all. Under such circumstances, the integration of reason and *ēthos* becomes wishful thinking.[22]

This chapter and the next show, however, that even in the best polis, the alignment of *ēthos* and *logos* in practical reason generally, and in rhetoric in particular, still has problems. It is hard to be virtuous, Aristotle reminds us in *Ethics* V.10. It is hard to keep one's reasoning in the service of *ēthos* and still have it be reasoning, with its own rational values, and not something purely instrumental. The rest of this book will expose and explore those permanent difficulties.

VI

MAKING DISCOURSE ETHICAL:
CAN I BE TOO RATIONAL?

Eloquence persuades because it is seeming prudence.

—Thomas Hobbes

When I hear a man discourse on aretē, *or on wisdom, one who is truly a man . . .
I am deeply delighted as I behold how both the speaker and his words become each
other* [preponta] *and are suited* [harmottonta] *to each other.*

—*Laches* 188c–d

At this point we have a pair of problems. One is textual. In the last three
chapters, I have explored in some detail Aristotle's examination of two of
the three sources of proof, *logos* and *pathos*. We have to see why there is no
parallel section of the *Rhetoric* that concentrates on *ēthos*.[1] Of course that
textual problem is only part of a bigger problem (one that still lies within
Aristotle's own text), the question of the interrelations of the three sources
of proof.

But there is a second problem generated by this argument, which extends
beyond analysis of Aristotle's text to the philosophical problems it generates.
I have argued that rhetorical argument is argument that is ethical throughout. In the last chapter I said that rhetorical argument had better be ethical,
because if it isn't, the rhetorical power will be quite dangerous—and the
more powerful Aristotle makes rhetoric the more dangerous. I have shown
how these resources for logical and pathetic proof allow rhetoric to prove
opposites in quite a thoroughgoing sense. We therefore have to see how
such a power for arguing does not degenerate into pure license and the
ability to argue for or against anything at all. Will the missing component of
rhetoric, *ēthos* in a specifically rhetorical sense, be enough to make rhetorical
argument ethical, or will we need moral control from outside?

I want to approach these problems about *ēthos* by looking at a series of
passages from the *Rhetoric* that seem to posit a range of incompatible-
looking relations between *logos* and *ēthos*. That is, I want to approach the

philosophical problems by way of the textual ones. These passages, plus the concerns we bring to them, generate a series of four problems that are worth keeping in mind as we go. First, we have to understand how *logos* and *ēthos* can sometimes be allies and sometimes opponents, how argument can be at the center of rhetoric, while some speakers can fail by using argument. It looks as though speakers can fail by being too logical and argumentative. Does that mean that they fail by being too artful? Second, we need to know why Aristotle, in the passages I cite, seems quite indifferent whether he is talking about making discourse ethical or making discourse *appear* ethical. Third, Aristotle will offer some instructions for directly "making discourse ethical"—that is his expression—and we will have to see why offering means for making discourse ethical is not an inherently immoral activity, an art of disguise and deception. Finally, when Aristotle is not talking about how directly to make discourse ethical, he seems forced to a no less problematic position, in which the most important thing of all, our discourses being ethical, will be an incidental by-product of something else.

The Problem and the Evidence

Our analytical performance becomes automatically suspect if it is openly pressed into the service of moral conviction; and conversely, moral conviction is not dependent on analytical argument and can actually be weakened by it, just as religious belief has on balance been undermined rather than bolstered by proofs of God and their intellectual prowess. The matter has been best expressed by the great German poet Hölderin in a wonderfully pithy, if rather plaintive, epigram . . .

> *If you have brains and a heart, show only one or the other,*
> *You will not get credit for either should you show both at once.*
> —Albert O. Hirschman, *Essays*, 296–97

The difficulty of Aristotle's project is symbolized his affirming two central but apparently contradictory theses. On the one hand, he says that the enthymeme is the strongest (*malista*) of rhetorical proofs (I.1.1355a5) and the body of proof (1354a15). On the other, he tells us, a page later, that character (*ēthos*) is the most persuasive (*kuriotaten*) kind of proof (*pistis*) (I.2.1356a13; cf. I.9.1366a28). I want to bring the issue to a head by looking at his use of the expression, "making discourse [*logos*] ethical." He uses it in ways that are not easy to put together, either with each other or with my thesis. Taken together, however, these passages will do justice to the complexity of the relation between *logos* and *ēthos*. The more rational rhetoric looks, and the more I have been able to exhibit the resources Aristotle's text makes available, the less plausible that harmony between *logos* and *ēthos* appears.

Our arguments are ethical when listeners infer from the speech to the character of the speaker:

> Character is what makes us ascribe moral qualities to the agents (*Poetics* 6.1450a5).

> The narration ought to be indicative of character [*ēthikēn*]. This will be so if we know what makes character [*ēthos*]. One way, certainly, is to make deliberative choice [*prohairesis*] clear: what the character is on the basis of what sort of deliberative choice [has been made]. And choice is what it is because of the end aimed at (*Rhetoric* III.16.1417a15–18).

Not only are people ethical, but *logoi* are too. Part of the problem I want to explore in this chapter is how equivocal it is to apply the same adjective, "ethical," to people and arguments.[2] There are three uses of the phrase "making discourse ethical," and each seems to make a different point. First, he says:

> Since characters [*ēthē*] as found under [different] constitutions have been discussed earlier—as a result, the definition of how and through what means one ought to make speeches ethical [*ex hōn ēthikous tous logous endechetai poiein*] should be complete (II.18.1391b26–27).

The same expression is also used just before the beginning of this passage at II.18.1391b23 (cf. I.8.1365b23–1366a12; *Politics* IV.4.1292a18, VI.1.1317a39). These lines echo the opening lines of I.9:

> After this, let us speak of virtue and vice and honorable and shameful; for these are the points of reference for one praising or blaming. Moreover, as we speak of these, we shall incidentally also make clear those things from which we [as speakers] shall be regarded [*phanein*] as persons of a certain quality in character, which was the second form of *pistis;* for from the same sources we shall be able to make both ourselves and any other person worthy of credence [*axiopiston*] in regard to virtue (1366a23–28).

Knowing the forms of government in II.18 and the noble in I.9 is knowing the ends at which people aim. Such knowledge, is, "incidentally," knowing how to make discourse appear ethical, according to those passages. That the same methods produce both *logos* and *ēthos* is also indicated in the transition

passage at the beginning of Book II: "The means by which one might appear prudent and good are to be grasped from analysis of the virtues; for a
person would present himself (*phanein*) as being of a certain sort from the
same sources that he would to present another person" (II.1.1378a16–19).
On this understanding of the relation of *logos* and *ēthos*, the speaker makes
discourse ethical by making it practical, that is, by reasoning toward ends.
Making discourse ethical is a *by-product* of making it rhetorical. The point
of the *Rhetoric* is precisely to establish such an intimate relation between
them. If the enthymeme is the body of proof, *ēthos* is its soul.[3] To bring one
into existence is to create the other.

In Book III, however, making discourse ethical and making it logical
seem to be in opposition:

> Nor should you seek an enthymeme when the speech [*logos*] is
> being "ethical" [*ēthikos*]; for logical demonstration has neither *ēthos*
> nor moral purpose [*prohairesis*]. Maxims should be used both in a
> narration and in a proof; for they are "ethical" [*ēthikon*]; "I should
> have given [the money], though knowing one should not trust"
> (III.17.1418a15–19; cf. I.15.1376a13–16).

Here argument and the expression of character are at odds. Argument is
unethical. The more the art of rhetoric succeeds at restricting persuasion to
argument, the less persuasive it becomes.

The remaining relation between *logos* and *ēthos* that Aristotle asserts seems
to make a more complicated point still. In my last quotation he recommended the use of maxims. In II.21, maxims are a device for making discourse ethical, and so of *overcoming* the opposition of *logos* and *ēthos*. Use of
the maxim (*gnōmē*) is recommended because it

> makes the speech "ethical" [*ēthikous gar poiei tous logous*]. Speeches
> have character insofar as deliberative choice [*prohairesis*] is clear, and
> all maxims accomplish this because one speaking a maxim makes a
> general statement about preferences, so that if the maxims are mor-
> ally good, they make the speaker seem to have a good character
> (II.21.1395b13–17).

In the passage from II.18, referring back to Book I, making rhetoric argumentative is sufficient to make discourse ethical. In the passage from III.17,
making rhetoric argumentative is opposed to making it ethical. In II.21, the
maxim is singled out from example and enthymeme because it is the
method *par excellence* for making discourse ethical.

Putting all those passages together will be difficult.[4] But however the
details turn out, the very idea of making discourse ethical might seem disturbing. This might not be a victory we want. Everyone wants practical

reasoning to *be* ethical, but there is something troubling about directly and artfully *making* reasoning ethical. It might even be that aiming directly at making argument ethical is self-defeating, and aiming at it makes *logoi* unethical, since any *ēthos* that can be the product of art can't be real *ēthos*. Not only does learned rhetoric appear to produce the same results as virtue and *phronēsis,* it leads to the same results produced by the same means. My citations seem to speak indifferently about making arguments ethical and making them *appear* ethical. Aristotle seems to be, against his wishes, proving Plato's case that rhetoric is an art of appearance.

Making *logoi* ethical is a specifically practical and rhetorical problem, not faced by the other arts. All the arts, as rational *dynameis,* can cause opposites. Only rhetoric *proves* opposites. It is the very perfection of the art of rhetoric, its argumentative capacity, that makes it fail to achieve its given end, persuasion. An art which proves opposites creates mistrust.

Whether or not the term *ēthos* can be applied both to arguments and to people, the term *pistis* certainly can. Applied to arguments, it can mean proof or appeal; applied to the effects of argument, it can mean belief, conviction, or commitment; applied to arguers, it can mean credibility. And applied to both speakers and the effects of speech, it can mean trust. *Rhetorical* argument, and not argument in general, needs *ēthos* because it depends on trust. To quote again the crucial passage I used in the last chapter:

> [There is persuasion] through character [*ēthos*] whenever the speech is spoken in such a way as to make the speaker worthy of credence [*axiopiston*]; for we believe [*pisteuomen*] fair-minded people to a greater extend and more quickly [than we do others] on all subjects in general and completely so in cases where there is not exact knowledge [*akribes*] but room for doubt. . . . character is almost, so to speak, the controlling factor in persuasion (I.2.1356a5–13).

The more indeterminate the situation, and the more necessary rhetoric is, the more fundamental the need for *ēthos* and trust. Because the audience has to trust the speaker, the speaker has to display *ēthos.* Put that way, it is not obvious that the *ēthos* the speaker has to display to win the audience's trust is the same *ēthos* he needs to ground his discursive ability in practical experience. Rhetorical *ēthos* and practical *ēthos* might have nothing in common. In the passage I just quoted, Aristotle stresses that the *ēthos* he is talking about is the artful *ēthos* found in the speech itself. It does not appear that that has to be the same *ēthos* the deliberator needs for finding out what to do. Unless they are the same, however, that discursive facility would be indistinguishable from mere cleverness, and appearing good and wise a mere cloak. *Ethos* is applied to people and to *logoi.* It is applied to people *qua* speakers and people *qua* doers. How much of this is equivocation?

What is the connection between formulating wise advice and winning an audience's trust? Both good deliberation and winning an audience's trust requires something that could be called *ēthos,* but is it the same *ēthos* in the two cases? Does the audience think it is trusting an *ēthos* which is an incidental by-product of artful argument? Whether the *ēthos* the *phronimos* needs and the *ēthos* the audience relies on are the same or not is the crucial question.

Aristotle moves in a different direction from what one might expect. One could respond to indeterminate practical situations otherwise than by saying that they call for trust. One could say, on the contrary, that since practical judgment depends on nontransferable experience, audiences should rely on hard evidence as an alternative because trust means depending on experience that is not their own, and that is an impractical and amoral thing to do. The more indeterminate the situation, the more it calls for suspicion, not trust. Or, one could say that since apparent character is all we get in rhetoric, we should simply discount appeals to character altogether. Trust and authority, that is, are more appropriate in science than in morals.[5]

But that is not Aristotle's response at all. It is by seeing an essential place for trust that Aristotle can simultaneously affirm both his theses, that the enthymeme is the body of proof and that character is the most persuasive of appeals.

Character and Rhetorical Invention

We may call it then the normal state of Inference to apprehend propositions as notions; and we may call it the normal state of Assent to apprehend propositions as things. If notional apprehension is most congenial to Inference, real apprehension will be the most natural concomitant of Assent
—John Henry Newman, *Grammar of Assent,* 51–52

The purpose of inference is to lead to assent, yet inference can also weaken assent. That problem is at the center of the *Grammar of Assent.* Aristotle faces a similar problem. Speakers might fail by being insufficiently logical and overly ethical, but that is not a likely result of the art of rhetoric. Being insufficiently logical and over ethical comes from not being artful enough. But being too logical and therefore not ethical is a danger specific to the art of rhetoric. Reaching the guiding end of the art of rhetoric might mean failing to achieve the given end; argument makes the speaker less persuasive. If reaching the guiding end makes us fail to achieve the given end, it cannot be a guiding end, and the enthymeme could not be the center of the art of rhetoric.

Being unpersuasive through being too logical and argumentative is an example of Veblen's "trained incapacity."[6] It is not just that developing one kind of talent makes a person worse at doing something else, the way skill at advocacy might make a lawyer unfit to be a judge, or the talents that make for an inspiring revolutionary work badly when the revolution has succeeded and consensus building is what is called for.[7] Here it is a skill which practiced to perfection seems to backfire, to cause failure of the very purposes for which it was designed. Persuasion is artful when it is argumentative, but persuasion can also *fail* through being argumentative. My quotation from III.17 at the beginning made *ēthos* and *logos* into contraries, and at that point in the *Rhetoric* such an artful failure is Aristotle's concern:

> And do not speak from calculation [*dianoias*], as they do nowadays, but from moral principle [*prohaireseos*]: [not] "I desired it" and "For I chose this" [but] "Even if I gain nothing, it is better so." The first [two examples] are the words of a prudent man [*phronimou*], the last of a good one [*agathou*]; for the quality of a prudent man consists in pursuing his own advantage, that of a good man in pursuing the honorable (III.16.1417a24–28).

> If one has logical arguments, one should speak both "ethically" and "logically"; if you do not have enthymemes, speak "ethically." And to seem virtuous suits a good person more than an exact argument does (III.17.1418a37–b1).

How can Aristotle reconcile the thesis that *ēthos* and enthymeme live harmoniously together with the evident fact that sometimes persuasion fails by being "too rational"? Excessive rationality is unpersuasive because it makes us suspicious rather than trustful of the speaker. Reason can drive out *ēthos*. If reason is something whose excess, as well as whose deficiency, makes persuasion unsuccessful, then there must be something wrong with Aristotle's identifying artful persuasion with argument. When argument fails by being too logical, it fails by being *too strong*. Such an idea is impossible in logic—validity is the top of the scale, not a mean. Rhetorical arguments can be so strong, though, that they stop being persuasive. They are so strong that they eliminate the speaker and hearer from the decision process. Demonstrations, he says (II.1.1377b16) are insufficient for rhetoric, because the object of rhetoric is judgment, and therefore *ēthos* and *pathos* have to be involved. The remedy is not making the arguments weaker, or disguising one's art in order to look natural and sincere, but making them ethical.[8] Persuasiveness does not consist of a moderate amount of rationality. One avoids the "trained incapacity" not by being less logical but more ethical.

Rhetoric has two parents to whom it owes continued fidelity and re-spect, logic and politics. Excessive devotion to logic can rupture its relations to politics. Even worse for Aristotle's project, excessive devotion to argu-ment is a concentration on the internal end of rhetoric to the exclusion of the external, given, end. Attention to argument is supposed to make us better at persuading audiences, or at least not significantly worse. Under-standing the right relation between *logos* and *ēthos* means constructing the right relation between internal and external end.

There is something parallel in the *Ethics* to this conflict between internal and external ends, between argument and persuasion. Justice too seems a victim of its own success. The law is reason without desire. The separation of reason from desire is an achievement, a purification of the rational from irrational biases and distractions. Nevertheless, Aristotle wants to think of justice as an ethical virtue, that is, as a habit of choosing, and not as a *technē* or an *epistēmē*. Rationality, then, must be an ethical state, a quality of one's desires and not just of their absence. The paradox of justice is that justice is a state of character, and yet the law is reason without desire.

Similarly for the paradox of a trained incapacity for rhetorical reasoning. Making persuasion into a matter of argument is an achievement. Aristotle could fairly call it his principal achievement in the *Rhetoric*. And yet making persuasion into argument threatens to reduce rhetoric to logic. And so Aris-totle insists at the beginning of Book II that rhetorical argument issues in judgment, and therefore requires *ēthos* and *pathos* as well as *logos*. Bringing in these other methods of proof is not a concession to weak audiences, but a recognition of the difference between the faculties of rhetoric and logic. In *Ethics* V, the problem is to understand rationality as an ethical state, a quality of desires and not just of their absence. So here: although reasoning can fail by being too logical, the remedy is not to make it less logical, but more ethical. Therefore the question: Is the rationality which is a quality of desires, i.e., practical rationality, the same rationality which logic governs?

We can answer the question about whether there is one *logos* or two by looking at the ambiguities of *ēthos*. Character is the most effective and sover-eign of the kinds of proof. When we trust a speaker, the real object of trust is the speaker's character. So Aristotle says that character is the greatest cause of *pistis*. What do the speaker's *arguments* have to do with that? How can he, again, also affirm that the enthymeme is the center of his art? More precisely, what is the connection between finding in each case the available means of persuasion—achieving the guiding end of rhetoric—and having one's *logoi* be ethical and convincing?

The practical and civic rhetorician needs *ēthos* to find in a given case the available means of persuasion because finding the relevant *rhetorical* resources is part of what it means to deliberate well. One cannot be fully virtuous or practically wise without deliberating well. But Aristotle needs the converse here, which is much more powerful: to deliberate well and so argue well takes *phronēsis* and *ēthos.* Deliberating well takes character. Arguing persuasively means showing that one is deliberating well and therefore showing character. Justice which is disembodied and unconnected to the desires of the good man is *rationally* inadequate. Argument alone is *argumentatively* inadequate, not just unpersuasive, but unpersuasive for good reason. An argument that is not ethical not only fails to achieve the given end—it does not persuade the audience; it also fails to achieve the guiding end—it does not find the available means of persuasion. Its failure to attain the internal end is the problem of the "trained incapacity" for rhetoric.

From the beginning I have been stressing the way the nobler and more civic and practical an art, the more the internal end becomes dominant. An art of rhetoric never stops being a capacity for arguing both sides of a question. As a *technē* it never stops being indifferent to the external ends for which it is deployed. But the dominance of those internal ends is necessary for rhetorical invention. Because internal ends guide our perception, we need *ēthos* for good deliberation and intelligent argument. As I noted before, it is impossible to point to objects of perception which exist for the good and wise man but which the rest of us do not see. The internal ends of rhetoric, the objects of rhetorical invention, are not entities that are normally invisible but which suddenly become visible through the illumination of art. The good man sees differently because he sees what to do. "Intelligence, this eye of the soul, cannot reach its fully developed state without virtue . . . For inferences about actions have an origin . . . And this [best good] is apparent only to the good person" (*Ethics* VI.12.1144a29–34). What Amélie Rorty says about the virtues is equally true for the practical art of rhetoric:

> When a virtue is central to a person's character—when its exercise is organizationally dominant—the thoughts and categorical preoccupations that are central to that virtue form interpretations of situations: they focus attention and define what is salient. It is not enough that the virtuous person acts and reacts in specific ways when the occasion arises. She must also have a certain cast of mind. This is not primarily a matter of purity of heart or intention, not a matter of nobility or disinterest: it is the very practical matter of seeing situations in such a way as to elicit actions and reactions. A virtue of action is worthless without sensitivity to the conditions that require it.[9]

In Chapter 1 I argued that persuading (*pistis*) in the speaker was identical to belief (*pistis*) in the audience, because each is identical to the enthymematic argument. Argument is a middle term which is the cause of the connection between persuading and being persuaded. The speaker's act of persuading and the audience's being persuaded are as identical as the builder building is to the building being built. Here I have to argue something even stronger, that *ēthos* in the speaker is identical to the *trust* engendered in the audience. *Ethos* does not cause trust, nor is it the effect of trust. They are identical. To summarize: artful rhetoric is argument. To invent practical arguments the speaker needs *ēthos*. When an audience is persuaded, it imputes *ēthos* to the speaker, because it realizes that *ēthos* is necessary for practical argument. But is that *ēthos* the *ēthos* the speaker has? Can what is essential to the speaker be a by-product to the audience?

The rhetorical problem of making discourse ethical has the same puzzling structure as the questions raised in the *Ethics* about the relation between moral virtue and *phronēsis*. The paradox of justice is only its most obvious manifestation. In fact, the problem pervades the *Ethics*. (In the last chapter, I suggested that it pervades the *Metaphysics* as well.) Somehow, Aristotle has to be able to say that *phronēsis* is not simply the incidental by-product of moral virtue, while at the same time he cannot give it any very independent status. *Phronēsis* is nothing but the *orthos logos* of the moral virtues, and yet there is a little more to be known about it—its distinction from *technê*, its connection to *eubolia, gnōmē,* and *synesis,* and its relation to cleverness and natural virtue give the idea of *phronēsis* some more content than what is supplied just by its connection to the moral virtues. Similarly, *ēthos* in the *Rhetoric* is not just the incidental by-product of intelligent deliberation, but exists independently as well. In the last chapter, I looked at the dangers that arise when *logos* seems to separate itself from practical purposes and take on its own life and independent power; this chapter concerns what happens when *ēthos* similarly seems to burst free of its ties to *logos*.

At least, audiences think there is more to character than its existence as a by-product would imply. Aristotle validates that judgment of audiences. The audience attributes character to a speaker as a by-product of their perception of intelligent deliberation. Audiences confidently make this imputation because they think that the speaker needs *ēthos* in order to effect good deliberation, and therefore it cannot just be a by-product.

The rhetorical experience that generates this chapter's problem offers a strong proof that *logos* and *ēthos* must be connected. Speakers failing by being too argumentative shows something stronger than the obvious fact that *logos* and *ēthos* can be distinct. *Logos* could not destroy *ēthos* unless *ēthos* meant something more than possessing the right given ends. That something more must be essential to the argumentative work of deliberation.

Why Rhetoric Needs Ethos

The great merit of Aristotle was in developing this link between the rhetorical concept of persuasion and the logical concept of the probable, and in constructing the whole edifice of a philosophy of rhetoric on this relationship.
— Paul Ricoeur, *The Rule of Metaphor,* 12

We have some resources from the last chapter for understanding how *logos* and *ēthos* can fall apart. Rhetorical argument, unlike logical argument, is argument *to* someone. For that reason, Aristotle says, it needs *ēthos* and *pathos* in addition to *logos*. Logical argument has forms that are distinct from their purposes; its argument forms can therefore be used for a variety of purposes. When it comes to the *Rhetoric,* however, it appears that Aristotle's success in discovering this independence of form from function in logic produces the possibility of failure: the speaker fails to persuade by being too logical and so not ethical. Loss of trust is an argumentative failure.

In the last chapter I noted that rhetorical arguments, unlike logical ones, but like virtuous actions, are partly constituted by their circumstances. I argued there that our criteria for individuating and classifying arguments must not be purely logical, but ethical as well, because circumstances and purpose are part of what they are. The "same" argument is different when advanced by smokers and by nonsmokers, just as the "same" act done by the virtuous and nonvirtuous man are in fact different actions.

Rhetorical argument is addressed by someone to someone for some end, and those circumstances—speaker, hearer, situation, purpose—are part of what it means to be *this* argument. The practicing rhetorician cannot simply adopt argumentative values and methods from dialectic. That is why I said that this is a trained incapacity, that when *logos* drives out *ēthos,* the speaker not only fails to succeed at the given end, persuasion, but fails also to achieve the guiding end, finding the available means of persuasion.[10] And it is a *trained* incapacity, and not a natural one, since Aristotle indicates, in lines I quoted earlier, that the use of *logos* without *ēthos* is a recent aberration: "Do not speak from calculation (*dianoias*), as they do nowadays, but from moral principle (*prohaireseos*)" (III.16.1417a24–25).

That is the root of the tension between the techniques of formal logic and actual practical argument, between rhetoric as the counterpart of dialectic and rhetoric as an offshoot of politics. If rhetoric is the child of politics and logic, it is hard to see how that marriage can have a viable issue. Logic and scientific reasoning cannot be too rational, but that is the possibility Aristotle has discovered for rhetoric. That is why practical reason sometimes looks as thought it has its own logic, or that is aspires to "real logic" but falls short of that ideal. It is the task of a civic art of rhetoric to make judgments determinate by making them particular and circumstantial. In the last chapter, I argued that rhetoric will not be reducible to logic because rhetorical arguments are essentially intentional, and so ethical. Rhetorical argument is not reducible to logical argument, but it does not for that reason fall short of a logical ideal.

But we also have to face the corresponding problem on the other side. The artful *ēthos* of the speaker is not reducible to a real *ēthos* that would be the subject of ethics and politics. Yet the circumstantial nature of rhetorical argument does not make it less "ethical" in any sense of the term that has some relation to its use outside rhetoric. Just as rhetorical reasoning does not fall short of logic because it is not reducible to it, so artful *ēthos* does not necessarily fall short of a real *ēthos* because Aristotle denies that reduction too. Making the best case in particular circumstances cannot, to the disappointment of those who hope for one sort of use of reason to govern practical affairs, be accomplished by filling in further premises to produce a watertight argument, and so removing the need for *ēthos*.[11] As I mentioned in the last chapter, the fallacy of *secundum quid* is the last "apparent [as opposed to real] enthymeme" discussed in *Rhetoric* II.24, and the only one for which Aristotle points out that it is used in sophistical disputations. He thinks that this fallacy is at the center of the "art" of the sophists (cf. *Phaedrus* 273b–c). It is a character flaw, not just a logical mistake, to make things appear inevitable when they are not, to make judgment and character seem unnecessary by making the facts seem fully determinative. That is how *logos* drives out *ēthos*.

My parallel to the analysis of justice in *Ethics* V is apposite again. To rule on the basis of the law alone is a character flaw. Aristotle condemns the man who stands on his rights in demanding an ethically excessive sort of precision concerning justice in the distribution of goods (V.10.1137b34–1138a3). Similarly here. To argue on the basis of reason alone is a character flaw, a failure of *ēthos*, and therefore a failure to persuade. Excessive precision is in both cases unethical because it takes something which should be within the range of praxis and judgment and makes it into a subject for more precise, scientific determination.

An argument that audiences may trust is a piece of reasoning permeated by *ēthos*, not necessarily one intended simply to serve a good end. Aristotle is rejecting instrumental experts just as Plato did, rejecting people who offer their services in helping others attain ends selected independent of and prior to deliberation on how to acquire them.[12] But it remains unclear why such an instrumental role is impossible in rhetoric. Why cannot the end of an argument be given by the client, or by antecedent reasoning distinct from the reasons presented in the speech?

For Aristotle to save a civic function for rhetoric, a side of practical reason that cannot be made into a commodity or delegated to experts, he must show that such instrumental reasoning is somehow inadequate. Its insufficiency will lie in an inability to make reasoning determinate and particular without engaging the character. Probabilities and signs, the materials of rhetoric, are, as data, ethically weighted. Without character the speaker will not be able to *see* different weightings, and so he will be consigned to practicing the sophistic art in which all the things that can be otherwise, the things that form the subject of practical reason, are equally probable.[13] That is why the fallacy of *secundum quid* is not just a particular logical fallacy, but an ethical failing. Without character, there is no ethical knowledge. Without ethical knowledge, one is left with empty technique. Even artful rhetoric can still be in the service of further ends—it is still an art, not a virtue. Having an internal end does not prevent the speaker from having an external one also. The artful speaker still wants to win. The trouble with the sophists is not that they have external ends but that those are the *only* kinds of end they can have. But rhetoric has to embody character, and therefore ends, so that the speaker can apprehend particulars. Without *ēthos,* argument will be pure calculation, and an art of argument nothing but technique. In both the *Ethics* and the *Rhetoric,* Aristotle has to show exactly how *logos* and *ēthos* need each other, how it takes character to reason well and intelligence to pursue good ends.

When, at the beginning of the *Rhetoric,* he attacks the sophists for being devoted solely to irrelevant passions, that criticism is of a piece with the neglect of both argument and character. I claim that the overriding achievement of the *Rhetoric* is to align art, argument, and *ēthos* so that we primarily make discourse ethical by making argument artful. Aristotle certainly affirms that the absences of *ēthos* and of *logos* go together. The sophists were not artful because they failed to pay attention to argument and therefore did not deal with *ēthos.* Only on an understanding of argument tied to art, praxis, and *ēthos* could they be accused of neglecting argument. If enthymeme means those formal aspects of argument—"formal" in the theoretical sense—then that claim is hard to swallow. But if enthymeme is the organizing and actualizing form of signs and probabilities, its neglect is caused by the absence of character.

To say that the sophists neglected *ēthos* is as improbable as saying that cleverness does not involve choice. But the difference between cleverness and *phronēsis* is just that: "though they are closely related in definition, they differ in [so far as *phronēsis* requires the right] decision [*diapherein de kata tēn prohairesin*]" (VII.10.1152a13–14). Similarly, choice is absent in sophistic and professional rhetoric, and since choice is absent, so too is *ēthos,* and hence *logos.*[14]

Aristotle accuses the sophists of neglecting both enthyeme and character, and we now see why those two absences go together. Discourse is ethical if it is civic; discourse is merely logical if it is professional. Logical form is indifferent to matter. Of course the sophists did not neglect the logical in that sense. They paid a great deal of attention to it. They *therefore* neglected the enthymeme. They neglected character. Their arguments did not take up into form the crucial property of praxis. They did not make discourse ethical. That was *their* trained incapacity.

In Chapter 3 I asked whether rhetoric, the offspring of logic and politics, had any emergent properties, properties that were not simply derivative from its parents. The inquiry into making discourse ethical has shown that the answer must be yes. Rhetorical argument has logical properties and ethical properties, but the logical and ethical cannot be separated. *Logos* and *ēthos* will be specifically rhetorical *logos* and *ēthos*. If they could be separated, rhetorical argument would either be simply derivative from logic, or rhetoric—and practical reason—would have its own logic distinct from the logic studied by "logic," and we might wonder whether it was really logical or rational after all.

The prospects on the side of *ēthos* are, if anything, even worse. Rhetorical *ēthos* would either simply depend on the actual *ēthos* of the speaker *qua* moral agent, instead of *qua* speaker, or it would have such autonomy that we would have to wonder why it was called *ēthos* at all. Aristotle therefore seems to be forced into an uncomfortable dilemma, to which he responds, in part, by that seeming indifference to whether he is talking about *ēthos* or only apparent *ēthos,* which I noted as my second puzzle, and the similar dilemma—my third and fourth questions—that rhetorical argument is ethical either through direct intervention or as a by-product with trouble either way. (Therefore in the next chapter we will have to ask whether a specifically rhetorical and artful *ēthos* is really enough to address the ethical problems we bring to rhetoric.)

Rhetorical argument, consequently, cannot be achieved by combining two independent existents, the ethical and the logical. The young, according to Aristotle, are argumentative and they have noble ends, but that combination does not make them prudent. They have the right given ends, but no guiding ends. In the *Ethics* Aristotle shows that ethical virtue is the guiding end at which we should aim and through which we do our best to achieve the given end of happiness. Happiness, the second actuality, is not within our power nor within the scope of deliberation. Virtue, the first *energeia,* is at least indirectly within our power (*Ethics* III.5) and is the object of deliberation.[15]

The young cannot understand the relation between virtue and happiness, because such understanding comes only through the experience of deliberating about how to do what I can to achieve my ends. This guiding end too has to be grasped through the experience of deliberation. The young cannot be prudent because they lack knowledge of particulars acquired through deliberation. They therefore lack knowledge of the guiding ends, and cannot do good for its own sake. In the first chapter I used Aristotle's analogy to the doctor, and it is useful again here. The doctor and patient share a given end, a loose conception of health, but only the doctor possesses the guiding end at which he or she aims, since such an end is unintelligible, and sometimes invisible, apart from the experience of deliberation. Guiding ends represent the integration of knowledge and character. Knowledge and character can easily coexist in disputatious youths who have their hearts in the right place. Integration, therefore, cannot be taken for granted. The integration of thought and character means more than their coexistence.

The distinction between given and guiding end solves the problem in the *Ethics* of why *phronēsis* is about the means, moral virtue the end, and yet *phronēsis* is necessary for leading the good life. It is through calculating how to obtain a given end that we come to formulate a guiding end. The guiding end therefore comes about only through the cooperation of desire and thought. The guiding end shows what is good about the given end. It shows how much of the given end is good, and which parts of the given end are otherwise unobserved. When Dewey says that ends are means, he is saying that our ends in view, the guiding ends we can do something about, are the means to securing the things we ultimately desire, but that our energies and attention are directed not to the objects of ultimate desire but the guiding ends.[16]

Similarly, the instrumental rhetorician can have a good end—whether his or her own or that of the client—and have logical skill. But possessing those two is not the same as having an art of rhetoric, where the art is defined as a faculty for finding in a given case the available means of persuasion. *Phronēsis* is not moral virtue *plus* cleverness. The order of exposition in *Ethics* VI is significant: after defining *phronēsis,* he discusses cleverness and natural virtue as fallings away from *phronēsis,* but he does not present *phronēsis* as a combination of a natural affection for good ends and an ability to calculate means to given ends. The very fact that *logos* can drive out *ēthos* shows that there can be no such clean separation of means and ends, calculative ability and right desires. Rhetoric must be subordinate to politics, but that subordination is different for practical arts, like rhetoric, than it is for the purely poetic arts that Aristotle takes as his model for *technē,* that is, arts where there is a product that can be judged, and used, apart from who makes it or for what purpose. Rhetoric is not subordinate to politics, or to its users, the way the saddle maker is subordinate to the captain of the cavalry, but rather as the *politēs* is to the lawmaker, the *nomothete,* in *Ethics* VI.8: "Of *phronēsis* as regards the state, one kind, as supreme and directive, is called legislative science (*nomothetikē*), the other, as dealing with particular occurrences (*kath' hekasta*) has the name, political science (*politikē*), that really belongs to both kinds. The latter is concerned with action and deliberation" (1141b25–27). Politics may be subordinate to lawmaking, but it cannot simply operate as a technician following the lawmakers' orders with no judgment, or *phronēsis,* of its own. The same holds for rhetoric: it cannot just borrow ends from another and execute them.

We therefore have some answer to the first on that list of four questions at the beginning of this chapter. We needed to understand how *logos* and *ēthos* could sometimes be allied and sometimes at odds, so that speakers could fail by using argument, although argument was the center of the art. We now see that if argument did not sometimes destroy *ēthos* and trust, *logos* and *ēthos* would be completely independent. *Ethos* could not then be argumentative or, therefore, artful. The trained incapacity, in which argumentative facility drives *pistis* out, is proof of the ethical efficacy of argument.

An art that makes alternatives equally probable—the sophistic art which according to Aristotle centers on the *secundum quid* fallacy—would not need knowledge of particulars. The foreigner and the parvenu could do as well as the citizen in such a debate, because there is nothing ethical about the arguments. The sophistic art has the sort of appeal seen today, and in all times, in arguments that deny the integrity and autonomy of arguments from probability and signs, the basic material of rhetoric. Such arguments claim that once one leaves the certainty of science and eternal truths, what one person says is as good as another, making everything a matter of free and arbitrary decision: probability, as failed necessity, becomes reduced to chance. Recall the example of "creation science" from my last chapter.

The enthymeme is made up of probabilities and signs; it is formal, as any pattern of reasoning must be, because it organizes those materials by bringing them to bear on a given case. It actualizes data into a reasoned practical judgment. But the enthymeme is the form of those materials, and not a form that exists, *qua* reasoning, independent of them, just as *phronēsis* in the *Ethics* is the form, the *orthos logos,* of the virtues of character. Aristotle's advice on how to make discourse ethical is not a guide for manipulation, because the task of making discourse ethical is necessary for the construction of credible arguments, not just for making some given arguments credible.

The art of rhetoric will have to be a faculty capable of adopting ends outside itself. It is a rational *dynamis* and proves opposites. But the operations of this art of rhetoric must incorporate an end. The philosophical importance of rhetoric is that it is an art that is noble and yet serves ends outside itself by proving opposites. The art has to be formal, like any art, but this will be a form in each instance tied to matter and purpose. That is how *ēthos* and the *logos,* the two parents of rhetoric, will be integrated.

The art of rhetoric has two aspects, which we can associate with *logos* and *ēthos*. It is a rational *dynamis* and proves opposites, just as dialectic does; all the arts are powers for producing opposites. But rhetoric, like any art, is part of the intellectual virtue of art: it is the good functioning of the thinking part of the soul. Of course one could say that it is good functioning of the *thinking* part of the soul and not the desiring and choosing part, and so not a desirable state of *character*. But I regard that response as an inadequate evasion. Taking it seriously would result in a large independence between parts of the soul. Such a separation might work for the other arts: being a skilled physician does not involve *ēthos,* but it cannot work for rhetoric.

Ethos and Trust: Speaker and Audience

Rhetorical theory dealt very early with the artificial arousal of emotions. It treated ethos only casually, for [it] cannot be aroused.
—Friedrich Nietzsche, "Description of Ancient Rhetoric," 131

I have been trying to show that rhetorical argument, *qua* argument, is necessarily ethical, because it requires deliberation, and deliberation requires the habits of desire and perception which constitute character. Is there not, however, a fallacy here? Just because rhetorical argument, unlike the proofs of geometry, is *about* ethical matters, about choice and character, it does not follow that rhetorical argument must itself *be* ethical. Movies about the boredom and emptiness of modern life should not themselves be boring and empty. Aristotle seems to commit just such a fallacy: "Mathematical works do not have an *ēthos* because they do not show deliberative choice [*prohairesis*] (for they do not have a [moral] purpose [*to heneka*]), but the Socratic dialogues do (for they speak of such things)" (III.15.1417a19–21).

If that mode of argument is fallacious, Aristotle is in a lot of trouble, because it is at the heart of some of his most crucial argumentative moves. For example: "For when the beings are of different kinds, the parts of the soul naturally suited to each of them are also of different kinds, since the parts possess knowledge by being somehow similar and appropriate [to their objects]" (*Ethics* VI.1.1139a9–12). This sentence follows and grounds the claim that there are two rational faculties, "one whereby we contemplate those things whose principles are invariable, and one whereby we contemplate those things which admit of variation." There is a likeness between faculties and their objects; if rhetorical argument and *phronēsis* are about variable particulars, then they must themselves have variability and particularity. If they are about ethical matters, they have to be ethical. If this is a fallacy, Aristotle does not fall into it by accident, but uses it intentionally.

Once logical and rhetorical argument start to diverge, there can be conflict. Logical arguments cannot be too strong, but rhetorical arguments can. Logical form is a form independent of purpose, and so is not a form of any particular matter; rhetorical form is tied to end and matter. Hence my question about emergent properties. Isn't there a conflict between a logic that is indifferent to matter and purpose, and rhetorical argument, which is argument to someone, and so a form tied to matter and purpose? Isn't there, similarly, a conflict between the artful *ēthos* necessary for good argument and the more fully political and ethical *ēthos* the audience attributes to a speaker it trusts?

Because of this difference between logic and rhetoric, an art of rhetoric cannot be a substitute for *phronēsis* by becoming a sort of organon for *phronēsis,* a study which detaches *phronēsis* from its dependence on the moral virtues. Here Aristotle is on Newman's side when Newman says:

> In concrete reasonings we are in great measure thrown back into
> that condition, from which logic proposed to rescue us. We judge
> for ourselves, by our own lights, and on our own principles. . . . It
> is this distinction between ratiocination as the exercise of a living
> faculty in the individual intellect, and mere skill in argumentative
> science, which is the true interpretation of the prejudice which
> exists against logic in the popular mind.[17]

I think that the way to approach these questions is by seeing just how uniquely rhetorical the issues are. *Ethos* and trust are not always desirable, let alone essential. They are critical only in rhetorical situations, only within praxis. Sometimes, instead, I want *logos* untouched by *ēthos.* I would like biology and physics to be judged by reason alone. I want my accountant to be honest, but I don't want him to have my welfare in mind in making his calculations. He needs an *ēthos* which makes me trust him, but he doesn't need an *ēthos qua* accountant.[18] The difference between kinds of thought that can do without *ēthos* and practical *logoi* that need it is the difference between the "rational man" of modern economics and the "reasonable man" of the law. It is the difference between arts whose status as intellectual virtues is unproblematic, and rhetoric, which cannot have such a title and still be only a faculty for proving opposites.

Good choice and good character consist in seeing and choosing the right amounts of the things we deliberate about. Without such weightings, the speaker, the practical deliberator, must reason instrumentally toward given and therefore "thin" ends stipulated outside his own reasoning. Such reasoning must take a form something like cost-benefit analysis, with its homogenizing of all means into costs and all ends into benefits. Probabilities—and their rhetorical associate, confidence—are transformed into their modern meaning based on predicting regularities. When *ēthos* disappears, so does trust. An audience can still assent, but there is nothing for it to trust without ethical argument. Aristotle notes that *eunoia* arises only from friendships of virtue, not of utility or pleasure (*Ethics* IX.5.1167a12–14); the latter kinds of friendships might generate relationships that are perfectly predictable, but there is no trust in them. I can have a friendship of utility toward my accountant. I depend on him. I count on him. I rely on him. But I neither trust nor distrust him. *Ethos* is not essential to the calculation or decision of the accountant. Someone might have so much "continence" (*enkratia,* self-control) that his actions would be more predictable than any virtuous person's could be, but I would not trust the continent person, only the virtuous one. *Logos* is the enemy of *ēthos* when regularity is the enemy of trust. That is how an argument can be too strong. Where trust was, there predictability will be.

To return again to my running example of the advocate of bilingual education and public financial support for church schools: the perfectly predictable advocate might be consistent, but would anyone trust such a person? The person who makes all decisions on the same values may be consistent, but is not very ethical—predictable, but not reliable. If rhetoric develops the ability to argue for both sides of a question, and for apparently contradictory decisions in different cases, then consistency cannot be the automatically ultimate value in practical reason that it is in theoretical reason. And that raises as an urgent question—what replaces consistency?[19] If not consistency, what prevents this rhetorical power from becoming license to clothe in argument whatever preferences and desires one might have? *Ethos* is the only available candidate, and the question is whether Aristotle's presentation of *ēthos* in the *Rhetoric* can do the job. Trust has a heavy burden here.

There is another analogy to the moral virtues in the *Ethics* that I think helps. Courage, to take one of the virtues, is a praiseworthy state of character. But there is no universal rule that I should always prefer a courageous person over a professional soldier to stand next to me in the trenches. Sometimes a professional skill detached from character is just what we want in accountants and soldiers. I would probably prefer to have the predictable, professional soldier standing next to me rather than the trustworthy, courageous man. Aristotle says that the best fighters are not the most courageous men, but those who have the least to lose (III.9.1117b17–21), and he ridicules those who think that it is dishonorable to rely on devices like fortifications instead of true courage. If in a given case one can hit the given end directly without the intervention of artful or virtuous action, with its own autonomous end, as the professional soldier can, there is no reason not to do so. Aristotle recommends neither moral nor artistic fastidiousness. His remarks about fortifications in the *Politics* are apposite here too:

> The fortification of cities by walls is a matter of dispute. It is sometimes argued that states which lay claim to military excellence ought to dispense with any such aids. This is a singularly antiquated notion. . . . When the question at issue is one of coping with an enemy of similar character, which is only slightly superior in numbers, there is little honor to be got from an attempt to attain security by the erection of a barrier of walls. But it sometimes happens—and it is always possible—that the superiority of an assailant may be more than a match for mere courage, human or superhuman; and then, if a state is to avoid destruction, and to escape from suffering and humiliation, the securest possible barrier of walls should be deemed the best of military methods (VII.11.1330b32–1331a2, Barker's translation).

Sometimes, consequently, a professional *ēthos* of detachment and competence will be persuasive and appropriate. There is no universal rule that we should always make discourse ethical, nor even that making discourse ethical always makes our appeals more persuasive. These judgments are limited to the sphere of deliberation and praxis.

What looked like a fallacy on Aristotle's part is not. Where the subject for decision calls for deliberation, there deliberation, and hence *ēthos,* should be involved. Where the subject for decision calls for other forms of calculation, in which matter and end are irrelevant, then *ēthos* is out of place. There is, then, no universal rule that we should always aim at the guiding end and never approach the given end directly.

In rhetoric and practical judgment, then, *ēthos* is necessary for finding and formulating arguments, and not just presenting them. The probabilities and signs that are the materials of rhetoric and deliberation are accessible to ethical perception. When I deliberate, I am, implicitly or explicitly, adjusting proposed choices to pictures of who I think I am, or want to be, or want to be seen to be. In deciding what to do, I decide what *I* should do. That is what it means in the *Ethics* to act for the noble, and that is why ethical deliberation is permeated by *ēthos,* and is not just calculation toward an ethically good end.[20] For that reason it is not enough to have good ends or borrow them from one's client. *Logos* and *ēthos* are integrated.

My parallel between the problem of relating *logos* and *ēthos* at this point in the *Rhetoric* and the relation between the ethical virtues and *phronēsis* in the *Ethics* can help here. In both cases, there is a mutual implication and interdependence between the two terms. We trust a speaker, and impute *aretē* and *phronēsis* to him, when he presents us with a cogent and intelligent argument. We infer from *logos* to *ēthos*. But rhetorical arguments are about indeterminate matters. So, in order to regard an argument as cogent and intelligent, we have to trust the speaker. That is why *ēthos* cannot be a by-product of argument. We need trust to perceive the argument correctly. We infer from *ēthos* to *logos*.

It is the interdependence of *ēthos* and *logos* that prevents such inferences from becoming a vicious circle. Most enthymemes are presented with some premise absent, and the audience has to fill it in. Whether they add a premise that makes the argument cogent and believable or one that makes it incredible is up to the audience. They will insert the premise most to the speakers's advantage if they trust the speaker. If I think you are opposing bilingual education but supporting the diversion of tax revenue to religious schools because you will benefit, I will supply one set of missing premises; if I think you are deliberating about what is best for the country as a whole, I will supply a different set. As William James puts it, "In truths dependent on personal action . . . faith based on desire is certainly a lawful and possibly an indispensable thing."[21] In Aristotle's own words, "no one cares about reputation [in the abstract] but on account of those who hold an opinion of him" (II.6.1384a23).

The central finding of chapter 1, once more, was that the *logos* of an artful speech was shared between speaker and audience, and that consequently the act of the speaker persuading was identical to that of the hearer being persuaded. I have said that the stakes are now higher, because an identity between *ēthos* in the speaker and trust in the audience is more difficult to achieve than that identity of *logos*. I do not possess an *ēthos* when I trust someone else's, the way I share an argument in following it, and for that reason logical and ethical proofs do not seem parallel. Even though I, as a member of the audience, can simply take over the speaker's argument while his *ēthos* is not similarly transferable, I trust him because he is arguing ethically. I can understand and share his argument. I cannot share his *ēthos;* I have to trust it.

The middle term that connected *pistis,* an act of persuasion engaged in by a speaker, and *pistis,* the state of being persuaded in an audience, was argument. If the speaker's persuading was argumentative, it could then be identical to the audience's being persuaded. Similarly, it is art and argument that is the middle term connecting the two senses of *ēthos,* the one the speaker uses and the one the audience trusts. Therefore, back in I.2 when he said that *ēthos* is the most persuasive method of proof, he also insisted that it is artful *ēthos* that is involved, the *ēthos* of the speaker *qua* speaker, not *qua* human being, citizen, or ethical agent. It is the speaker's argumentative and deliberative ability that creates *ēthos* as a by-product. That *ēthos* is not the accumulation of previous praxis, as the *ēthos* of the moral virtues is. It is that act of deliberation that the audience trusts, not the speaker's ethical reputation. When both are tied to art, the *ēthos* the speaker uses and the one the audience trusts are identical. That is why there is no vicious circle in our inferences between *logos* and *ēthos*.

Artful Ethos and Real Ethos

The power of speaking, and that of acting [dynamis tou legein, tou prattein] [*are among the things considered good*], *because they produce many good things* [poietika gar panta ta toiauta agathon].
— *Rhetoric* I.6.1262b19

It seems to me impractical and possibly even counterproductive to issue guidelines to social scientists on how to incorporate morality into their scientific pursuits and how to be on guard against immoral "side effects" of their work. Morality is not something like pollution abatement that can be secured by slightly modifying the design of a policy proposal. Rather, it belongs in the center of our work; and it can get there only if the social scientists are morally alive and make themselves vulnerable to moral concerns—then they will produce morally significant works, consciously or otherwise.
— Albert Hirschman, *Essays*, 305

I want to go back to my original trio of sets of quotations, in which *logos* and *ēthos* were first allies, then enemies, and finally independent enough for there to be specific directions on how to use maxims to make *logoi* ethical. We now should be in a position to understand the first and the second. We should now understand why *logos* and *ēthos* go together, that is, why trusting a speaker and following his practical argument go together. We should also understand why being logical is sometimes to fail to be ethical, and so to fail to be persuasive. Ethical argument is still argument; there is no separate practical logic. And yet, ethical and rhetorical argument differ from logical argument in having another kind of form, a form tied to purpose, speaker, and matter. In the next section I will finally be able to look at the third set of citations, concerning the methods for making discourse ethical through devices like the maxim.

First, however, we need to attack another of the quartet of problems I listed at the beginning. We now understand how *logos* and *ēthos* can sometimes be allies and sometimes opponents, how argument can be at the center of rhetoric, while some speakers can yet fail by using argument. We have three questions left. In this section I want first to show why the most important thing of all, making discourse ethical, can be an incidental by-product of something else, as my first set of quotations claims. I will then answer the question of why Aristotle seems to be quite indifferent whether he is talking about making discourse ethical or making discourse *appear* ethical. In the next section we will tackle the last question and try to see why presenting means for directly making discourse ethical is not an inherently immoral activity, an art of disguise and deception.

The relation between *ēthos* and *logos* that I have established shows, to the puzzlement and frustration of commentators, that there is no special art of presenting character, while there is a special part of the art devoted to *eunoia* and the emotions. I.4–14 are about *logos;* II.2–11 are about *pathos.* We now can see why *ēthos* can receive no comparable distinct treatment. Character may be the most persuasive kind of appeal, but the artful and methodical approach to character must be via the enthymeme. If there was a special method for achieving *ēthos,* we could argue about ends. The similarity of this relation between character and enthymeme to the relation of prudence and the moral virtues is apposite once again. We do not, for the most part, acquire prudence directly, because it is nothing but (or almost nothing but) the form, the *orthos logos,* of good choices and good character. Explicit instructions for making discourse ethical seem to create the possibility of an independent life for *ēthos,* and, similarly, for the *orthos logos.* There is no art for hitting the given ends of deliberation. The art of calculating how to do what one can to achieve the given end is simply the art of achieving the guiding end.

We make our discourse ethical by making our *ēthos* argumentative. *Ethos* is an incidental result of argument in the same way that *phronēsis* is an incidental result of ethical virtue and happiness is an incidental result of virtue. In none of these cases does "incidental" or "by-product" mean that the result in not important. It just means that it cannot be directly the end of an action. We cannot aim at *ēthos*—with the exceptions of the methods Aristotle gives us for doing just that—and there are no methods for *phronēsis* or happiness. *Phronēsis* is the culmination of the moral virtues, and therefore cannot be approached directly. Happiness is the *energeia* of virtue and therefore can only be obtained through exercising the virtues. Incidental does not mean unimportant. It means that it cannot be the direct object of deliberation and action. Therefore we make discourse ethical by arguing about what to do.

I think that the peculiar status of *ēthos,* as opposed to *logos* and *pathos,* can be brought out by a thought experiment. I am persuaded to do something by a rhetorician. You ask me to explain the reasons for my decision. My explanation for rational persuasion can simply repeat or reenact the logos in the original speech. That is what it means for speaker and hearer to share the *logos,* as I showed in the first chapter. With regard to *pathos,* I can explain why I was angry, pitying, etc., because I can give the arguments into which pathetic appeals are translatable. That was the burden of chapter 4. The *pathos* is not shared between speaker and hearer, but its form is. The speaker possesses the form alone, the hearer has the form enmattered. The audience being moved emotionally is in that way like the patient being healed: physician and patient share a form; the doctor possesses the form alone, the patient the enmattered form.

But what do I say in accounting for how I was persuaded by *ēthos?* The principal thing I would have to point to would be, once again, the *logos* of the speech. It is the primary evidence for the speech's *ēthos.* Turning attention to *ēthos* would not make me simply repeat what I said about *logos,* however. Approaching the arguments ethically would change the focus slightly. The speaker's *ēthos* would, in addition, answer such questions as: Why choose this decision and argument and not another? Why this example? Why these probabilities and signs and why weight them as you did? I would generalize my choice in explaining it. Generalizing is exactly what maxims do, and that is why they make discourse ethical. Turning to *ēthos* does not turn attention away from *logos;* it just broadens the understanding beyond logical values like cogency toward ethical values of trust. *Ethos* differs from *pathos* and *logos,* then, by *not* being a separate source of conviction.

With the exception of devices like the maxim, there are no special methods for *ēthos,* as there are for *pathos* and *logos.* There is, of course, a simple reason why most of our presentation of character should be indirect, via argument: this is an instance in which what is most artful also seems most successful. Attempts to persuade directly through an appeal to character are prone to backfiring, as in the notorious, "Trust me; I'm not a crook." Attempts to teach *ēthos* are likely to backfire too, leading to an ability to talk about values and good ends but not act on them. To the extent that the *Rhetoric* can be read as a reply to Isocrates, this is how the response would go.

Once again, however, I am imputing to Aristotle the stronger claim that the best displays of character are argumentative not just because they succeed, but because concentration on argument is more inventive. The chief way in which one displays a character is by presenting an argument: one acquires, uses, and displays character through deliberation and choice, and argument is a pattern of deliberation and choice. The chief way in which one acquires an *ēthos* is through deliberating about what to do.

Through the connection that Aristotle posits between character and argument our puzzle about whether the *Rhetoric* is concerned with real or only apparent character receives a clear resolution. The appearance/reality distinction looks different when the appearance in question is an argument or a character. An apparent argument *is* an argument: a piece of deliberation presented in aid of persuasion *is* a piece of deliberation, even though the speaker might be presenting it with some further end in view.

While an apparent argument, or an argument presented for some ulterior and hidden purpose, is still an argument, an apparent character seems to lie at greater distance from a real character. The distance between appearance and reality is bridged by argument. Argument can always be evaluated by how it achieves the guiding end, independent of external purpose and given end. When the best method of presenting one's character is through presenting an argument, then an apparent character, for practical purposes, *is* a character. Rhetorical audiences should judge the argument *qua* argument, and that means that they should judge the speaker's *ēthos* as it is embodied in the enthymeme.

It is a mistake, thus, to infer to a real character distinct from such artful character. Once a citizen understands the relation between *ēthos* and *logos* presented in the *Rhetoric,* he will see that the responsibility for the mistake lies not in the rhetorician—he is not doing anything he shouldn't—but in the hearer who wrongly infers from apparent, artful character to real character. I will return to this placement of responsibility below, but the rhetorician need not be acting deceptively by manifesting an artful *ēthos*. This kind of *ēthos* is apparent, but it, like an apparent argument, is not the appearance of some deeper reality.[22]

The *ēthos* which the audience trusts, then, is the artificial *ēthos* identified with argument. It is not some real *ēthos* the speaker may or may not possess. It is an *ēthos* not necessarily tied to past experiences of the speaker, not an *ēthos* acquired through performing similar actions in the past. It may be *likely* that the good speaker is able to deliberate intelligently because of past experiences, but it is not *ēthos qua* product of past experience that the audience trusts, but *ēthos* as exercised in some particular argument.

Insofar as audiences do actually draw that further inference about moral character, demonstrating its superfluousness should be seen as a contribution the *Rhetoric* makes to political science and legislation. More sophisticated, politically wise, audiences trust a speaker *qua* speaker, but not therefore *qua* man. "Rhetoric dresses itself up (*hypoduetai*) in the form (*to schema*) of politics, as do those who pretend to a knowledge of it, partly from lack of education, partly from boastfulness, and other human causes" (I.2.1356a27–30).

The *Rhetoric* licenses inferences from argument to artificial *ēthos* but bars further inferences from artificial *ēthos* to real *ēthos*. I don't think that the *Rhetoric* runs into any great conflict with the ordinary judgments audiences make. I am not convinced that inferences from artful *ēthos* to real *ēthos* are all that common, and so I side with Aristotle in not seeing rhetoric as threatening to the moral and political order. When listening to an able lawyer defending a client, I think most people can respond to the practical intelligence displayed by a lawyer *qua* advocate without thinking either that the lawyer believes what he or she says or that the practical intelligence shown in the speech is any reason at all to trust the lawyer in other contexts. The argumentative *ēthos* is artificial, but not for that reason unreal. We do not infer that the lawyer *qua* man is really a *phronimos,* but that is not necessarily a reason to suspect him or his arguments, or to doubt the *phronēsis* of his arguments. Because *ēthos* is artificial, it is often—more in forensic and epideictic situations than in deliberative ones—conventional, and audiences learn the conventions. No one expects the advocate to "mean what he says."

The inference from artful character to real character is an argument from signs, and is fallible and defeasible in the way such arguments are. "Proof from signs is expressive of character, because there is an appropriate style for each genus and moral state" (III.7.1408a25–27).[23] By framing the question as one of real vs. apparent character, we are forced to frame it as: Why is apparent character good enough? Aristotle instead poses the issue as artful character vs. its opposite. Then we don't need to make artful character a *pis aller.* We need not and should not look for character in any stronger sense.[24]

But this explanation is surely more plausible for judicial and epideictic rhetoric than for deliberation. No one expects the legal advocate to "mean what he says," but people make just that inference all the time for political orators. I quoted Hobbes at the beginning of the chapter saying "Eloquence persuades because it is seeming prudence." Don't we have enough evidence to say that political eloquence is often far more persuasive than it ought to be, that we frequently and mistakenly make inferences from the *ēthos* in a speech to the *ēthos* of a moral agent who can make intelligent and effective choices? Haven't we elected leaders because they are fluent speakers and then discovered that they couldn't govern?

I want to approach that question by looking at the details of Aristotle's advice on how to use maxims to make *logoi* ethical. I will then be able in the conclusion to look more carefully at how people reason from the *ēthos* expressed in a speech and tied to argument to an actual *ēthos* of the speaker *qua* moral agent.

How Maxims Make Discourse Ethical

Maxims bring to a head a central problem with rhetorical argument. I have constructed that problem by trying to triangulate the three uses of the expression, "making discourse ethical": *logos* and *ēthos* are sometimes opposed; sometimes making discourse ethical is a side effect of making arguments;

and sometimes, in maxims, making discourse ethical is a distinct challenge for the rhetorical art.

I consequently asked why presenting means for directly making discourse ethical, as Aristotle does with maxims, is not an inherently immoral activity, an art of disguise and deception. Given the difficulty and sophistication of the problem I have constructed for Aristotle and the importance of the idea of making discourse ethical, his actual treatment of the maxim in II.21 looks, like much of the rest of the *Rhetoric,* so straightforward and unproblematic that he seems unaware of the difficulty and significance of what he is talking about. Nowhere does he draw attention to the apparent discrepancies I have noted among my three sets of initial citations. He clarifies the idea that maxims make speech ethical by saying that "speeches have character insofar as deliberative choice is clear (*en hosios dele hē prohairesis*)" (II.21.1395b14)," and he seems to think that that is all the explication that the expression "ethical speeches" needs.

Something of what he means comes from my last section, where I pointed out that practical judgments are decisions not only that something is best, or should be done, but that *I* ought to do it. Making one's choices clear is to take that kind of responsibility for the decision. That is the contrast between thought and *ēthos* that Aristotle brings out in a passage I quoted earlier:

> Do not seem to speak from thought [*dianoias*] as men now do, but from choice [*prohaireseos*]. Say, for example, "I wished this. Indeed, I *chose* this. But if I gained nothing, still this is better." For the one way of speaking is the mark of a practically wise man [*phronimou*], the other way is the mark of a good man [*agathou*]. The practically wise man is involved in pursuing the advantageous, but the good man in pursuing the noble (III.16.1417a24–28).

Ethos can be a product of the speech, and like any product, it can be an externally given end at which a speaker aims. When *ēthos* is such a product, it exists as a state of trust, *pistis,* in the audience, the terminus of a *kinēsis.* The speaker can aim at that condition equally through argument or through unartful means such as appealing to past exploits, wearing one's combat uniform, or fighting back tears. Any of these things can give hearers confidence in a speaker.

Any goal can be made into a given end toward which we calculate means. Any method, even those constitutive of a practice or art, can be exploited for further purposes.[25] Guiding ends, however, are constituted by the actions we perform to accomplish them. Unlike given ends, they cannot be defined apart from those means, and cannot exist apart from them either. If *ēthos* is a guiding end, then it is limited to art and argument. Therefore it is a kind of *ēthos* evoked through ethical argument, and ethical argument alone. If maxims aim directly at evoking trust and belief the way wearing a uniform does, then they will indeed be devices for directly achieving something we thought could only be reached through argument. They will therefore be inartistic and fall outside the art of rhetoric. They will produce the guiding end, but certainly not *qua* guiding end.

Maxims, like any other method or technique, can be used for purposes outside the art, and purposes contrary to the art. There are no facets of rhetoric, or any other art, that can be protected from such usurpation. Abuses are always possible. The question is whether the use of maxims to make discourse ethical is *inherently* deceptive and inartistic. The relation between artful *ēthos* and real, or practical, *ēthos* is the heart of the relation between the art of rhetoric and the intellectual virtue of *phronēsis*. The precise issue takes this kind of complicated framing.

I think that my invocation of Veblen's idea of trained incapacity helps to separate maxims, along with the other methods internal to the art of rhetoric, from true *atechnoi* such as military campaign medals. Losing trust through being argumentative is a problem specific to the art of rhetoric. I can also lose trust for many other reasons—because the audience is prejudiced against me, or because they are distracted by empty stomachs after listening to a long speech by my opponent. These are factors not generated by the art of rhetoric, and Aristotle thinks of them as matters of necessity not intrinsic to rhetoric's guiding end. If the way maxims makes *logoi* ethical is a response to the specifically artistic problem of *logos* driving out *ēthos,* then it will not be an instrumental device for achieving a given end, but part of the internal project of rhetoric merging *logos* and *ēthos.*[26] But the availability of a speaker's *ēthos* to such a direct approach is reason to keep speaker's *ēthos* and agent's *ēthos,* the one connected to *technē* and the other to *phronēsis,* distinct.

Maxims are the one place where the speaker can see, and control, a distinction between the logical and the ethical. Maxims show ways in which *logos* and *ēthos* can be contraries, and how their opposition can be exploited by the speaker. The rest of the *Rhetoric* shows how they go together. Maxims are arguments which exhibit simultaneously their logical and ethical natures. The trouble is that they therefore seem to appeal to a sense of *ēthos* distinct from art and argument.

The striking fact about Aristotle's treatment of maxims, and therefore of the prospect of directly making discourse ethical, is how casual it is. He moves from maxims' value in achieving the given end, persuasion, to achieving the guiding end, integrating *ēthos* and *logos,* very casually indeed.

> Maxims make one great contribution to speeches because of the uncultivated mind of the audience; for people are pleased if some-one in a general observation hits upon opinions that they them-selves have about a particular instance. . . . Thus, one should guess [*stochazesthai*] what sort of assumptions people have and then speak in general terms consistent with these views. This is one useful aspect of employing maxims, and another is greater; for it makes the speech "ethical." Speeches have character insofar as deliberative choice [*prohairesis*] is clear, and all maxims accomplish this because one speaking a maxim makes a general statement about preferences (II.21. 1395b1–17).

Guessing things about one's audience is the surest mark of aiming at the external end of persuasion; yet maxims serve that purpose and, almost as an afterthought, are also said to produce trust and the integration of *ēthos* and *logos* by making speeches ethical. It is one thing to say that we incidentally become happy by aiming at virtue, or that we come to know how to appear ethical in the course of learning how to argue about character in others. In those cases calling the achievement of a given end "incidental" just shows how smoothly that accomplishment follows reaching the guiding, internal end. It is quite another to say that we make our discourse ethical by trying to win a case through guessing our audience's opinions.

The positions of guiding and given ends appear here to be reversed. We achieve the guiding end of rhetoric and integrate *logos* and *ēthos* by directing hitting the external end, persuading some particular audience. We are not supposed to be able to accomplish constitutive ends that way. That is why such a method is inherently deceptive in appearance. Being ethical seems *incompatible* with direct effort. Like happiness, it seems the sort of thing that can only be approached indirectly, via wise argument. If it cannot be achieved directly, then methods for making discourse ethical, such as the maxim, will be methods of appearing ethical without being so.

I want to approach this difficulty in the *Rhetoric* by an analogy to another aspect of the *Ethics*. There is something which, like ethical speech in the *Rhetoric,* is part of the constitutive end of moral virtue, virtuous activity, and which therefore cannot be approached directly, namely, controlling our passions. While the virtues of character concern both actions and passions, we give a right relation to our emotions by choosing right actions, not the other way around. One becomes more courageous by choosing right ac-tions, not by trying to master the passions, except to a secondary degree.[27] That is, there is no art or method for mastering the passions, having the right amount of them, or feeling them in connection with the right objects in the right circumstances. We are not praised or blamed for our passions, but for standing well or badly with regard to them. There is a method for the guiding end of choosing what to do. By choosing an action, we are doing the best we can toward achieving the end of rightly feeling passions. The young are ruled by their passions. They do not overcome this deficiency by learning methods of self-control, but by gaining experience in action and choice (*Ethics* I.3.1095a1–8). To make arguments ethical by direct application of a technique is like becoming virtuous by developing the right passions without orienting one's choices to good ends.

The casual way Aristotle observes that maxims also make discourse ethical suggests that accomplishing the given end—external success at persuading the audience—and achieving the guiding end, merging *logos* and *ēthos*, are not very far apart. Given the naturalness of the polis, that is as it should be. There is no grand conflict in Aristotle between success and morality. It would take a different kind of political theory to understand and regulate practices in a world in which success and morality are regularly in conflict.

Therefore we might, in circumstances different from Aristotle's, evaluate differently a method like the maxim or any means of directly producing trust. If in contemporary politics, voters function less like citizens and more like consumers and judges of theatrical performances, it is no wonder that our inferences from eloquence to virtue should go wrong so regularly. That is an inference people have never been good at, as the frequency with which people fall in love with movie stars, and television news broadcasters, indicates. There are circumstances, that is, in which artful *ēthos* becomes apparent *ēthos* as opposed to real *ēthos*, and in which we should not trust eloquence. A hermeneutics of suspicion and a politics of distrust are more appropriate.[28]

Aristotle himself recognizes the possibility of such degeneration. On the one hand, he criticizes other rhetorical arts because they neglect the art of delivery. Those who pay attention to delivery usually win. "Those [performers who give careful attention to these] are generally the ones who win poetic contests; and just as actors are more important than poets now in the poetic contests, so it is in political contests because of the sad state of governments" (III.1.1403b32–35).

If the inferences from discursive *ēthos* to practical *ēthos* are less smooth and more dangerous for us than they were for Aristotle, we might think about turning elsewhere for further exploration of this line of problems. Aristotle may not be able to take us further. It might be more useful, for example, to think about the inferences from author to moral agent that Lionel Trilling invites in talking about some writers as "figures": "In modern English literature there have been many writers whose lives were demonstrations of the principles that shaped their writing. They lead us to be aware of the moral personalities that stand behind the work."[29]

I would also diagnose contemporary political problems as stemming from an independence of political and epideictic rhetoric, so that people vote for candidates who express the "right values" while those same voters disagree with all of their chosen candidates' policy recommendations. That is, in what Aristotle would view as our unnatural politics, it is false to say that "praise and deliberations are part of a common species [*koinon eidos*] in that what one might propose in deliberation becomes an encomium when the form of expression is changed" (I.9.1367b36–1368a1). Using the maxim to make *logoi* ethical is not ethically troublesome when political and epideictic rhetoric are as interdependent as that. Under those circumstances Aristotle is right to say that maxims make discourse ethical because they make the speaker's moral purpose or choice (*prohairesis*) clear. If pronouncing maxims has no connection with choices, when epideixis and deliberative rhetoric are distinct, then artificial *ēthos* becomes merely an apparent and deceptive *ēthos*.

Rhetoric, Cleverness, and *Phronēsis*

At the beginning of this chapter, I identified four questions generated by the idea of making discourse ethical, and want to end by giving direct answers to each of them. First, Aristotle noticed that *logos* and *ēthos* are allies in artful rhetoric, but that there are times when they are contraries. Argument can be at the center of rhetoric, yet some speakers can fail by using argument.

Naturally, then, I asked how to make sense of this picture of a harmony between *logos* and *ēthos* interrupted periodically by contradiction between them. The reason, I argued, for this trained incapacity is that rhetorical form differs from logical form by being a form tied to purpose and therefore to matter. Who is persuading whom are not factors extrinsic to the argument, but part of it, *qua* rhetorical argument. Therefore logic and persuasion are allies, and to be logical is to be persuasive, when our arguments are ethical. When our arguments are not ethical, they are not practical either, and so not rhetorical. The enthymeme is the body of proof, and *ēthos* is its soul.

Because of this complicated relation between *logos* and *ēthos*, making our arguments ethical is the constitutive end of the art of rhetoric. Concerning the subjects of deliberation, finding the available means of persuasion is an ethical activity, requiring character. Second, therefore, I asked how attaining this important goal can be, for the most part, an incidental by-product of something else. The given end of ethics and politics is happiness and the good life. The lesson of the *Ethics* and *Politics* is that we should almost never aim at that given end, but instead turn attention to the guiding ends, virtue and justice, of those sciences. As I mentioned, our passions, pleasures, and pains are not directly within our power; our actions are. We become happy and we live well by making choices about what to do and what laws to institute. Similarly here. The end of rhetoric is persuasion; we are persuasive when audiences trust us, but we rarely aim directly at such trust. The art of rhetoric teaches us to aim instead at the guiding end of rhetoric, argument.

As I stressed in the first chapter, there must be a general overall harmony between given and guiding ends, such that for the most part we reach those external ends best through aiming at the constitutive ends of practices, arts, and virtues. Rhetoric is, however, a rational *dynamis,* a power of proving opposites, and therefore *logos* not only creates *ēthos;* it can have an independent existence. Aristotle has to recommend devices like maxims which reintegrate *ēthos* and *logos.*[30] In the last chapter I showed how *logos* could have independent force. Here we see how, in quite a different way, *ēthos* has independence, too.

That is the answer to our third question. I wanted to know why presenting devices for directly making discourse ethical is not an inherently immoral activity, an art of disguise and deception. Showing how to use maxims to make arguments ethical is giving directions for hitting the given end, persuasion, instead of the guiding end, finding the available means. If given and guiding end are more divergent, as they might be in other circumstances, then the same advice Aristotle gives could in those circumstances be manipulative and even immoral. So might an art that allowed people directly to find the mean about passions without acting on them.

It turns out that there is a plot to my three original sets of citations. First and for the most part, we make discourse ethical by making rhetoric argumentative. However, there is something about rhetoric as a rational *dynamis* that makes it possible for form to be separated from function, so that *logos* and *ēthos* are at odds. Consequently, there is room for techniques specifically designed to make discourse ethical. They are of minor importance in the *Rhetoric* compared to the methods for making rhetoric argumentative and emotional, but they still have a place. They have that place because they exhibit the connection between *logos* and *ēthos,* and so exhibit the connection between trustworthiness and *ēthos* in the speaker and trust in the audience. So long as they are minor, rhetoric stays subordinate to politics.

Finally, I raised the question of why Aristotle seems quite indifferent whether he is talking about making discourse ethical or making discourse *appear* ethical. As I said before, Aristotle would reject this way of posing the issue. The relevant *ēthos* is an artful *ēthos, ēthos* insofar as it is tied to *logos* and art. The real issue, then, is why call such a thing *ēthos,* if it is not a manifestation of the speaker's real character? I think the answer is that this quality in the speaker, and this quality of argument, is called ethical simply because it produces trust in the audience, and because there is an essential connection between *ēthos* and trust.

The powers exercised in constructing a persuasive speech, especially in indeterminate situations calling for judgment and action, are just the powers the *phronimos* has to call on in deciding what to do. The difference is in the context for the possession and exercise of those powers. The persuasive speaker as such lacks the connections to experience, habit, and action that the *phronimos* has. The institutional context and purposes of rhetoric have to serve instead. His explanation in the *Ethics* about the relation between cleverness and *phronēsis* applies here to the relation between the rhetorical art, including its ability to make discourse ethical, and *phronēsis*:

> There is a capacity [*dynamis*], called cleverness, which is such as to be able to do the actions that tend to promote whatever goal is assumed and to achieve it. If, then, the goal is base, cleverness is unscrupulousness [*panourgia*]; hence both intelligent [*phronimous*] and unscrupulous people are called clever. . . . *Phronēsis* is not the same as this capacity [of cleverness], though it requires it. *Phronēsis,* this eye of the soul, cannot reach its fully developed state [*hexis*] without virtue (*Ethics* VI.12.1144a24–31).

The key sentence is the penultimate one: "*Phronēsis* is not the same as this capacity [of cleverness], though it requires it." Similarly *phronēsis* and the *dynamis* of rhetoric are not identical, but the *phronimos* must use the same skills as those embodied in the art of rhetoric. Facility at rhetoric will not, Aristotle explains in that passage, make someone a *phronimos,* but the *phronimos* needs a *dynamis* very much like that of rhetoric. Small wonder that we infer from artful *ēthos* to practical *ēthos*.

Because of the institutional settings of the three kinds of rhetoric, Aristotle thinks that fallacious inferences from the *ēthos* of the speaker and speech, *qua* artful *ēthos,* are not a great danger. Earlier I quoted Aristotle as saying that "proof from signs is expressive of character, because there is an appropriate style for each genus and moral state" (III.7.1408a25–27). I want finally to look at a similar argument from signs: "Thus, one should take coincidences and chance happenings as due to deliberative purpose (*prohairesis*); for if many similar examples are cited, they will seem to be a sign of virtue and purpose" (I.9.1367b24–26). Similarly here. If someone repeatedly gives advice that warrants trust, an audience could well come to trust the person, not just *qua* speaker but *qua* moral agent. If such an argument from signs is not refuted by broadening the scope and looking at the rest of the person's acts, *qua* moral agent, then it is not such a fallacious inference after all. Artful *ēthos* and artful trust go together, and artful *ēthos* can lead to positing an actual *ēthos*. By itself, that is an argument from signs, not a fallacy.

There are certainly ethical contexts in which the inference from luck to purpose and virtue would be dangerous, and even immoral. A moral theory quite different from Aristotle's, existing in a different moral world, might find that inferences from fortune to virtue threatened the heart of its enterprise. In the same way, other conceptions of *ēthos* and *technē* could be threatened in a way that Aristotle's are not. Even for Aristotle, these inferences are always defeasible, and ask for more evidence. But success is a sign of design, and repeated success a reasonably reliable sign. And fortune as a sign of virtue supplies a useful analogy for us now in a further way. Fortune is a noncircular sign of virtue. Someone's actions are validated by something outside those actions. To follow that side of the analogy out, the persuasive speaker not only has to give advice that sounds good and which people accept. It has to be good advice: we must win the war. If someone regularly and dependably gave sound advice, that would create a presumption that his artful *ēthos* was evidence for real *ēthos*. Someone would have to rebut that presumption by supplying strong reasons to believe the opposite, that in this case sound advice, for specific reasons, was offered by someone not himself or herself sound.

The two concluding chapters of my book will explore the relation between artful *ēthos* and real *ēthos*, and between rhetoric and *phronēsis*, in more detail. In this chapter, I have followed Aristotle in applying the predicate, *ēthikōs*, to both people and arguments. The next chapter begins by following Aristotle in distinguishing people from arguments.

VII

HOW TO TELL THE RHETORI-
CIAN FROM THE SOPHIST,
AND WHICH ONE TO BET ON

ODYSSEUS: *As the occasion demands, such a one am I. When there is a competition of men to see who is just and good, you will find none more scrupulous than myself. What I seek in everything is to win.*

— *Philoctetes*, 1048–1051

Energeia and Praxis

As I have been moving through this presentation of Aristotle's civic art of rhetoric, I occasionally picture a reader who sees my argument as a process of delayed gratification in which the delay easily outweighs the gratification. Whenever I talk about the *Rhetoric,* audiences ask me about rhetorical deception and fraud, about the morality of rhetoric, and about how to tell a good rhetorician from a sophist. I am sure that readers who share the concerns of those audiences have felt periodically that I have been on the verge of talking about the morality of rhetoric. They must have wondered how the legislator's political decisions, which have been my focus, can really replace the moral judgments they are looking for.

The first and most important thing to say about the *Rhetoric* in connection with such questions of the morality of rhetoric is that Aristotle has very little to say about them, and, as far as I can tell, very little interest in them. Contemporary readers of the *Rhetoric* see people constantly duped by slick commercial and political advertisements, and hope that the *Rhetoric* can help them become conscious of hidden persuasion, or able to make more morally based discriminations between decent appeals, which they should trust, and immoral ones, which they should reject. Rhetoric is often promoted today as an equivalent to defensive driving. It is worth asking why these questions have so little interest for Aristotle.

People today not only see rhetorical strategies deployed to achieve ends

206

they deplore; worse, they assume that the sophist, unrestrained by moral or artful considerations, will best anyone who answers to Aristotle description of a rhetorician as someone whose appeals are limited to rational argument. Sophists appeal to the emotions and ignore rational appeals. The sophist asks to be acquitted because he is truly sorry, was just following orders, has learned his lesson, just couldn't help himself because he had such a terrible childhood. He'll appear in a military uniform, with wife and children at his side. The prosecuting orator who does nothing but provide evidence hasn't a chance. To be guided by knowledge and one's rhetorical faculty is to argue with one hand tied behind one's back. The rhetorician follows the demands of his art, the sophist will do anything to win. Art, with its limited means and ends, here seems not to improve practice, but to make things worse.

Aristotle has a simple answer to questions about the morality of rhetoric: he distinguishes the rhetorician and the sophist. What sets the sophist apart from the rhetorician is not a "difference in faculty [*dynamis*] but in moral purpose [*prohairesis*]" (I.1.1355b18; see *De Sophisticis Elenchis* 1.165a30). Keep straight the difference between sophist and rhetorician, and all moral problems will evaporate. He certainly does not think telling them apart needs great philosophical development or exquisite ethical judgment. Distinguishing them requires neither *phronēsis* nor familiarity with the *Rhetoric*. He gives his distinction all the explanation he thinks it needs by saying:

> In the case of rhetoric, however, there is the difference that one person will be [called] *rhētor* on the basis of his knowledge [*kata tēn epistēmen*] and another on the basis of his deliberative choice [*kata tēn prohairesein*], while in dialectic *sophist* refers to deliberative choice [of specious arguments], *dialectician* not to deliberative choice [*ou kata tēn prohairesin*], but to ability [*kata tēn dynamin*] [at argument generally] (b19–21).[1]

But his distinction between the rhetorician and the sophist seems too off-hand for such weighty issues. We have to wonder why he thinks it adequate.

In the first chapter I noted that the legislator must have one set of policies to govern rhetoric's effects, and other policies for the activity of rhetoric itself. He or she has to distinguish occasions which call for one sort of regulation or the other. The distinction between the rhetorician and the sophist directs the legislator's attention to the *effects* of sophistic rhetoric. There is nothing in the activity of sophistic itself that warrants attention, since there is nothing unique to sophistic *qua* activity. The effects of bad rhetoric are out there to be treated just like anything else in the polis that is bad; they are not uniquely rhetorical or sophistical problems. We might construe analogous problems as problems for moral assessment, but Aristotle approaches them as problems calling for political deliberation.

So the problems of the "ethics of rhetoric," which interest so many modern readers, fall between stools. There are no special problems with the ethics of the effects of rhetoric; those problems are simply subsumed under general legislation about bad consequences. There are no ethical problems with sophistic *activity*, either, because *qua* art and activity, rhetoric and sophistic are not different. They only differ in motives and purposes, not in the activities themselves. The moral problems that may have generated modern interest in the *Rhetoric* in the first place seem to have disappeared. I want to reconstruct the approach to rhetoric that would make such a casual dismissal of the difference between the rhetorician and the sophist plausible.

Arts, as I argued in the first chapter, differ from other skills that Aristotle, and Plato, would classify as *empeiriai,* because arts, like the moral virtues, possess internal, guiding, constitutive ends, and consequently internal standards of excellence. Both for the virtues and for arts such as rhetoric and medicine, guiding ends do not simply replace given ends. When I act courageously, I subordinate my feelings of fear and confidence to my desire for the noble, but I never forget that I am also trying to win a military victory. States come into existence for the sake of life, but once they reach their *telos* of existing for the good life, they do not start neglecting the need for merely staying alive. In persuading artfully, I am presenting a proof with its own standards of excellence and completeness, but I never forget that I am trying to get the audience to decide things my way.

Artful rhetoric has an internal purpose, finding in any given case the available means of persuasion. Artful rhetoric also shares with its less scrupulous competitors an external end, winning an audience's assent. Why should we not conclude that concentration on the internal end makes one *less* able to achieve the external end? What MacIntyre says of the virtue seems to hold for artful rhetoric as well: "Virtues stand in a different relationship to external and to internal goods. The possession of the virtues—and not only of their semblance and simulacra—is necessary to achieve the latter; yet the possession of the virtues may perfectly well hinder us in achieving external goods."[2]

Aiming at the guiding end can sometimes help a speaker, or any agent, in accomplishing the given end by offering a goal within one's power and a restricted set of techniques and instruments about which it is easier to deliberate. But having a restricted set which points toward an internal end means that there are some ways of achieving the external end that are not available to the art. Not everything that someone could do to accomplish the given end also counts as a part of the guiding end. Aristotle says that good laws not only forbid emotional appeals but also success based on delivery (II.25.1402b32–35) and says that the speaker should not cause pain or delight (III.1.1404a4–5). If these methods were not successful, they would not be worth condemning. But we cannot condemn the rhetorician for wanting to win. Aristotle himself realizes this and therefore gives advice on how to reach such external ends, instead of the guiding ends of the art. Speakers "guess [*stochazesthai*] what sort of assumptions people have and then speak in general terms consistent with those views" (II.21.1395b10–11).

The Internal Ends of Art and Virtue

[Among the] things that must necessarily be good . . . are the powers of speaking and acting [dynamis tou legien, tou prattein], *for these powers produce many goods.*

—*Rhetoric* I.6.1362b10–19

The possibility that the sophist who aims directly at the external end might reach it more successfully than the rhetorician who sticks to his art is only half the problem, however. There are some things that might successfully bring about persuasion but which lie outside the art of rhetoric. There apparently are, in addition, some things that might successfully bring about persuasion but which no good man would stoop to. Is the restriction to means and resources that achieve the guiding end of the art of rhetoric a restriction to means and resources that are noble, that is, the sort of things the good man would do? In other words, do artful and moral restrictions coincide?

Argument, as something that can be accomplished *in* an act of speaking and which has its own standards of success, is analogous to virtues which are their own end. But rhetorical argument and virtuous actions are not identical. The art of rhetoric has constitutive ends of its own, but the art still should not be assimilated to the virtues. All *energeiai* are complete in themselves, and therefore have standards of excellence and values apart from achieving their instrumental purposes. Rhetorical arguments and virtuous actions both have guiding ends as well as given ends. But not all guiding ends are the same, or even necessarily consistent with each other.

Plato and Aristotle both raise questions about the unity of the virtues, that is, whether there is in fact a single constitutive end for all of them, or that they at least form a consistent set. Here I am raising an analogous question about the relation between two sets of guiding ends, those of the virtues and those of the arts, or at least of rhetoric, the noblest and most practical art. Can the unity of the virtues extend still further, to a unity of the virtues *and* the arts? That is what it would mean for artistic and ethical limitations to coincide.

Actually, it seems at least possible that a conflict between rhetoric and morality would be aggravated, not removed, once rhetorical activity discovers its own internal values. It might be easier to subordinate rhetoric to moral concerns if rhetoric had no intrinsic values of its own. Once gain, the *Rhetoric* might be a victim of its own success. Therefore my question: Do artful and moral restrictions coincide?

Issues of the morality of rhetoric are worries first about the relation between its guiding and given ends, and then between the artful and ethical guiding ends of praxis. If there were a complete identity between artful and ethical guiding ends, then the abilities which comprise the art of rhetoric, and which carve it off from the wider set of powers that could accomplish the given end of persuasion, would simply coincide with what a decent man would do anyway. The good man would not stoop to winning a case by inflaming the passions of his audience. Neither would the artful rhetorician, not because it isn't decent or moral, but because it is not part of the art. The artful rhetorician would forbear to do certain morally objectionable things because doing them would not help to accomplish the internal, guiding end of the art: doing whatever is in one's power to persuade the audience. It is in one's power *qua* man to win by getting the audience angry or impatient, but not within one's power *qua* rhetorician or *qua* man of moral virtue.

But simply to state the identity between moral and artistic constitutive ends, and so moral and artistic restrictions, is to suggest its implausibility. If they were the same, Aristotle could never say: "Such [speakers] are most artful and unjust [*technikotatoi kai adikotatoi*]" (III.15.1416b6–7), a combination of properties which echoes Medea's "Men say we women are most helpless for all good [*amechanotatai*] but of evil most cunning [*kakon panton tektones sophotatai*]." If all ethical standards and constraints were already present as demands and limitations dictated by art, character and nobility would be supererogatory. All we would need would be technical skill in all areas of life, and no one would do anything underhand. The artful rhetorician *qua* rhetorician would respect the audience's autonomy, and no further moral problems would exist.

It is easy to imagine a practical world in which the guiding ends of the arts were sufficient for all the important ends of life, so that there was no central role for further ethical virtues and ends. Technology would replace character; *logos* without *ēthos* would solve all our problems. Morality would come into play only where the result did not matter, a possibility I alluded to in chapter 1. Art and morals, making and doing, would be related as they are in Socrates' refutation of Polemarchus in *Republic* I. There Polemarchus agrees that he would go to an investment counselor if he wanted to make more money, and to a just man if he wanted to keep the money he had, from which it follows that justice is useful only if the thing that justice concerns is useless. There is a clear danger of something like that happening in the relation of art and morals, especially in arts like rhetoric. The ambitious speaker will be guided by success, not moral considerations, except when success is not a factor—as, say, in a hopeless case or one where victory is already a foregone conclusion—and then he can afford the luxury of responding morally.

Therefore there is good reason for Aristotle to stop at the unity of the virtues and not press further to a putative unity of the virtues and the arts. Even in the natural world of the polis, such unity is too much to expect. Today, where we have good reason to doubt the unity of the virtues, these problems about the morality of rhetoric have a greater seriousness than they did for Aristotle.

To repeat: when the rhetorician—like a practitioner of any virtue or art—tries to achieve internal goods, he or she does not stop pursuing external ends. The doctor who understands health as constituted by an internal balance of humors still wants patients to feel better. But when that overall thesis is applied to rhetoric, a surprising conclusion emerges, which makes rhetoric look different from the other arts. Powers like rhetoric and dialectic prove opposites, and powers in general bring about opposite results because they are rational potencies (*dynameis*). "Every rational *dynamis* is capable of causing both contraries, but every irrational potency can cause only one; for example, heat can cause only heating, but doctoring can cause sickness as well as health" (*Metaphysics* IX.2.1046b5–7).[3] Rational potencies are potencies for contrary results. When a doctor poisons someone, we usually blame the doctor, not the art of medicine. But when a lawyer helps a guilty client go free, or when we fall yet again for a politician's tricks, we typically blame rhetoric as well as those particular rhetoricians. I am stirred by someone's arguments against bilingual education, and equally persuaded by the same person's arguments in favor of public support for religious education. When I later become angry that I didn't notice that the two appeals were contradictory, should I only blame the speaker, or may I turn part of my outrage on the art of rhetoric itself? If both are arts, and so rational *dynameis,* why do we respond differently?

I think Aristotle's distinction between internal and external ends, *kinēseis* and *energeiai,* and between rational and irrational *dynameis,* can help us to look on these problems in a new way. Rational powers can bring about contrary effects *because* they are rational. When rhetoric becomes an art with internal, autonomous values, it does not stop being a power which proves opposites. The restriction to artistic proofs is a limitation on *means,* not ends. The restriction of persuasion to argument does not stop rhetoric from proving opposites; it fulfills and completes the ability to prove opposites! There is, then, no reason to think that concentration on the constitutive end of rhetoric will make speakers act more "morally." Art and virtue are distinct masters.

From the outside, confining rhetoric to argument looks like a restriction, and so I considered at the beginning of the chapter the possibility that practicing rhetoric artfully might make the speaker less persuasive than the competition. But the restriction to argument simply displays what is essential to rhetoric as a faculty for proving opposites. Therefore, despite this ethically troubling status, rhetorical activity, *qua* activity—*qua* actualization of such a rational *dynamis*—will be part of the good life, and the good polis. Someone prevented from developing and exercising the capacity for argumentative persuasion would have a part of his or her life unfulfilled. Rhetorical activity, as activity, is in itself valuable because it actualizes essential human powers.

Rhetorical activity, then, is in itself valuable, even if not all its products are desirable. A valuable power that often produces questionable products presents grave ethical problems. But note that that predicament is the opposite of the one with which we started. Rhetoric, and the other arts, initially seemed to be valued only for their results, for achieving their given ends. The arts were not worth having for oneself if one were rich and powerful enough to hire someone else. Now the worries come from rhetorical activity being valued while we have doubts about its products.

Even if rhetorical activity is a part of the good life, then, there is no guarantee that the *products* of that activity will be similarly welcome, and good reason to think that they will not. That lack of guarantee is a fundamental difference between the arts, including rhetoric, and the virtues, including *phronēsis*. The prospect that good activity can have undesirable products is a reason why, for Aristotle, rhetoric can never become *phronēsis*. For this reason, Aristotle says that there is excellence in art, but not in *phronēsis* (*Ethics* VI.5.1140b21–24). There is excellence, and its contrary, in art, because we cannot presume that its products are always excellent. No such separation of activity and product can exist for *phronēsis*. After the constitutive ends of rhetoric are understood, there will still be the need for external regulation of those products and consequences. There is unity to the virtues, but the virtues and the arts do not form a comfortable unity.

In *Ethics* II.6 Aristotle says that a virtue both "causes its possessors to be in a good state and to perform their functions well" (1106a17–18). Such a claim that the thing and its function are both good is trivially true for all irrational *dynameis*. To make something good *qua dynamis* is to make it perform its function well, because that is the good condition of a *dynamis*. You cannot say that my body is healthy but I am unable to perform the functions that healthy bodies exercise (external circumstances apart). My car heater pours out heat, and you can't distinguish its being good from its doing well. But the same claim can be false for rational *dynameis* in general, which is why there is no unity of the arts. My medical power can be in wonderful shape, and I can use it to make a lot of money in cosmetic surgery for movie starts or in degrading or useless medical experiments. I am then not performing the function of medicine well.

My good *dynamis* produces bad *energeiai* because, as Aristotle's distinction between rhetorician and sophist makes clear, I am supplying the wrong *prohairesis*. Rational *dynameis* differ from irrational ones because they need a *prohairesis* to move from potency to act. Since they are indeterminate, the claim from II.6 can be false for the arts, including rhetoric.[4] Possessing the art of rhetoric might "render the thing itself [the power to persuade] good," without causing "it to perform its function well." That is why the fact that rhetoric can be misused seems to pose problems that are not motivated by the parallel fact that courage too often causes trouble. "If a man is foolish or unjust or profligate he would gain no profit from using [things that are truly good], any more than an invalid would benefit from using the diet of a man in good health or a weakling and disabled person from the equipment of a healthy man and of a sound one" (*Eudemian Ethics* VIII.3.1248b31–34).

The situation is the same with dialectic as it is with rhetoric, and the comparison might help. Rhetoric and dialectic are faculties, rational powers for producing opposites. Therefore—and here I want to stress the direction of inference—facility at either, the *energeia* of either *dynamis,* will not, Aristotle says, constitute wisdom. That does not mean that the powers engaged in rhetoric and dialectic are not the same powers when engaged in practical and theoretical wisdom. They are, just as *phronēsis* requires the *dynamis* of cleverness (VI.12.1144a24–31). It does mean, however, that no one is wiser simply by exercising rational faculties (I.2.1356a32–34). Aristotle therefore appeals to the same *topos* of *dynamis* vs. *prohairesis* in the *Metaphysics* to distinguish among sophistic, dialectic, and philosophy:

> Sophistic and dialectic treat the same *genos* as philosophy, but philosophy differs from sophistic by the kind of *dynamis,* and from dialectic in its *prohairesis* of a way of life. Dialectic treats as an exercise what philosophy tries to understand [*gnoristikē*], and sophistic seems to be philosophy, and is not (*Metaphysics* IV.2.1004b23–27; see also *Politics* III.16.1287a33-b3).

The Art and Virtue of Truth-telling

Someone's character determines what he says and does and the way he lives, if he is not acting for an ulterior purpose.
—*Ethics* IV.7.1127a26–27

In explicating the distinction between rhetorician and sophist I want to turn for help to an unlikely parallel in the *Ethics*. Aristotle's claim in the *Rhetoric* is so brief and causal-sounding that turning to other Aristotelian texts makes sense. The passage from the *Ethics* I refer to is not straightforward, and with it I cannot offer any sudden illumination of the *Rhetoric*. Its complications are interesting and relevant, however, in sorting out the relation between faculty and choice, between doing something for its own sake and for a purpose, and, eventually, between rhetoric and sophistic. Turning to the *Ethics* and noting a similar analysis is no way an argument that rhetoric is a virtue, a moral activity, or part of the good life. I am interested instead in the relation between two distinct and possibly competing *energeiai*, rhetorical activity and virtuous activity, and therefore two distinct and possibly competing *dynameis*, the art of rhetoric and the *hexeis* of virtue. In fact, it will turn out that the moral virtues in Aristotle's hands look more like rhetorical and strategic skills than a modern reader might expect, not the other way around. If we judge that Aristotle is wrong to see no problem with the morality of rhetoric, the problem could be with Aristotle's conception of ethics, not rhetoric.

My ethical analogue to the rhetorician/sophist distinction appears in an unlikely place, the description of the boastful man in *Ethics* IV.7. There too Aristotle makes a distinction between *dynamis* and *prohairesis*, in a one-sentence parenthetical explanation: "It is not a person's *dynamis*, but his *prohairesis*, that makes him a boaster [*alazon*]; for this state of character [*hexis*] makes a person a boaster" (1127b14–16; Irwin trans.). Many editors put this sentence in parentheses because it is not clear what it has to do with the rest of the argument. *Aletheia*, truth-telling, truthfulness, or sincerity, as it is sometimes translated, is a virtuous mean between boasting and ironizing self-deprecation. All these kinds of actions "may be done with or without an ulterior purpose [*heneka*]; and someone's character determines what he says and does and the way he lives, if he is not acting for an ulterior purpose" (IV.7.1127a26–27; cf. III.7.1115b18–22). To act with an "ulterior motive" is precisely what the sophist does in acting from *prohairesis* rather than a *dynamis*. Aristotle's evaluations of boasting, truth-telling, and ironizing will, I think, reveal a fair amount about his evaluations of rhetoric and sophistic.[5]

Truth is a good thing, and so truth-telling is a virtue. But truth-telling is not a virtue simply because truth is a good. If truth-telling is a virtue, then the value of the guiding end for the practice of truth-telling is not derivative from the given end, truth. One sign of the complicated relations between given and guiding end here is that the extremes are not vices, as they should be according to the general definition of virtue. If truth is a good, then falsity is bad, and those who choose falsity are vicious: "Falsehood is base and blameworthy, and truth is fine and praiseworthy" (a28–30). Yet boasters and ironizers are not vicious. Telling the truth is good, but its goodness is not self-evident.

Instead, Aristotle has to explain why truth-telling, and truth, are good things. He questions their value, not because he is skeptical that they might not be good, but because the nature of their goodness is not evident. What, in other words, is bad about boasting and ironizing? Are they bad because they misrepresent things, or because they do so for a bad motive? Are liars objectionable, or is it lies? Similarly, is the motive or the truth-telling itself the locus of praise for truth-telling? Do I praise the truth-teller because I value the truth or the telling? Is the locus of evaluation the act, or its motives, or its results? All these questions come up because, although truth-telling is a virtue, the extremes between which it is a mean are not vices.

Aristotle begins his account of truth-telling by excluding truth-telling in business matters or justice, since those are covered by other virtues. The subject here is truthful representation in one's "words and in actions, i.e. in their claims [about themselves] [*en logois kai praxesi kai toi prospoiemati*]" (a20), or, as he puts it at 1127b2, "someone who is truthful both in what he says and in how he lives [*en logoi kai en bioi*]." What is good about the person who faithfully presents himself? What is the real object of condemnation in someone who shows a different face to the world?

Aristotle declares that truthfulness is a virtue because "a lover of the truth who is truthful even when nothing is at stake will be keener to tell the truth when something is at stake [*en hois diapherei*], since he will avoid falsehood as shameful [*aischron*] [when something is at stake] having already avoided it in itself [when nothing was at stake]. And this sort of person is praiseworthy" (1127b5–8).[6] Aristotle then hedges: the sincere man "inclines to tell less, rather than more, than the truth; for this appears more suitable [*emmelesteron*], since excesses are oppressive" (b8–9).

Acting nobly and acting in good taste hardly seem to be the same. At the beginning I announced that my analogy between rhetoric and the virtue of truth-telling was not designed to make rhetoric into a virtue, and warned that the opposite was closer to the mark. Here· truth-telling seems to become a rhetorical, strategic problem rather than one that requires character and acting virtuously for its own sake.

Truth-telling is not the only virtue Aristotle makes into a matter of taste and judgment, rather than finding the mean. In a similar way, the just man will take less than his legal share (V.10.1137b34–1138a3). The just man is not *akribodikaios*. Excessive precision is a character flaw, not just the mistake in argument we are warned against elsewhere in Aristotle.[7] Precision is not a logical property but an ethical one. The overprecise speaker is not persuasive because excessive accuracy is a sign of vice, not virtue. What does it take to be sincere and just? Are these virtues matters of character or taste? Are truth and tact conflicting standards? Both the truthful and the just person, by being ironical and imprecise, seem to be doing something other than what is right.

It is easier to say why boasting is a bad thing than why truth-telling is good, and this discrepancy will become important when we get to the third member of the trio, irony. I have already reported the whole of the little Aristotle had to say about the truth-teller, but the braggart allows more description. There are two possibilities: someone can boast with or without ulterior motive. Someone who, for no particular reason, claims merit he does not possess "appears more foolish than vicious" (*mataios* vs. *kakos*) (1127b11; see the similar remark about the prodigal man at IV.1.1121a26–28, and about the vain and "small-souled man" at IV.3.1125a18–19; cf. *Metaphysics* V.29.1025a1–13).[8]

It is foolish, not vicious, to state what is false for its own sake. Can it be virtuous, rather than smart or tasteful, to tell the truth for its own sake? The man who boasts without further motive is foolish, and that is all Aristotle has to say about him. How much blame accrues to the man who boasts with an ulterior object in view depends not on the falsehood but on that object. Boasting to gain honor is not so bad, but boasting to get money is more unseemly (*aschemonesteros*) (b14), because "honor is the greatest of external goods" (IV.3.1123b20, 1124a17). Those who boast for profit "claim the qualities that gratify other people and that allow someone to avoid detection when he claims to be what he is not, e.g. a wise man (*sophia*) or doctor" (IV.7.1127b19–21; see also *De Sophisticis Elenchis* 11.171b25–35, *Charmides* 173a-d). Rhetoric falls within this class of things that are useful but in which fraud is likely to succeed: the fields of pretense and of bragging (*prospoiountai kai alazoneuontai*) (b21). "Rhetoric assumes the appearance of politics and rhetoricians the appearance of political expertise, some through a lack of education, and others because of boastfulness" (*Rhetoric* I.1.1356a27–30).

Unfortunately, the nobler and more desirable some activity is for its own sake, the harder it is to detect fraud. By this point in our exploration of the *Rhetoric,* we are in a position to see why arts like prophecy, wisdom, and medicine should be both useful and hard for us to evaluate. One would think that Aristotle should say, with Plato, that "in the case of justice and the honourable many would prefer the semblance without the reality in action, possession, and opinion, yet when it comes to the good nobody is content with the possession of the appearance but all men seek the reality, and the semblance satisfies no one here" (*Republic* VI.505d–e see *Theaetetus* 172). Aristotle can say instead that the things we value most are also the easiest to fake because the more an internal end dominates a practice, the less it can be judged by external success, and so the more room for fraud.[9] The arts of prophecy, philosophy, and medicine exemplify this pair of qualities.

The contrast between boasting for an ulterior motive and virtuously telling the truth corresponds to the distinction between the sophist and the rhetorician, the one acting for an external end and the other exercising a *dynamis*. The sophist does not correspond to the foolish man who brags without further purpose but to the one who boasts for money or honor. The first member of each pair—braggart and sophist—has an external object that motivates and explains his actions. The sincere man tells the truth for its own sake—that is what makes him virtuous. The artful rhetorician persuades according to the demands of his art.

In neither of the latter cases does aiming at such an internal, constitutive end preclude having a further end in mind. To act virtuously is not to be a narcissist or aesthete, or to value formal, procedural goods of following rules at the expense of desirable results.[10] The truth-teller does not go up to strangers and list his merits and defects. The artful rhetorician can still try to win his case.

To say that the external end is not of the essence of rhetoric, or of virtue, is not to say that that end is irrelevant. Dialecticians and rhetoricians do not act with no external purpose at all in mind, but the quality of their arguments comes from the faculty of dialectic and rhetoric rather than whatever purpose they have. The sophist acts in accordance with some choice distinct from his rhetorical faculty. Rhetoricians and sophists both have external ends. When Aristotle says that the rhetorician differs from the sophist this way, he is saying that the rhetorician's arguments are answerable to, and should be evaluated according to, standards of the art, while the sophist's appeals are judged by their purpose.

I want to pursue this analogy between rhetorical argument and virtuously telling the truth, and between sophists and boasters, a step further. Identifying what is blameworthy about boasting with the goals one has for boasting suggests that truth-telling is not inherently valuable. At least it shows that truth-telling's intrinsic value is not enough to ground our evaluations of true and false conduct; the value of the guiding ends does not follow from the value of the given end. The boaster is identified by his motive, as the sophist is by the *dynamis/prohairesis* distinction in the *Rhetoric,* but, as in that passage, the truthful man seems identified by his lack of motive, rather than by any particular attachment to the truth or to the noble. In this respect too, truth-telling resembles the virtue of justice; Aristotle initially characterized both by the lack of ulterior motive, and not by any sense of intrinsic value.

That suspicion, that truth and falsity have purely instrumental value and external justification, seems confirmed when Aristotle turns to the ironist. Most other virtues are means between two vicious extremes. Here the one extreme, boasting, is not itself a vice except when impelled by a base motive. The other extreme, irony, is not an object of blame at all. Ironists are more refined (*chariesteroi*) than boasters, because of the motive for their insincerity, which is not gain but dislike of ostentation.

By the time he is done it is unclear whether there are in fact three kinds of character here or only two. Irony and truth-telling collapse into a single virtue, because irony is a virtuous way of telling the truth. That lack of clarity is captured in the summary at the end of the chapter: "It is the boaster who appears to be opposed to the truthful person, because he is the worse [*antikeisthai ho alazon phainetai toi aletheutikoi. keiron gar*]" (1127b33–34). Everything turns on what it is worse than, but the structure and position of the sentence suggest that boasting is simply worse than the (single) alternative. If boasting has only one opposite, then truth-telling and ironizing are the same.[11]

There is an ironic vice, but that vice has to do with disavowing trivial qualities. Such self-denial, Aristotle says, is really a kind of boasting. Denying esteemed qualities, as Socrates does, is graceful (*charotenēs*) (1127b31). To pursue the analogy between the virtues of truth-telling and justice, Aristotle initially posits a distinction between legal justice and equity, but once the just man is characterized as taking less than he legally could, the equitable becomes the just, and mere legal justice, like telling some previously defined truth, is no longer a mark of virtue. From being an exceptional phenomenon, at play only when legal justice breaks down, equity becomes the norm. Here too a virtue is first defined by the external goods it achieves or preserves, and then becomes the measure of those goods. The constitutive end takes over from the external end. That does not happen with most of the other moral virtues, and therefore the extremes between which they fall are vices.

We can now fill in a little of what Aristotle means when he says, "when a man is acting without further purpose, his words, actions, and conduct always represent who he is" (IV.7.1127a26–27). Truth-telling is not a matter of transparency or accuracy of representation of thoughts in words but of appropriate self-presentation, finding the right amount to put forward about oneself in the circumstances. Even though the extremes are not vices, the virtue is still a habit of choosing a mean.

For that reason, Aristotle begins the ethical treatment of truth-telling by talking about virtue and achieving an external goal, but he ends by talking about tact, taste, and refinement. If truth-telling were an openness that let others see the truth about oneself, then it would be impossible to be artfully sincere, and the rhetorician would be faced with a series of choices between truth and accommodation to audience. Once truth-telling and ironizing are assimilated, the possibility for artful yet truthful self-representation becomes a live one.[12] To act artfully and to act virtuously need not be alternatives. These two *dynameis,* the art of rhetoric and the virtue of telling the truth, can issue in a single *energeia*. Technique and *ēthos,* not just artful *ēthos* defined within the act of persuasion, but real *ēthos,* can coexist.

Increasingly, it looks as though truth-telling is not a virtue but a rhetorical skill. How one can artfully show oneself and actually *be* ethical and truthful is one of the central issues in my analysis of the *Rhetoric*. Here we see that the issue is not unique to rhetoric but extends to the moral virtues.

People are suspicious of rhetoric because they think that art and truth are fundamentally incompatible. Indeed when the internal end becomes dominant, what by other standards could be called "truth" may be sacrificed to art. But not only is that not vicious for Aristotle, it is virtuous.

The assimilation of truth and irony makes this virtue unusual for the *Ethics,* because when Aristotle is done there is no longer a difference between a mean and one of its extremes: we are left with the alternatives of boasting and something called either truthfulness or irony. Although unusual, it is the product of a kind of argument that Aristotle uses in his treatment of all the virtues. The internal end gradually emerges as authoritative. Courage, for example, is the ability cheerfully to withstand fear in battle, to stand rather than flee. But staying to fight is not the measure of courage; by the end of Aristotle's argument, the courageous man is the measure of whether someone should fight or flee. In chapter 1, I suggested that the existence of internal ends allows the doctor to tell the patient, "You may think that you're healthy, but you're not," and wondered whether that could extend to rhetoric: could the rhetorician say to an audience, "You may think my opponent was more convincing, but really, I had the more persuasive argument." Wherever there is a internal end, whether in the arts or the virtues, such possibilities for conflict exist. The courageous man can say, "You, the noncourageous observer, might think that the person who always fights and never runs is more courageous than I; but in fact he's foolhardy to stay in these circumstances. It is right to run."

For that reason, as I noted in the last chapter, the treatment of courage ends on the note that "it is quite possible for brave people not to be the best soldiers. Perhaps the best will be those who are less brave, but possess no other good; for they are ready to face dangers, and they sell their lives for small gains" (III.9.1117b17–21). (Similarly, the liberal man is easy to cheat, so he is not the most successful person in financial matters. IV.1.1121a4–5, 1120a14–20.) There is a discrepancy between courage's external, given end of military victory and its constitutive end of mastering fears. There is nothing unique to rhetoric in the prospect I noted in the beginning of the chapter, that the sophist might beat the rhetorician. In the first chapter, I noted that difference between the courage required for fighting foreign and for fighting civil wars, and said that in the first case, where the external goal was all, the professional, or, in the lines I just quoted, the man who has nothing to lose, might be preferable, but in truly civic activities, we need virtues, because we are aiming at an internal, constitutive end.

Consequently, internal and external ends provide distinct standards of evaluation for both the virtues and for rhetoric. It is better to *be* courageous than to be someone who risks his life because he has little to lose. But although I would rather be courageous, I might prefer to be protected by soldiers of the latter kind. Similarly, the just man will take less than he can claim, and so although I would like to *be* just, justice might not figure in my job description for a tax accountant.

The analogy to rhetoric is obvious. I would rather *be* the artful rhetorician who persuades through the exercise of practical intelligence, but I might choose to hire a trial lawyer of the other kind. Aristotle is untroubled by the prospect of hiring others to do something it would be ignoble to do oneself. There is nothing in Aristotle approaching the doctrine that if one wills the end one must also will the means. If I need something done, and if doing it is ignoble, I should simply get someone else to do it for me. There's nothing ignoble in that. Nobility and slavishness are not transitive properties (see *Politics* III.2.1277b3–7).

Such a divergence between points of view shows a discrepancy between and internal and external ends characteristic of all true practices, whether virtuous or artful. It sets peculiar problems for the legislator, to whom Aristotle assigns the job of making the decisions we attribute to moral judgment. To make citizens virtuous is to teach them to concentrate on the internal goods of practices, but such concentration cannot be to the full exclusion of external goods. Legislators have to be concerned that the external and internal ends do not diverge too much. Otherwise, courage, liberality, and artful rhetoric no longer have practical value. When all wars are foreign wars, when law is transformed from being reason without desire into a series of commercial treaties, when success is all, there are no longer any civic activities, and no longer any polis.

At the beginning of the discussion of truth-telling, virtue looked easy. It simply depended on the absence of a base motive. When virtue becomes the measure of how much of the given goal we should aim for, the virtue of truthfulness determines how much truth to tell, and how we should present ourselves. Virtue is no longer just a matter of avoiding ulterior motives, but of intelligently and sensitively figuring out what to say and do. Once again, there is a parallel between truth and justice:

> Since human beings think that doing injustice is up to them, they think that being just is also easy, when in fact it is not. . . . Knowing how actions must be done, and how distributions must be made, if they are to be just, takes more work than it takes to know about healthy things (V.9.1137a5–13).

Similarly, rhetoric, a *dynamis,* or art, has its own standards for goodness not reducible to success, or to some antecedent standards of good behavior. There is more to being a good rhetorician than refraining from sophistic tricks. From the outside—and that is the point of view I might adopt in hiring someone to argue for me—virtue and the art of rhetoric are both systems of restraints by internal standards. From the outside, the sign of the sophist is his *prohairesis.* The *energeiai* of rational *dynameis* need additional determination from *prohairesis*. Rational *dynameis* are not self-actualizing; the sophist's powers are for sale, which shows that his *dynamis* and what he does with it are independent. That is why, as Socrates noted in his challenge to Protagoras, the ability to teach is the mark of other forms of knowledge, but the offer to teach is here grounds for suspicion (see *Ethics* X.9.1180b33–1181a3).

From the inside, the essence of artful rhetoric is not its lack of such motive, but the presence of a subject matter and internal end for art, namely the enthymeme. From the outside, the audience is the measure of successful rhetoric; from the inside, the art of rhetoric can criticize the judgments of the audience, just as the courageous man can look down on the fellow who is willing to risk his life because it isn't worth much. In the case of irony, from the outside there are three states of the soul, from the inside only two. From the outside, it looks as though justice is a mean between taking too much and too little of good things; from the inside, the just man takes less than he could, and becomes the measure of what things are good. From the outside, artful rhetoric, truth-telling, and justice are all characterized by the absence of motive. From within, it is the dominance of the internal end.

The argument in both the *Ethics* and the *Rhetoric* moves from outside to inside, as Aristotle discloses the true nature of art and virtue, moving, as he characterizes scientific inquiry, from things better known by us to things better known in nature (e.g., *Posterior Analytics* I.2.71b33–72a5; *Ethics* I.3.1095a31–b4, I.7.1098a34–b8, VII.1.1145b1–7). "To the same persons different things are more intelligible at different times—first of all the objects of sense-perception, and then, when their knowledge becomes more accurate, the converse occurs" (*Topics* VI.4.142a1–3). From the outside point of view, virtue is a mean located by its intermediate position between extremes; this is what Aristotle calls natural virtue. It is not hard to be good. From the inside, where natural virtue is replaced by a virtue informed by *phronēsis*, the right state of character is what we use to define the extremes. Virtue now is difficult, and praiseworthy.

The Moral Point of View and the Rhetorical Point of View

PROTARCHUS: *Gorgias regularly said, Socrates, that the art of persuasion was greatly superior to all others, for it subjugated all things not by violence but by willing submission.*

—*Philebus*, 58a

So far, I think I have softened the charges of immorality concerning rhetoric, by showing how analogous problems exist within the moral virtues themselves. But that is not enough. What does any of this have to do with distinguishing the rhetorician from the sophist, which I promised it would, and with the difference between Aristotle's rhetoric and an art of deception? Are we now in any better position to respond to the charge that the artful rhetorician hasn't a chance against the clever sophist?

If the difference is not one of art but motive, then there are no aspects of the art that cannot be used sophistically for external purposes. There is no distinction between rhetoric and sophistic, only between the rhetorician and the sophist. Everything the rhetorician does artfully, the sophist can also use for ulterior motives. There is no art of sophistic, only a sophistic use of the art of rhetoric. "Only one of a pair of contraries is needed to discern both itself and its opposite. For instance, by that which is straight we discern both straight and crooked; for the carpenter's rule is the test of both, but the crooked tests neither itself nor the straight" (*De Anima* I.5.411a3–7). Everything, all the arts and virtues, can be done for some external purpose. There is nothing unique to rhetoric in that. Men interested in excessive enjoyment, he tells us, "use every ability [*dynamis*] in a way not consonant with its nature. The function of courage is not to produce money but confidence; neither is this the aim of the military or medical art; the one has the function of producing victory, the other that of producing health. But they turn all such capacities into forms of the art of acquisition" (*Politics* I.9.1258a10–14).

In any given case there are some things that the sophist will do and the rhetorician will not. But these particular acts of restraint on the part of the artful rhetorician do not add up to a pattern of restrictions. The same things that only a sophist would do in one case can fall within the art of rhetoric on a different occasion: "Vote for me and I'll make you rich" can be either a rational appeal to self-interest or a bribe. As we have seen, the same emotions that Aristotle says in *Rhetoric* I.1 should be excluded from rhetoric by good laws are the emotions treated in Book II, and there is no simple demarcation between real and apparent enthymemes.

The sophists, at least when they are selling their talents, claim that they have an esoteric set of techniques to teach, but they are wrong. That is false advertising. What ability they have is parasitic on the actual art of persuasion analyzed in *Rhetoric*. There is no art of poisoning; it is just an abuse of the art of healing.

There are only two places in the entire corpus where Aristotle claims originality. He states at the beginning of the *Rhetoric* that this is the first rhetoric to focus attention on the enthymeme, and he ends the *Organon* by claiming to be the first to isolate the syllogism. Both rhetoric and logic are universal faculties and common *tropoi*, not specialized sciences. In these faculties, there is no gradual scientific development; there is simply the isolation of an artistic object and artistic end. The sciences have histories, and Aristotle uses dialectic to explore those histories in the first books of the *Physics, De Anima,* and the *Metaphysics,* as well as in *Politics* II. There is nothing parallel for rhetoric or dialectic. The sophists and their professional art of rhetoric ignore this *koinon tropon* and pretend instead to develop an esoteric art. By claiming to be the first to make the enthymeme central to rhetoric, Aristotle is not simply saying that he is establishing a new rhetoric alongside the competition. He claims to be the first to analyze rhetoric at all. It is not a novel presentation of a new, esoteric art. It is a novel presentation of an art everyone practices. There is nothing only an artful rhetorician can do and nothing the artful rhetorician would never do.

Once Aristotle has constructed an art of rhetoric, he can say that to the extent that sophists are successful, they are practicing, and abusing, the art of rhetoric, not practicing a separate art of their own. Since they are practicing rhetoric only accidentally—since they have no clear conception of it, and especially of its end—they are not likely to do it very well. Aristotle sees no threat in the sophists and the rhetoricians the way Socrates does. He does not need to promise that his own art will improve practice. The so-called arts of rhetoric produced by the sophists are not in Aristotle's eyes so much immoral as intellectually vacuous.[13]

But intellectual vacuity does not prevent the sophists from being practically powerful. In any given case, the sophist has things as his disposal that the rhetorician does not. Overall, however, the rhetorician has something the sophist lacks. From an external point of view, the art of rhetoric seems to put the rhetorician at a disadvantage, arguing with one hand tied behind his back. The surprising lesson of the *Rhetoric* is that that point of view has it backwards, in the case of rhetoric just as in the case of the virtues, especially the virtues of my examples, truth-telling and justice. Rhetorician and sophist both aim at the given end of rhetoric, persuading an audience. The sophist aims at nothing but that given end, while the rhetorician in addition aims at the artful end, finding in each case the available means of persuasion. Instead of the image of arguing with one hand tied behind one's back, I suggest a different picture. In the first chapter I used geometric proof as my paradigm for argument as *energeia.* I remember the feeling of arbitrary constraints in beginning geometry, where I was told that only straightedge and compass were permitted in constructions, not rulers and protractors. There were, I quickly learned, some things I wanted to do which I couldn't do under the rules such as to trisect an angle. Learning geometry is learning that the limitation to straightedge and compass is not an arbitrary and perverse restriction but a limitation partly constitutive of geometry. The art of rhetoric offers a similar kind of restriction. That is why, even if sometimes I choose to hire a sophistical lawyer, and even vote for sophistical politicians, I would rather not be one, preferring to be an artful rhetorician instead.

Just as the courageous man aims not only at military victory but at being a certain kind of person, and as the truthful man possesses not only the given goal of telling the truth but the constitutive goal of presenting himself well, the artful rhetorician will aim at persuasion by aiming at finding in a given case the available means of persuasion. Aristotle's insight, in both the *Rhetoric* and the *Ethics,* is that the constitutive end of these practices guides and *perfects* the achievement of the initially given end by offering a guiding end whose achievement is within the agent's power and which comprises— on the whole although not in each individual case—doing what is within one's power to persuade. The rhetorician *qua* rhetorician is in each instance constrained by his art or *dynamis,* because someone can always point to some sophistic trick he isn't considering. In good states, much of that constraint is institutionalized by good laws. It is a sign, then, that someone is persuading rhetorically when there are things he could but will not do. (The doctor sees more opportunities for killing than I do.) But such a sign is no more the essence of the rhetorical art than morality's struggle against inclination is its essence in Kant. There, struggle against inclination is a good sign of morality, but it would be a mistake to define morality by the struggle. Similarly, it would be a mistake to define rhetoric by the sophistic things it will not stoop to.

It is wrong to think that the rhetorician selects from among all the things that the sophist does those appeals that are admissible by his own standards of art. It looks that way to the sophist, no doubt. In fact, because of his own artful, constitutive end, the rhetorician has things to think about that the sophist does not. Specifically, he thinks about rhetorical argument. Consequently the "arts" of the sophists are pretty meager affairs which Aristotle can describe, consistent with this line of argument, as the presentation of a collection of products, rather than any actual art:

> Of this inquiry, it was not the case that part of the work has been thoroughly done before, while part has not. Nothing existed at all. For the training given by the paid professors of contentious argument was like the treatment of the matter by Gorgias. For they used to hand out speeches to be learned by heart, some rhetorical, others in the form of question and answer. . . . Therefore the teaching they gave their pupils was ready but rough. For they used to suppose that they trained people by imparting to them not the art but its product, as though any one professing that he should impart a form of knowledge to obviate any pain in the feet, were

then not to teach a man the art of shoe-making or the sources whence he can acquire anything of the kind, but were to present him with several kinds of shoes of all sorts; for he has helped him to meet his need, but has not imparted an art (*De Sophisticis Elenchis* 34.183b37–184a7).

As I showed in the last chapter, lack of art and lack of attention to argument go together. The claim that earlier writers on rhetoric neglected argument could be true on one condition: that it is possible to engage in rhetorical *argument* only if one is aiming at artful persuasion instead of persuasion over-all. Aristotle says that "proofs are the only things in rhetoric that come within the province of art," and I am claiming the converse, that proofs *only* come about artistically. Aiming directly at the external end, persuasion, is incompatible with arguing because the only direct relation a speaker can have with the external end, persuasion, is that of productive, efficient cause to effect.[14] To be a sophist is to be governed by *prohairesis* rather than the rhetorical *dynamis,* and that precludes argument in favor of moving the mind of the audience instead. Only the rhetorician can argue, just as only the geometer, not the empirical craftsman who will rely on any tool that will work, can prove anything.

The *Ethics'* discussion of truth-telling is, again, apposite, here to the question of who has the advantage, rhetorician or sophist. Telling the truth for its own sake is virtuous. When Aristotle begins talking about that virtue, he speaks as though there are psychic qualities each of us possesses, and sincerity consists in matching one's words and deeds to those qualities. If so, all it would take for sincerity is the absence of an effective motive to do otherwise. Virtue is easy: "anyone who is not deformed [in his capacity] for virtue will be able to achieve happiness through some sort of learning and attention" (I.9.1099b18–20; cf. I.2.1095b7; *Prior Analytics* I.30.46a17). Similarly, it is easy to distinguish sophist from rhetorician and truth from false-hood (*Rhetoric* I.1.1355a17, a31; see also *Topics* I.1.100b29–101a1: "Usually the nature of untruth in eristic arguments is immediately obvious to those who have even a small power of comprehension"). By the end of *Ethics* IV.7, when irony and sincerity are assimilated, he is denying a distinction between personal qualities and their expression. Initially, a preexistent truth—a correspondence between quality and expression—is the measure of virtue, but once the virtuous character is articulated, character becomes the measure of truth. Shaping one's self-presentation is truthful to oneself in relation to circumstances, including the circumstances of other people and their expectations. "The *lexis* will be appropriate if it expresses emotion and character and is proportional to the subject matter" (*Rhetoric*

III.7.1408a10–11). In that case, the virtuous man can see that there are on occasion better modes of self-presentation than what from the outside looks like truth. There are alternatives to truth-telling other than lying, such as reticence. The virtuous man will, of course, never be vicious, but he will do things that others may regard as vicious.

I have developed an analogy between the virtue of irony and the art of rhetoric, and have tried to avoid assimilating them. Without using the parallel to irony to claim that rhetoric is a virtue, I have been pointing to a parallel structure in their arguments. The movement from the prephilosophic understanding of irony as a vice to the philosophic conception in which irony and sincerity are indistinguishable is a microcosm of the argument of the *Rhetoric*. Artful rhetoric is artful. As with irony—and this is the reason I have used irony as the point of comparison—rhetoric's art is sometimes a decorous and tactful presentation; at other times it has an ulterior motive, and then the packaging becomes disguise. If Aristotle's *virtues* can look morally ambiguous, it is all the more likely that his arts, especially the art of rhetoric, will be morally ambiguous too.

The Moral Ambiguity of Rhetoric, and the Moral Ambiguity of Morality

Anyone who feels moral discomfort with the *Rhetoric* should be equally troubled by Aristotle's other writing. The *Topics,* far more than the *Rhetoric,* contains advice about how to win that seems unconnected to the higher motives of dialectic, and the *Politics* is full of practical maxims aimed at success rather than achieving a fuller embodiment of justice. Part of the discomfort readers experience with the *Rhetoric* comes from failing to see how wide most of its difficulties spread, and how little is specific to rhetoric.

I want to make thing still worse by juxtaposing two more passages, one from the *Ethics,* in the discussion of magnanimity and the other from the account of anger in the *Rhetoric.* Irony turns up in both. The great-souled man has all the virtues, knows that he has them, and acts, in Aristotle's eyes, accordingly.

> He must be open in his hatreds and his friendships [*phaneromise kai phanerophilon*], since concealment is proper to a frightened person. He is concerned for the truth more than for people's opinion. He is open [*phaneros*] in his speech and actions, since his disdain [*kataphronetikon*] makes him speak freely. And he speaks the truth,

except when he speaks ironically to the many, [because he is moderate], not because he is self-deprecating (IV.3.1124b27–31; see also 1125a9 [where he is seen committing acts of *hybris*]).

Here it is the same lack of motive that characterized the truthful and ironic man in IV.7 that is again the mark of a virtue of openness. The only difference is that openness comes not from no motive at all but from the absence of a specific motive, namely, fear. Truth and irony are not different conditions of the soul, but different manifestations of the single virtue of magnanimity in different circumstances. All that is of a piece with the earlier discussion of truth-telling. But one of the properties of people at whom we are angry, he notes in the *Rhetoric,* is that they use irony "when we ourselves are serious, for irony is contemptuous" (II.2.1379b25). Irony is offensive not because it dissimulates some truth, as boasting does, it is offensive because it discloses. It looks as though we are supposed to be aware of our superiority, but not display the awareness. That's what happens when internal and external standards of success diverge.

By making truthfulness into a *virtue,* rather than the *product* of the ideal communicative situation, Aristotle highlights the double nature of irony as both decency and deception, and the double nature of truth both as disclosure and as appropriate statement. Irony is one particular manifestation of the double nature of rhetorical accommodation to circumstances, where— throughout the history of rhetoric—accommodation is either a compromise of one's ideals and standards with necessity, or a way of making one's purposes real and effective. That double nature is symptomatic of Aristotle's overall project: everything, he says (e.g., *Politics* I.9.1257a8), has a double nature, and can be used either in accordance with its function or as an exchangeable good, commensurate with everything else (*Nicomachean Ethics* I.3.1094b18–19; *Eudemian Ethics* VIII.1.1246a26–35; *Politics* I.3.1258a6– 14). Rhetoric is no exception: as a faculty, or art, it has a function, but it can also be used, bought and sold, rented and hired. Persuasive activities can be the actualization of the *dynamis* of rhetoric, or can spring from an ulterior motive. All the techniques of the art of rhetoric can be used in order to win a debate, as well as to fulfill the function of the art. Consequently, the same technique will sometimes be displayed, and recommended, as part of the good functioning of the art in the *Rhetoric,* yet can, in another passage, be condemned and excused as simply trying to win at all costs. In the one case, it is the *dynamis* of rhetoric that is the basis of evaluation, in the other, the agent's *prohairesis.*

All the ambiguities and puzzles about the morality of rhetoric come from the relation Aristotle constructs between these internal and external ends for the virtues and the arts. To show they all have the same root, however, does not in any way solve the problems. It only lets us ask them in Aristotelian language and so avoid begging questions. I have framed the distinction between rhetoric and sophistic as the difference between an internal and an external principle of action. Earlier I noted that Aristotle says there is excellence in art but not in *phronēsis* (*Ethics* VI.5.1140b21–24). From that Aristotle infers that "in *technē* voluntary error [*hamartia*] is not so bad as involuntary, whereas in the sphere of *phronēsis* it is worse, as it is in the sphere of the virtues" (see *Metaphysics* V.29.1052a10–13). Because he sees these problems as questions of adjustment either between internal and external end, or between competing candidates for internal end, he can address the problems without moralizing them. He does not attend to this kind of problem in the *Rhetoric*, but he does devote *Poetics* 25 to questions of this kind. I want to end this chapter by quoting at some length from that chapter, since it is the fullest treatment Aristotle offers of these questions:

> The standard of what is correct [*orthotēs*] is not the same in poetry as it is in politics or any other art. In poetry itself [*autēs*] there are two kinds of errors [*hamartia*], essential and accidental [*kath' autēn, kata symbebekos*]. If a man meant to represent something and failed through incapacity [*adynanamian*], that is an error within the art. But if his error is due to his original conception being wrong and his portraying, for example, a horse advancing both its right legs, then that is a technical error in some special branch of knowledge. . . . Or else some sort of impossibility has been portrayed, but that is not an essential error either.
>
>   Let us first take the charges against the art of poetry itself. If an impossibility has been portrayed, an error has been made. But it is right [*orthos*] if the poet thus achieves the object [*telos*] of poetry. . . . If the object could have been achieved better or just as well by artistic resources and the art itself, then it is not right [*orthos*] (1460b13–28).

And most apposite for our purposes:

> Any impossibility may be defended by reference to the poetic effect [*pros tēn poiesin*] or what is better [*pros to beltion*] or to current opinion [*pros tēn doxan*]. For poetic effect a convincing impossibility [*pithanon adynaton*] is preferable to that which is unconvincing though possible [*apithanon kai dynaton*] (1461b9–12; see also *Ethics* II.6.1106b14–15: "Virtue, like nature, is more accurate and better than art.").

Intentional error is possible and justifiable in art because there is a difference between an art's powers and ends and an artist's powers and ends: one can violate the internal demands of art for the sake of the further end. Art does not deliberate (*Physics* II.8.199b26). Since there is no such further end in *phronēsis*, there can be no justification, and so no voluntary error. Chapter 25 of the *Poetics* therefore is a series of instructions on how to uphold in argument internal values against accusations against a poem for violating external standards. The possibility of intentional error is just what prevents reducing ethical virtue or *phronēsis* to knowledge or craft (cf. *Eudemian Ethics* VIII.1.1246a32–46b4). And, therefore, intentional error is legitimate in art but not in *phronēsis* because an art itself does not have to take all facets of the concrete individual into account, whereas *phronēsis* always does (e.g., *Metaphysics* I.1.988a13–24).[15] All along I have been claiming that the *logoi* of the *phronimos* and of rhetorical argument must be *logoi enhyloi;* another way of putting that is to say that these *logoi* have a different sort of relation to particulars than the *logoi* of the crafts, one in which authority is divided between the *logoi* and particulars. That is why there can be no *technē* for *phronēsis,* and why the idea of a *technē* for rhetoric must be so paradoxical.

There are no absolute moral rules in Aristotle (apart from a few categorical prohibitions such as that against adultery, which are not part of Aristotle's theories but marginal background for them). Irony done to deceive is illiberal and corrupt, but irony can not only conceal the truth but advance it. The internal standards of rhetoric *qua* art are not moral standards. Whether the goods of art and the internal goods of morality coincide, or even overlap significantly, is a political question concerning the place of rhetorical activity in the community. Indeed I claimed in the first chapter that it is *the* political question which makes the legislator turn to the *Rhetoric.*

In distinguishing rhetorician from sophist by drawing attention first to the *dynamis* and then to the *prohairesis,* Aristotle places the blame for unscrupulous argument on the speakers, and not on the art. The distinction between internal and external ends earns Aristotle the right to claim on a principled basis something analogous to "Guns don't kill people; people kill people" (see *Gorgias* 456c–457b). There is no ethics of rhetoric, there is only an ethics of rhetoricians, and that is just ethics itself.

The distinction between the rhetorician and the sophist helps us to make a further stab at my running example of the advocate of public aid for religious schools who also opposes bilingual education. I have tried to show that that pair of arguments cannot just be dismissed as inconsistent, because rhetoric provides resources for arguing for opposites, and otherwise confronting shifting particulars. A person of integrity, someone with *aretē, phronēsis,* and *eunoia,* can well argue for both these policies. The kinds of rhetoric, the various forms of topical argumentation, and legitimate appeals to emotions all make it possible to be against bilingual education yet in favor of public support for religious education.

But of course many people without *aretē, phronēsis,* and *eunoia* have more interested, less principled, grounds for the same stance. They do not see themselves as benefiting from bilingual education but as directly profiting from public financial aid for parochial education. They do not want policies to help others but wish to support policies that help them. There is nothing immoral in promoting policies from which one will benefit. And there is nothing inherently wrong with the arguments they might use. There *is* something wrong, however, with the combination of motive and argument.

People who think that way may have a vision of what education should look like, and they may use whatever arguments they can to advance that vision. The arguments are just weapons.[16] Their arguments can be principled in the sense that they are rationally defensible, and the people can be principled in the sense that their policy preferences spring from deeply held convictions that are themselves worthy of respect, but their use of arguments is not principled. Arguing from utility constitutes defensible grounds for making a decision on policy, but apparently they think that such calculations of utility require coloring in the language of high principles of justice and freedom, and of American history and values. They don't want to be seen to claim that "my desires count, yours don't."

That resolution, that arguments can be principled, even when arguers are not, echoes Aristotle's distinguishing not the art of rhetoric from sophistic, but the rhetorician from the sophist. It is also meant to signal something of the difficulty and delicacy of the issues here. Rarely are there debate-closing arguments concerning the question of whether a given argument is special pleading or not.

The distinction between *dynamis* and *prohairesis* that Aristotle casually uses to distinguish the rhetorician and the sophist is just what distinguishes civic from professional activities in general, and civic from professional rhetoric in particular. Aristotle's question throughout the *Rhetoric* concerns what a civic art of rhetoric would look like, where "civic" means in the first instance fit for citizens as civic activity. It is this interest in articulating a civic art of rhetoric that accounts for the ease with which Aristotle dismisses sophists and the dangers of deception.

In the first chapter, I stressed the way issues that do not seem to trouble Aristotle become fundamental for us today, and explained that shift by the way Aristotle's inquiry depends for its coherence on the naturalness of the polis, which frequently offers middle terms and connections that are not available to us. Within the natural context supplied by the polis, there is no need to worry whether good audiences will see the true and the false for what they are, and will prefer truth. Outside the polis, such confidence might have to be replaced by inquiry. Along similar lines, the question of whether artful and moral *energeiai* (and consequently, the restrictions pertaining to each) coincide seems to me yet another question whose answer depends on circumstances and context. The relation between the internal, autonomous values of a particular artistic activity and the internal or autonomous values of ethics and politics depends on the place of a particular art, and of both its given and guiding ends, in the moral and political whole.

Therefore a single art, such as rhetoric, can generate radically different answers to the question of whether artistic and moral restrictions coincide, when that single art is practiced in different political circumstances. But that is the question that generates most of the worries about the morality of rhetoric. If Plato seems much more than Aristotle to share our concerns about the morality of rhetoric, it is because he stands with us in not sharing Aristotle's premises about the naturalness of the polis.

In the final chapter I want to look more closely at how we can read, and use, the *Rhetoric* in circumstances different from those of the polis. The last thing we need today is another book that shows us how badly we live, and how much better the Greeks did. I think that the bearing of the *Rhetoric* on our own problems is more subtle than that. The *Rhetoric* offers an organon, a set of resources and insights, through which we can approach current problems. Each point at which what is natural for Aristotle looks contingent or questionable for us is a crucial point for self-criticism. More than that, however, the *Rhetoric* also offers a picture of a coherent whole, an art of rhetoric which has rich, complicated, yet stable relations to logic and to the ethical side of politics.

ARISTOTLE'S *RHETORIC* AND
THE HISTORY OF PRUDENCE

If theory can transform practice, then it can be tested in the quality of the practice it informs. What makes a theory right is that it brings practice out in the clear; that its adoption makes possible what is in some sense a more effective practice.
—Charles Taylor, "Social Theory as Practice," 104

The good practical use of reason has a history, which I want to call the history of prudence. Aristotle's formulation of the intellectual virtue called *phronēsis* is one especially important event in that history, important both for its own intellectual richness and for the ways it helped set a direction for the rest of the history of prudence. While the influence of the *Rhetoric* on the subsequent understandings of *phronēsis* has been negligible, I offer it here as a resource for better understanding Aristotle's conception of *phronēsis* and the history of prudence more generally. It can make a major contribution to our understanding of the history of prudence, even if its participation in that history has been minimal. I think that this history of prudence constructs a usable past, so that the *Rhetoric* becomes a resource for helping us to understand what practical wisdom could look like for us today.

That the good practical use of reason has a history is not, I think, self-evident. Some might think instead that the good practical use of reason stays constant over time, and others could argue that the changes in what counts as good uses of practical reason have no intelligible pattern of development. Here I have not traced prudence's progress, but I have tried to historicize the *Rhetoric* by placing it in the context in which it is intelligible. I see this project as a contribution to what Dewey meant by "reconstruction in philosophy." He repeatedly historicized logic and scientific method. He argued that as the materials and instrumentalities of reasoning changed, so must reasoning's methods. There can be no eternal organon. Logic has a history.[1] Practical reason and practical wisdom have a history too, a claim that is as far from obvious as the thesis that logic has a history. As the materials and instrumentalities of practical reason change, so must its methods and its standards. Prudence has a history in which the relation between *phronēsis* and rhetoric is a central theme because *phronēsis* alternately defines itself in contrast to *technē* and to the ethical virtues. If I have shown a connection between rhetoric, via *phronēsis*, to the human good and the human function, then these things too, contrary to Aristotle's own designs, have a history.

I have consequently stressed the way my inquiry differs from Aristotle's own enterprise in the *Rhetoric*. The polis is natural, and rhetoric consequently occupies a reasonably stable and unproblematic place in civic life. For us, there is no polis; our lives are therefore in Aristotle's eyes unnatural, and we have no grounds to be confident that rhetoric could occupy a safe place in what passes for civic life today. Without a polis, we have to reformulate the relations between theory and practice and between intelligence, craft, and character. Therefore *phronēsis* has to be something different for us than it was for Aristotle. For that reason, the *Rhetoric* is of greater philosophical interest today than it was for Aristotle. Its very lack of fit makes it all the more illuminating for what *phronēsis* was and what contemporary *phronēsis* might be.

Where Aristotle saw nature, I see, and have indicated, contingencies of connection between internal and external end, between internal artful end and internal ethical ends, between rhetorical functioning and political function. The points of contingency I have stressed can become topics for political criticism. That is a use of rhetoric in the reconstitution of practical reason and *phronēsis*. In particular, I have stressed the way the *Rhetoric* offers resources for arguing about plural, conflicting, and incommensurable choices and goods. For Aristotle, the power to prove opposites was not of major ethical significance because rhetoric was subordinate to politics. For us, that same power is ethically fundamental, because the argumentative facility of rhetoric has no politics to be subordinate to.

Phronēsis today must be simultaneously less political and more historical than it could have been for Aristotle. It is less political because, to repeat, there is no politics in Aristotle's sense for rhetoric to be subordinate to. It is more historical because contemporary *phronēsis* has to function within an expanded range of possibilities that are not tied to any given stable practical situation. That is, whatever *phronēsis* can mean today, it will not be, as it was for Aristotle, only the *orthos logos* of the ethical virtues. The more *phronēsis* is detached from the moral virtues, the more difficult it is to distinguish it from *technē*.[2] We might admire Aristotle's integration of *logos* and *ēthos*, but it may not be a real possibility for us.

When *phronēsis* becomes so difficult to distinguish from *technē*, two possibilities emerge. The art of rhetoric and *phronēsis* might, first, be even further apart today than they were for Aristotle. Discursive power is even less reliable as a sign of *phronēsis*. Rhetorical power has to be reined in more than ever. Or, they might instead grow closer together—cleverness may be just what good decisions need. It is out of free debate that truth can emerge. We mistrust cleverness only because we think there should be something more. That both these possibilities seem, prior to inquiry, equally likely is good reason for the instability and ambivalence with which we regard the relation between rhetoric and prudence.

I want to turn in this conclusion to Charles Taylor's article, "Social Theory as Practice," to help show the role of rhetoric in the history of prudence. Taylor, as the epigraph for this chapter shows, is quite careful in the benefits he promises for good social theory. A theory will make practice "in some sense more effective." A more extended quotation from that article is apposite:

> I want to argue that to have a better theoretical self-definition is to understand better what we are doing; and this means that our action can be somewhat freer of the stumbling, self-defeating character which previously afflicted it. Our action becomes less haphazard and contradictory, less prone to produce what we did not want at all. In sum, I want to say that, because theories which are about practices are self-definitions, and hence alter the practices, the proof of the validity of a theory can come in the changed quality of the practice it enables. Let me introduce terms of art for this shift of quality, and say that good theory enables practice to become less stumbling and more clairvoyant (p. 111).

Good theory does not necessarily improve practice, since laying bare a structure does not necessarily make that structure more accessible to manipulation. Aristotle never claims that studying the *Rhetoric* will make someone a more successful speaker. "Less stumbling and more clairvoyant" need not mean more efficient at achieving the given external end, persuasion. Even for purely poetic arts, the rational artisan is not necessarily more successful than the empiric, who works without understanding. "With a view to action experience seems in no respect inferior to art, and men of experience succeed even better than those who have theory without experience" (*Metaphysics* I.1.981a13–15; *Ethics* VI.11.1143b12–17, but see VI.12.1143b23–28). In the *Metaphysics* he says that the person who has an art is *wiser* than the one who acts by experience alone (I.1.981a24–30), but wiser is not equivalent to more effective. Whether theory plus experience provides an advantage over experience alone is a question on which Aristotle is silent. Moreover, in purely poetic arts, Aristotle further allows the possibility that nature, in addition to experience, can be a better source of success than art. He does not allow for the possibility of natural genius in praxis as he does for poiesis. Natural virtue is ethical virtue *minus phronēsis*.

But we may not be able to exclude the possibility of natural virtue today so easily.

Even if the *Rhetoric* could make its readers better speakers, it is surely not the most efficient way of doing so. I have, consequently, assumed that instead of doing that job badly, Aristotle is in fact trying to accomplish something else. I see him exhibiting the internal values and standards of rhetorical argument to legislators and citizens. Such analysis makes practice "in some sense more effective." The precise sense in which rhetorical practice becomes more effective comes from Aristotle's exhibitions which make "more clairvoyant" the relations between internal and external end, and between artistic and ethical internal ends. That is an effectiveness which is not to be measured solely in terms of its external end.

An art of rhetoric can fail to make its practitioners more successful for two reasons. As I argued in the first chapter, an art can fail either if the art wrongly articulates an internal end, so that that guiding end is not related to the given end as first *energeia* to second, or if political circumstances prevent the achievement of the internal end from leading regularly to accomplishing the external end. If the *Rhetoric* were nothing but a *technē*, the first reason would be the only one of interest. A *technē* starts with a given end, and figures out a way of producing it reliably and efficiently. That "way"—*methodos*—becomes the goal within the agent's power. Such a *technē* cannot blame the world for its own failures. But if the *Rhetoric* articulates an internal end, then there is at least the possibility that the fault lies in the world, not the art.[3] It is in fact because these two sources of failure are so different, and because it is so important to the legislator to distinguish their effects, that the legislator has to understand the practice of rhetoric in such detail as the *Rhetoric* presents.

Since they have internal ends, practical arts such as rhetoric share with the moral virtues this second kind of success, and therefore a second kind of failure. In the last chapter, I pointed to Aristotle's claim that a virtue "causes its possessors [both] to be in a good state and to perform their functions well" (*Ethics* II.6.1106a17–18), and noted that those two forms of achievement are inseparable in the virtues, but not in the arts. Arts can render the "thing itself," the thinking part of the soul, good, without necessarily enabling it to perform its function well. Rhetoric today, or rhetoric anywhere outside the polis, might fail because it is not functional. Good public deliberation might be like calligraphy in no longer producing significant practical effects. Calligraphy is no less a manifestation of skill and technical intelligence when its only uses are display rather than communication. It is still an art, but it is obsolete. It might be that its lack of connection to important practical ends makes it become the province for professional artisans, or that its lack of utility makes it a badge of privilege and status. In either case, the skill and intelligence it requires remains unchanged while its place in life more generally changes. It has no function to perform well.

But if rhetoric today does not have uses that are as politically central as Aristotle makes out, it would be wrong to call good deliberation and rhetorical argument obsolete the way calligraphy is. Calligraphy can blame the world because it no longer has a function, but the lack of function for calligraphy is hardly a defect in the way we live now.

Rhetoric is a noble and practical art because its exercise is an essential part of the human function. Therefore, if there are no circumstances today in which rhetoric can achieve its internal end, then part of the human function cannot be fully actualized. The absence of contemporary circumstances in which rhetoric can achieve its internal end constitutes a criticism of current social and political arrangements, not an indictment of artful rhetoric, and not just the occasion for nostalgia like that occasioned by calligraphy being replaced by printing. There is a dimension of essential human communicative activity missing from our lives. People have no opportunity to deliberate together and persuade each other about the most consequential decisions. While I think Aristotle's ideas of a human function and a best life have to be historicized, that is not to endorse a surrender to whatever current conditions allow. We equally have to be able to say that political circumstances prevent human development and flourishing from being complete. The *Rhetoric* permits such criticism.

The *Rhetoric* therefore offers specific political critique and detailed resources for understanding our own imperfections. It offers more than just the occasion for laments about the loss of the polis and nostalgia for a world of virtue. The more we understand the internal end of rhetoric, the more we understand what we are missing. As we see better the contingent connections between internal and external end, we see better what to do about it. I said in the Introduction that to us Aristotle might look naive, while to Aristotle we would look not sophisticated but unnatural. My goal has been to make both those points of view available as real possibilities without assuming that either mode of thought is inherently superior.

According to Taylor, "good theory enables practices to become less stumbling and more clairvoyant." But Taylor's insight can be taken a step further. Good theory not only lays bare the workings of a practice, it lays bare and articulates the nature of the manifold to which a given practice is applied, the circumstances in which it is appropriate or intelligible. The art of rhetoric makes practice more effective and "clairvoyant." In current circumstances, there is no reason to think that its effectiveness and clairvoyance make artful rhetoric persuade its audiences more reliably than do sophistic, deceptive, or immoral appeals. If a practical art has no function today, the problem is not that the practical art is obsolete but that our lives are unnatural.

The most noble arts are the most revealing about the human ergon and human nature. These are practical arts. Nothing can be further from Aristotle's idea of practical art than the popular contemporary claim that rhetoric is epistemic and that metaphor is the most revealing thing in rhetoric. Today people try to find a connection between human nature and a poetic art, sometimes even a poetic art of rhetoric, by finding links between creativity, metaphor, insight, and essential humanity. That inclination is not confined to contemporary rhetorical theorists. Hermeneutics is similarly attracted to poetic arts: Gadamer and Arendt both try to approach *phronēsis* from a discussion of aesthetic judgment. Kuhn models scientific revolution on discontinuous changes in perception, not action or argument. They are all consequently committed to a picture of rationality which identifies reasoning with having or following a rule, and then have to relate perception, application, interpretation, and action to those rules.[4]

In the Introduction, I promised that this exploration of the *Rhetoric* could inform, and perhaps transform, contemporary projects concerning *phronēsis* and rhetoric. Here is one way I can make good on that promise. For Aristotle, practical arts are more tied to the human ergon than poetic ones. That, for Aristotle, is almost a conceptual truth. Praxis allows inferences back to the agent, while makings do not (*Ethics* II.4.1105a26, V.8.1135a15). When the noble is allied naturally with the practical, then it is also easy to see that the higher arts are the ones more tied to the human function.

The dimensions of the *Rhetoric* that are most tied to praxis, which are the dimensions I have emphasized in this book, are the ones connected to the human function, while the more poetic side, such as the discussion of style and arrangement in Book III, is not. The current direction of rhetorical research and discussions of *phronēsis* is another reason to see a lack of connection between the human good and the contemporary circumstances for its exercise.[5] The trouble is that the most praxis–oriented aspects of the *Rhetoric* are also the ones most tied to the context of the polis, while style, metaphor, etc. are more easily adapted to current interests. That is, the side of rhetorical activity, and of Aristotle's inquiry, that is most closely connected to the human ergon is also most closely connected to its specific political context.

It is not rhetoric's fault that it has no politics to be subordinate to. (Of course, the fact that it is no fault of rhetoric does not mean that it is not dangerous and that there is no need for us to take precautions.) In the first chapter, I argued that it is only in rhetorical argument about the particulars of deliberation, and not in persuasion generally, that cause and effect, arguing and being persuaded, are identical and that persuasive activity has internal ends. In the following chapter I argued further that such identity of cause and effect can only be located in the kinds of rhetoric, not in rhetoric in general. Therefore rhetoric as practice makes sense only under certain particular political circumstances, where such practices are possible. An internal end that is not significantly connected to external success loses its own purposiveness and value. An attempt at communication becomes calligraphy. Similarly, in rhetoric the enthymeme is displaced from the center by metaphor. Rhetoric is such a high practical art for Aristotle that it is sometimes mistaken for politics itself. That dignity of rhetoric, and consequent similarity to politics, is contingent, dependent on connections that are natural in the polis but not universally. Within Aristotle's context, the connection is a natural one, while in my analysis, it is contingent. Its contingency makes my analysis of the *Rhetoric* part of the history of prudence.

Thus in the Introduction I noted that one of the unique, very Aristotelian features of the *Rhetoric* was that it directed attention to rhetoric as an activity, instead of looking at the motives that might inspire a rhetorician or the effects these practices cause. Rhetoric as an activity has its own values and criteria for success and failure. I also suggested that it is easy to imagine practical worlds in which this emphasis would be counterproductive, and in which we would be better off concentrating instead on motives or effects. Even in the days of the polis, Thucydides and Euripides at least thought their emphasis on intentions was more appropriate than Aristotle's focusing on the activity itself. Appropriateness to circumstances, then, does not mean an appeal to neutral, pretheoretical brute experience. Still, Aristotle either observes or constructs a world in which rhetoric as *energeia* has coherence and plausibility.

Without a polis, *energeiai* such as rhetoric are impossible. Things that have no end outside themselves because they were done for their own sake become pointless. Subduing one's fear of death in battle is its own end; subduing one's fear of death by climbing Mount Everest without oxygen is in Aristotle's eyes pointless. Virtue becomes virtuosity. Persuading through argument alone is simply fastidious restraint. Seeing something as good means seeing it as more than just one's own preference, and that requires impersonal standards. For Aristotle, impersonal standards mean political standards. Without them, as we saw in the last chapter, rhetoric becomes a weapon deployed for purposes outside itself. It cannot be its own end.

Throughout I have been claiming that the *Rhetoric* is a work of political theory or political science. That is, the *Rhetoric* shows the internal workings of the practice of rhetoric so that the legislator can make intelligent political decisions about it. For citizens and legislators, the need to understand rhetoric is not a narrowly practical need. All citizens, he says in the *Politics,* need training in drawing, which permits them better to "judge the works of artisans" (VIII.3.1338a17–19). But he then notes that civic education must have a broader justification than that:

> They should be educated in drawing not so that they may not make errors in their private purchases and avoid being deceived in the buying and selling of wares, but rather because it makes them expert at studying the beauty connected with bodies. To seek everywhere the element of utility is least of all fitting for those who are magnanimous and free (1338a40–b2).

Similarly for rhetoric, regardless of political circumstances. Part of citizenship, and part of practical wisdom, is the ability to reflect and theorize about human affairs. The *Rhetoric* can be a contribution to contemporary *phronēsis* even if it is only the occasion for such reflection and has no practical application at all. This analysis of the *Rhetoric* offers a series of occasions for reflection that should be part of the political judgment of any mature person. The relations between *technē*, ethical virtue, and *phronēsis,* the relations between internal and external ends, and between ethically and artfully guiding ends, are central topoi for the *phronimos* in any circumstances. Serious theorizing about the human function and the human good is as difficult to practice as political reform is. Such theorizing is as essential a part of *phronēsis* as political reform is, and just as absent from contemporary life: the history of prudence is part of prudence.

Part of such practical reflection considers the relation between the practical art of rhetoric and the manifold in which it operates. Contemporary *phronēsis,* unlike Aristotle's, has to be historical. The contemporary *phronimos,* unlike Aristotle's, has to have a historical consciousness. I therefore want to look more specifically at the relation between the *Rhetoric* and the *Politics* to get a better understanding of the relation between this practical art and its political circumstances.

In the first chapter I appealed to the treatment of music in *Politics* VIII as an analogy. I said that his distinction between professional and civic musical education and performance, and the effects of each on the souls of practitioners, was the closest explicit parallel in Aristotle to the claims I want to make about the *Rhetoric.* On the present question of the relation between a practical art and its relevant circumstances, this analogy suggests trouble. The considerations in Book VIII are suited to the ideal polis of Books VII and VIII and not to the whole range of poleis examined in the *Politics.* Although he briefly notes that the question of which modes and other musical practices should be developed varies with the type of state—e.g., martial music for martial states—he does not present a general analysis of music and its place in the polis. *Politics* VIII is not about the place of music in the polis but about the place of music in the specific, best, kind of polis found in *Politics* VII and VIII.

What about the *Rhetoric*? It seems to differ drastically from the analysis of music in this respect, and to be tied to no polis in particular, even if it does require some polis or other. To what range of poleis is it suited? Neither the *Rhetoric* nor the *Politics,* which says nothing at all about rhetoric, explicitly says anything about the political context for understanding the *Rhetoric.*

I think the answer is that the *Rhetoric* has the same range, and the same political function, as the *Nicomachean Ethics.*[6] On this point the *Ethics* as a whole is a better analogy than the section on music in *Politics* VIII. Although the *Politics* is silent about rhetoric, the political presence of rhetoric is even more pervasive than that of music; rhetoric and ethics are coextensive, since both are concerned with deliberation and deliberation is coextensive with the polis. It is the mark by which slaves, no matter how good they might be at technical calculation, are excluded from citizenship and living well.[7]

Music has a more restricted political significance. It is a political issue only where education, and therefore musical education, is public and state-sponsored. That is why Aristotle talks about it only in Book VIII and not in his analysis of inferior states, where education is considered the responsibility of parents. Music might be essential to political education, but if education is private, then it is not subject to political deliberation. Rhetoric, however, is unavoidable as a political issue, regardless of how good or bad the state is.

The *Ethics,* like the *Politics,* is a political inquiry. The *Ethics* is about the best life for man. The best life must be in a polis, but the *Ethics* is not a picture of life in any particular polis. I would like to argue the same for the *Rhetoric,* that the artful rhetorical activity Aristotle describes must be in some polis, but not any particular polis. The politician needs the same understanding of the good for man, the good human being, and living well, regardless of whether he or she is making decisions concerning the ideal state or not. In those rare cases where the good man and the good citizen coincide—the best state *haplōs*—the *Ethics* can be applied in a straightforward way. Where there is a divergence between the good man and the good citizen, that same analysis of the good man will help the statesman in several different ways. It can help show how to move the partial justice of the given *polis* closer to full justice, how to move it instead closer to the justice appropriate to that form of constitution, how to make it more stable and inclusive, how to adjudicate competing claims about justice, etc. It can even serve the *phronimos* as pure theory, giving legislators and citizens "an observant eye for beauty of form and figure." The *Ethics* is a description of the good man, and so can be normative for politics. Politics would otherwise have to rest with a definition of the good citizen fully relative to the polis in which he lived. But just how ethics is normative for politics will vary.

Something of the same sort will obtain for the *Rhetoric*. Aristotle's *Rhetoric* is about rhetoric at its best, parallel to the best human life in the *Ethics*. The *Rhetoric* presupposes circumstances in which there is no great gap between internal and external ends. It is set in a world where in general the best way to persuade successfully is by artful persuasion, where the audiences are decent enough that truth will usually win out over falsity. Deliberative audiences are not rent by faction or ideological differences, but are in general agreement over what is good, and only in doubt about how best to secure it. If there is a human ergon and a human good, then what is best for me is not in principle different from what is best for you. In its manifold of application there are no huge discrepancies between artful *ēthos* and practical *ēthos*, nor between the demands of *ēthos* and those of *logos*. The *Rhetoric* makes sense for circumstances in which Aristotle can confidently assert that deliberative rhetoric is the model for rhetoric in general, and in particular that deliberation is authoritative over forensic rhetoric. None of those features of rhetoric holds universally. I see no reason to think that any of them holds today.

In an ideal state, the *Rhetoric* could be an accurate picture of actual practice. In most actual states artful rhetoric and successful rhetoric will not coincide as thoroughly as the *Rhetoric* makes out, just as the good man of the *Ethics* and the good citizen of the *Politics* rarely coincide. In most real circumstances the *Rhetoric* then becomes less descriptive and more normative. What politicians do with that knowledge of norms will itself vary with circumstances. The *Rhetoric* and *Ethics,* then, extend beyond the ideal state of *Politics* VII and VIII to the entire range of poleis considered in the *Politics*.

But they do not extend as far as I want to take them, beyond the polis altogether to the contemporary world. In trying to understand the *Rhetoric* today, we are taking the text beyond Aristotle's intention, and beyond his possible imagination. There's nothing illegitimate about exceeding Aristotle's intentions, but there is the danger of incoherence.

Aristotle, however, offers some resources for avoiding that incoherence and extending his understanding of *phronēsis, technē, ēthos,* and rhetoric beyond circumstances he could imagine. If we only had the *Ethics* and not the *Politics,* we might think that Aristotle in the *Ethics* presented the moral virtues as essential components of the human function, such that if any of them was missing, one's life could not be complete. Although such an interpretation is true, the *Politics* helps us to see that it is also incomplete, since one can live well in poleis where some of the virtues need not be developed and exercised. Similarly, I have argued that the three species of rhetoric are the only kinds of rhetorical activity that are fully *energeiai,* from which one could conclude that only in those political settings is rhetoric part of the human function. Since the existence of these species depends on the polis, functional rhetoric then does not exist today. If we take the *Rhetoric,* like the *Ethics,* as self-contained, its value for *phronēsis* today is negligible.

But the *Politics* gives some room for criticism of the good life presented in the *Ethics,* and, in similar fashion, of the good operation of the faculty of rhetoric presented in the *Rhetoric.* To show how the *Rhetoric* can not only offer a reference point, but also itself be subject to historical and political criticism, I want to turn for my comparison from calligraphy back to the ethical virtue of courage, which I have used in contrast to rhetoric in earlier chapters. Rhetoric as a practical art occupies middle ground between pure *technai* like calligraphy and the moral virtues like courage. While calligraphy is no less an art when pointless and does not fit into a whole, courage *is* less of a virtue when it is exercised in climbing Mount Everest without oxygen, or in forgoing modern weapons in order better to display one's manliness. If its exercise is no longer connected to the human function and the human good, it is not longer a virtue. When courage is a moral virtue, the fact that it is not evaluated solely as a means to an external end makes courageous action its own end, worth pursuing for its own sake. When courage is a test of oneself divorced from external ends, far from being its own end, it becomes pointless.

One could argue that since courage is part of the human function, a life without opportunities for courage is an incomplete and distorted life. But that conclusion seems to me too quick. A world without war might be a better world, even though there is no longer room for the virtue of courage. Skills are still skills regardless of their circumstances of execution. Virtues do not stay virtues when they no longer have a place in a greater political whole. If their external end is not valued, then the internal end is no longer an end either. What was done for its own sake then is done in vain. That is why Aristotle, once again, says that while there is such a thing as excellence in art, there is no such thing as excellence in *phronēsis,* and why I have been saying that there can be no unity of the arts parallel to the unity of the virtues. The more tied to praxis rhetoric is, the more it, like courage, depends for its intrinsic value on external circumstances. Only with a fit between the value of the external end and of the internal end can Aristotle say, in the lines I quoted in the last chapter, that the virtues both "render the thing itself good, and also cause it to perform its function well" (II.6.1106a17–18).

I think a strong case can be made that the absence of artful and functional rhetoric from today's world is a deformation of *phronēsis* and of the human good. But that hypothetical narrative about courage stands as a caution against too easily using Aristotle's judgments as a standard. The *Politics* takes categorical pronouncements from the *Ethics*—courage is an essential part of the human good—and relativizes them to specific kinds of poleis. I think it gives us ammunition for doing the same to the features of rhetoric which in the *Rhetoric* look essential.

This is a surprising reversal of the way the *Ethics* and *Politics* are usually read, and I hope my presentation of the *Rhetoric* contributes to this reversal. Typically, the *Ethics* is seen as embodying timeless wisdom whereas the *Politics* is tied to its historically bound subject matter, the polis. That is why the *Ethics* has been studied so much more than the *Politics*.

I see it the other way around. The *Ethics* offers a complete picture of the human good with no room for practical self-criticism. (I limit the claim to *practical* self-criticism to allow for the role of *theoria* in casting a different perspective on the life of virtue.) *Phronēsis* in the *Ethics* is nothing but the *orthos logos* of the ethical virtues. The *Politics* has a flexibility which does allow for internal self-criticism. Political *phronēsis* is not tied to the moral virtues as *phronēsis* is in the individual, because the statesman has to make citizens morally virtuous. It is thus *less* historically bound than the *Ethics*!

I want to show how the *Politics* in fact offers an orderly way of engaging in such criticism, but first I want to place the *Rhetoric* alongside the *Ethics* and the *Politics* in this discussion. Where does the *Rhetoric* fit in this contrast between the *Ethics* and the *Politics*, where the *Politics* opens up more possibilities for criticism than the *Ethics*? Like the *Ethics*, the *Rhetoric* is subordinate to the *Politics*. They both present pictures of activities that are politically located but independent of any particular polis. But the *Rhetoric*, like the *Politics* and unlike the *Ethics*, exhibits shifting lines between the noble and the necessary within its own account of an art. As he puts it in the *Posterior Analytics:* "The same effect may obtain both for a purpose and as a necessary consequence" (II.11.94b27; cf. *De Sophisticis Elenchis* 4.165b35).[8]

The *Politics* exploits the shifting boundary between purpose and necessity. The sharp line drawn in the *Ethics* between *praxis* and *poiēsis* is replaced in the *Politics* by a more flexible account. That is what I meant by saying that the *Ethics* presents a self-contained picture of the good life while the *Politics* allows for internal criticism. In the *Ethics*, there are necessary connections between praxis, *energeia*, and the noble as opposed to *poiēsis*, *kinēsis*, and the banausic, or instrumental. In the *Politics* those necessities are seen as ideals and are presented in the context of variability—the line between what is civic and what is banausic, between the parts of the state and its mere necessary conditions, shifts, and therefore what are sharp distinctions in the *Ethics* become matters of degree.[9]

I can illustrate this aspect of the *Politics* by returning to an example I used in the first chapter. At the beginning of the first chapter I showed how

Aristotle says that there is no art of mastering slaves, because being a master was a matter of the kind of person one was, and not of a technique. That looks like a sharp distinction between the civic and the banausic. But he then softens that claim by conceding that that there may be such an art, but an ignoble and unimportant one.

The *Politics* is full of such transformations. My use of courage as the analogy to rhetoric is no accident, since it is part of this larger picture. Courage in the *Ethics* is a moral virtue, and an essential part of the human good. In the *Politics,* at least in the ideal state of *Politics* VII and VIII, however, war is said to be for the sake of peace, and courage therefore only hypothetically desirable and praiseworthy. As I mentioned in the last chapter, Aristotle does question the value of the virtue of truth-telling in the *Ethics.* He could, but in the *Ethics* never does, raise the same question about the goods pursued by the other moral virtues. One could wonder what is good about military victory, but its value is simply taken as given for the discussion of courage. Generosity depends on property being held privately and in unequal shares, but the examination of the virtue of generosity in the *Ethics* takes for granted that such distribution is beyond question.[10]

The *Rhetoric,* like the *Ethics,* takes its goods for granted, while the *Politics* at least leaves room for such critique. The human function, the human good, *phronēsis*—none of these is a historically variable phenomenon for Aristotle, but the variability within the *Politics* gives resources for extension. The *Rhetoric,* like the *Politics,* repeatedly shows how the same resource can be used to achieve the internal end of rhetoric or used out of necessities dictated by the corruption of the audience. Where Aristotle sees no great philosophical significance to that double duty, I see these points as an opportunity to extend the *Rhetoric* beyond its own designs.

A political extension of the *Rhetoric* to contemporary problems of rhetoric and *phronēsis* might open up some surprising possibilities. It could be that, where courage is necessary rather than good in the best polis, rhetoric is necessary instead of good in the most *corrupt* poleis, or in communities so unnatural that they are not even poleis. We might think that we are now so civilized that courage is no longer a virtue. But if rhetoric is no longer noble, that might not be grounds for self-congratulation. It might not be a sign of our excellence but of our disconnection to the human ergon. We have to be alive to the possibility that we aren't good enough to be able to afford rhetoric as part of our human good.

Rhetoric is more closely tied to *phronēsis* than courage is, despite the fact that rhetoric is an art, whereas courage is a virtue. Because of this close alliance to *phronēsis,* rhetoric is less likely to disappear from human flourishing than is manliness. Rhetoric is a noble activity. It is so noble that it sometimes passes for politics. It therefore seems to me unlikely that it could suffer the same fate as courage. It is hard for me to imagine a polis so good, or so bad, that the practice of public deliberation moves from the set of good activities to the list of merely necessary ones. Different moral and political circumstances call for changing kinds of *phronēsis,* and hence for changing versions of artful civic rhetoric. Their intellectual, as opposed to ethical, nature, gives *phronēsis* and rhetoric a certain independence from circumstances that courage lacks. While progress might move courage off the battlefield and onto the snowfields of the Himalayas, those same advances don't make rhetoric irrelevant, but rather, destructive.

I suggest that the way the *Politics* exhibits shifting boundaries between the good and the necessary is an Aristotelian resource for extending Aristotle beyond himself to the history of prudence. The *Rhetoric,* like the *Politics* and unlike the *Ethics,* exhibits shifting boundaries between reason and necessity as the inquiry proceeds. I have explored several examples as we have gone along. Appeals to the passions and attention to style are denigrated, and then he shows how they are part of the art of rhetoric. The speaker is told to formulate maxims by guessing at the opinions of his hearers, and then we learn that those maxims make arguments ethical. The *Rhetoric* shows these shifting lines between the noble and the necessary within a single complex activity. The *Rhetoric,* then, can equip us even better than the *Ethics* or *Politics* can to make such historical extensions.

The *Rhetoric* is designed, I have been claiming, to present legislators with an understanding of the civic art of rhetoric. It is not very useful to practitioners of the art, and it does not offer legislators any ready-made solutions to the problems of understanding and regulation they confront. I think that the *Politics* offers the best formula for seeing the uses of the *Rhetoric.* Aristotle offers the following programmatic remarks at the beginning of *Politics* IV:

> In all arts and sciences which have not arisen on a partial basis but are complete with respect to some one type of thing, it belongs to a single one to study what is fitting in the case of each type of thing. In the case of training for the body, for example, it belongs to it to study what sort is advantageous for what sort of body; which is best (for the best is necessarily fitting for the body that is naturally the finest and is most finely equipped); which is best—a single one for all—for most bodies (for this too is a task of gymnastic expertise); and further, if someone should desire neither the disposition nor the knowledge befitting those connected with competitions, it belongs no less to the sports trainer and the gymnastic expert to provide this capacity as well (IV.1.1288b10–19)

It is a single art or science that has all these different functions in different circumstances. If the *Rhetoric* is one of those arts that is "complete in relation to some one class of subject," then it will allow the legislator to do those different jobs. I said before that legislators will make use of the *Rhetoric* in a variety of ways. That variety is so great that it produces these four meanings for "best." The same reasoned capacity for making serves a series of different purposes marked off in this passage by different senses of "best." It will determine what kind of rhetoric most suits different kinds of people and kinds of poleis, what rhetoric looks like in the best of circumstances, what kind of rhetoric will be suitable to a wide variety of circumstances, and how to use rhetoric to make the best out of a situation which is itself not desirable.

To be able to do all those jobs, the *Rhetoric* would have to pay careful attention to changing relations between internal and external end. It will therefore have to appear, to those who ignore this understanding of a complete art, to be wavering in purpose between a pious moralizing that blithely wishes for the best and a cynical and manipulative attitude. Parts of the *Rhetoric,* especially the first three chapters, give a moral defense of rhetoric. Parts, including most of the text, show how to practice it, regardless of one's end. Without integrating those two, the first seems just a prayer designed to ward off a punishment the second would otherwise draw down, like Agamemnon declaring he is ashamed before committing an act of *hybris.* Law schools and business schools today offer ethics courses that (to an uncharitable viewer) seem designed to give those schools a rationale for avoiding responsibility for what their students do—"Don't blame us. We have an ethics course."

Those different appearances are part of a single whole: the idealistic side of the *Rhetoric* comes from those occasions where Aristotle shows how the internal end leads smoothly to the external end, and the amoral and empirical side from the occasions when he looks directly to the external end, as the fourth sense of "best" ordains. I said in the Introduction that I was going to avoid questions of the composition of the *Rhetoric* and be guided instead by the hypothesis that it is best read as a unified argument. I said that the two questions of historical composition and philosophical analysis were logically independent. They are not, of course, independent in other ways. One of the prime sources of attraction and evidence for separating strata of composition is the contradictions readers find in the work as we have it. If in my approach those contradictions for the most part evaporate, the project I ignored does not become invalid, but it does lose much of its importance.

In the *Politics,* that final sense of best is the meaning appropriate for doing the best in corrupt poleis liable to faction and revolution. The challenge of *Politics* V is to see what "the best" means in such circumstances. It is plausible to suspect that an approach that is designed for circumstances farthest from the ideal would be the approach most suitable for using the *Rhetoric* to inform a contemporary inquiry into practical wisdom. If that is the case, then we are left with the tantalizing and disturbing prospect that the most manipulative side of artful rhetoric is the most informative and relevant today. The *Rhetoric* would then offer not so much an ideal to aim toward as a series of resources for getting the best out of our current lack of connection between argumentative excellence and practical success, and the current distance between *ēthos qua* rhetorical artifact and *ēthos* as reflected in a person's actual practical choices.

For just one example, in chapter 6 I quoted III.1, where Aristotle notes that in more corrupt states, "actors count for more than poets" in dramatic contests, and similarly for political contests. What does that analogy really mean for politics? Poets are masters of plots, while actors are masters of the art of delivery. Similarly, presumably, argument, the rhetorical analogon of plots, gives way to delivery. Aristotle's further comment on this change suggests that the parts of rhetoric that confront necessity rather than the good are the parts most relevant today:

> Those performers who give careful attention to these [volume, change of pitch, and rhythm] are generally the ones who win poetic contests; and just as actors are more important than poets now in the poetic contests, so it is in political contests because of the sad state of governments. An art concerned with [the delivery of oratory] has not yet been composed, since . . . it seems a vulgar matter when rightly understood. But since the whole business of rhetoric is with opinion [*doxa*], one should pay attention to delivery, not because it is right [*orthos*] but because it is necessary, since true justice seeks nothing more in a speech than neither to offend nor to entertain (III.1.1403b32–1404a5).

If, because of the unnatural character of our lives, those crucial connections that Aristotle sees between power and activity, between internal and external end, between artful and ethical internal ends, between *logos* and *ēthos* and between artful and practical *ēthos,* if all these connections are severed, then an art of rhetoric today becomes an art of necessity rather than an art dominated by its own internal purposes. But seeing the whole art, in the flourishing condition Aristotle presents, can help us to design lines of improvement.

All this by way of conclusion must be taken as merely suggestive and oversimplified. Throughout the book, I have relied on comparisons to the *Ethics* and the *Politics* to illuminate the *Rhetoric*. At the same time, I have claimed that the *Rhetoric* in turn clarifies the *Ethics* and *Politics*. It therefore should be clear that a full account of the *Rhetoric* really would require equally full treatment of the *Ethics* and *Politics,* which I obviously have not attempted. By saying that I end on a merely suggestive note does not mean that I have doubts whether my conclusions are true and defensible; it is to recognize that I have not yet fully defended them.

There are always dangers in referring to history, and especially to Aristotle, to address contemporary philosophic and practical problems. There is the danger of nostalgia for a lost golden age of the polis. There is the danger of removing history from history by making the past easily available to the present, thinking that because some possibility is desirable it therefore really is an available alternative. I think that my exploration of the *Rhetoric* avoids those dangers. I do not think one can abstract the parts of Aristotle one likes, or which seem useful, from the entirety of his argument, and so I have stressed its coherence. The *Rhetoric* is tied to the polis. The polis has its attractions, but is not the ideal world Aristotle takes it to be. I would not want to live there myself, even if I could peek through the veil of ignorance and be sure I was a citizen and not a slave or a woman. The more completely one understands the *Rhetoric*—or any other work of Aristotle's—the less directly available and applicable it is. Knowing what we cannot have, however, is useful. And the most useful side of the *Rhetoric* may well be its most manipulative and suspect side, not its noblest.

Rhetoric is the noblest, and most dangerous, of arts. It is the most rational art: other arts cause opposites, but only rhetoric proves opposites, because proof is its characteristic mode of causation and making. Rhetoric can be called the art of arts in that in rhetoric rationality fully dominates the art. Just as politics is the architectonic art, so rhetoric is the most artistic of arts. An art which proves opposites creates mistrust. Today we don't need to be reminded of this mistrust. But we do need to know about its nobility.

NOTES

INTRODUCTION
Aristotle's *Rhetoric* and the Professionalization of Virtue

1. For a couple of representative comments by philosophers, see, first, W. D. Ross, *Aristotle*, 275: "The *Rhetoric* may seem at first sight to be a curious jumble of literary criticism with second rate logic, ethics, politics, and jurisprudence, mixed by the cunning of one who knows well how the weaknesses of the human heart are to be played upon." See also G. E. R. Lloyd, *Aristotle: The Growth and Structure of His Thought*, 273: "In the *Rhetoric* he discusses the tricks of the trade, the various devices the public speaker may use to win his case."

2. Gerald F. Else, *Aristotle's Poetics: The Argument*, 443; Jakob Wisse, *Ethos and Pathos from Aristotle to Cicero*, 12. For criticism of this interpretive strategy as applied to the *Poetics*, see Jonathan Lear, "Katharsis," esp. p. 336, n. 10: "The *Poetics* was not meant to be a self-contained universe; it was an integral part of Aristotle's philosophy."

3. I began with the immodest-sounding claim that this is the first philosophical treatment of Aristotle's *Rhetoric*. I have to compound that assertion with the equally immodest-sounding claim that the field to which I hope my book is a contribution is a field with little growing in it so far. (An earlier such contribution of mine was *Machiavelli and the History of Prudence* [University of Wisconsin Press, 1987].)

4. "Aristotle," *Proceedings of the British Academy* 11 (1924).

5. Alasdair MacIntyre, *Whose Justice? Which Rationality?* (University of Notre Dame Press, 1988), 28.

6. Charles Taylor affirms the fundamental difference between Aristotle's practical reason and a practical reason that assumes one of its major tasks to be the refutation of skepticism: "Our modern conceptions of practical reason are shaped—I might say distorted—by the weight of moral skepticism. Even conceptions which intend to give no ground to skepticism have frequently taken form in order best to resist it, or to offer the least possible purchase to it. In this practical reason falls into line with a pervasive feature of modern intellectual culture, which one could call the primacy of the epistemological: the tendency to think out the question of what something *is* in terms of the question of how it is *known*" ("Explanation and Practical Reason," 208). We read a similar story, with the fundamental change occurring

at the same time, in Thomas M. Conley, *Rhetoric in the European Tradition,* 162: "The seventeenth-century trend away from Renaissance conceptions of rhetoric as an instrument of *controversia*—what we called . . . the management of uncertainty—to the faculty of apprehending the means of persuasion through affect to action." Conley notes, for example, that Hobbes changes Aristotle's definition of rhetoric and treatment of emotion by an "emphasis on 'winning'" (p. 166). See also p. 177: "In rhetoric and political philosophy alike, as we have seen in the instances of Lamy and Hobbes above all, the traditional understanding of reason as self-motivating and a faculty that can control the passions and direct the will is replaced by a new model. In the old model, reason proposes goods to the agent and provides that agent—a rational agent—with grounds for action. In the new model, reason is inert, incapable of moving to action. Only affect can do that."

7. Jonathan Lear, *Aristotle: The Desire to Understand,* 196, expresses a similar judgment—that Aristotle is not to be considered naive just because he is unalarmed by skepticism. "One advantage of Aristotle's approach to ethics, then, is that it defuses skepticism in a completely novel way. Instead of stepping outside of the ethical and trying to convince a skeptic in his own terms that he has reason to be ethical, Aristotle shows those who are already living an ethical life that they have good reason to be doing so. However, such an approach also has its pitfalls. The main danger is that one will be insufficiently critical. In commending the ethical life by pointing to the ethical life that is actually lived, there is the danger that one will end up defending the status quo. For if one does not step outside the society in which one lives, how can one subject any aspect of it to criticism?

"If Aristotle is to naturalize human freedom, reflection ought to be an activity in which the human animal can plausibly engage. There is no substitute for moving around critically within one's values: investigating, say, the value of nobility and its dependence on a society of masters and slaves; testing this against one's commitment to justice and equality; learning about other societies and other ethical systems; using one's imagination."

8. Immanuel Kant, *Critique of Judgment,* sec. 53, 198/328 n. 63.

9. John Dewey, *The Public and Its Problems,* 126. "There are too many publics and too much of public concern for our existing resources to cope with. The problem of a democratically organized public is primarily and essentially an intellectual problem, in a degree to which the political affairs of prior ages offer no parallel."

CHAPTER 1
Aristotle's *Rhetoric:* Between Craft and Practical Wisdom

1. Except where I am talking about the *Eudemian Ethics,* when I refer to "the *Ethics,*" I mean the *Nicomachean Ethics.* Sometimes the *Eudemian Ethics* offers something useful for the *Rhetoric,* and I use it. But I do not find important differences between the two *Ethics* that are relevant for illuminating the *Rhetoric.* Most of my references to Aristotle's *Ethics* are to the books the two *Ethics* have in common anyway. So I generally refer to the *Nicomachean Ethics,* as it is better known to most readers.

2. Whether an indefinite end disqualifies rhetoric from being an art has been raised repeatedly in the history of rhetoric. See, e.g., Sextus Empiricus, *Against the Professors* 1.187–96: "Since every art has an end which is fixed and stable, like philosophy or grammar, rhetoric too, if it is an art, will have to profess one or the other of these. But is has not an end which is always stable . . . and therefore it is not an art." See also Cicero, *De Oratore* 1.3.12.

3. There is something else that my treatment is not about. I follow Aristotle in leaving only implicit the historical and political context of the *Rhetoric*. For a few recent book-length works I have found helpful in understanding the actual historical context, see K. J. Dover, *Greek Popular Morality in the Time of Plato and Aristotle*; Cynthia Farrar, *The Origins of Democratic Thinking*; Carnes Lord, *Education and Culture in the Political Thought of Aristotle*; and Josiah Ober, *Mass and Elite in Democratic Athens*. In the background of my understanding is Hannah Arendt, *The Human Condition*.

4. Plato's name occurs only at I.15.1376a10, II.23.1398b31 and III.4.1406b32; Socrates at II.20.1393b4, III.14.1415b30. I think that Richard McKeon gets exactly right the reasons for this absence. "Rhetoric and Poetic in Aristotle," 205–7: "Aristotle reports that reflection on philosophic method and the application of such considerations of method to the treatment of moral questions were no older than the inquiries of Socrates, but he makes no mention of the pioneer work of Socrates in analyzing rhetoric and the arts. On the contrary, he refers to no previous philosophic inquiries into that subject in the *Rhetoric* . . . . both Socrates and Plato are quoted [only] for examples and precepts of rhetoric. His silence concerning the treatments of rhetoric and poetry in Plato's dialogues, notwithstanding his tendency to criticize Plato on all other subjects, is to be taken rather as a sign that he thought his own departure from previous methods to have been radical to the point of making the example of his predecessors irrelevant to the problems of poetic and rhetoric as he conceived them."

For one example of the very widespread assumption that the *Rhetoric* is a response to Plato, see W. Rhys Roberts, "References to Plato in Aristotle's Rhetoric." Roberts sees Aristotle's first sentence, "Rhetoric is the counterpart of dialectic" as echoing "Socrates' annoying observation in the Gorgias (465d) that 'rhetoric is the counterpart of high-class cookery'" (344), and concludes that Aristotle, "with half-malicious, half-playful exaggeration, opens fire" in the *Rhetoric* by an allusion, "meant to be 'vocal to the wise'" (344–45) to Plato's arguments. But Roberts's claims makes my case all the stronger, since such Platonic echoes do not take seriously the charges against rhetoric that Plato raises. For another, more recent, commentator who see strong influence of Plato on the *Rhetoric,* see William W. Fortenbaugh, "Aristotle's Attitude toward Delivery." Even Wesley Trimpi, whose use and judgment of evidence is much more acute, seems to agree: p. 18. "Whatever the similarities and differences between the two competing rhetorical systems, one seems always to overhear Aristotle in conversation, not with Isocrates, but with Plato" (*Muses of One Mind,* 18).

Here too I see the situations of the *Rhetoric* and the *Poetics* as similar. Readers of the *Poetics,* like readers of the *Rhetoric,* often assume that the *Poetics* must be a response to Plato. For example, Brian Vickers, *In Defence of Rhetoric,* 160: "Having, in the *Poetics,* defended tragedy from Plato's strictures, in the *Rhetoric* he answered part of his master's indictment of the sister art, although agreeing with him on some issues." For counterargument against the similarly common assumption that the *Poetics* must be a response to Plato, see Paul Woodruff, "Aristotle on *Mimesis,*" esp. 73–75.

5. I reject for the *Rhetoric* the "confident assumption" expressed, for example, by Stephen G. Salkever, "Tragedy and the Education of the *Demos:* Aristotle's Response to Plato," 277: "We may confidently assume that however much Aristotle's solutions differ from Plato's, his notion of what problems require solving and much of his vocabulary for solving them are drawn from Platonic sources."

On rhetoric itself as a Platonic invention, see Thomas Cole, *The Origins of Rhetoric in Ancient Greece,* and Edwin Schiappa, *Protagoras and Logos.* (I have reviewed Cole's book in *Philosophy and Rhetoric* 25 (1992): 306–10). For *pathos,* see Thomas Gould, *The Ancient Quarrel between Poetry and Philosophy,* xii, n. 11. With four nearly contemporary exceptions (Democritus, Thucydides, Gorgias, Xenophon), "the evidence points to a Platonic origin for this use of *pathos.*"

6. For art supplementing nature, see *Politics* VII.17.1337a1–3: "All art and education wish to supply the element that is lacking in nature." For *technē* replacing luck, see *Eudemian Ethics* VIII.2.1247a13–17: "Wisdom is not irrational but can give reasons why it acts as it does, whereas [lucky men] cannot say why they succeed." The liberal definition of art seems applied to the art of war in *Politics* I.8.1256b23; even more apposite is the art of delivery, something like modern speech act theory, mentioned in *Poetics* 19.

7. I have rarely found other readers of the *Rhetoric* who share my sense of scandal at the lack of argument that rhetoric is a *technē.* For one, see Alexander Nehemas, "Pity and Fear in the *Rhetoric* and the *Poetics,*" 292–309.

8. Sarah Broadie, *Ethics with Aristotle,* 330: "Aristotle mentions a stock objection to the claim that pleasure is the good: there is no craft for producing pleasure (1152b18–19), whereas [it is assumed that] every kind of good is the product of a corresponding kind of craft. Aristotle replies that, by that argument, no activity can be good because there can be no crafting of an activity. For an activity cannot be a product; only the condition for it can. That is why there is no craft of pleasure, since pleasure is an activity." Just as he seems to make a concession here, and admits arts of perfumery and cookery—the very arts Socrates compares to rhetoric in the *Gorgias*—so he makes a similar concession in the discussion of arts of despotism and slavery after rejecting them. I will discuss that concession below, but I think in both cases the point of the concession is to avoid arguing about the meaning of words to focus attention on what is at stake in calling something an art, namely the relations between technical intelligence and ethical virtue.

9. *Pistis* is used to refer both to the effect aimed at (e.g., I.2.1355a5, I.9.1367b29) and to the process of proof that brings persuasion about (e.g., I.1.1354a14, I.2.1356b6–8, II.20.1393a21–24). Grimaldi (*Studies,* 58ff). sees three relevant meanings of *pistis:* "(1) *pistis* as a state of mind, i.e., belief or conviction, which results when a person accepts a proof or demonstration; (2) *pistis* as source material, material which comes from the *logical analysis* of the subject, from the study of the *character* of the speaker or audience, and from the study of the *emotional context* potentially present for this audience in this subject and situation. As the source of

conviction *pistis* in each meaning—which is *ēthos, pathos,* and not enthymeme but what I call *pragma,* the logical aspect of the subject—carries probative force either in itself, or most effectively when it is organized in a form of deductive or inductive inference; (3) *pistis* as source material." (pp. 58–59). Similarly, Kennedy, in his note on this passage (30, n. 9), where he leaves *pistis* untranslated, says: "*Pistis* (pl. *pisteis*) has a number of different meanings in different concepts: 'proof, means of persuasion, belief,' etc. In 1.2.2–3 Aristotle distinguishes between artistic and nonartistic *pisteis,* and divides the former into three means of persuasion based on character, logical argument, and arousing emotion. Here in chap. 1 readers familiar with dialectic have no knowledge yet of persuasion by character or emotion and will assume that *pistis* means 'logical proof.' In 3.17.15 *pistis* means 'logical argument' in contrast to character presentation."

See also Quintilian, *De Institutio Oratoria* 5.10.8: "To all these forms of argument the Greeks give the name of *pistis,* a term which, though the literal translation is *fides,* 'a warrant of credibility,' is best translated by *probatio,* 'proof.'"

I will turn to this last, and most fundamental, meaning of *pistis* as *fides,* or trust, in later chapters. For now, see Alexander Mourelatos, *The Route of Parmenides,* 136, n. 1: "Semantic studies tend to concentrate on either of the two branches of this family [of *peith-* words], viz. *peitho, -omai, peitho* on the one side, and *pistos, pistis,* etc., on the other. . . . This split, though understandable as a reflection of divergent scholarly interests in the history of rhetoric and of theology, respectively, can be misleading. For it allows us to overlook the fact that 'persuasion' and 'fidelity' or 'faith' are modes of one and the same concept for the Greeks." See also Barthes, "The Old Rhetoric," 53. "We shall keep the word [proofs as a translation for *pisteis*] out of habit, but for us it has a scientific connotation whose very absence defines the rhetorical *pisteis.* It would be better to say: convincing reasons, ways of persuasion, means of credit, mediators of confidence (*fides*)."

10. For the relation between external and internal ends in the moral virtues, see my "Aristotle's Genealogy of Morals." Rhetoric, and other *technai,* qualify as what MacIntyre (*After Virtue*) calls "practices": "By a 'practice' I am going to mean any coherent and complex form of socially established cooperative human activity through which goods internal to that form of activity are realized in the course of trying to achieve those standards of excellence which are appropriate to, and partially definitive of, that form of activity, with the result that human powers to achieve excellence, and human conceptions of the ends and goods involved, are systematically extended" (p. 187). "What is distinctive in a practice is in part the way in which conceptions of the relevant goods and ends which the technical skills serve—and every practice does require the exercise of technical skills—are transformed and enriched by these extensions of human powers and by that regard for its own internal goods which are partially definitive of each particular practice or type of practice" (p. 193). I will also rely on the terminology, and analysis, of given and guiding ends in Broadie, *Ethics with Aristotle,* esp. pp. 190–98. E.g.: "Health as ordinarily conceived is the starting-point of medical deliberation about how to treat a patient, in the sense of being the raison d'être of all steps taken with a view to treatment, including the deliberation; but the technical goal presented in the leading premiss is the starting-point that guides the physician to one conclusion rather than

254 NOTES TO ONE

another. The former starting-point is what justifies engaging at all in the deliberation with a view to taking whatever action it will indicate; the latter explains why *this* conclusion was reached and *this* action taken" (p. 195).

11. Bacon also remarks on the two kinds of success, interestingly distinguishing the doctor, who in his mind can only be judged by results, from the lawyer and rhetor: "The subject [of medicine] being so variable has rendered the art more conjectural, and left the more room for imposture. Other arts and sciences are judged of by their power and ability, and not by success or events. The lawyer is judged by the ability of his pleading, not the issue of the cause; the pilot, by directing his course, and not the fortune of the voyage; whilst the physician and the statesman have no particular act that clearly demonstrates their ability, but are principally censured by the event" (*Advancement of Learning,* ed. Kitchin, 157–58).

12. The contrast between the *endechomena* and *ek pantos tropou* is also made in the *Topics:* "We shall fully possess the method when we are in a position similar to that in which we are with regard to rhetoric and medicine and other such powers (*dynameis*); that is to say, when we carry out our purpose with every available means (*ek ton endechomenon*). For neither will the rhetorician seek to persuade nor the physician to heal by every expedient (*ek pantos tropou*); but if he omits none of the available means (*ton endechomenon*), we shall say that he possesses the science adequately" (I.3.101b5–10). My formulation therefore depends on the hypothesis that Aristotle is drawing the same distinction in those three passages, those at the end of the first chapter and the beginning of the second of the *Rhetoric*, and at *Topics* I.3. The two passages in the *Rhetoric* are obviously connected, since the one summarizes the results of the first chapter, and the other is the definition that begins the second chapter; hence my claim, by triangulation among those three passages, that *ton endechomenon* and *ta huparchonta* are equivalent. The first passage in the *Rhetoric,* which refers to "existing means" of persuasion (*ta huparchonta*), claims that rhetoric is in this respect parallel to medicine, while the passage from the *Topics* says that dialectic is in this respect similar to rhetoric and medicine; in both cases, the parallel consists in the distinction between succeeding and exercising a function, although that exercise is described in the one case as limited to "existing means" of persuasion (*ta huparchonta*), and in the other to "available means," *ek ton endechomenon*. The definition of rhetoric in *Rhetoric* I.2 and the passage from the *Topics,* finally, both use the phrase "available means," *ek ton endechomenon,* in delimiting their respective powers, *dynameis.* That both the *Rhetoric* and the *Topics* make this distinction between existing means and other devices is, in addition to the fact that both are available to everyone and that both prove opposites, a key respect in which rhetoric is said, in the first line of the *Rhetoric,* to be the antistrophe of dialectic.

13. A similar conflict between internal and external ends appears in the *Poetics.* Some think epic superior to tragedy because it is less vulgar and appeals to a better audience. But Aristotle refuses to endorse this criterion and instead says that tragedy is more powerful because it better achieves the constitutive end (26.1461b26–1462a15).

14. Cope, *The Rhetoric of Aristotle* I.83:"This technical term [*he energeia*], and the opposition of *dynamis* and *energeia* . . . pervades Aristotle's entire philosophy." I.261.

"On the subject of *dynamis* and *energeia*, physical, moral, and metaphysical, the fundamental and all pervading antithesis of the Aristotelian Philosophy, a commentary on Rhetoric is not the place to enter. . . . Aristotle himself nowhere gives a complete and intelligible description of this antithesis and its bearings, but assumes the knowledge of it in all his writings."

15. Motions are incomplete actualities (*energeiai*): *Physics* III.2.201b31–32; see also VIII.5.257b7–9 and *De Anima* II.2.417a1–17, III.3.431a6–7. Like Aristotle, I will sometimes contrast motions with *energeiai,* but this is not to deny that motions are *energeiai* too, only incomplete ones.

16. The recent literature on the *energeiai/kinēseis* and *praxis/poesis* distinctions is huge. I have made my own contribution in "Aristotle's Metaphysics of Morals," which has a bibliography.

17. Samuel Gorovitz and Alasdair MacIntyre, "Towards a Theory of Medical Fallibility," is an extended treatment of what Aristotle makes into the distinction between "internal" and "external" success, between acting properly as a doctor and bringing about a cure. They dissociate the concept of injury ("external" failure) from that of malpractice ("internal" failure), and they point out that such a distinction makes sense only because medicine is not the application of a known body of knowledge, an applied science, but instead what Aristotle means by an art or power. See also MacIntyre, *After Virtue,* 188. "We call [goods] internal for two reasons: first . . . because we can only specify them in terms of chess or some other game of that specific kind and by means of examples from such games . . . ; and secondly because they can only be identified and recognized by the experience of participating in the practice in question. Those who lack the relevant experience are incompetent thereby as judges of internal goods."

18. As usual, Aristotle complicates things (14.1453b1–7: "Fear and pity sometimes result from the spectacle and are sometimes aroused by the actual arrangement of the incidents (*systaseos tōn pragmatiōn*) [equivalent to plot], which is preferable and the mark of a better poet. . . . To produce this effect by means of an appeal to the eye is inartistic (*atechnoteron*) and needs adventitious aid."

19. My insistence on the internal end as constitutive of an art of rhetoric shows how unaristotelian an understanding of rhetoric is imputed to Aristotle in Michael Heim, "Philosophy as Ultimate Rhetoric": "While judicial speakers can hide their genuine selves and still attain their persuasive ends, the deliberate rhetorician must *express himself,* viz. his own deepest interest, if he is to provide the strongest arguments for convincing other participants in the deliberation. That is, fellow deliberants are more likely to be convinced if the speech of the rhetor has a dimension of self-involvement or self-implication."

20. Dorothea Frede, "Necessity, Chance, and 'What Happens for the Most Part' in Aristotle's *Poetics,*" 217, n. 12: "Uniformity can at best tell us *that* something cannot be otherwise, it is not sufficient to show *why* it should be so."

21. Whether these conflicts produce problems for a "morality of rhetoric" is the subject of Chapter 7. For a different conception of the relation between the rational and the stochastic, see William W. Fortenbaugh, "Aristotle's Conception of Moral Virtue and Its Perceptive Role," 82.

22. Stephen G. Salkever notes that this discrepancy between internal and external ends means that politics cannot, in Hume's words, be reduced to a science. Deliberation is always necessary. "Aristotle's Social Science," 492: "If those nomoi which were best suited to achieving the ultimate aim of politics (virtuous persons) were also those most appropriate for achieving its proximate goals (peace and integration), then social science could in principle provide precise answers to questions concerning the sorts of nomoi which could best serve the ends of the polis. Unfortunately, the antecedent of this hypothesis is usually not the case; at the heart of the problem of human affairs sits a tension which does not admit of precise theoretical resolution."

The relation between two kinds of end is well captured in David Luban's analysis of the work of Hannah Arendt. David Luban, "Explaining Dark Times," 221–22: Arendt's "conception of politics can seem adolescent to us; it seems to overlook the fact that political actions are customarily undertaken for specific purposes and not to satisfy a yen to do something great. But Arendt recognizes this. She sharply distinguishes between the *meaning* of an action and its *end,* and attacks as monstrous the confusion of the two. (It is monstrous because it is the root of totalitarian ideology, which thinks of 'the meaning of history' as something we can consciously aim at as if it were an end.) The end is the particular goal of an action, while its meaning is general. But, she argues, we can keep these sorted out by noticing the difference between the expressions 'for the sake of . . .' and 'in order to. . . .' A carpenter performs his actions *in order* to make a table, but 'his whole life as a carpenter is ruled by something quite different, namely an encompassing notion 'for the sake of' which he became a carpenter in the first place' (*Between Past and Future,* [New York: Viking, 1963], p. 79). Keeping this in mind, it is no paradox to say that political communities are founded for the sake of immortalizing their inhabitants, not in order to fulfill certain specific purposes; or that political action is undertaken for the sake of glory. And this seems to be Pericles' conception of the matter."

23. *Whose Justice?* 28.

24. *Metaphysics* VII.7.1032a32–1032b33. Lear, *Aristotle: The Desire to Understand,* 33. "There are at least three ways in which forms are transmitted in the natural world: by sexual reproduction, by the creation of artefacts, and by teaching." I am here arguing that we should extend "teaching" to cover artful rhetoric.

25. For an earlier observation on the relation between *peitho* and performative utterances, see Mourelatos, *The Route of Parmenides,* 142–144.

26. For enthymeme as body and form, see, e.g., Grimaldi, *Studies,* 137: "When Aristotle calls the enthymeme *sōma tēs pisteōs* (1354a15) it certainly appears that it is in this sense of inferential form, something which is able to contain and give form to the *pisteis.*"

27. I have argued this claim in detail in "The Moral Virtues and the Two Sides of *Energeia.*"

28. See, e.g., Hintikka, *Knowledge and the Known,* 88, in which the intentionality of communication leads him to note the existence of two standards of success analogous to those in *Rhetoric* I.1: "In an international production of an outcome a double creation as it were seems to be taking place. Besides bringing about the result in a purely causal sense (when successful) the agent creates through his knowledge,

his beliefs, and his expectations a kind of framework in which the result can be discussed even when the agent is unsuccessful." For something similar in a very different idiom, see Michel de Certeau, "What We Do When We Believe," 200. "In order to presume its object (the expected thing) believable, belief must also presume that the other, in a certain sense, also 'believes' and that he considers himself obligated by the gift given to him. It is a belief in the belief of the other or in what he/one makes believe that he believes, etc. A belief of the other is a postulate of a belief in the other."

29. In the same way, the *Poetics* declares that plot, with the soul of tragedy, is not an obvious empirical datum or an immediate end of artistic effort 6.1450a30–35: "Those who try to write tragedy are much sooner successful in language and character-study than in arranging the incidents, and it is the same with almost all the earlier poets." This is proof that the plot is the soul and essence of tragedy.

30. For parallel reasons, honesty and avowability will do as little as rationality in contrast to emotion to define artful persuasion. Mill gives a good reason why these sorts of differentiae do not work. "Honesty" and similar criteria become harder to judge fairly the more important the case. *On Liberty*: "It is fit to take some notice of those who say, that the free expression of all opinions should be permitted, on condition that the manner be temperate, and do not pass the bounds of fair discussion. Much might be said on the impossibility of fixing where these supposed bounds are to be placed; for if the test be offense to those whose opinion is attacked. I think experience testifies that this offence is given whenever the attack is telling and powerful, and that every opponent who pushes them hard, and whom they find it difficult to answer, appears to them, if he shows any strong feeling on the subject, an intemperate opponent. But this though an important consideration in a practical point of view, merges in a more fundamental objection. Undoubtedly the manner of asserting an opinion, even though it may be a true one, may be very objectionable, and may justly incur severe censure. But the principal offences of the kind are such as it is mostly impossible, unless by accidental self-betrayal, to bring home to conviction. The gravest of them, is to argue sophistically, to suppress facts or arguments, to misstate the elements of the case, or misrepresent the opposition opinion. But all this, even to the most aggravated degree, is so continually done in perfect good faith, by persons who are not considered, and in many other respects do not deserve to be considered, ignorant or incompetent, that it is rarely possible on adequate grounds conscientiously to stamp the misrepresentation as morally culpable; and still less could law presume to interfere with this kind of controversial misconduct."

31. Broadie, *Ethics with Aristotle,* 209. "Although any given production must as a matter of fact be particular if it occurs at all, its particularising conditions are external and accidental to its *nature* as a that-sort-of-production. But the particulars of an action belong to its essence as action, since these are features of *what* it is that is judged good or not. The verdict depends on the when, the where, the agent's relations with those affected, the forseeable consequences, the cost, the alternatives sacrificed etc."

32. The standard view is that Book III was joined to the first two books not by Aristotle but by a later editor. Wisse has recently suggested that, while written

separately, the three books may have been put together by Aristotle. Apart from the evidence of later doxographers and biographers, the main datum is that Books I and II never refer to anything in III, except for the transitional passage at the end of II.

I don't think any of this matters for my purposes. It is, I think, admitted by all that III is relatively independent of the first two books, and, on the other hand, that their compilation into a single work at least makes more sense than appending Book III to any of Aristotle's other works. In other words, one could write transitions, etc. that could go some way toward making a single work out of the three books, but it will not be a single work with the strong kind of unity that the first two books have. That moderate position is enough for my purpose, which is to treat Books I and II as a sustained argument and occasionally appeal to III for amplification.

For more data and theories, see Jakob Wisse, *Ethos and Pathos from Aristotle to Cicero*, 333–36, William Grimaldi, *Studies*, 49–52, Carnes Lord, "On the Early History of the Aristotelian Corpus," and Paul Moraux, *Les listes anciennes des ouvrages d'Aristotle*.

33. See also *Physics* II.2.194a33–b7: "The arts make their material (some simply 'make' it, others make it serviceable), and we use everything as if it was there for our sake. . . . The arts, therefore, which govern the matter and have knowledge are two, namely the art which uses the product and the art which directs the production of it. That is why the using art also is in a sense directive; but it differs in that it knows the form, whereas the art which is directive as being concerned with production knows the matter. For the helmsman knows and prescribes what sort of form a helm should have, the other from what wood it should be made and by means of what operations."

34. *Pace* Grimaldi, *Studies*, 8, n. 8: "It is difficult to see how the rhetorician is not, as far as Aristotle is concerned, as much a maker as the poet."

35. Historically, there is an association between the professional art of rhetoric and foreigners. See Dover, "Freedom of the Intellectual," 52: "Athenians had very good reason for thinking of the typical intellectual as a visiting foreigner dependent on the patronage, hospitability and generosity of a small number of rich and distinguished families. . . . And we should consider the probability that foreign intellectuals were widely regarded as exercising, through their wealthy Athenian patrons, great influence over Athenian policy, while not themselves accountable for the execution of policy. As foreigners, they could be regarded as not owing their primary loyalty to the Athenian demos and therefore as comparatively indifferent to such antagonism as might arise between the demos and the gods in consequence of the spread of sceptical rejection of traditional practices. It is even possible that an Athenian, such as Damon or Socrates, who gained a reputation as 'teacher' of wealthy and powerful men, incurred special odium inasmuch as he was felt to have alienated himself from the community by choosing a foreigner's role—rather as a citizen who prostituted himself incurred severe penalties, while a male prostitute of foreign birth incurred none."

36. III.4.1277b2–7: "Now the works of those ruled in this way should not be learned by the good [man] or the political [ruler] or the good citizen, unless he does it for himself out of some need of his own (for then it does not result in one person

becoming master or another slave)." See also *Rhetoric* I.9.1367a30–31: "Not to work at a vulgar trade [is honorable]; for it is characteristic of a free man not to live in dependence on another." "The magnanimous person cannot let anyone else, except a friend, determine his life" (*Ethics* IV.3.1124b31–1125a2).

37. That practices associated with internal goods cannot be delegated is explained in Allen E. Buchanan, "Assessing the Communitarian Critique of Liberalism," 869: "Internal goods . . . are not ends of communal activity characterizable independently of the communal relationship itself, as if that relationship were valued simply as the means towards them. Moreover, although these goods are, in the economist's parlance, jointly produced, they are not public goods because they are excludable—indeed, intrinsically excludable. In other words, internal goods require the contribution of two or more people, but by their nature they are not available to non-contributors. . . . Because internal goods are not in principle available to those who only feign contribution to them, no free-rider problem threatens their production as it does with public goods. To the extent that the distinctive goods of community are goods of participation, goods intrinsic to the cooperative process itself, non-contributors cannot hope to achieve them."

38. The people in law schools who worry about whether advocacy is just a technique use the same test when they argue that law is corrupting not because of the uses to which it is put—anything can be put to bad uses—but because of its effects of the souls and characters of practitioners. I have learned the most from James B. White, *The Legal Imagination, When Words Lose Their Meaning, Heracles' Bow: Essays on the Rhetoric and Poetics of Law*, and *Justice As Translation: An Essay in Cultural and Legal Criticism*. See also John O. Cole, "The Socratic Method in Legal Education: Moral Discourse and Accommodation;" William Epstein, "The Classical Tradition of Dialectics and American Legal Education"; William C. Heffernan, "Not Socrates, but Protagoras: The Sophistic Basic of Legal Education"; David Luban, *Lawyers and Justice: An Ethical Study*; Luban, "Partisanship, Betrayal, and Autonomy in the Lawyer-Client Relationship"; and Joseph Vining, *The Authoritative and the Authoritarian*.

39. Cf. *Politics* II.5.1273a21–38. "The easy use of words and phrases and the avoidance of strict precision is in general a sign of good breeding; indeed, the opposite is hardly worthy of a gentleman" (*Theaetetus* 184c). Alasdair MacIntyre, *Whose Justice?* 113: "It is in part in this aristocratic carelessness about consequences that the nobility, the fineness of the exercise of such virtues resides."

CHAPTER 2
The Kinds of Rhetoric

1. That the three kinds of rhetoric was Aristotle's own innovation, and not something obvious by inspection is noted by Peter J. Crook, "Language, Truth and Law in Ancient Greece," *Language and Communication* 5 (1985): 241. "Until Aristotle identified three distinct kinds of rhetoric—forensic, deliberative and epideictic (epideictic being a catch-all term for anything not forensic or deliberative)—the rhetorical theorists must have been somewhat handicapped in their search for methods of

persuasion appropriate to different audiences; for there did not seem to be any iden-
tifiable or significant differences between their audiences." Obviously, I disagree
with the parenthesis. Crook also notes the significance of the identification of species, p. 242: "The claim that there are only three types of rhetoric, or rather, three
types of context in which rhetoric is found, also leads to the idea that rhetorical
theory was viewed as that which provided anyone with the right thing to say to
anybody in any context." Kennedy (p. 75) gives speeches by ambassadors as a kind
of rhetoric not mentioned; any reader of Thucydides must think that these are
pretty important examples of rhetoric.

2. In addition to the comments of Jonathan Lear that I have already cited, for
further exploration of this difference between Aristotle and us see Paul Feyerabend,
"In Defence of Aristotle."

3. For more on the *haplōs/tini* distinction in Aristotle's *Ethics,* see Paula Gottlieb,
"Aristotle and Protagoras." In later rhetorics, such as the *Ad Herennium,* this distinction becomes the distinction between absolute and assumptive issues.

4. X.5.1176a3–10: "Each kind of animal seems to have its own proper pleasure,
just at it has its own proper function. . . . Hence animals that differ in species also
have pleasures that differ in species; and it would be reasonable for animals of the
same species to have the same pleasures also. In fact, however, the pleasures differ
quite a lot, in human beings at any rate." *Politics* VII.13.1332b3–8: The other animals live by nature above all, but in some slight respects by habit as well while man
lives also by reason (for he alone has reason); so these things should be consonant
with the other."

5. Bernard Williams, *Ethics and the Limits of Philosophy,* 126: "*Ought* cannot be
deduced from *is* if the *ought* is taken to be the same as the *should* that occurs in the
practical question 'what should I do?' and in the 'all things considered' answer to it.
Such an answer, the conclusion of a piece of practical reasoning, cannot be logically
deduced from the premises that support it."

6. Similarly quick inference is the cause of faction and revolution in the *Politics.*
For just one example: "All fasten on a certain sort of justice, but proceed only to a
certain point, and do not speak of the whole of justice in its authoritative sense. For
example, justice is held to be just, and it is, but for equals and not for all; and
inequality is held to be just and is indeed, but for unequals and not for all: but they
disregard this element of persons and judge badly (III.9.1280a8–13).

John Finnis, *Fundamentals of Ethics,* 70: "The history of moral philosophy, especially in the centuries during which it has sought to distinguish its method from the
method proper to theology, is the history of a search for the missing *intermediate
principles.* This search for principles, to guide the transition from judgments about
human goods to judgments about the right thing to do here and now, has been
waylaid by all sorts of intellectual, spiritual and cultural confusions. Note particularly
the unhappy tendency to find a spurious, or at best only partial, unity of ethical
thought, by casting a single principle as the master principle or axiom from which
all ethical conclusions are to be derived, or in terms of which all moral virtues are
to be explained."

7. Michael Stocker, "Some Problems with Counter-Examples in Ethics," 281:
"Some think that it is conceptual of the notion of *intrinsic value* that if a value v is

intrinsic anywhere, it is intrinsic everywhere. Some also think that what is not good just everywhere is, therefore, only instrumentally good where it is good. But these are simply confusions of *intrinsic* value with *absolute* or *unconditional* value." See also James D. Wallace, *Moral Relevance and Moral Conflict,* and Christine Korsgaard, "Two Distinctions in Goodness."

8. For a clear statement of some of the differences, see Thomas Conley, "Ancient Rhetoric and Modern Genre Criticism."

9. On the way the function is embodied primarily in the species, not in the genus, see *Metaphysics* X.8.1057b37–1058a5: "For by genus I mean one identical thing which is predicated of both and is differentiated in no merely accidental way, whether as matter or otherwise. For not only must the common attach to different things, e.g., not only must both be animals, but this very animality must also be different for each (e.g., in one case equinity, in the other humanity, and so this common is specifically different for each from what it is for the other." See also *De Anima* II.3.414b20–32. For a treatment of the way the genus is actualized in its species, see James Lennox, "Aristotle on Genera, Species, and 'the More and the Less,'" esp. 337ff. "Voice is the genus and matter, but its differentiae make the species, i.e., the letters, out of it" *Metaphysics* VII.12.1038a7–8.

10. I argue this in detail in "The Human Function and Aristotle's Art of Rhetoric."

11. David Keyt, "Distributive Justice in Aristotle's *Ethics* and *Politics,*" 34: "One thing is an accessory of another if, and only if, the one is indispensable for the existence of the other but does not enter into the essence of the other. Thus a particular group is an accessory of a polis if, and only if, the group is indispensable for the existence of the polis but does not enter into the essence of the polis. . . . A particular group would not enter into the essence of a polis if the life characteristic of that group is incompatible with the sort of life that defines a polis, namely, a life of moral and intellectual virtue." For more information about the use of *symperilambanein,* see Lionel Pearson, "Characterization in Drama and Oratory."

12. I have explored this particular example in more detail in "He Does the Police in Different Voices: J. B. White on the Criminal Law."

13. See also the causal and conceptual connection between justice and advantage at *Ethics* V.1.1129b13–17: "Whatever is lawful is in some way just; for the provisions of legislative science are lawful, and we say that each of them is just. Now in every matter they deal with the laws aim either at the common benefit of all, or at the benefit of those in control, whose control rests on virtue or some other such basis." *Ethics* V.4.1132a21–25: "Hence parties to a dispute resort to a judge, and an appeal to a judge is an appeal to what is just; for the judge is intended to be a sort of living embodiment of what is just. Moreover, they seek the judge as an intermediary, and in some cities they actually call judges mediators, assuming that if they are awarded an intermediate amount, the award will be just. If, then, the judge is an intermediary, what is just is in some way intermediate." Justice varies from one state to another, in the *Politics,* because of variations in whose advantage is aimed at.

14. One interesting possibility for conflict in the *Rhetoric* echoes the *Gorgias:* "Also just things and works justly done [are honorable] (but not things justly suffered; for in this alone of the virtues what is justly experienced is not always

honorable, but in the case of being punished, to suffer justly is more shameful than to suffer unjustly)" (I.9.1366b30–33).

15. Adam Smith notes some differences between decisions that we think should be determined by rules alone and those where being guided by nothing but rules seems a character flaw. *The Theory of Moral Sentiments,* 172: "All those graceful and admired actions, to which the benevolent affections would prompt us, ought to proceed as much from the passions themselves, as from any regard to the general rules of conduct. A benefactor thinks himself but ill requited, if the person upon whom he has bestowed his good offices, repays them merely from a cold sense of duty, and without any attention to his person. . . . The contrary maxim takes place with regard to the malevolent and unsocial passions. We ought to reward from the gratitude and generosity of our own hearts, without any reluctance, and without being obliged to reflect how great the propriety of rewarding: but we ought always to punish with reluctance and more from a sense of the propriety of punishing, than from any savage disposition to revenge."

See also Robert Trivers, "The Evolution of Reciprocal Altruism," 50: "Selection may favor distrusting those who perform altruistic acts without the emotional basis of generosity or guilt because the altruistic tendencies of such individuals may be less reliable in the future." Owen J. Flanagan, Jr., *Varieties of Moral Personality,* 37: "Some people are guided by benevolent sentiments to such a degree that they need no philosophical motive for extending charity to unconnected others. Indeed, replacing their benevolent motivation with a philosophical rationale for benevolence in terms of utility would constitute a deep change in the kind of person they are. Other sorts of persons, however, often need belief-based motives and principled rationales in order to want to be certain kinds of persons or do certain kinds of things. Unless we are being excessively moralistic, it seems unfair to judge such persons as morally defective compared to more spontaneously benevolent types. Outside of those segments of life which are undermined if they are too motivated by conscious, ulterior aims or principled rationales—for example, love and friendship—philosophical reasons seem perfectly suitable, indeed necessary, as motives for certain persons in certain domains."

16. Broadie has an explanation for how epideixis and deliberation can be convertible, yet epideixis extends further than the scope of deliberation. *Ethics with Aristotle,* 127–28: "When Aristotle says that praise and censure apply to actions which issue from virtue and vice . . . he is not, I think, forgetting the voluntary actions of the immature. Rather, the statement is about the terms *in which* we praise and find fault. Praise and censure, all along the line, send the following message: this is what a good/bad (brave/cowardly, honest/dishonest, etc.) person would do. Obviously, the message is applied to the actions of those whose characters we considered to be formed, and in that context it implies that these persons *are* good or bad. But the *undeveloped* agent, too, is meant to absorb the same lesson in connection with his own behavior, though here it does not carry the same categorical judgment of him as he actually is. Praise encourages him to play the part of a good person by telling him that doing this or that is playing that part, and correspondingly for discouragement by reprimand."

17. That such surpluses are functional in creating useful barriers to translation

and reduction is suggested by Mario Biagioli, "The Anthropology of Incommensurability," 184: "Both Kuhn's paradigm and Darwin's species refer to *populations* of individuals who interbreed either sexually (in Darwin's case) or intellectually (in Kuhn's case). Consequently, the barrier of sterility among species observed by Darwin could be compared to the incommensurability Kuhn has perceived among competing paradigms. In the same way that the barrier of sterility is an antiswamping device which prevents the characters of the new species from being absorbed back into the old one, incommensurability could be seen as a form of intellectual sterility—as the impossibility of breeding intellectually."

18. David B. Wong, "Three Kinds of Incommensurability," 156: "The most interesting and substantial cases for evaluative incommensurability arise, not from our inability to make sense of another people's beliefs, but precisely from those situations in which we understand and see how different their beliefs are from our own. The question of evaluative incommensurability arises, not because their beliefs appear bizarre to us, but because we can understand how they are tied to a life that [some] people would want to live. . . . These cases for evaluative incommensurability need not arise from skepticism about the lack of an independent and neutral standard for judging between theories, but rather from a solid sense of what it is satisfying in alternative forms of life." See also Jonathan Lear, "Ethics, Mathematics, and Relativism."

19. Sabina Lovibond, *Realism and Imagination in Ethics,* 182. "The different policies we can adopt in response to moral contradiction reflect the varying extent to which our cognitive control is threatened by the existence of the alternative view. Thus if the threat is severe, we may prefer not to 'let the contradiction stand,' when reasoned argument fails us, but to switch to an objectifying treatment of the anomalous opinion which will enable us to consider it in terms of its causal origins. If the threat is light or negligible, on the other hand, we may not see fit to give the matter any more thought." This, though, is a strangely voluntary description of the process.

See also Albert R. Jonsen and Stephen Toulmin, *The Abuse of Casuistry,* 295: "If 'theories' . . . were opposed to one another as a matter of logic, supporters of any one account would then be intellectually obliged to forswear all the others. But because the points at issue between them rest, rather, on considerations of rhetoric, the only question left to answer is, 'What makes appeals to one of the accounts cogent and appropriate on one particular occasion, while appeals to another will carry more conviction on a second occasion?'"

William A. Galston, *Justice and the Human Good,* 23: "Contradiction has practical force in arguments because the telos of theoretical speech is truth, and it is impossible for all components of a contradiction to be true simultaneously. But the telos of a political community may be compatible with practices the justifications of which contradict one another. Machiavelli traced the strength and glory of Rome to the enduring struggle between patricians and plebeians. Practices may be opposed to one another or mutually limiting, but it is a mistake to say that they contradict one another. Underlying the faith in immanent critique is the preference for a harmonious, rational community, the component practices of which can be justified in a mutually consistent manner—an admirable goal, perhaps, but one the justification

264   NOTES TO THREE

of which lies outside the process of the critique." See, finally, Amélie Rorty, *Mind in Action*, 65: "Whether conflicts are so formulated that a policymaker must regard them as contradictory already reveals something about his identity. In choosing policies, a person also has some unexpected latitude in determining the logical relations between them. Some, but not all, of the difference between being conflicted and facing a contradiction lies in the way in which a policy has been formulated."

20. Probably the most extensive use of Aristotle to explore contemporary problems of plurality and commensurability is in Michael Stocker, *Plural and Conflicting Values*. Also relevant are David Wiggins, "Weakness of Will, Commensurability, and the Objects of Deliberation and Desire" and Martha Nussbaum, *The Fragility of Goodness*.

21. A similar pair of arguments is noted by Michael W. McConnell, "Religious Freedom at the Crossroads." McConnell notes that "some would expand the scope of the Free Exercise Clause by treating the free exercise right as a right of personal autonomy or self-definition. Rather than understanding religion as a matter over which we have no control—the demands of a transcendent authority—it has become common to regard religion as valuable and important only because it is *what we choose*" (172). "There is an interesting and important parallel to the analysis of homosexual rights reflected in the general shift from the term 'sexual preference' to the term 'sexual orientation.' It used to be thought that sexuality was entitled to constitutional protection because each person should be free to choose the objects of his or her affection. Now it is more often argued that sexuality is entitled to constitutional protection because it is *not* a choice, but something inherent in the person's nature, which cannot be changed" (173n.250).

CHAPTER 3
Rhetorical Topics and Practical Reason

1. I will offer further explications of the analogy that enthymeme is to *ēthos* as body to soul in chapter 6.

2. Offshoot is a better translation of *paraphues* than child would be. Cope, in his note, says that it "properly denotes either a branch or a separate plant 'growing alongside' of the parent plant, and proceeding either from the stem or the root, as a scion or offshoot" (p. 33). Although Cope notes that a *paraphues* properly only has one parent, I think it would be a mistake to push the metaphor further and say that logic is the male parent, supplying the form, and politics the female, furnishing the matter. For a history of interpretations of the relations of rhetoric to politics and dialectic, see Lawrence D. Green, "Aristotelian Rhetoric, Dialectic, and the Traditions of *Antistrophos*" and William Wallace, "Aquinas on Dialectic and Rhetoric."

3. For a subtle analysis of Plato's encounter with rhetoric's being about *logoi*, see Terry Penner, "Socrates on the Impossibility of Belief-Relative Sciences," 266: "Each of rhetoric, cookery, cosmetology, and the art of interpreting Homer involve in a crucial way, as part of their subject matter, *beliefs*—beliefs, moreover, where it is officially irrelevant to the alleged science in question *whether the beliefs are true or*

false. Rhetoric aims to get you to accept the belief that a certain course of action would be good. And it is officially indifferent to the science of rhetoric whether the belief is true or false. (Not only that; we will also see that the persuader *does not even have to know, himself or herself,* whether the belief in question is true or false.)" (Also p. 267): "Socrates has an idea about the sciences that, looked at from a sophisticated modern point of view, may seem rather primitive. His idea is that a science concerning *beliefs,* or *desires,* or other similar psychological states, has to be in a certain way *transparent.* That is, the science must 'look through' the psychological states in question to the reality towards which the psychological states are directed." See also Jon Moline, "Plato on Persuasion and Credibility."

4. I have tried to explicate the meaning of these passages in "Aristotle's *Rhetoric* on Unintentionally Hitting the Principles of the Sciences."

5. Paul Ricoeur, *The Rule of Metaphor,* 29–30. "Rhetoric cannot become an empty and formal technique, because it is linked to what is contained in the most highly probable opinions, that is, what is admitted or endorsed by the majority of people. Now with this connection between rhetoric and non-critical subject matter goes the risk of turning rhetoric into a sort of popular science. This collusion with *accepted ideas* throws rhetoric into a scattered and dissipating pursuit of argument-motifs or 'positions,' which amount to so many recipes to protect the speaker from being taken by surprise in debate—a collusion, then, between *Rhetoric* and *Topics,* which was doubtless one of the causes of the former's death."

6. For example, de Pater speaks of the topics as directions for research, "formules de recherche," *Les Topiques d'Aristote,* 122.

7. Compare the opening lines of *Politics* V: "Nearly everything else that we intended to speak of has been treated. What things bring about revolutions in regimes and how many and of what sort they are; what are the sources of destruction for each sort of regime and into which sort of regime a regime is most particularly transformed; further, what are the sources of preservation both [for regimes] in common and for each sort of regime separately; and further, by what things each sort of regime might most particularly be preserved—these matters must be investigated in conformity with what has been spoken of" (V.1.1301a19–25).

8. Kenneth Burke, *A Rhetoric of Motives,* 56.

9. See also Eugene F. Ryan, "Aristotle's *Rhetoric* and *Ethics* and the Ethos of Society."

10. Thus the contrast that Fortenbaugh gives in the following is not quite right. William Fortenbaugh, "Aristotle's *Rhetoric* on Emotions," 226–27, n.24: "The definitions of individual emotions are not external to a method that can be mastered independently of the definitions. While it is possible to master persuasion 'through demonstration' without mastering any particular set of premises, persuasion 'through the hearers' cannot be mastered apart from an understanding of individual emotions. While the former mode of persuasion belongs to the man who is able to 'syllogize,' the latter mode belongs to the man who is able to investigate and so understand the nature of emotional response (1356a21–25). The definitions and analyses of individual emotions are not external to the mode of persuasion but rather what a man learns when he learns the mode." Aristotle does supply premises here in chapter 5, and also in chapter 9 as well. The difference, and it is an important

one, is that the premises of Book I can be used by the orator because the audience holds them, while the premises that are the definitions of the emotions can be used by the orator because they are true—otherwise their use would not evoke the appropriate emotions.

11. Thomas Cole, *The Origins of Rhetoric in Ancient Greece*, 91.

12. For connections between topics and Toulmin's inference warrants, see Otto Bird, "The Tradition of the Logical Topics," and "The Re-Discovery of the 'Topics': Professor Toulmin's Inference-Warrants." Joseph L. Cowan, "The Uses of Argument—An Apology for Logic," notes that the intertranslatability between modes of inference and principles fails for Toulmin's warrants, just as they should according to this analysis of the relation between practical reason and logic.

13. See, for example, Michael W. McConnell and Richard A. Posner, "An Economic Approach to Issues of Religious Freedom."

14. Rorty, *Mind in Action*, p. 274: "When we are conflicted, we are not torn by the large dichotomized conflicts between altruism and egoism, or between principles of morality and the psychology of desire and interest. Our conflicts are those between particular thoughtful desires or thoughtful habits that cannot all be simultaneously realized or enacted, because they eventually undermine each other. The resolutions of such conflicts rarely involve denying or suppressing one side, for both sides of intrapsychic conflicts, like both sides of political conflicts, represent functional contributions to thriving."

John Dewey, *Human Nature and Conduct*, 193: "The occasion of deliberation is an *excess* of preferences, not natural apathy or an absence of likings. We want things that are incompatible with one another; therefore we have to make a choice of what we *really* want, of the course of action, that is, which most fully releases activities. Choice is not the emergence of preference out of indifference. It is the emergence of a unified preference out of competing preferences."

15. Criticism of arguments of this kind can be found in Michael W. McConnell, "Religious Freedom at the Crossroads."

16. The emotions often function to allow a continuing role for reasons that are not directly acted upon. For details, see chapter 4.

17. Cass R. Sunstein, "Free Speech Now," 313.

18. Ernest de Sousa, *The Rationality of Emotion*, 286: "Unlike true and false, [the tragic and the comic] are not contradictories, since the number of formal objects of emotions is large, whereas there is only one formal object of belief. This disanalogy makes axiological correctness more difficult to understand than truth. Good is already more complicated than true, in that it is subject to the 'Monkey's Paw' phenomenon': something good can turn out bad because of what it is conjoined with; by contrast, nothing true can turn out false because of what it is conjoined with."

Bernard Williams, "Political Philosophy and the Analytical Tradition," 66–67: "An important aim, and certain consequence, of systematizing in these areas is to reduce or eliminate conflict among our ideas and sentiments; and before we set out doing that, and while we are doing it, we should reflect on the significance of conflict. Conflict in our moral sentiments and beliefs is, first, a historically, socially, and probably psychologically conditioned phenomenon, the product of such things as pluralistic societies and rapid cultural change as well as, perhaps, more generally

disturbed psychological needs which tend to conflict. We can, to some extent, understand *why* we have conflicting sentiments, but that does not mean, or should not
mean, that we therefore withdraw our loyalty from them. Second, it is not true that
any situation in which there is no such conflict is better than one in which there is,
or even—what is perhaps more plausible—that conflict-reduction is an aim which
always has a very strong priority. In the case of belief-conflict and of explanatory
theories, conflict-reduction is an undoubted aim: whether it be for the pragmatist
reason, that conflict-elimination itself defines the aim of the explanatory endeavor,
or for the realist reason that conflicting beliefs cannot both, in some more substantial
sense, be true. But the articulation of our moral sentiments does not necessarily
obey these constraints, and to demand that they be schooled by the requirement of
system is to alter our moral perception of the world, not just to make it in some
incontestable sense more rational."

19. The differences between dependability and logical validity are well brought
out in Ronald Beiner, "Do We Need a Philosophical Ethics?" 235–36: "Part of the
explanation for the primacy of *ēthos* is that in order for moral convictions to have
force within the life of concrete societies, ethical intuitions must possess a great
deal more self-certainty than they could possibly gather from merely theoretical
demonstrations. (An insight of this kind is present in Hegel's and Nietzsche's analyses of Socrates, whose very appearance is seen as a symptom of moral decline within
the polis.) As even Habermas concedes, 'the difference between what we always
claim for our rationality and what we are actually able to explicate as rational can
in principle never be eliminated.' But for the demands of situated praxis, this is
simply not enough. One must act *as if* unreflectively, embodying a sure sense of
what is good and right; one must command a kind of practical assurance that even
the strictest, most rigorous set of arguments fails to supply. This is something made
available only by character and habituation, never by rational argument as such. As
an Aristotelian would say, in order to live virtuously and to make the right choices,
one's soul must be shaped by certain habits of virtuous conduct, in a way that ren-
ders superfluous recourse to strict arguments. Judged by these purposes, the
achievements of theory always fall short."

20. For another complication, in *Poetics* 25, epic and tragedy have the same
species (*eidē*) and parts (*merē*), apart from song and spectacle, which are unique to
tragedy (1459b7–9).

21. Richard McKeon, "Dialectic and Political Thought and Action," 26: "Like
the use of reason in the natural sciences, its use in practical affairs is an inference. . . .
The inference is not from a proposition to a prediction, however, except in an
analogical sense. Principles, theories, and statements are only one ingredient in the
premises from which a practical inference proceeds. They are inferences and are
made precise, in so far as they enter serious consideration, not by their truth but by
their reliability as statements of intention, granted the circumstances, history, and
character of their proponents. . . . Reason in application to practical questions
therefore has, in addition to its direct inferential function of relating assumptions to
conclusions [the function assumed in the so-called practical syllogism and in productive action], an inverse inferential or imputative function of relating proposals to
the character and attitude form which they flow." Kenny, *Will, Freedom, and Power,*

p. 89: "In theoretical argument it is reasoning to necessary conditions—deductive theoretical logic—which is *conclusive,* in the sense of ensuring that the conclusion has the value which the reasoning aims at, namely truth; only deductive inference makes it certain that if the premises are true the conclusion is also. Inference to the best explanation, or inductive logic, as a host of philosophers of science have insisted, is never conclusive in the sense of showing that it is logically impossible for the premises to be true and the conclusion false. On the other hand, in practical inference it is only the logic of satisfactoriness which is *conclusive,* in the sense of ensuring that the conclusion has the value that the reasoning aims at, namely the satisfaction of the reasoner's wants. The logic of satisfaction—reasoning to necessary conditions for satisfaction—is never conclusive in the sense of ensuring the arrival of what is wanted."

22. Cf. Richard McKeon, "Literary Criticism and the Concept of Imitation in Antiquity."

23. For two other places that depend on a similarly multivariant causal analysis see: "Factional conflicts arise, then, not over small things but from small things—it is over great things" (V.4.1303b17). There he identifies three causes of revolutions: "One should grasp what condition [men] are in when they engage in factional conflict; for the sake of what they do so; and thirdly, what the beginning points are of political disturbances and of factional conflicts among one another" (V.2.1302a16–22). And see also the treatment of the emotions in *Rhetoric* II, each of which must be delimited by three causes, the "disposition of mind" (*pōs*), the persons that are the object of the emotion (*tisin*), and the "occasions that give rise" to the feeling (*poiois*) (II.1.1378a24–25). I will discuss this aspect of Aristotle' analysis of the emotions in the next chapter.

24. II.24.1402a3–8: "Further, just as in eristics an apparent syllogism occurs in confusing what is general [*haplōs*] but some particular (for example, in dialectic that nonbeing exists, for what-is-not *is* what-is-not; and that the unknown is known, for it is known about the unknown that it is unknown), so also in rhetoric there is an apparent enthymeme in regard to what is not generally probable but probable in a particular case." And Aristotle ends that chapter on apparent enthymemes by saying: "And this is 'to make the weaker seem the better cause.' Thus, people were rightly angry at the declaration of Protagoras; for it is a lie and not true but a fallacious probability and a part of no art except rhetoric and eristic" (1402a23–27).

25. Compare to the separation of the kinds of rhetoric in I.3.1358b30–37. There Aristotle used practices of concession and taking a stand to establish the autonomy of the three *eidē* of rhetoric. Here the same practices lead not to genres but to individual controversies. There are passages in Book III on similar subjects that have led some scholars, including Cope, to see an anticipation of the later rhetorical doctrine of *stasis.* See III.15.1416a6–33, III.16.1416b19–1417a12, III.17.1417b16–25.

26. For one interesting example, see Richard Posner, "The Homeric Version of the Minimal State."

27. Roger Shiner, "Aristotle's Theory of Equity," 182: "The *elleipein* image, which . . . is an integral part of Aristotle's theory of equity, does not connote 'gaps' in the 'hole-in-a-doughnut' sense. The image, rather, connotes a distance between two things, a falling-short. Aristotle's use of the term *elleipein* and cognates in

theorising about practical judgment is focused on the celebrated doctrine of the mean, which recurs constantly in the *Nicomachean Ethics* and the *Politics*. "Virtue is a mean between two vices, the vices of exceeding the mean and of falling short of the mean [*kat' elleipsin*]; the vices fall short [*elleipein*] or exceed what is required in both passions and actions, while virtue finds and chooses that mean" (*Nicomachean Ethics* 1107a2–6).

28. In the *Ethics*, equity is confined to unavoidable errors, and therefore does not correct a law but only its use in a case. On that reading, judgments of equity cannot become precedents and are *ad hoc*. The distinction between voluntary and involuntary legislative errors is given a further interpretation by Hamilton in *Federalist* 87: "It is not with a view to infractions of the Constitution only, that the independence of the judges may be an essential safeguard against the effects of occasional ill humors in the society. These sometimes extend no farther than to the injury of the private rights of particular classes of citizens, by unjust and partial laws. Here also the firmness of judicial magistracy is of vast importance in mitigating the severity and confining the operation of such laws. It not only serves to moderate the immediate mischiefs of those which may have been passed, but it operates as a check upon the legislative body in passing them; who, perceiving that obstacles to the success of iniquitous intention are to be expected from the scruples of the courts, are in a manner compelled, by the very motives of the injustice they meditate, to qualify their attempts."

Even discretion is distinct from caprice, but the following treatment of discretion should make clear its difference from equity. Frank Easterbrook, "Criminal Procedure as a Market System," 299: "Prosecutors have absolute discretion. They may prosecute whom they please, for such crimes as they please. . . . They need not develop or follow any criteria for making such decisions. . . . Legal discretion is not the same as caprice in fact. The prosecutor's desire to maximize his returns, and his interactions with other actors, impose constraints as firm as any explicit system of rules."

29. The differences between considerations of justice and equity are mirrored in an interesting way in Adam Smith, 168. "Man is by Nature directed to correct, in some measure, that distribution of things which she herself would otherwise have made. The rules which for this purpose she prompts him to follow, are different from those which she herself observes. She bestows upon every virtue, and upon every vice, that precise reward or punishment which is best fitted to encourage the one, or to restrain the other. She is directed by this sole consideration, and pays little regard to the different degrees of merit and demerit, which they may seem to possess in the sentiments and passions of man. Man, on the contrary, pays regard to this only, and would endeavour to render the state of every virtue precisely proportioned to that degree of love and esteem, and of every vice to that degree of contempt and abhorrence, which he himself conceives for it."

30. Cf. Sabina Lovibond, *Realism and Imagination in Ethics*, 13: "The idea of moral judgments, not as statements of fact, but as expressions of the moral orientation of the individual, leads to a conception of morality itself as a kind of *partisanship*. This answers to the common-sense view that you have to stand up for your own values in face of the competition from the rival values endorsed by others. Individuals

are pictured as struggling to defend their own moral convictions, either within an institutional framework, or (possibly) by a trial of brute strength. Our 'factual' beliefs are not considered to need a militant defence of this kind, since they after all are (we hope) *true*—and, as such, can take care of themselves to some extent."

31. The last fifty years has seen a series of unsuccessful attempts to disentangle fact from value, objective description from the expression of emotions, etc. Aristotle's explication of topical argument might make this research project seem as unattractive as it is impossible. On the other side, for strong evaluation, see Charles Taylor, "What is Human Agency?" For metapreferences, see Harry Frankfurt, "Freedom of the Will and the Concept of a Person."

32. Charles Larmore, *Patterns of Moral Complexity,* 8: "The distinction between applying rules and acting on reasons that imply rules not given in advance is vital if we are to grasp the sense in which moral judgment responds to the particularity of a situation by going beyond the given content of the general rules that it applies. Observe that this distinction does not correspond to the one between explicit and implicit application of rules, since the latter implies that the rules were given in advance, but because of habituation did not figure in the agent's awareness." See also Broadie, 76: "The ungeneralisability of the *orthos logos* into a rule does not entail that it cannot be articulated by means of statements employing general terms. It is a *logos,* after all. What cannot be relied upon to hold good beyond the present case is its *orthotēs,* its correctness."

Vincent A. Wellman, "Practical Reasoning and Judicial Justification, 72–73: "Our expectations about the role of judges in the legal system suggest that complete consistency throughout the system is implausible. The consistency of a deductive system of logic implies that we may rely on indirect or *reductio ab absurdum* arguments. Yet, *reductio* arguments are unreliable in the law. When a judge decides a particular case he might be taken to have denied the validity of one party's arguments, but he is not necessarily understood to have decided that any other legal propositions are false. Consider, for example, the situation where there are two applicable but conflicting legal rules, but where the second is neither argued by any of the parties nor considered by the bench. The judge's use of the first does not entail the falsity of the second. Indeed, his decision does not even mean that the second rule was inapplicable." P. 76: "From the command, 'Post the letter,' it would be patently unacceptable to infer 'Post the letter or burn it,' no matter how valid the inference might have been among truth-bearing propositions with the same descriptive content. No commander who wants the letter posted would accept fulfillment of the inferred disjunction as fulfillment of the original order. On the other hand, while inferring 'Bring me a cloak' from 'Bring me something to keep me warm' may be an acceptable inference among commands, the corresponding inference among the related propositions would be invalid in deductive logic."

33. Ernest de Sousa, *The Rationality of Emotion,* 256–57: "What is peculiar about aesthetic arguments is that they are conducted without reliable major premises. If we construe aesthetic arguments on the model of the cognitive, then a major premise of an argument for an aesthetic conclusion might be of the form, 'Whenever such and such nonaesthetic properties are present, then we should expect such and such aesthetic properties to result.' But we seldom if ever know such a thing to be true."

For an extended argument against the existence of such major premises in aesthetic arguments, see chapter 3, "The Peculiar 'Logic' of Evaluative Criticism," in Wayne C. Booth, *The Company We Keep: An Ethics of Fiction,* 49–80.

This feature of the topics is related to the authority of particulars in praxis. T. E. Wilkerson, "Uniqueness in Art and Morals," 310: "Our judgments about aesthetic failures are clearly universalizable. The same mistakes are made, the same inadequacies are revealed, the same diagnoses are offered. Thus if I say that one of Barbara Cartland's novels is aesthetically unsatisfactory, because it is vapid and unimaginative, and because it positively impedes our understanding of the human condition, then I am logically committed to making the same judgment about any other novel that is relevantly similar, and for precisely the same reasons." P. 312: In both the moral and the aesthetic cases, "our judgments about the mundane are universalizable, and our judgments about the outstanding are not. . . . To the extent that works of art are necessarily unique, so too are certain morally significant actions or agents; to the extent that moral judgments are universalizable, so too are aesthetic judgments."

34. Anthony Kenny, *Will, Freedom, and Power,* 92: "Theoretical deductive reasoning is not defeasible in the sense that the addition of a premiss cannot invalidate a previously valid inference: if a conclusion follows from a given set of premisses it can be drawn from any larger set containing those premisses no matter how many are added to that set. With practical reasoning in the logic of satisfactoriness this is not so." John Ladd, "The Place of Practical Reason and Judicial Decision," 135–36. "One of the most interesting and important peculiarities of practical reasoning is what might be called its 'pluralism,' that is, the way it admits and deals with conflicts of premises or reasons. . . . Although an action that is based on one end X is incompatible with the pursuance of another end Y, the choice of that action does not eliminate or render unacceptable the end Y. This feature of practical inference stands out in contrast to the principle of ordinary propositional logic, which holds that, if two different premises entail contradictory conclusions, then one of them must be false."

CHAPTER 4
Deliberative Rationality and the Emotions

1. This is as good a place as any to warn the reader that, to signal their problematic status, I try frequently to leave *pathē* untranslated, and also translate it at different points as passions, emotions, and moral sentiments. The last term, which I prefer, is intended to be provocative anachronism. I believe, and hope, that nothing turns on their translation. For accounts of some complications in fixing a translation, see Amélie Rorty, "Aristotle on the Metaphyiscal Status of *Pathē,*" Stephen R. Leighton, "Aristotle and the Emotions"; William Fortenbaugh, "Aristotle's Rhetoric on Emotions," and "Aristotle: Emotion and Moral Virtue," esp. 178,n.3: "There is, of course, a general usage of pathos such that all psychic phenomenon [*sic*] may come under the label of pathos. See *De Anima* 430a3, 409b15, and R. D. Hicks, *Aristotle, De Anima* (Amsterdam: A. M. Hakkert, 1965), 117, 198, 474. It is not with *pathē* in

this wide sense that moral virtue is concerned but rather with that class of psychic phenomena which Plato had distinguished from itches and tickles, hungers and thirsts (*Philebus* 47e1-2) and which Aristotle distinguished from dynameis and hexeis and explained by means of an illustrative enumeration (*Nicomachean Ethics* 1105b21–23)."

2. See also Christopher Gill, "The *Ethos/Pathos* Distinction in Rhetorical and Literary Criticism." For a quite different distinction between *ēthos* and *pathos,* see *Politics* VIII.7.1342a3–5, where the contrast is between the most ethical harmonies and the most active and enthusiastic.

3. There is a similar development at *Politics* V.9.1309a33-b15, where he lists the differing demands that different offices require, and groups them under the three qualities of *philia,* competence (*dynamis*), and third, virtue and justice. See also VII.3.1325b13. In the *Ethics,* since its subject is the best life, it is not possible fully to possess *phronēsis* and lack *aretē* or conversely (e.g., IX.5.1167a19–21). For that reason, *eunoia* has no separate existence there either.

For one distinction between *phronēsis* and *aretē* in the *Rhetoric,* see III.16.1417a26–28. For an example of such a distinction in "ordinary Greek," see Herodotus I.4, in which he has "the Greeks" say: "It is the work of unjust men, we think, to carry off women at all; but once they have been carried off, to take seriously the avenging of them is the part of fools, as it is the part of sensible men to pay no heed to the matter: clearly, the women would not have been carried off had they no mind to be."

The distinction between failing through ignorance and through dishonesty is the theme of Diodotus's speech in Thucydides III.42–48, esp. 42: "Whosoever maintaineth that words are not instructors to deeds, either he is not wise, or doth it upon some private interest of his own. Not wise, if he think that future, and not apparent things, may be demonstrated otherwise than by words: interested, if desiring to carry an ill matter, and knowing that a bad cause will not bear a good speech, he go about to deter his opposers and hearers by a good calumniation."

For the distinction between *eunoia* and the others, see *Politics* III.16.1287a33–b3: "And the argument from the example of the arts may be held to be false—that it is a poor thing [for example] to heal in accordance with written [rules], and one should choose instead to use those who possess the art. For these do not act against reason on account of affection, but earn their pay by making the sick healthy; but those in political offices are accustomed to acting in many matters with a view to spite or favor. In any case, if doctors were suspected of being persuaded by a person's enemies to do away with him for profit, he would be more inclined to seek treatment from written [rules]. Moreover, doctors bring in other doctors for themselves when they are sick, and trainers other trainers when they are exercising, the assumption being that they are unable to judge what is true on account of judging both in their own case and while they are in a state of suffering." Also of interest is the distinction drawn between *eunoia* and the mere rule of the stronger as justifications for slavery at *Politics* I.6.1255a18. See also the trio parallel to Aristotle's offered by Socrates in *Gorgias* 487a, "knowledge, goodwill, and frankness" [*epistēmē, eunoia, parrēsia*]. At *Republic* III.412c we hear that the guardians must be "intelligent, capable, and careful of the interests of the state." Some distinction between *phronēsis* and *aretē* is also drawn at *Politics* III.4.1277a15, and the trio of knowledge, *ēthos,* and *alethos philkalon* at *Ethics* X.9.1179b7–9.

4. "For it is excusable [*sungnōmē*] that an angry person calls a wrong 'heaven-high' or 'monstrous.' And [this can be done] when a speaker holds his audience in his control and causes them to be stirred either by praise or blame or hate or love. . . . Those who are empassioned mouth such utterances, and audiences clearly accept them because they are in a similar mood [*homoios echontes*]" (1408b12–18). The importance of *eunoia* is also developed in Jacqueline De Romilly, "Eunoia in Isocrates."

5. *De Anima* III.10.433b5–6: "Appetites [*orexeis*] run counter to one another [only] when a principle of reason and a desire [*epithymia*] are contrary and [that in turn] is possible only in beings with a sense of time." Ernest de Sousa, *The Rationality of Emotion,* 189: "Rational coexistence is a matter of consistency, not compatibility. The latter concerns simultaneous satisfaction, whereas the former concerns simultaneous success. The two are easily confused, since they coincide for the case of beliefs. But they do not coincide for goodness, or for the different species of axiological appropriateness. Wants are consistent, not if their objects can all be *true* together, but if they can all be *good* together. Similarly, the condition of consistency for emotions is not whether their targets, motivating aspects, or propositional objects are compatible but whether their formal objects are logically consistent. And if each emotion has its own formal object, then the constraints of consistency will only relatively rarely have occasion to apply."

6. Note, also, the continuation of this passage: "The attitude which some require in their guardians—to be friendly disposed to all whom they know, and stern to all who are unknown—is the attitude of a high-spirited temper. Spirit is the faculty of our souls which issues in love and friendship; and it is a proof of this that when we think ourselves slighted our spirit is stirred more deeply against acquaintances and friends than ever it is against strangers. . . . This faculty of our souls not only issues in love and friendship: it is also the source for us all of any power of commanding and any feeling for freedom" (VII.7.1327b25–1328a6; cf. III.14.1285a16–22). The Europeans who while free are apolitical are the referent of "for the one who is such by nature has by this fact a desire for war, as if were an isolated piece in a game of chess" (*Politics* I.2.1253a7). They have, in the language of the *Ethics,* natural virtue (VI.13.1144b1–17), an orientation of the *thymos* to good ends, without *phronēsis.* For a similar piece of geography, see *Republic* IV.435e.

Carnes Lord, *Education and Culture in the Political Thought of Aristotle,* 164: "For Aristotle as for Plato . . . the phenomenon of spiritedness appears to be of fundamental importance for understanding of [the] nature of human sociality, and thereby the limits or the nature of political life in particular and for both the phenomenon of spiritedness is profoundly problematic. Spiritedness is indispensable for the best city just as it is an inescapable fact of political life as such; but it represents at the same time a grave danger, as it constantly threatens the predominance in politics of prudence or reason."

7. "A city is maintained by proportionate reciprocity. For people seek to return either evil for evil, since otherwise [their condition] seems to be slavery, or good for good, since otherwise there is no exchange" (*Ethics* V.5.1132b32–1133a2). See

also *Ethics* VIII.1.1155a22–30; *Politics* VII.6.1328a1: "Spiritedness is more aroused against intimates and friends than against unknown persons." Judith Shklar, *The Faces of Injustice,* 98: "Being a good citizen is not the same thing as being wise, unbiased, humane, or unusually independent. No such claims can or should be made for citizenship. Rousseau was on solid ground when he noted that the best citizens were xenophobic and bellicose. Passive injustice is a civic failing, not a sin or a crime. It refers to the demands of our political role in a constitutional democracy, not to our duties as men or women in general."

8. The different accounts of the emotions depending on context is explored in Leighton, "Aristotle and the Emotions."

9. Modrak, *Aristotle: The Power of Perception,* 140–41: "Aristotle's strategy for dealing with emotions and desires of all sorts is to reduce them to the experience of pleasure or pain in relation to a particular object or situation and to treat the awareness of pleasure and pain as a kind of perceptual activity (cf. *De Anima* 431a12–14)."

10. Arendt, *Eichmann in Jerusalem,* 106. The connection between coloring and emotional modifications, which has a long history in rhetoric after Aristotle, could be said to begin with *Metaphysics* V.14.1020b8–12. The idea of qualifications as "colorings" has a long history in subsequent rhetorical theory. Passions color judgments in the *Rhetoric* in the way character colors plot in *Poetics* 6.1450a20–23: "The end aimed at is the imitation not of qualities of character, but of some action; while character makes men what they are, it is their actions and sufferings that make them happy or the opposite."

11. A similar suggestion is made and rejected at II.23.1396b5–8, where Aristotle says that the same method should be used in emergencies as under other circumstances.

12. Rorty, *Mind in Action,* 287: "The immanence of thought in action affects the thick description of the ways the action is performed: subdominant or recessive alternatives can be expressed in voice, gesture, timing, without being denied or rejected. The etiology of an action—its rejected alternatives as well as its direct derivations, the psychological processes that articulated its intentional description— are expressed in the *petites actions* that form its tonality."

13. Irwin notes a similar function for the uses of pleasure and pain in assessing the voluntary and the involuntary. Aristotle "insists that forced action is always painful, so that what we enjoy cannot be forced (1110b11–13). . . . He denies that such behaviour is involuntary, even though the actual causal sequence is just the same as it would be in an involuntary action. . . . [Similarly] he argues that if I act because of ignorance, and do not regret my action, I have acted non-voluntarily, but not involuntarily; involuntary action requires regret as well as ignorance (1110b18–24, 1111a19–21). . . . The distinctions Aristotle draws are curious if he simply wants to identify the agent's actual causal relation to his action, [but] his distinctions are more reasonable if his primary concern is the relation of rational agency to the action. Though my pleasure and pain may make no actual difference to what happens, they indicate my attitude to the action, and so reveal my character (1104b3–11) and the decision that has formed it" (342–43). Irwin's observation is important in that it shows how our assessments of character are based on wider evidence than the person's choices alone.

14. See also *Politics* VIII.5.1340a18–24: "For in rhythms and tunes there are likenesses particularly close to the genuine natures of anger and gentleness, and further of courage and moderation and of all things opposite to these and of other things pertaining to character. This is clear from the facts: we are altered in soul when we listen to such things. But for habituation to feel pain and enjoyment in similar things is close to being in the same condition relative to the truth."

15. In the discussion of fear, for example, we learn how fear colors the perceptions of situations by the audience (II.5.1383a8–12): "whenever it is better [for the speaker's case] that they [i.e. the audience] experience fear. . . ." But we also learn how to make an audience draw a conclusion, either "You should fear" or "The person on trial was afraid" from premises that express likely causes of fear. For further examples see, e.g., II.3.1380b31–34, II.7.1385a31, II.11.1388b30; note generally all the arguments from signs contained in the instructions for evoking emotions.

16. Wisse notes seven places in II.2–11 where Aristotle "gives instructions about the use of his analysis" to construct arguments (pp. 21–22). His list is: II.2.1380a2–5, 3.1380b29–33, 4.1382a16–19, 5.1383a8–12, 7.1385a29–b10, 9.1387b17–20, 10.1388a25–28. Alexander Nehemas, "Pity and Fear in the *Rhetoric* and the *Poetics*," 297: "What makes a desire or emotion rational is not its content, which can have a complex propositional and evaluative structure, but the *grounds* on which that structure depends. Our states are rational if what causes us to be in them includes reasons for considering them appropriate."

17. Note the similarity to claims that pity and fear in the *Poetics* are features of the structure and plot of the tragedy. On my analysis, the traditional question of whether pity and fear are in the audience (e.g., 9.1452a2–3) or in the plot itself (11.1452a8–9) poses a false choice. Actual cause and actual effect are identical.

18. Charles Fried, "The New First Amendment Jurisprudence," 253: "The West Virginia Board of Education could not have imagined that by getting Jehovah's Witnesses to salute the flag they were instilling patriotism in them. Instead they were showing off their power by ramming their conception of patriotism down the schoolchildren's throats." See also Richard K. Sherwin, "Law, Violence, and Illiberal Belief," 1793, n. 26: "Lynch v. Donnelly, 465 U.S. 668, 688 (1984) (O'Connor, J., concurring) (governmental endorsement of religion is invalid to the extent that it 'sends a message to nonadherents that they are outsiders, not full members of the political community, and an accompanying message to adherents that they are insiders, favored members of the political community.)"

19. See also e.g., II.6.1383b11, II.7.1385a15–16. It is worth noting that the situation most resembling this account of the causes of the emotions occurs not in the discussion of *akrasia* in the *Ethics,* or indeed anywhere in the *Ethics:* The closest parallel is found, appropriately, in the discussion of factions in *Politics* V, which I cited in the last chapter.

20. Note, though, that *epithymia* is included under *pathos* in II.12.1388b33–34. As Wisse notes (p. 40, n. 151), "the exclusion of *epithymia* from the *pathē* in 2,2–11 is in line with 1,10,17–18 ([13]69b11–18), where *orgē* and *epithymia* are treated: for the first Aristotle refers to 2,2–11, for the second there is no such reference."

21. For the relative, but not full, independence of emotions from actions, see Troels Engberg-Pedersen, *Aristotle's Theory of Moral Insight,* 140: "If I feel pity for

someone, then even if I cannot do anything to alleviate his pain, it will remain the case that if I had been present when the painful thing happened and if I had been able to do something to prevent it from happening, I would have had at least some desire to do what I could to prevent the misery from occurring." Michael Stocker, "Dirty Hands and Conflicts of Values and of Desires in Aristotle's Ethics," 37: "The dirty features—the impossible oughts—are double counted. In determining the act to be done, they are taken into account. They tell against the act, but not with enough force to make it overall wrong. However, in focusing on these features as dirty, they are given moral weight all over again, now on their own—as, it seems, reasons against doing that act and as reasons for regretting doing it. They remain dirty even though justified."

22. For useful details on this neglected subject, see Michael Tanner, "Sentimentality." For another form of abuse, see David Hume, *An Inquiry Concerning the Principles of Morals*, 95: "Though much of our friendship and enmity be still regulated by private considerations of benefit and harm, we pay at least this homage to general rules, which we are accustomed to respect, that we commonly pervert our adversary's conduct by imputing malice or injustice to him, in order to give vent to those passions which arise from self-love and private interest. When the heart is full of rage, it never wants pretenses of this nature."

23. On the emotions as incipient desires, see Modrak, *Aristotle*, 141: "Since the object as presented is a component of the desire (there is no desiring without an object), the desire is itself a particular way of apprehending an object as well as an impulse to pursue or avoid that object."

24. "For men become angry whenever they are distressed; for the person who is distressed desires something" (II.2.1379a12). *De Anima* III.7.431a8–14: "When the object is pleasant or painful, the soul makes a quasi-affirmation or negation, and pursues or avoids the object."

25. Here I reach the opposite conclusion from the same data as Wisse, who says that "this principle of enumerating the elements subject, object and cause is in general consistently followed: all deviations are either natural or are explained" (p. 69). His note (n. 291) lists the deviations. "2,3 on *praoenesthal* (the cause is an absence of *oligoria*, which is explained in 2,2); 2,4 on *philia-echthra* (the subject is not explicit because everyone can experience this *pathos*; the essential point is the relationship with the other person involved, cf. 2,4,4:81a8–11, etc; cause and object are intimately connected and treated together in §§ 1–12: 82a21-b28); 2,5 on *tharrein* § 16–2: 83a12-b11) (it has no object, for it is absence of fear—cf. 83a14–15); 2,7 on *charis* (the three elements are closely related and treated together; cf. § 4, 85a30–31); 2,9 on indignation (like fear: §§ 7–11: 87a8-b4; cf. b24)."

It does not settle the issue between Wisse and me, but it is worth nothing that my account of the emotions in the *Rhetoric* is one with (at least my view of) the relation between the general statement about moral virtue lying in a mean between extremes and what Aristotle says about each particular virtue. There too I find a lack of fit between general program and the details. That discrepancy in the *Ethics* becomes important in my Chapter 7.

26. Nancy Sherman, *The Fabric of Character*, 137: "In acting out of kindness, our sympathy goes out to an individual because of the circumstances, and not because

of *who* the individual happens to be. The situation is different in friendship, when we act out of a specific concern for a *particular* person." See also Amélie Rorty, "The Historicity of Psychological Attitudes: Love Is Not Love Which Alters When It Alteration Finds," in *Mind in Action*, 121–34.

27. That distinction makes sense of the observation of Rorty, "Varieties of Rationality, Varieties of Emotion," 347: "Some emotions (joy, grief) are characteristically sensed or felt, and felt in characteristic ways: this tends to be true of such emotions as are strongly associated with pleasures and pains, in such a way that there is a presumption against the attribution of the emotion if the person is not aware of the feeling. Other emotions (hate or love) need not be consciously felt, and can sometimes just consist in the person's having a sequence of thoughts that are characteristic of the emotion. A person's jealousy can consist in his obsessively thinking about his exclusion and loss, without his experiencing those pangs and stabs that are characteristic of feeling jealous."

28. Leighton, "Aristotle and the Emotions," 169, n. 4, tries to explain these data away: "In his stated definitions of pity and indignation an aim is not explicitly announced. Rather, it is part of the larger concept of these emotions. We find the same thing in envy and emulation. Part of the concept of envy involves preventing one's neighbour from possessing certain goods, while emulation strives to make oneself fit for such goods (*Rhetoric* 1388a35–37). From these aims, which are part of the concept of emotion (but not part of their stated definitions), we still can explain certain changes of judgment." He admits, though, a problem with some of the emotions: Fear, shame and shamelessness "have no aim towards the realization of which our judgments might be bent."

29. Claudia Card, "Gratitude and Obligation," is especially interesting on the difference between being grateful *that* someone helped me and being grateful *to* that person. Among other things, people other than the recipient can be grateful that someone was helped, but not to the benefactor (except for getting the rest of us off the hook).

Stocker, "Emotional Thoughts," 62. "Holding constant all these beliefs and thoughts, my emotions may not hold constant. They can go from fear to pleased anticipation and back again, with, of course, the one shot through or modified by the other. Nor, need there be any change in my values. At all times, I keep the same evaluation of the danger and of facing it courageously. And I can at all times have the same desires." Similarly, Rorty, *Mind in Action*, 114: "The issue is whether there are emotions that are more properly evaluated as inappropriate or harmful than as irrational. If the intentional component of an emotion is always a belief, then the conservation of an emotion after a change of belief would always involve a conflict of beliefs." Judith Shklar. *The Faces of Injustice*, 89: "The English language is of some help . . . in showing us the difference between ourselves and our animal friends. The latter, no less than we, expect *that* something will be done because it always has been done, as effect follows cause, and if it is something we enjoy, they and we are sorely disappointed and frustrated if it fails to happen. People, however, also have expectations from or of each other, and these depend upon our roles and the social character of our mutual relations. We expect fairness *from* public officials, fidelity *from* our friends and the delivery of goods and services *from* those we have paid for them. We feel betrayed, not just upset, when these expectations are not met."

30. In Chapter 1 I quoted from Alexander Mourelatos, *The Route of Parmenides,* 136, n. 1, and the last part of the note is worth quoting again. "'Persuasion' and 'fidelity' or 'faith' are modes of one and the same concept for the Greeks." For the relation between faith as believing *that* something is true and as believing *in* someone in religious thought, see, among a large literature, Martin Buber, *Two Types of Faith*; H. H. Price, "Belief 'In' and Belief 'That'"; and Kenneth Seeskin, "Judaism and the Linguistic Interpretation of Jewish Faith."

31. "Poles have never come out against Jews 'because they are Jews' but because Jews are dirty, greedy, mendacious, because they wear earlocks, speak jargon, do not want to assimilate, and *also* because they *do* assimilate, cease using their jargon, are nattily dressed, and want to be regarded as Poles. Because they lack culture and because they are overly cultured. Because they are superstitious, backward and ignorant, and because they are damnably capable, progressive, and ambitious. Because they have long, hooked noses, and because it is sometimes difficult to distinguish them from 'pure Poles.' Because they crucified Christ and practice ritual murder and pore over the Talmud, and because they disdain their own religion and are atheists. Because they look wretched and sickly, and because they are tough and have their own fighting units and are full of *khutspah*. Because they are bankers and capitalists and because they are Communist agitators. But in *no* case because they are Jews." Konstantyn Jelenski, *Kultura* (Paris), May 1968, quoted in Sander Gilman, *Pathology and Difference,* p. 29.

Patricia S. Greenspan, "A Case of Mixed Feelings," 233: "Reasons cannot just be 'built into' emotions, in the way that they can be built into judgments. That is, even if I do feel happy for my rival, or happy about his winning *in that* it satisfies a desire of someone I identify with, I would normally still feel happy about his winning—*simpliciter*—so that my emotion cannot be said to be truly qualified. Hence emotions should not be identified with qualified evaluative judgments."

32. Thomas Conley, "*Pathē* and *Pisteis,* 312: "The warrants in the case of the defense are the contraries of those in the case of the prosecution, as, indeed, the motivating emotions in the one case are the contraries of those in the other. This brings out the real genius, I think, of the arrangement 'by contraries' which Aristotle uses in the discussion of ii.2–11, for by means of such an arrangement it is possible to derive arguments on both sides with maximum economy and efficiency."

33. That same narrowing of range occurs in the *Poetics*. Because of the interrelations of pity and fear, we can only fear for ourselves what we pity in others.

34. Carnes Lord, "Politics and Philosophy in Aristotle's *Politics,*" 348: "Aristotle agrees with Plato that spirit is necessary to the city or to the best city. But his analysis of spirit differs in some important respects. In the presentation of the *Republic, thymos* appears as a kind of harsh and warlike passion eminently suited to a class of warriors whose primary task is to defend the city against external enemies. When Aristotle suggests (1327b38–1328a1) that spirit is responsible not only for the guardians' harshness toward enemies but for their friendliness or gentleness toward fellow

citizens, he goes beyond the explicit teaching of the *Republic*: Plato had limited himself to requiring that the guardians possess, in addition to spirit, a 'philosophic nature.'"

35. For that reason such pleasures and pains cause a more shameful and vicious kind of error than being overcome by anger and *thymos* at *Ethics* VII.6.1149a25–b5. See also *Ethics* X.9.1180a22–24; "Besides, people become hostile to an individual human begin who opposes their impulses even if he is correct in opposing them; whereas a law's prescription of what is decent is not burdensome."

36. See, similarly, *De Sophisticis Elenchis* 2. These emotions, then, can make more plausible the quotation from *Politics* III cited above which appears to be purely wishful thinking on Aristotle's part: "The many, of whom none is individually an excellent man, nevertheless can when joined together be better—not as individuals but all together—than those [who are best], just as dinners contributed [by many] can be better than those equipped from a single expenditure. For because they are many, each can have a part of virtue and prudence, and on their joining together, the multitude, with its many feet and hands and having many senses [*aisthēsis*], be- comes like a single human being, and so also with respect to character and mind [*peri ta ēthe kai tēn dianoian*]. . . . All when assembled together have sufficient discern- ment [*aisthēsis*], but separately the individual is immature [or imperfect, undevel- oped] in judgment" (*Politics* III.11.1281b1–10). This process of addition must not only combine individual understandings, but individual feelings. See also *Metaphys- ics* II.1.993b1.

37. II.18 is presented as a summary of the section on the passions and a transition to the later subjects of common forms of reasoning and style and arrangement. Although the chapter is widely seen as corrupt, its emphasis on judgment, and its explicit indifference to whether it is an individual or collective judge, is in keeping with this treatment of the passions.

38. Cf. *De Anima* I.1.403a5: "In most cases it seems that none of the affections, whether active or passive, can exist apart from the body. This applies to anger, courage, desire and sensation generally, though possibly thinking is an exception." See also the statement about definitions at the beginning of the *De Anima,* using anger as the paradigm. "For the actual existence [of the form] there must be em- bodiment of it in a material" (I.1.403b3).

39. See, e.g., the interesting discussion in Kendall Walton, "Fearing Fictions."

40. David Hume, *Treatise of Human Nature*. Above, though, I suggested that this dependence of emotions on beliefs, such that when belief ceases, so too does the emotion, is not true for all the emotions, and is contradicted especially frequently by the experiences of love and hate. Lovers and haters often look around for new reasons for their feelings to replace those they can no longer affirm.

41. There is, of course, a large philosophical literature concerned with the para- dox of jointly asserting a belief and awareness of its falsity. It is sufficient to note here that it is a paradox, not a contradiction. See, among many others, Bernard Williams, "Deciding to Believe."

42. Nancy Sherman, *The Fabric of Character,* 62. "It is not an agent's desires *per se* that are among his reasons, since reasons are considerations which move one, and

it is less an agent's awareness of his affective state that moves him than an awareness of the *objects* of his desires."

CHAPTER 5
Why Reasoning Persuades

1. In the first chapter, I explored the meaning of *pistis* in the *Rhetoric*. In thinking about "why reasoning persuades," I believe it is important to say also that the relation between *pistis* and knowledge in Aristotle should not be assumed to be that commonly supposed between belief and knowledge in contemporary thought, as, for example, in the idea that knowledge is true justified belief. For some of the data for construing the relation between *pistis* and knowledge in Aristotle see *Posterior Analytics* I.2.72a26–72b4; *Ethics* VI.3.1139b32–34; VI.8.1142a18–21.

2. Newman, *Grammar of Assent*, p. 197, tells the story of the judge "who, when asked for his advice by a friend on his being called to important duties which were new to him, bade him to always lay down the law boldly—but never give his reasons—for his decision is likely to be right, but his reasons are sure to be unsatisfactory."

3. Roland Barthes's "The Old Rhetoric: An Aide-Mémoire" suggests an explanation to the double treatment of logical appeals in the *Rhetoric*, first in Book I and then again in these last chapters of Book II. He says that Book I "is the book of message-emitter, the book of the orator: it deals chiefly with the conceptions of arguments. . . . Book II is the book of the message- receiver. . . . it deals . . . once again with arguments, but this time insofar as they are *received* (and no longer, as before) *conceived*" (p. 22). In terms more harmonious with my own project, Book I, as I showed in the first two chapters, concerns why rhetoric and persuasion should be argumentative, while these last chapters of Book II instead ask why reason or argument is persuasive.

4. Christine Korsgaard, "Skepticism about Practical Reason," 13: "A practically rational person is not merely capable of performing certain rational mental operations, but capable also of transmitting motive force, so to speak, along the paths laid out by those operations."

5. I have explored these questions for the *Ethics* in detail in "Aristotle's Genealogy of Morals," and "The Moral Virtues and the Two Sides of *Energeia*."

6. Korsgaard, "Skepticism about Practical Reason," 9: "An *internalist* theory is a theory according to which the knowledge (or the truth or the acceptance) of a moral judgment implies the existence of a motive (not necessarily overriding) for acting on that judgment. If I judge that some action is right, it is implied that I have, and acknowledge, some motive or reason for performing that action. . . . On an *externalist* theory, by contrast, a conjunction of moral comprehension and total unmotivatedness is perfectly possible: knowledge is one thing and motivation another."

Loren Lomasky, in *Persons, Rights, and the Moral Community*, sees the necessity for an argument for the "transmissibility of practical reason," given the basis of practical reason in personal projects rather than some posited moral point of view. E.g.,

p. 64: "The transmission of practical reason . . . provides a bridge between someone's *having a reason* and *there being a reason,* that is, a bridge between personal value
and impersonal value. It does not, however, collapse the distinction between the
two." Harold Zyskind, in "The New Rhetoric and Formalism," 19, says: "Rhetoric's independence and distinctiveness lie in the mind's not being eliminable from
the process or context of proof, as it is in the depersonalized calculations of demonstrative reasoning (properly restricted). The special mark of rhetoric is thus that the
person's adherence to a proposition contributes to its value: and the process of justifying and judging amounts to stating one's position in a behavioral manner." The
distinction between beliefs, desires, and values existing *in potentia* in the premises
and data of deliberation, and the beliefs, desires and values manifested in an actual
decision to act is incorporated in Newman's reflections on assent in the *Grammar of
Assent,* as well as in L. Jonathan Cohen's important distinction between belief and
acceptance in *The Dialogue of Reason.*

7. The contemporary literature on internalist vs. externalist accounts of practical reason is vast. The following citation seems to me especially relevant here, because it ties that distinction to the distinction between given and guiding ends,
kinēseis and *energeiai.* Alasdair MacIntyre, "How Moral Agents Became Ghosts,"
301: "In the context of practices we do have to make a clear distinction between
what makes a good reason a good reason and what gives that reason force for any
particular agent. If I am playing chess with a sick child in order to entertain that
child, then 'Moving my bishop is the only way to avoid checkmate' may be a reason
for not moving my bishop. Only if I am playing chess for the sake of the goods
specific to chess in accordance with the standards of excellence which partially define the game of chess will it necessarily be a reason that has force for me."

For this differentiation of the various senses of the internal/external contrast, and
especially my distinction between the deliberative sense in which internal reasons
motivate and the judicial sense in which reasons are internal to a practice, see Mac-
Intyre's review of Williams's *Moral Luck*: "The Magic in the Pronoun 'My.'"

8. Aristotle notes this distinction: In the assembly "the judge judges about matters that affect himself, so that nothing is needed except to show that circumstances
are as the speaker says. But in judicial speeches this is not enough; rather, it is serviceable to gain over the hearer; for the judgment is about other people's business
and the judges, considering the matter in relation to their own affairs and listening
with partiality, lend themselves to [the needs of] the litigants but do not judge
[objectively]" (I.1.1354b28–1355a1).

9. There is a similar opposition between *ēthos* and *logos* in I.15 for the atechnical
proof of witnesses. Recent witnesses prove only what happened, but ancient witnesses and proverbs testify to the quality of an act. "On such matters, outsiders are
[objective] witnesses, and ancient ones the most credible; for they are incorrupt-
ible." (I.15.1376a16).

10. For details on the relations between a character as represented in an argument
and the character supposedly really possessed by the author, see Wayne C. Booth,
The Company We Keep.

11. See also Bacon, *De Augmentis* IX, 134: "Logic handles reason in truth and
nature, and rhetoric handles it as it is planted in the opinions of the vulgar. And

therefore Aristotle wisely places rhetoric between logic on the one side, and moral and civil knowledge on the other, as participating of both. For the proofs and demonstrations of logic are the same to all men; but the proofs and persuasions of rhetoric ought to differ according the auditors . . . which application and variety of speech, in perfection of idea, ought to extend so far, that if a man should speak of the same thing to several persons, he should nevertheless use different words to each of them." Cf. *Topics* VI.4.141b34–142a3 and *Metaphysics* II.3.994b32–995a17.

12. Donovan Ochs helped me to see this point. For a different approach to the cogency and persuasiveness of such arguments, see Jonathan E. Adler, "Even-Arguments, Explanatory Gaps, and Pragmatic Scales."

13. Laurence Thomas, "Trust and Survival," 35: "If a person is trustworthy, then we can make predictions about the individual's behavior. But . . . the converse is false. . . . It is a conceptual feature of trust that we believe that the individual would not wrong us although the person could do so without either detection or loss." Thomas, "Trust, Affirmation, and Moral Character," 239: "Because the predictions involving trust are tied to nondissembling self-presentation on the part of the other, we may think of them as intentionally manifested predictions." There are complications concerning what form such awareness must take. It must be something short of full consciousness, since we can trust people and arguments without knowing that we do. Intentional relations such as trust are opaque.

14. Contrast Philip Bobbitt, *Constitutional Fate*, 95: "There is an almost utter absence of the discussion of ethical arguments *as arguments* in the teaching of constitutional law. Either they are instead regarded as disreputable reflections of the moral and political positions of the judge who lacks sufficient willpower to keep them properly cabined or they are indulged by both the cynical and the sentimental for being what 'real' judging is all about, having little to do with the competition of arguments *per se*."

15. D. W. Hamlyn, "Aristotle on Dialectic," contains an interesting analysis of Aristotle's logical enterprise as concerned less with the transmission of truth than of acceptance and acceptability of the truth.

16. For just one relevant treatment of the difference between inference among propositions and among propositions as held by people, see Onora O'Neill, "Between Consenting Adults," 255: "Like other propositional attitudes, consent is opaque. Consent may not extend to the logical implications, likely results, or to the indispensable presuppositions of which is explicitly consented to. A classical and instructive example of this range of difficulties occurs in liberal political debates over how far consent to a particular political constitution (explicitly or implicitly given) signifies consent to particular governments formed under that constitution, and how far consent to a particular government or party constitutes consent to various components of government or party policy. The notion of loyal opposition is never more than contextually determinate."

This difference between relations among propositions and among propositions as held by people is the subject of what Mikhail Bakhtin calls dialogics. See, e.g., *Speech Genres*, 117: "*Dialogic relations* have a specific nature: they can be reduced neither to the purely logical (even if dialectical) nor to the purely linguistic (compositional-syntactic). They are possible only between complete utterances of various speaking subjects. . . . Where there is no word and no language, there can be no dialectic relations; they cannot exist among objects or logical quantities (concepts, judgments, and so forth). Dialogic relations presuppose a language, but they do not reside within the system of language. They are impossible among elements of a language." That dialogical relations are possible "only between complete utterances is prefigured in Aristotle's separation of affirmation and denial, in *Categories* 10, from other forms of contrariety. See also Don Bialostosky, "Dialogics as an Art of Discourse in Literary Criticism." "Dialectic concerns impersonal relations among terms that are independent of those who hold them—relations of confirmation and contradiction, antithesis and synthesis, and the like. Rhetoric concerns relations of practical agreement and disagreement among persons—relations that may be effected, despite ideological differences, in the formation of consensuses among divergent interests and parties. Dialogics concerns the relations among persons articulating their ideas in response to one another, discovering their mutual affinities and oppositions, their provocations to reply, their desires to hear more, or their wishes to change the subject."

17. Barthes, "The Old Rhetoric," 55. "A kind of quasi-esthetic difference, a difference of style, has been introduced between the example and the enthymeme: the *exemplum* produces a gentler persuasion, more highly prized by common people; it is a luminous force that charms through the pleasure inherent in any comparison; the enthymeme, more powerful, more vigorous, produces a violent, disturbing force, it enjoys the energy of the syllogism; it performs a veritable seizure, it is proof in all the force of its purity, of its essence."

18. Bernard Williams, *Ethics and the Limits of Philosophy*, 102. "It is one aspiration, that social and ethical relations should not essentially rest on ignorance and misunderstanding of what they are, and quite another that all the beliefs and principles involved in them should be explicitly stated. That these are two different things is obvious with personal relations, where to hope that they do not rest on deceit and error is merely decent, but to think that their basis can be made totally explicit is idiocy."

19. Contrast, though, *Politics* VIII.5.1340a21–25: "Rhythms and melodies contain representations of anger and mildness, and also of courage and temperance and all their opposites and the other moral qualities, that most closely correspond to the truth of these qualities (and this is clear from the facts of what occurs—when we listen to such representations we change in our soul); and habituation in feeling pain and delight at representations of reality is close to feeling them towards actual reality."

20. I regard this as the explanation for a phenomenon Grimaldi observes (*Studies*, 17, n. 27): "Those who accept that Aristotle gave us three distinct modes of rhetorical proof, i.e., *enthymeme* (rational), *ēthos* (ethical), *pathos* (emotional) never ask why Aristotle gave his attention to a formal discussion of the misuse of rational proof, namely his discussion of apparent enthymeme in book B, but never bothered to discuss formally or informally the misuse of ethical proof or emotional proof. There is certainly an equal demand for such a discussion, particularly in view of the extended discussion of *pathos* in book B. It is difficult to understand on what grounds the omission can be justified."

David Luban, "Explaining Dark Times," 228–29. "It is not just that it is difficult in practice to ascertain the objective state of affairs. The problem is rather that the objective state of affairs is radically decentered: if offers us no Archimedean point from which it can be comprehended, because every point is Archimedean. Every participant in politics is potentially an initiator of action based on his or her perspective: thus perspectival facts are among the objective facts of the matter. Conversely, no fact bearing on a situation can be translated into action without passing through the eye of the needle that each individual perspective is. Thus *only* perspectival interpretations are politically meaningful. As we have seen, moreover, the basic concepts of practical politics—strength, unity, support—refer not to unequivocal facts but to coincidences of perspective. This is why controlled experiment is impossible: in politics to control the variables is to erase the data. Theories are underdetermined because historical events are overdetermined."

21. As a consequences, when all alternatives all equally probable, all language is equally appropriate. III.2.1405b8: The third condition for using metaphors "refutes the sophistical argument; for it is not the case, as Bryson said, that no one ever uses foul language, if the meaning is the same whether this or that word is used; this is false, for one word is more proper than another, more of a likeness, and better suited to putting the matter before the eyes." Cf. *Phaedrus* 273b–c.

22. This detachment of *logos* from its functioning, so that it exercises a persuasive power independent of that function, is duplicated by the same thing happening to style, *lexis,* in Book III. Aristotle never says that the power or art of rhetoric is limited to verbal persuasion, but simply takes for granted that argument is embodied in words. When all is well, style has no independent existence or power. But, like *logos,* and like *ēthos* in my next chapter, it can have its own persuasive power that warrants consideration. As the circumstances of persuasion move farther away from Aristotle's, Book III historically becomes more influential.

CHAPTER 6
Making Discourse Ethical

1. Some commentators have tried to find a section devoted to *ēthos,* parallel to those that concern *logos* and *pathos.* William W. Fortenbaugh, "*Benevolentiam conciliare* and *animos permovere,*" 260, claims that Aristotle discusses the three modes of proof as follows: "first persuasion through argument (I.4–14), then persuasion through character (2.1) and finally persuasion through the hearers or emotional appeal (2.2–11)." Brian Vickers, *In Defence of Rhetoric,* 20, agrees. Wisse, *Ethos and Pathos,* 37, goes further, and limits the treatment of *ēthos* to II.1.5–7, that is, to thirteen lines of the *Rhetoric!*

It is *prima facie* unlikely that the most persuasive proof of all should be treated in a single chapter, especially one that seems so clearly propaedeutic. Yet explicit treatments of character are hard to find. Hence my claim that Aristotle here shifts the structure of argument. In the succeeding pages of his article, Fortenbaugh reasons, from much of the same data that I am appealing to, to different conclusions. Against Fortenbaugh and in favor of my reading is the fact that when this section ends,

Aristotle in II.18 introduces his next subject with a back reference to *ethikos*. See also I.9.1366a21–22: "After this, let us speak of virtue and vice and honorable and shameful; for these are the points of reference for one praising or blaming. Moreover, as we speak of these, we shall incidentally also make clear those things from which we [as speakers] shall be regarded as persons of a certain quality in character, which was the second form of *pistis*; for from the same sources we shall be able to make ourselves and any other person worthy of credence in regard to virtue." There have also been attempts to locate the section on *ēthos* in II.12–17. Since these chapters are about the character of the audience, not the speaker, I find that a difficult case to make.

2. In a note on one of my passages, II.21.1395b13–18, Kennedy calls it "an unusual expression for Aristotle; otherwise only persons have *ēthos*, though speeches may be 'ethical.'"

3. Kennedy (p. 30, n. 10), commenting on the passage, observers "*Body* is here contrasted with 'matters external' in the next clause. Though Aristotle does not say so, one might speculate that the soul, or life, of persuasion comes from ethical and emotional qualities."

A similar relation between thought and *ēthos* is found, according to Mary Whitlock Blundell, in the *Poetics,* in a place that explicitly derives from the *Rhetoric.* In "*Ethos* and *Dianoia* Reconsidered" she writes: "The rhetorical role of the enthymeme forges an inextricable link between *ēthos* and *dianoia* as 'parts' of tragedy. *Qua* form of argument, enthymemes belong to the *dianoia* of the play. But they employ maxims, general statements about what is to be chosen, and are thus indicative of *prohairesis* and hence of personal *ēthos*." See also A. M. Dale, "Ethos and Dianoia: 'Character' and 'Thought' in Aristotle's *Poetics.*"

4. I do not think that these problems can be evaded by pointing out that *ēthos* is merely ambiguous. Many of the perceived ambiguities in the term are simply differences between *ēthos* as potency and as actuality, e.g., *ēthos* as a source of proof and as a resultant state of trust in the audience. Other ambiguities are perceived because of the problems I have indicated, and not on independent grounds. For a recent thorough treatment, see Wisse, 60–65, which summarizes much of the earlier analysis. For a history of the term, see Charles Chamberlain, "From 'Haunts' to 'Character'." For *ēthos* in the *Poetics,* with much reference to usage outside Aristotle, see Elizabeth Belfiore, *Tragic Pleasures,* and Mary Whitlock Blundell, "*Ethos* and *Dianoia* Reconsidered."

5. Reasoning along these lines can be found, for example, in Richard Posner. "The Jurisprudence of Skepticism," 860: "American judges today are subject to exquisitely refined and elaborate rules on disqualification for conflict of interest. The tiniest conflict is disqualifying. This would make no sense if legal reasoning (including the resolution of factual disputes) were as transparent and reproducible as scientific reasoning and experimentation, for then an erroneous decision would be perceived and corrected and the judge ridiculed for having yielded to temptation. So there is an evident lack of confidence in the ability to detect judicial errors. Consistent with this point, the rules on conflict of interest have been growing stricter in lockstep with the decline of consensus in law and the concomitant growth in judicial discretion. The greater the consensus, the easier it is for judges to fix the premises of decision and thus transform the process of legal reasoning into something

approximating logical deduction. Because legal reasoning is more powerful in a consensus setting, conflict of interest rules are less needful in that setting to prevent bias from operating."

6. For the application of Veblen's idea to rhetoric in a different way, see Kenneth Burke, *Permanence and Change*. Another phrase for the same phenomenon is Robert Bolgar's "natural fanaticism of expertise," in "Humanism as a Value System with Reference to Budé and Vives," 208.

7. "You may take Martin Luther or Erasmus for your model, but you cannot play both roles at once; you may not carry a sword beneath a scholar's gown, lead flaming causes from a cloister. Luther cannot be domesticated in a university. You cannot raise a standard against oppression, or leap into the breach to relieve injustice, and still keep an open mind to every disconcerting fact, or an open ear to the cold voice of doubt. I am satisfied that a scholar who tries to combine these parts sells his birthright for a mess of pottage; that when the final count is made, it will be found that the impairment of his powers far outweighs any possible contribution to the causes he has espoused. If he is fit to serve his calling at all, it is only because he has learned not to serve in any other, for his singleness of mind quickly evaporates in the fires of passions, however holy." Learned Hand, "On Receiving an Honorary Degree," quoted by Philip B. Kurland in "The True Wisdom of the Bill of Rights," 8.

8. I reject the idea that failing through being excessively argumentative suggests the possibility that good practical rationality is a mean between excessive and insufficient reasoning. The *Eudemian Ethics*, unlike the *Nichomachean Ethics*, posits just such an understanding of *phronēsis* when it places *phronēsis* as a mean between "rascality" or "unscrupulousness" (*panourgia*) and "simpleness" or "unworldiness" (*euetheia*) in the table of virtues and vices (II.3.1221a12), but Aristotle never does anything with that trio in the later discussion of *phronēsis*. The strangeness of the idea of *phronēsis* as a mean is captured in Woods's note on the passage: "Although the unworldly (*euethes*) man may lack the intelligence with which the practically wise man is properly endowed, that is surely not something with which it is possible to be overendowed; hence there is no symmetry in the characteristics of the unscrupulous and unworldly man *vis-à-vis* the man of practical wisdom" (p. 115). Contrast Socrates in the *Phaedrus*: "To *you* perhaps it makes a difference who the speaker is and where he is from. For you do not consider this alone, whether what he says is or is not the case" (275b).

9. *Mind in Action*, 300–301.

10. My favorite example of successful reasoning—successful by the standards of logic—destroying trust is Mr. Collins's marriage proposal in *Pride and Prejudice*. "My reasons for marrying are, first, that I think it is a right thing for every clergyman in easy circumstances (like myself) to set the example of matrimony in his parish; secondly, that I am convinced it will add very greatly to my happiness; and thirdly— which perhaps ought to have mentioned earlier, that it is the very particular advice and recommendation of the very noble lady whom I have the honor of calling patroness. . . . Thus much for my general intention in favor of matrimony: it remains to be told why my views were directed to Longbourn instead of my own neighborhood, where I assure you there are many amiable young women. But the

fact is, that being, as I am, to inherit this estate after the death of your honored father . . . I could not satisfy myself without resolving to choose a wife from among his daughters, that the loss to them might be as little as possible. . . . This has been my motive, my fair cousin, and I flatter myself it will not sink me in your esteem. And now nothing remains for me but to assure you in the most animated language of the violence of my affection."

11. John Dewey, "Logical Method and Law," 22. "Again to quote Justice Homes, 'General propositions do not decide concrete cases.' No concrete proposition, that is to say one with material dated in time and placed in space, follows from any general statements or from any connection between them."

Aquinas points out that not only can general propositions not be made completely determinate in this way, but that the more one tries, the worse the formulation becomes. "From the principle [that one should art in accord with reason] there follows a particular conclusion: that things entrusted to one are to be returned. And this, in most cases, is true. But it is possible that in a particular case it will be harmful and therefore irrational actually to return the deposit; for instance, if someone were seeking to overthrow his country. And this sort of principle will be found to fail more often, the more particularly we formulate it: for instance, if we said that deposits are to be returned with such and such warnings or in such and such way: Because the greater the number of particular conditions added, the more ways there are for the principles to fail, so that it will not be right either in indicating that the things are to be returned or in indicating that the things are not to be returned" (*Summa Theologica* 1–2, 94, 4c). (I owe this reference to James R. Ross, in "Justice Is Reasonableness.")

12. Sarah Broadie, *Ethics with Aristotle*, 81: "Aristotle's reference to the prohairetic state is by implication a reference to those very emotions, urges, pleasures and pains which seem to be left out of the definition—the relation being this: what characterises a prohairetic state (as distinct from, say, a skill) is that is shows itself in the agent's acting and failing to act *because of his feelings*. Fear might prevent the craftsman from functioning properly as a craftsman; it might hinder his dexterity or warp his judgment in some way; but if we know the situation we shall not assess his *skill* on the basis of that response. Conversely, if we do assess someone as a bad performer on the basis of a performance which we know fell short because of fear, lust, or anger, then we are assessing his quality as a prohairetic agent. Emotional excitements, like physical handicaps, tend to excuse the craftsman, in the sense that his skill is not impugned by performances spoiled by these conditions." For Plato's rejection, see, among other things, Terry Penner, "Desire and Power in Socrates."

13. Pierre Bourdieu, *Outline of a Theory of Practice*, 77: "Unlike the estimation of probabilities which science constructs methodically on the basis of controlled experiments from data established according to precise rules, practical evaluation of the likelihood of the success of a given action in a given situation brings into play a whole body of wisdom, sayings, commonplaces, ethical precepts ('that's not for the likes of us') and, at a deeper level, the unconscious principles of the ethos, which, being the product of a learning process dominated by a determinate type of objective regularities, determines 'reasonable' and 'unreasonable' conduct for every agent subjected to those regularities." See also Hilary Putnam, *Measuring and the Moral*

Sciences, 72: "It is a feature of 'scientific' knowledge . . . that we *use measuring instru-ments that we understand*. . . . It is a feature of *practical* knowledge that we often have to use *ourselves* (or other people) as the measuring instruments—and we do *not* have an explicit theory of *those* interactions."

My favorite example of the ethical precept Bourdieu quotes, 'that's not for the likes of us,' blocking a too quick inference from end to action occurs somewhere in Trollope. Someone says of a character that he's not a gentleman, and, when asked to explain, says, "He's the sort of man, who, if he discovered that horseflesh was good to eat, would eat it."

One central example of an apparently benign, progressive replacement of rhetor-ical by scientific argument is the invention of the modern sense of probability, re-placing the older, specifically rhetorical one. For details, see Ian Hacking, *The Emer-gence of Probability.*

14. Aristotle uses *prohairesis* in two different ways that we have to keep distinct here. In this quotation from the *Ethics* only praxeis, and only virtuous praxeis at that, involve *prohairesis* because only good praxeis are chosen for their own sakes. (Note that at *Ethics* II.4.1105a33, "chosen" and "chosen for its own sake" seem connected by hendiadys.) In passages that will be my proof text for the next chapter, however, *prohairesis* extends much more widely, so that the sophist is distinguished from the rhetorician by the fact that whereas the rhetorician actualizes his *dynamis,* the sophist acts from *prohairesis.* I have worried about some of the subtleties of *pro-hairesis* in "The Moral Virtues and the Two Sides of *Energeia.*"

15. For virtue as a first actuality and happiness as a second, see my "Aristotle's Metaphysics of Morals." See esp. *Ethics* I.13.1100b35–1101a8.

16. John Dewey, *Human Nature and Conduct,* 249–50: "The object desired and the attainment of desire are no more alike than a signboard on the road is like the garage to which it points and which it recommends to the traveler. Desire is the forward urge of living creatures. When the push and drive of life meets no obstacle, there is nothing which we call desire. There is just life-activity. But obstructions present themselves, and activity is dispersed and divided. Desire is the outcome. It is activity surging forward to break through what dams it up. The 'object' which then presents itself in thought as the goal of desire is the object of the environment *which, if it were present,* would secure a re-unification of activity and the re̅storation of its ongoing unity. The end-in-view of desire is that object which were it present would link into an organized whole activities which are now partial and competing. It is no more like the actual end of desire, or the resulting state attained, than the coupling of cars which have been separated is like an ongoing single train. Yet the train cannot go on without the coupling."

17. John Henry Newman, *An Essay in Aim of a Grammar of Assent,* 240.

18. Raimond Gaita in "Virtues, Human Good, and the Unity of a Life," 412: "The virtues are external to the primary dimension of assessment of some modes of thought, whereas for other modes they are not. . . . A scientist requires certain vir-tues of character if he is to do worthwhile work, but the primary dimension of assessment of that work is determined by a conception of truth and falsehood which can be explicated without reference to those virtues. It is a conception of truth and

falsehood which philosophers express when they speak of 'truth-value.' It is different if a person's thought is criticized as sentimental, for then virtues of character are internal to the primary dimension in which the thought is judged."

19. Charles Taylor, "Rorty in the Epistemological Tradition," 260–61: "What makes consistency? Now there is a story which was injected into our philosophical bloodstream by the Vienna School that consistency is a matter of logic. Propositions are consistent, and they are so when they fail to contradict each other. But this doesn't get to the interesting questions. We use logical inconsistency to point up and articulate what's wrong with a position, but that's not how we identify it as wrong. For instance, we might say to a holder of a self-indulgent view: 'How nice and convenient! In your artistic and love life, you're always quoting Sartre, and rejecting any human essence. Then when you want to denounce the Junta, suddenly you're talking about their violating this essence. You can't have it both ways."

20. Richard Sorabji, "Aristotle on the Role of Intellect in Virtue," 206: "Whatever other roles practical wisdom may or may not play, I suggest that one role is this. It enables a man, in the light of his conception of the good life in general, to perceive what generosity requires of him, or more generally what virtue and *to kalon* require of him, in the particular case, and instructs him to act accordingly."

21. William James, *The Will to Believe,* abridged in Amélie Rorty, *Pragmatic Philosophy: An Anthology,* 193: "The previous faith on my part in your liking's existence is in such cases what makes your liking come. But if I stand aloof, and refuse to budge an inch until I have objective evidence, until you have done something apt, as the absolutists says, *ad extorquendum assensum meum,* ten to one your liking never comes. How many women's hearts are vanquished by the mere sanguine insistence of some man that they *must* love him! He will not consent to the hypothesis that they cannot. The desire for a certain kind of truth here brings about that special truth's existence. . . . There are, then, cases where a fact cannot come at all unless a preliminary faith exists in its coming. *And where faith in a fact can help create the fact,* that would be an insane logic which should say that faith running ahead of scientific evidence is the 'lowest kind of immorality' into which a thinking being can fall. Yet such is the logic by which our scientific absolutists pretend to regulate our lives!"

See also Bacon, *Advancement of Learning* II.XXV.1, p. 209: "If we believe only that which is agreeable to our sense, we give consent only to the matter, and not to the author, which is no more than we would do towards a suspected and discredited witness; but that faith which was accounted to Abraham for righteousness was of such a point as whereat Sarah laughed, who therein was an image of natural reason."

22. In a paper whose concerns parallel mine, Anthony T. Kronman first argues, citing Aristotle, that character is essential to persuasion, and hence essential to the successful lawyer. He then faces the question of why the fake appearance of character is not a threat to law and justice. "Living in the Law," 869: "It might be objected that all anyone really needs in order to be successful in debate is a reputation for practical wisdom and not the trait itself. But a person's character is more difficult to conceal than this cynical advice implies. Our characters reveal themselves in all we do and are open to view, on the public surface of our lives, for everyone to see. Indeed, a person's character is often the first thing we feel with any confidence that

we know about him. The reason is that our characters (unlike our beliefs and intentions, which are more easily concealed) have a dispositional dimension—more exactly, they consist in a set of dispositions or habitual desires. What we desire is
generally harder to hide than what we think or intend, and the most difficult desires
to conceal are those that have congealed into habits." In other words, according to
Kronman, *argument* is easier to fake than character!

23. Further evidence that Aristotle is untroubled by a merely apparent character
as opposed to real character can be draw from the *Politics,* where he says that "habituation to feel pain and enjoyment in similar things is close to being in the same
condition to the truth" (VIII.5.1340a23–25). This remark comes in the context of
Aristotle's arguing that music, unlike the visual arts, imitates character, and "has the
power of producing a certain effect on the moral character of the soul" (1240b1–3).
See also VIII.5.1339a23: "Just as gymnastic makes the body of a certain quality, so
also is music capable of making the character of a certain quality by habituating it
to be capable of enjoying in the correct fashion."

24. We have to avoid anachronistic conceptions of the relation between appearance and reality here. K. J. Dover, *Greek Popular Morality,* 226: "An Athenian's 'I
wanted to be regarded as honest' is equivalent to our 'I wanted to be honest.' In
such cases there was no intention, of course, of drawing a distinction between disguise and reality; it was rather that goodness divorced from a reputation for goodness was of limited interest." Among Dover's examples are *Demosthenes* 1vi 14: "We
thought it best to put up with a certain disadvantage and come to an agreement, so
as not to be regarded as litigious" and *Isocrates* xvii 1: "The issue at stake for me is
not simply the recovery of a large sum of money, but the avoidance of being thought
to have coveted dishonestly what is not mine; and that is the most important consideration for me."

See also Hannah Arendt, *On Revolution,* 94: "In politics, more than anywhere
else, we have no possibility of distinguishing between being and appearance. In the
realm of human affairs, being and appearance are indeed one and the same."

25. Stephen Levinson, *Pragmatics,* 112–13: "There is a fundamental way in which
a full account of the communicative power of language can never be reduced to a
set of conventions for the use of language. The reason is that wherever some convention or expectation about the use of language arises, there will also therewith
arise the possibility of the non-conventional *exploitation* of that convention or expectation. It follows that a purely conventional or rule-based account of natural
language usage can never be complete, and that what can be communicated always
exceeds the communicative power provided by the conventions of the language and
its use."

26. If, on the other hand, I can make a better case for maxims, we will at the
least have to be more cautious in the future about ascribing manipulative purposes
to Aristotle for much of the rest of the advice he offers in the *Rhetoric* about how
to win. I have already quoted these lines form Book III, for example: "The proper
lexis also makes the matter credible [*pithanoi to pragma*]: the mind [of the listener]
draws a false inference [*paralogizetai*] of the truth of what the speaker says because
they [in the audience] feel the same about such things, so they think the facts to be
so, even if they are not as the speaker represents them" (III.7.1408a20–23); "Seize

an opportunity in the narration to mention whatever bears on your own virtue" (III.16.1417a2). It is not simple to decide whether these things are more like maxims or more like displaying one's combat medals.

27. Amélie Rorty, "Two Faces of Courage," 162: "The best preparation for courageous action is the preparation for action: competence and confidence in competence. Dangerous and fearful actions form a heterogeneous class, with distinctive problems of attention and competence. But competence is always specific and confidence without competence is folly. Often the skills of the courageous are those of proper focusing, cognitive habits specific to the actions they must perform." See also my "The Moral Virtues and the Two Sides of *Energeia*," for more details.

28. Kenneth Burke's definition of democracy as "government by interference, by distrust," is apposite here. *Counterstatement,* 119.

29. Lionel Trilling, Introduction to *Homage to Catalonia,* by George Orwell, ix. See also Wayne C. Booth, *The Company We Keep.*

30. As a consequence, an independent development and life of both *phronēsis* in the *Ethics* and of character (in the speech, not in some antecedent speaker) in the *Rhetoric* is problematic. At the margins, the exhibition of character can be developed independent of the enthymeme, in the later part of Book II and in Book III, through use of the maxim and through arrangement and style. Similarly, at the margins, I believe the development and partially independent existence of *phronēsis* can be shown, in addition to the argument I give above, through the minor intellectual virtues of *Nicomachean Ethics* VI.9–11, *synesis, gnōmē,* and *eubolia.*

CHAPTER 7
Deception in Aristotle's *Rhetoric:* How to Tell the Rhetorician from the Sophist, and Which One to Bet On

1. The relation of sophistic to rhetoric is slightly different from the relation of sophistic to dialectic. I think that the difference asserted here is that sophists do not stop being rhetoricians on adopting ulterior motives, but they do stop being dialecticians. This semantic difference reflects the fact that there is no neutral position from which one can arbitrate boundary disputes in rhetoric, while there is in dialectic. To be neutral is to take a position politically, but not dialectically. Accusing someone of being a sophist always has a rhetorical point, but not a dialectical one. There is a "logical" distinction between dialectic and sophistic, such that sophistic deserves distinct treatment in the *Organon,* but there is no parallel "rhetorical" distinction between rhetoric and sophistic, and no rhetorical counterpart to the *De Sophisticis Elenchis.* For more on the tactical uses of the *dynamis/prohairesis* distinction in the *Topics* see also IV.4.126a30–b11.

2. MacIntyre, *After Virtue,* 196.

3. Cf. *Eudemian Ethics* II.10.1227a23–32: "There are some things that cannot be employed for something other than their natural objects, for instance, sight—it is not possible to see a thing that is not visible, or to hear a thing that is not audible, but a science does enable us to do a thing that is not the object of the science. For

health and disease are not the objects of the same science in the same way: health is its object in accordance with nature, and disease in contravention of nature. And similarly, by nature good is the object of wish, but evil is also its object in contravention of nature; by nature one wishes good, against nature and by perversion one even wishes evil." I have discussed the rational/irrational *dynamis* distinction from the *Metaphysics* in connection with the definition of the moral virtues as *hexeis prohairetikē* in "Aristotle's Metaphysics of Morals," cited above.

4. Broadie, *Ethics with Aristotle*, 195. "Health as ordinarily conceived is the starting-point of medical deliberation about how to treat a patient, in the sense of being the raison d'être of all steps taken with a view to treatment, including the deliberation; but the technical goal presented in the leading premiss is the starting-point that guides the physician to one conclusion rather than another. The former starting-point is what justifies engaging at all in the deliberation with a view to taking whatever action it will indicate; the latter explains why *this* conclusion was reached and *this* action taken."

5. "It makes a difference, too, for the sake of what one does or learns something. What is for one's own sake or for the sake of friends or on account of virtue is not unfree, while the person who does the same thing on account of others would often be held to do something characteristic of the laborer or the slave" (*Politics* VIII.2.1337b17–22). See also III.4.1277b2–7; *Rhetoric* I.9.1367a29; *Ethics* IV.3.1124b31–1125a2, all cited in chapter 1. See also *Eudemian Ethics* II.11.1228a11: "We praise and blame all men with regard to their purposes rather than with regard to their actions, although activity is a more desirable thing than goodness."

6. Compare *Rhetoric* I.9.1367b5–6: "For if a person meets danger unnecessarily, he would be much more likely to do so where the danger is honorable." The trouble is that that is an argument, as I noted before, that Aristotle calls a fallacy, a *paralogistikon ek ten aitias*.

7. E.g., *Metaphysics* I.2.982a25–26, I.3.995a11; *Ethics* I.3.1094b11–27, I.7.1098a26–33, II.2.1104a7–10, II.4.1106b9–10; *Politics* VII.1328a18; *Rhetoric* I.10.1369b31–32, III.12.1414a7–18, 17.1418a2–4. Similarly we are told at *Republic* VI.486a that *smikrologia* is incompatible with a philosophical nature. See also *Republic* I.340e, where Thrasymachus accuses Socrates of such excessive precision: *su akribologei*. Shorey's note for the Loeb edition on this passage is instructive: "For the invidious associations of *akribologia* (1) in money dealings, (2) in argument, cf. Aristotle, *Metaphysics* 995a11, *Cratyl* 415a, *Lysias* vii. 12, Antiphon B 3, Demosth. xxiii. 148, Timon in Diog. Laert. ii. 19." In addition, we are told in *De Anima* ii.9 that smell is less *akribes* than hearing and sight because we do not sense smells without either pleasure or pain (421a11–13); presumably those senses are more precise which can experience objects as they are apart from their causing pleasure and pain. For the later history of the contrast between precision and truth, see Wesley Trimpi, *Muses of One Mind*.

8. None of these virtues seems to fit Aristotle's general account of virtue as a mean between two extreme vices. In fact, all the moral virtues present problems *vis-à-vis* the general account, just as each of the emotions in *Rhetoric* II presents discrepancies with the general account of II.1. I have explored a few of those problems for courage in "The Meaning of *Thrasos* in Aristotle's *Ethics*." For still more

troubles, see Charles Young, "Aristotle on Justice," and "Aristotle on Temperance." I am especially indebted to Young for his usual troubling comments on this chapter.

9. Bacon observes that fields where the internal end is dominant are the fields of pretence and bragging: "The subject [of medicine] being so variable has rendered the art more conjectural, and left the more room for imposture. Other arts and sciences are judged of by their power and ability, and not by success or events. The lawyer is judged by the ability of his pleading, not the issue of the cause; the pilot, by directing his course, and not by the fortune of the voyage; whilst the physician and the statesman have no particular act that clearly demonstrates their ability, but are principally censured by the event." *Advancement of Learning,* 157–58.

10. Alasdair MacIntyre, "Moral Rationality, Tradition, and Aristotle," 463: "Virtues practiced only for their own sake become exercises in moral narcissism." See also John Dewey, who calls "spiritual egoists" people who are "preoccupied with the state of their character, concerned for the purity of their motives and the goodness of their souls. . . . The needs of actual conditions are neglected, or dealt with in a half-hearted way, because in the light of the ideal they are so mean and sordid." Dewey, *Human Nature and Conduct,* 7–8.

11. Irwin consequently supplies his own interpretation in amplifying the translation, adding the passages in brackets: "It is the boaster [rather than the self-deprecator] who appears to be opposed to the truthful person, because he is the worse [of the two extremes]."

12. Annette Baier, "Why Honesty is a Hard Virtue," 268: "The honesty of virtuous truth telling, and with it due trust in what others say, is at least as convention-dependent as the honesty of respect for others' property, along with proper trust in others' honesty. Honest speech is a special case of respect for rights—namely for another person's right to occasional access to one's own naturally private states of mind. This is as complex a right as the right to have a debt paid. It is the right to get from another what is currently in their secure possession."

13. For one place where Socrates seems to be on Aristotle's side, see *Republic* III.409c: "That cunning fellow [*deinos*] quick to suspect evil, and who has himself done many unjust acts and who thinks himself a smart trickster, when he associates with his like does appear to be clever, being on his guard and fixing his eyes on the patterns within himself. But when the time comes for him to mingle with the good and his elders, then on the contrary he appears stupid."

14. James B. White, "The Ethics of Argument," 878: "One cannot be a propagandist in the service of truth or an advocate in the service of justice, for the character and the motives are wrong. And character and motives are for these purposes everything, for 'truth' and 'justice' are not abstract absolutes, to be attained or not in materially measurable ways; these are words that defined shared motives out of which a community and a culture can be built and a character made for the individual and his world. They express an attitude, imply a process, and promise a community."

15. Sarah Waterlow Broadie, "The Problem of Practical Intellect in Aristotle's *Ethics,*" 250: "The fundamental difference between the reasoning of the craftsman and of the ethical agent is not that the former is concerned only with means, but rather that there is a limit in the case of craft, but not in the ethical case, to the

kinds of consideration that might reasonable claim the agent's attention. The fact that a certain drug has unhealthy side effects is a relevant consideration for the physician *qua* physician; the fact that it is expensive is not."

16. Cynthia Farrar, *The Origins of Democratic Thinking*, 101: "[In Euripides' *Hecuba*], persuasion and rhetoric are not means to express and secure common values, but rather to manipulate others in pursuit of one's private aims, often by appealing to the very values one is in the process of violating (see lines 816f., 118f., 1246f.). Once communal trust and openness, and the sense of participating in a common project, have been corroded, the practices that comprise the political order created by man cease to be constitutive of his identity and become mere contrivances, ways of securing personal advantage within a system which can no longer secure the collective good. Men are thrown on to their own resources and look to values or standards or goals independent of the political order."

CHAPTER 8
Aristotle's *Rhetoric* and the History of Prudence

1. John Dewey, *Reconstruction in Philosophy*, 2d ed. x: "An important aspect of the reconstruction that now needs to be carried out concerns the theory of knowledge. In it a radical change is demanded as to the subjectmatter upon which that theory must be based; the new theory will consider how knowing (that is, inquiry that is competent) is carried on."

2. Richard Bernstein, *Philosophical Profiles*, 71–72: "Gadamer stresses how all such principles and laws require judgment and phronēsis for their concrete application. This makes good sense when there are shared nomoi that inform the life of a community. But what happens when there is a breakdown of such principles, when they no longer seem to have any normative power, when there are deep and apparently irreconcilable conflicts about such principles, or when questions are raised about the very norms and principles that ought to guide our praxis? What type of discourse is appropriate when we question the "universal" element—the *nomoi*— that is essential for the practice of phronēsis?" P. 157: "As Aristotle stresses, and Gadamer realizes, *phronēsis* presupposes the existence of *nomoi* (funded laws) in the polis or community. This is what keeps *phronēsis* from degenerating into the mere cleverness or calculation that characterizes the *deinos* (the clever person). Given a community in which there is a living, shared acceptance of ethical principles and norms, then *phronēsis* as the mediation of such universals in particular situations makes good sense."

3. Anthony Kenny, "Practical Inference," 68: "Suppose that the possible state of affairs described in the sentence does not, in fact, obtain. Do we fault the sentence, or do we fault the facts? Do we, for instance, call the sentence false; or do we call the state of things unsatisfactory? If the former, then we shall call the sentence assertoric; if the latter, let us call it imperative. . . . Assertoric sentences are like invoices and plans in guidebooks; imperative sentences are like orders and architects' plans." Bernard Williams, "Conflicts of Values," 224–25: [In "tragic" choices] "it

must be a mistake to suppose that what we have here is a case of logical inconsistency, such that the agent could not be justified or rational in thinking that each of these moral requirements applied to him. This is to misplace the source of the agent's trouble, in suggesting that what is wrong is his thought about the moral situation, whereas what is wrong lies in his situation itself—something which may or may not be his fault."

4. Stanley Cavell, *The Claim of Reason*, 307: "No rule or principle could function in a moral context the way regulatory or defining rules function in games. It is as essential to the form of life called morality that rules so conceived be absent as it is essential to the form of life we call a game that they be present."

5. Similarly, Perelman's abandoning of rhetoric's concern for particular audiences in favor of a dialectic for a universal audience attempts to purchase truth through a loss of practical determination. See Chaim Perelman and L. Olbrecht-Tyteca, *The New Rhetoric*.

6. I noted at the beginning that for the most part I was relying on the *Nicomachean Ethics* because it is more familiar and because I did not think consideration of the *Eudemian Ethics* would produce significantly different results. Since in this conclusion I am not only drawing on Aristotle's *Ethics,* but presenting a picture of its overall enterprise, I think I need to reiterate my conviction that, for the purposes of my inquiry, there are no fundamental differences between the two *Ethics* in their relations to either the *Politics* or the *Rhetoric*.

7. For details see my "Aristotle's Natural Slaves: Incomplete *Praxeis* and Incomplete Human Beings."

8. See the definitions of necessity in *Metaphysics* V.5. "We call 'necessary' (1) (a) that without which, as a condition, a thing cannot live . . . ; (b) the conditions without which good cannot be done or come to be, or without which we cannot get rid or be freed of evil; e.g., drinking the medicine is necessary in order to be cured of disease, and a man's sailing to Aegina is necessary in order that he may get his money" (1015a20–26).

9. "It has been argued in the *Ethics* (if the argument used there has any value) that felicity is the activity [*energeia*] and practice [*chrēsis*] of goodness, to a degree of perfection, and in a mode which is absolute and not relative. By 'relative' we mean a mode of action which is necessary and enforced; by 'absolute' we mean a mode of action which possesses intrinsic value. Consider, for example, the case of just actions. To inflict a just penalty or punishment is indeed an act of goodness; but it is also an act which is forced on the agent, and it has value only as being a necessity. (It would be better if neither individuals nor states ever needed recourse to any such action.) Acts done with a view to bestowing honors and wealth are in a different category: they are acts of the highest value" (VII.13.1332a12–22).

10. For some reflections on the way generosity as a virtue depends on unequal distributions of property that make it necessary, see T. H. Irwin, "Generosity and Property in Aristotle's *Politics*."

BIBLIOGRAPHY

The listing that follows is something more than a list of works cited, and quite a bit less than a full bibliography of relevant works on Aristotle's *Rhetoric* or on Aristotle or on rhetoric in general. Nor is it an exhaustive bibliography of works on practical reason. While it is essentially a list of works cited, I have added some of the works I referred to in earlier drafts, as well as works from which I have learned the most.

For a Greek text of the *Rhetoric* I have relied on Rudolph Kessel's edition, listed below under Aristotle; quotations in English from Aristotle's works are based on the translations there listed. For other classical works I have relied on the Loeb Classical Library for text and translation.

Adkins, A. W. H. *"Aretē, Technē,* Democracy and Sophists: *Protagoras* 316d–28d." *Journal of Hellenic Studies* 93 (1973): 3–12.

Adler, Jonathan E. "Even-Arguments, Explanatory Gaps, and Pragmatic Scales." *Philosophy and Rhetoric* 25 (1992): 22–44.

Aeschylus. *Eumenides. The Oresteia by Aeschylus.* Translated by David Grene and Wendy Doniger O'Flaherty. University of Chicago Press, 1989.

Arendt, Hannah. *Between Past and Future.* New York: Viking, 1963.

———. *Eichmann in Jerusalem.* New York: Viking, 1963.

———. *The Human Condition.* University of Chicago Press, 1958. Reprint. Anchor Books, 1959.

———. *On Revolution.* New York: Viking, 1962.

Aristotle. *Aristotelis Ars Rhetorica.* Edited by Rudolph Kassel. Berlin, 1971.

———. *Aristotle's Eudemian Ethics, Books I, II, and VIII.* Translated and edited by Michael Woods. Oxford: Clarendon Press, 1982.

———. *De Anima.* Translated and edited by R. D. Hicks. Cambridge University Press, 1907.

———. *Aristotle: Nicomachean Ethics.* Translated by Terence C. Irwin. Indianapolis: Hackett, 1985.

———. *The Politics.* Translated by Carnes Lord. University of Chicago Press, 1984.

———. *On Rhetoric: A Theory of Civic Discourse.* Translated with Introduction, Notes, and Appendixes by George A. Kennedy. New York and Oxford: Oxford University Press, 1991.

Arnhart, Larry. *Aristotle on Political Reasoning: A Commentary on the "Rhetoric."* DeKalb: Northern Illinois University Press, 1981.

————. "The Rationality of Political Speech: An Interpretation of Aristotle's *Rhetoric.*" *Interpretation* 9 (1981): 141–54

Bacon, Francis. *The Advancement of Learning.* Edited by G. W. Kitchin. London: Dent, 1973.

————. *Essays.* Edited by G. W. Kitchin. London: Dent, 1972.

————. *Works.* Edited by J. Spedding, R. L. Ellis, and D. D. Heath. 7 vols. 1857–61.

Baier, Annette. "Why Honesty Is a Hard Virtue." In Owen Flanagan and Amélie Oksenberg Rorty, eds., *Identity, Character, and Morality: Essays in Moral Psychology,* 259–84. Cambridge: MIT Press, 1990.

Bakhtin, Mikhail. *Speech Genres.* Austin: University of Texas Press, 1986.

Barker, Ernest. *The Political Theory of Plato and Aristotle.* New York: Dover, 1959.

Barthes, Roland. "L'ancienne rhétorique: Aide-mémoire." *Communications* 16 (1970): 172–229.

————. "The Old Rhetoric: An Aide-Mémoire." In Roland Barthes, *The Semiotic Challenge,* translated by Richard Howard, 11–94. New York: Hill & Wang, 1988. (Translation of the above.)

Beiner, Ronald. "Do We Need a Philosophical Ethics? Theory, Prudence, and the Primacy of *Ethos.*" *Philosophical Forum* 20 (1989): 230–43.

Belfiore, Elizabeth. *Tragic Pleasures: Aristotle on Plot and Emotion.* Princeton University Press, 1992.

Benoit, William. "Isocrates and Aristotle on Rhetoric." *Rhetoric Society Quarterly* 20 (1990): 251–60.

Berns, Laurence. "Spiritedness in Ethics and Politics: A Study in Aristotelian Psychology." *Interpretation* 12 (1984): 334–48.

Bernstein, Richard. *Philosophical Profiles.* Philadelphia: University of Pennsylvania Press, 1986.

Biagiolo, Mario. "The Anthropology of Incommensurability." *Studies in the History and Philosophy of Science* 21 (1990): 183–210.

Bialostosky, Don. "Dialogic, Pragmatic, and Hermeneutic Conversation: Bakhtin, Rorty and Gadamer." *Critical Studies* 1 (1989): 107–19.

————. "Dialogics As an Art of Discourse in Literary Criticism." *PMLA* 101 (1986): 788–97.

Bird, Otto. "The Re-Discovery of the 'Topics': Professor Toulmin's Inference-Warrants." *Proceedings of the American Catholic Philosophical Association* 34 (1960): 200–205.

————. "The Tradition of the Logical Topics: Aristotle to Ockham." *Journal of the History of Ideas* 23 (1962): 307–23.

Bitzer, Lloyd. "Aristotle's Enthymeme Revisited." *Quarterly Journal of Speech* 45 (1959): 399–408.

Blundell, Mary Whitlock. "*Ethos* and *Dianoia* Reconsidered." In Amélie Oksenberg Rorty, ed., *Essays on Aristotle's "Poetics,"* 155–76.

Bobbitt, Philip. *Constitutional Fate: Theory of the Constitution.* New York and Oxford: Oxford University Press, 1982.

Bolgar, Robert. "Humanism as a Value System with Reference to Budé and Vives." In A. H. T. Levi, ed., *Humanism in France at the End of the Middle Ages and in the Early Renaissance,* 199–215. Manchester University Press, 1970.

Booth, Wayne C. *The Company We Keep: An Ethics of Fiction*. Berkeley: University of California Press, 1988.

Bourdieu, Pierre. *Outline of a Theory of Practice*. Cambridge University Press, 1977.

Brandes, Paul D. "Evidence in Aristotle's *Rhetoric*." *Speech Monographs* 28 (1961): 21–28.

————. *A History of Aristotle's Rhetoric, with a Bibliography of Early Printings*. Metuchen, N.J.: Scarecrow Press, 1989.

————. "Printings of Aristotle's *Rhetoric* during the Fifteenth and Sixteenth Centuries." *Communication Monographs* 52 (1985): 368–76.

Brennan, William. "Reason, Passion, and 'The Progress of the Law.'" *Cardozo Law Review* 10 (1988): 3–23.

Brinton, Alan. "The Outmoded Psychology of Aristotle's *Rhetoric*." *Western Journal of Speech Communication* 54 (1990): 204–18.

Broadie, Sarah Waterlow, *Ethics with Aristotle*. New York and Oxford: Oxford University Press, 1991.

————. "Nature, Craft and Phronesis in Aristotle." *Philosophical Topics* 15 (1987): 35–50.

————. "The Problem of Practical Intellect in Aristotle's *Ethics*." In John Cleary, ed., *Proceedings of the Boston Area Colloquium in Ancient Philosophy*, vol. 3, 229–52. Lanham, Md.: University Press of America, 1988.

Buber, Martin. *Two Types of Faith*. London: Routledge & Kegan Paul, 1951.

Buchanan, Allen E. "Assessing the Communitarian Critique of Liberalism." *Ethics* 99 (1989): 852–82.

Burke, Kenneth. *Counterstatement*. 2d ed. Berkeley: University of California Press, 1968.

————. *A Grammar of Motives*. New York: Prentice-Hall, 1945.

————. *Permanence and Change*. 2d rev. ed. Indianapolis: Bobbs Merrill, 1968.

————. *A Rhetoric of Motives*. New York: Prentice-Hall, 1950.

Burke, Richard J. "Politics as Rhetoric." *Ethics* 93 (1982): 45–55.

Burnet, John. "Aristotle." *Proceedings of the British Academy* 11 (1924): 109–24.

Card, Claudia. "Gratitude and Obligation." *American Philosophical Quarterly* 25 (1988): 115–27.

Cavell, Stanley. *The Claim of Reason*. New York and Oxford: Oxford University Press, 1979.

Certeau, Michel de. "What We Do When We Believe." In Marshall Blonsky, ed., *Signs*, 192–202. Baltimore: Johns Hopkins University Press, 1985.

Chamberlain, Charles. "From 'Haunts' to 'Character': The Meaning of *Ethos* and Its Relation to Ethics." *Helios* 11 (1984): 97–108.

Christensen, Johnny. "The Formal Character of *koinoi topoi* in Aristotle's Rhetoric and Dialectic Illustrated by the List in *Rhetoric* II.23." *Cahiers de l'Institut du moyen âge grec et latin* 57 (1988): 3–10.

Classen, C. Joachim. "Aristotle's Picture of the Sophists." In G. B. Kerferd, ed., *The Sophists and Their Legacy*, 7–24. Wiesbaden: Steiner Verlag, 1981.

Cohen, L. Jonathan. *The Dialogue of Reason: An Analysis of Analytical Philosophy*. Oxford: Clarendon Press, 1986.

Cole, John O. "The Socratic Method in Legal Education: Moral Discourse and Accommodation." *Mercer Law Review* 35 (1984): 867–90.

Cole, Thomas. *The Origins of Rhetoric in Ancient Greece.* Baltimore: Johns Hopkins University Press, 1991.

Conley, Thomas M. "Ancient Rhetoric and Modern Genre Criticism." *Communication Quarterly* 27 (1979): 47–53.

———. "The Enthymeme in Perspective." *Quarterly Journal of Speech* 70 (1984): 168–87.

———. "*Pathē* and *pisteis:* Aristotle *Rhet.* II.2–11." *Hermes* 110 (1982): 300–315.

———. *Rhetoric in the European Tradition.* University of Chicago Press, 1990.

Consigny, Scott. "Dialectical, Rhetorical, and Aristotelian Rhetoric." *Philosophy and Rhetoric* 22 (1989): 281–87.

———. "The Rhetorical Example." *Southern Speech Communication Journal* 41 (1976): 121–34.

Cope, Gerald E. M. *The Rhetoric of Aristotle.* 3 vols. Revised by J. E. Sandys. Cambridge University Press, 1877.

Cowan, Joseph L. "The Uses of Argument: An Apology for Logic." *Mind* 73 (1964): 27–45.

Crem, Theresa. "The Definition of Rhetoric According to Aristotle." *Laval théologique et philosophique* 11 (1955): 233–50.

Crook, Peter J. "Language, Truth and Law in Ancient Greece." *Language and Communication* 5 (1985): 231–63.

Dale, A. M. "Ethos and Dianoia: 'Character' and 'Thought' in Aristotle's *Poetics.*" In *Collected Papers.* Cambridge University Press, 1969, 139–55.

Depew, David. "Politics, Music, and Contemplation in Aristotle's Ideal State." In David Keyt and Fred D. Miller, Jr., eds., *A Companion to Aristotle's Politics,* 346–80. Oxford and Cambridge: Blackwell, 1991.

De Romilly, Jacqueline. "From Aphorisms to Theoretical Analyses: The Birth of Human Sciences in the Fifth Century, B.C." *Diogenes* 149 (1988): 1–15.

———. "Eunoia in Isocrates; or, The Political Importance of Creating Good Will." *Journal of Hellenic Studies* 78 (1958): 92–101.

———. *Magic and Rhetoric in Ancient Greece.* Cambridge University Press, 1975.

de Sousa, Ernest. *The Rationality of Emotion.* Cambridge: MIT Press, 1987.

Dewey, John. "The Future of Liberalism." In Jo Ann Boydston, ed., *The Later Works of John Dewey, 1925–1953,* vol. 11, 289–95. Carbondale: Southern Illinois University Press, 1987.

———. *Human Nature and Conduct: An Introduction to Social Psychology.* New York: Modern Library, 1930.

———. "Logical Method and Law." *Cornell Law Quarterly* 10 (1924): 17–27.

———. *The Public and Its Problems.* New York: Henry Holt, 1927. Reprint. Chicago: Gateway Books, 1946.

———. *Reconstruction in Philosophy.* Enlarged [2d] edition with a new introduction by the author. Boston: Beacon, 1948.

Dover, K. J. "Freedom of the Intellectual in Greek Society." *Talanta* 7 (1976): 24–54.

———. *Greek Popular Morality in the Time of Plato and Aristotle.* Oxford University Press, 1974.

Dunne, Joseph. "Aristotle after Gadamer: An Analysis of the Distinction between the Concepts of Phronesis and Technē." *Irish Philosophical Journal* 2 (1985): 105–23.

Easterbrook, Frank. "Criminal Procedure as a Market System." *Journal of Legal Studies* 12 (1983): 289–332.

Eden, Kathy. "Hermeneutics and the Ancient Rhetorical Tradition." *Rhetorica* 5 (1987): 59–86.

―――. *Poetic and Legal Fiction in the Aristotelian Tradition.* Princeton University Press, 1986.

Else, Gerald F. *Aristotle's Poetics.* Translated with an Introduction. Ann Arbor: University of Michigan Press, 1970.

―――. *Aristotle's Poetics: The Argument.* Cambridge: Harvard University Press, 1957.

Engberg-Pedersen, Troels. *Aristotle's Theory of Moral Insight.* Oxford: Clarendon Press, 1983.

Epstein, William. "The Classical Tradition of Dialectics and American Legal Education." *Journal of Legal Education* 31 (1981): 399–423.

Erickson, Keith V. *Aristotle's "Rhetoric": Five Centuries of Philological Research.* Metuchen, N.J.: Scarecrow Press, 1975.

―――. "The Lost Rhetorics of Aristotle." *Communications Monographs* 43 (1976): 229–37.

―――, ed. *Aristotle: The Classical Heritage of Rhetoric.* Metuchen, N.J.: Scarecrow Press, 1974.

Farrar, Cynthia. *The Origins of Democratic Thinking: The Invention of Politics in Classical Athens.* Cambridge University Press, 1988.

Feyerabend, Paul. "In Defence of Aristotle: Comments on the Condition of Content Increase." In Gerard Radnitzky and Gunnar Anderson, eds., *Progress and Rationality in Science,* 143–80. Dordrecht: Reidel, 1978.

Finnis, John. *Fundamentals of Ethics.* New York and Oxford: Oxford University Press, 1983.

Flanagan, Owen J., Jr. *Varieties of Moral Personality: Ethics and Psychological Realism.* Cambridge: Harvard University Press, 1991.

Fortenbaugh, William W. "Aristotle and the Questionable Mean-Dispositions." *Transactions of the American Philological Association* 99 (1968): 203–31.

―――. "Aristotle: Emotional and Moral Virtue." *Arethusa* 2 (1969): 163–85.

―――. *Aristotle on Emotion.* New York: Barnes & Noble, 1975.

―――. "Aristotle's Conception of Moral Virtue and Its Perceptive Role." *Transactions of the American Philological Association* 95 (1964): 77–87.

―――. "Aristotle's Platonic Attitude toward Delivery." *Philosophy and Rhetoric* 19 (1986): 242–54.

―――. "Aristotle's *Rhetoric* on Emotions." *Archiv für Geschichte der Philosophie* 52 (1970): 40–70. Reprinted in Keith V. Erickson, ed., *Aristotle: The Classical Heritage of Rhetoric,* 205–34. Metuchen, N.J.: Scarecrow Press, 1974.

―――. "*Benevolentiam conciliare* and *animos permovere*: Some Remarks on Cicero's *De oratore* 2.178–216." *Rhetorica* 6 (1988): 259–73.

―――. "Cicero's Knowledge of the Rhetorical Treatises of Aristotle and Theophrastus." In William W. Fortenbaugh and Peter Steinmetz, eds., *Cicero's*

Knowledge of the Peripatos, 39–60. New Brunswick and London: Transactions Publishers, 1989.

Frank, Robert H. *Passions within Reason: The Strategic Role of the Emotions.* New York: Norton, 1988.

Frankfurt, Harry. "Freedom of the Will and the Concept of a Person." *Journal of Philosophy* 68 (1971): 5–20.

Frede, Dorothea. "Necessity, Chance, and 'What Happens for the Most Part' in Aristotle's *Poetics.*" In Amélie Oksenberg Rorty, ed., *Essays on Aristotle's "Poetics,"* 197–220. Princeton University Press, 1992.

Fried, Charles. "The New First Amendment Jurisprudence: A Threat to Liberty." In Geoffrey R. Stone, Richard A. Epstein, and Cass. R. Sunstein, eds., *The Bill of Rights in the Modern State,* 225–54. University of Chicago Press, 1992.

Gaita, Raimond. "Virtues, Human Good, and the Unity of a Life." *Inquiry* 26 (1983): 407–24.

Galston, William A. *Justice and the Human Good.* University of Chicago Press, 1980.

Garrett, Jan Edward. "Aristotle's Non-Technical Conception of *Technē.*" *Modern Schoolman* 64 (1987): 283–94.

Garver, Eugene. "Aristotle's Genealogy of Morals." *Philosophy and Phenomenological Research* 48 (1984): 471–92.

———. "Aristotle's Metaphysics of Morals." *Journal of the History of Philosophy* 27 (1989): 7–28.

———. "Aristotle's Natural Slaves: Incomplete *Praxis* and Incomplete Human Beings." *Journal of the History of Philosophy* 32 (1994): 1–22.

———. "Aristotle's *Rhetoric* on Unintentionally Hitting the Principles of the Sciences." *Rhetorica* 6 (1989): 381–93.

———. "He Does the Police in Different Voices: J. B. White on the Criminal Law." *Rhetoric Society Quarterly* 21 (1991): 1–11.

———. "The Human Function and Aristotle's Art of Rhetoric." *History of Philosophy Quarterly* 6 (1989): 133–46.

———. *Machiavelli and the History of Prudence.* Madison: University of Wisconsin Press, 1987

———. "The Meaning of *Thrasos* in Aristotle's *Ethics.*" *Classical Philology* 77 (1983): 282–332.

———. "The Moral Virtues and the Two Sides of *Energeia.*" *Ancient Philosophy* 9 (1989): 293–312.

Gastaldi, Silvia. "Discorso della citta e discorso della scuola." *Ricerche sulla "Retorica" di Aristotele.* Florence: La nuova Italia, 1981.

———. "*Pathē* and *Polis:* Aristotle's Theory of Passions in the *Rhetoric* and the *Ethics.*" *Topoi* 6 (1987): 105–10.

Gellrich, Michelle. *Tragedy and Theory: The Problem of Conflict since Aristotle.* Princeton University Press, 1988.

Gill, Christopher. "The Character-Personality Distinction." In Christopher Pelling, ed., *Characterization and Individuality in Greek Literature,* 1–31. Oxford: Clarendon Press, 1990.

———. "The *Ethos/Pathos* Distinction in Rhetorical and Literary Criticism." *Classical Quarterly* 34 (1984): 149–66.

————. "The Question of Character and Personality in Greek Tragedy." *Poetics Today* 7 (1986): 251–73.

Gilman, Sander. *Pathology and Difference*. Ithaca: Cornell University Press, 1985.

Goldhill, Simon. "Character and Action, Representation and Reading: Greek Tragedy and Its Critics." In Christopher Pelling, ed., *Characterization and Individuality in Greek Literature*, 100–127. Oxford: Clarendon Press, 1990.

Gorovitz, Samuel, and Alasdair MacIntyre. "Towards a Theory of Medical Fallibility." *Journal of Medicine and Philosophy* 1 (1976): 51–71.

Gottlieb, Paula. "Aristotle and Protagoras: The Good Human Being As the Measure of Goods." *Apeiron* 24 (1991): 25–46.

Gould, Thomas. *The Ancient Quarrel between Poetry and Philosophy*. Princeton University Press, 1990.

Green, Lawrence D. "Aristotelian Rhetoric, Dialectic, and the Traditions of *Antistrophos*." *Rhetorica* 8 (1990): 5–27.

Greenspan, Patricia S. "A Case of Mixed Feelings: Ambivalence and the Logic of Emotion." In Amélie Oksenberg Rorty, ed., *Explaining Emotions*, 223–50. University of California Press, 1980.

Grimaldi, William. "The Aristotelian Topics." *Traditio* 14 (1958): 1–16.

————. *Aristotle, Rhetoric I: A Commentary*. New York: Fordham University Press, 1980.

————. *Aristotle, Rhetoric II: A Commentary*. New York: Fordham University Press, 1988.

————. "*Semeion, Tekmerion*, and *Eikos* in Aristotle's *Rhetoric*." *American Journal of Philology* 101 (1980): 383–98.

————. *Studies in the Philosophy of Aristotle's Rhetoric*. Wiesbaden: Franz Steiner Verlag, 1972.

Hacking, Ian. *The Emergence of Probability*. Cambridge University Press, 1975.

Halliwell, Stephen. "Traditional Greek Conceptions of Character." In Christopher Pelling, ed., *Characterization and Individuality in Greek Literature*, 32–59. Oxford: Clarendon Press, 1990.

Hamlyn, D. W. "Aristotle on Dialectic." *Philosophy* 65 (1990): 465–76.

Hauser, Gerald. "The Example in Aristotle's Rhetoric: Bifurcation or Contradiction?" *Philosophy and Rhetoric* 1 (1968): 78–90.

Heffernan, William C. "Not Socrates, but Protagoras: The Sophistic Basis of Legal Education." *Buffalo Law Review* 29 (1980): 399–423.

Heim, Michael. "Philosophy As Ultimate Rhetoric." *Southern Journal of Philosophy* 19 (1981): 183.

Hicks, R. D. *Aristotle, De Anima*. Amsterdam: A. M. Hakkert, 1965.

Hill, Forbes. "The Amorality of Aristotle's *Rhetoric*." *Greek, Roman and Byzantine Studies* 22 (1981): 133–47.

Hintikka, Jaakko. "Practical vs. Theoretical Reason: An Ambiguous Legacy." In *Knowledge and the Known*, 80–97. Dordrecht: Reidel, 1974.

Hirschman, Albert O. *Essays in Trespassing: Economics to Politics and Beyond*. Cambridge University Press, 1981.

————. "Morality and the Social Sciences: A Durable Tension." In N. Haan, Robert N. Bellah, Paul Rabinow, and William M. Sullivan, eds., *Social Science as Moral Inquiry*, 21–32. New York: Columbia University Press, 1983.

————. *The Rhetoric of Reaction: Perversity, Futility, Jeopardy.* Cambridge: Harvard University Press, 1991.

Hobbes, Thomas. *Leviathan.* Indianapolis and New York: Bobbs-Merrill, 1958.

Hume, David. *An Inquiry Concerning the Principles of Morals.* Edited by Charles W. Hendel. Indianapolis: Library of Liberal Arts, 1957.

————. *Political Essays.* Edited by Charles W. Hendel. Indianapolis: Bobbs-Merrill, 1953.

————. *Treatise on Human Nature.* Edited by L. A. Selby-Bigge. London: Oxford University Press, 1888.

Hursthouse, Rosalind. "Acting and Feeling in Character: *Nicomachean Ethics* 3.i." *Phronesis* 29 (1984): 252–66.

————. "A False Doctrine of the Mean." *Proceedings of the Aristotelian Society* 81 (1980): 57–72.

Huseman, Richard C. "Aristotle's System of Topics." *Southern Speech Communication Journal* 30 (1965): 243–52.

Hutchinson, D. S. "Doctrines of the Mean and the Debate concerning Skills in Fourth-Century Medicine, Rhetoric, and Ethics." *Apeiron* 21 (1988): 17–52.

IJsseling, Samuel. *Rhetoric and Philosophy in Conflict: An Historical Survey.* The Hague: Martinus Nijhoff, 1976.

Irwin, T. H. "Generosity and Property in Aristotle's *Politics.*" *Social Philosophy and Policy* 4 (1987): 37–54.

————. "Moral Science and Political Theory in Aristotle." In P. A. Cartledge and F. D. Harvey, eds., *Crux: Essays in Greek History,* 150–68. London: Duckworth, 1985.

James, William. *The Will to Believe.* Abridged in Amélie Rorty, ed., *Pragmatic Philosophy: An Anthology.* Garden City, N.Y.: Doubleday Anchor Books, 1966.

Johnstone, Henry. *Philosophy and Argument.* University Park: Pennsylvania State University Press, 1959.

————. "Rationality and Rhetoric in Philosophy." *Quarterly Journal of Speech* 59 (1973): 381–89.

Jonsen, Albert R., and Stephen Toulmin. *The Abuse of Casuistry: A History of Moral Reasoning.* Berkeley: University of California Press, 1988.

Kane, Francis I. "Peitho and the Polis." *Philosophy and Rhetoric* 19 (1986): 99–124.

Kant, Immanuel. *Critique of Judgment.* Translated by Werner S. Pluhar. Indianapolis: Hackett, 1987.

Kenny, Anthony. *Action, Emotion, and Will.* London: Routledge & Kegan Paul, 1963.

————. "Practical Inference." *Analysis* 26 (1966): 65–75.

————. *Will, Freedom and Power.* Oxford: Blackwell, 1975.

Keyt, David. "Distributive Justice in Aristotle's *Ethics* and *Politics.*" *Topoi* 4 (1985): 23–45.

Korsgaard, Christine. "Skepticism about Practical Reason." *Journal of Philosophy* 83 (1986): 5–25.

————. "Two Distinctions in Goodness." *Philosophical Review* 92 (1983): 169–96.

Kronman, Anthony T. "Alexander Bickel's Philosophy of Prudence." *Yale Law Journal* 94 (1985): 1567–1616.

————. "Aristotle's Idea of Political Fraternity." *American Journal of Jurisprudence* 25 (1979): 114–38.

————. "Living in the Law." *University of Chicago Law Review* 54 (1987): 835–76.

————. "Practical Wisdom and Professional Character." *Social Philosophy and Policy* 4 (1986): 203–34.

Kurland, Philip B. "The True Wisdom of the Bill of Rights." In Geoffrey R. Stone, Richard A. Epstein, and Cass R. Sunstein, eds., *The Bill of Rights in the Modern State*, 7–12. University of Chicago Press, 1992.

Ladd, John. "The Place of Practical Reason in Judicial Decision." In Carl J. Friedrich, ed., *Rational Decision*, 126–44. New York: Atherton Press, 1964.

Larmore, Charles. *Patterns of Moral Complexity.* Cambridge University Press, 1987.

Lavency, M. "La technique des lieux communs de la rhetorique grecque." *Les études classiques* 33 (1965): 113–26.

Lear, Jonathan. *Aristotle: The Desire to Understand.* Cambridge University Press, 1988.

————. "Ethics, Mathematics, and Relativism." In Geoffrey Sayre-McCord, ed., *Essays on Moral Realism*, 76–94. Ithaca: Cornell University Press, 1988.

————. "Katharsis." In Amélie Oksenberg Rorty, ed., *Essays on Aristotle's "Poetics,"* 315–40. Princeton University Press, 1992.

Leighton, Stephen R. "Aristotle and the Emotions." *Phronesis* 27 (1982): 144–74.

————. "Aristotle's Courageous Passions." *Phronesis* 33 (1988): 76–99.

Lennox, James. "Aristotle on Genera, Species, and 'The More and the Less'." *Journal of the History of Biology* 13 (1980): 321–46.

Levinson, Stephen. *Pragmatics.* Cambridge University Press, 1963.

Lloyd, G. E. R. *Aristotle: The Growth and Structure of His Thought.* Cambridge University Press, 1968.

Lomasky, Loren. *Persons, Rights, and the Moral Community.* London and Oxford: Oxford University Press, 1987.

Lord, Carnes. "Aristotle's Anthropology." In Carnes Lord and David K. O'Connor, eds., *Essays on the Foundations of Aristotle's Political Science*, 49–73. Berkeley: University of California Press, 1991.

————. "The Character and Composition of Aristotle's *Politics*." *Political Theory* 9 (1981): 459–78.

————. "On the Early History of the Aristotelian Corpus." *American Journal of Philology* 107 (1986): 137–61.

————. *Education and Culture in the Political Thought of Aristotle.* Ithaca: Cornell University Press, 1982.

————. "The Intention of Aristotle's *Rhetoric*." *Hermes* 109 (1981): 326–39.

————. "Politics and Education in Aristotle's *Politics*." In *Aristoteles' "Politik": Akten des XI. Symposium Aristotelicum*, 203–16. Göttingen: Vandenhoeck & Ruprecht, 1990.

————. "Politics and Philosophy in Aristotle's *Politics*." *Hermes* 106 (1978): 336–57.

Lovibond, Sabina. *Realism and Imagination in Ethics.* Minneapolis: University of Minnesota Press, 1983.

Luban, David. "Explaining Dark Times: Hannah Arendt's Theory of Theory." *Social Research* 50 (1983): 215–48.

————. *Lawyers and Justice: An Ethical Study.* Princeton University Press, 1988.
————. "Partnership, Betrayal, and Autonomy in the Lawyer-Client Relationship." *Columbia Law Review* 90 (1990): 1004–1044.
McBurney, James H. "The Place of the Enthymeme in Rhetorical Theory." *Speech Monographs* 3 (1936): 219–74.
McConnell, Michael W. "Religious Freedom at the Crossroads." In Geoffrey R. Stone, Richard A. Epstein, and Cass R. Sunstein, eds., *The Bill of Rights in the Modern State,* 115–94. University of Chicago Press, 1992.
McConnell, Michael, and Richard A. Posner. "An Economic Approach to Issues of Religious Freedom." *University of Chicago Law Review* 56 (1989): 1–60.
MacIntyre, Alasdair. *After Virtue.* 2d ed. Notre Dame, Ind.: University of Notre Dame Press, 1984.
————. "How Moral Agents Became Ghosts; or, Why the History of Ethics Diverged from That of Philosophy of Mind." *Synthèse* 53 (1982): 295–312.
————. "How Virtues Become Vices: Values, Medicine, and Social Context." In H. T. Engelhardt, Jr., and S. F. Spicker, eds., *Evaluation and Explanation in the Biomedical Sciences,* 97–111. Dordrecht: Reidel, 1975.
————. "The Magic in the Pronoun "My."" *Ethics* 94 (1983): 113–25.
————. "Moral Rationality, Tradition, and Aristotle." *Inquiry* 26 (1983).
————. "Objectivity in Morality and Objectivity in Science." In H. T. Engelhardt, Jr., and Daniel Callahan, eds., *Morals, Science, and Sociality,* 21–39. Hastings-on-Hudson: Hastings Center, 1978.
————. *Whose Justice? Which Rationality?* Notre Dame, Ind.: Notre Dame University Press, 1988.
McKeon, Richard. "Aristotle's Conception of Moral and Political Philosophy." *Ethics* 51 (1941): 253–90.
————. "Dialectic and Political Thought and Action." *Ethics* 65 (1954): 1–33.
————. "Literary Criticism and the Concept of Imitation in Antiquity." *Modern Philology* 34 (1936): 1–35. Reprinted in R. S. Crane, *Critics and Criticism: Ancient and Modern,* 147–75. University of Chicago Press, 1952.
————. "Renaissance and Method." *Studies in the History of Ideas* 3 (1935): 37–114.
————. "Rhetoric and Poetic in Aristotle." In Elder Olson, ed., *Aristotle's "Poetics" and English Literature,* 201–36. University of Chicago Press, 1965.
————. "Rhetoric in the Middle Ages." *Speculum* 17 (1942): 1–32.
Madden, Edward H. "Aristotle's Treatment of Probability and Signs." *Philosophy of Science* 24 (1957): 167–72.
————. "The Enthymeme: Crossroads of Logic, Rhetoric, and Metaphysics." *Philosophical Review* 61 (1952): 368–76.
Mara, Gerald. "The Role of Philosophy in Aristotle's Political Science." *Polity* 19 (1987): 375–401.
Mill, John Stuart. "On Liberty." Reprinted in *Collected Works of John Stuart Mill,* vol. 18. University of Toronto Press, 1977.
Modrak, Deborah K. W. *Aristotle: The Power of Perception.* University of Chicago Press, 1987.

Moline, Jon. "Aristotle on Praise and Blame." *Archiv für Geschichte der Philosophie* 71 (1989): 257–82.

———. "Plato on Persuasion and Credibility." *Philosophy and Rhetoric* 21 (1988): 260–78.

Moraux, Paul. *Les listes anciennes des ouvrages d'Aristote.* Louvain: Editions Universitaires de Louvain, 1951.

Mourelatos, Alexander. *The Route of Parmenides.* New Haven: Yale University Press, 1970.

Nehemas, Alexander. "Pity and Fear in the *Rhetoric* and the *Poetics.*" In Amélie Oksenberg Rorty, ed., *Essays on Aristotle's Poetics,* 291–314. Princeton University Press, 1992.

Newman, John Henry. *An Essay in Aim of a Grammar of Assent.* Garden City, N.Y.: Doubleday, 1955.

Nietzsche, Friedrich. "Description of Ancient Rhetoric." In *Friedrich Nietzsche on Rhetoric and Language,* 2–193, edited and translated by Sander L. Gilman, Carole Blair, and David J. Parent. New York and Oxford: Oxford University Press, 1989.

———. *Twilight of the Idols.* In Walter Kaufmann, ed., *The Portable Nietzsche.* New York: Viking, 1954.

Nussbaum, Martha. "The Discernment of Perception: An Aristotelian Conception of Private and Public Rationality." In John J. Cleary, ed., *Proceedings of the Boston Area Colloquium in Ancient Philosophy,* vol. 1, 151–201. Lanham, Md.: University Press of America, 1986.

———. *The Fragility of Goodness.* Cambridge University Press, 1986.

Ober, Josiah. *Mass and Elite in Democratic Athens: Rhetoric, Ideology, and the Power of the People.* Princeton University Press, 1989.

Oehler, Klaus. "Logic of Relations and Inference from Signs in Aristotle." *Ars Semiotica* 4 (1981): 237–46.

Olian, J. Robert. "The Intended Uses of Aristotle's *Rhetoric.*" *Speech Monographs* 33 (1968): 137–48.

O'Neill, Onora. "Between Consenting Adults." *Philosophy and Public Affairs* 14 (1985): 252–77.

Pater, W. A. de. "La fonction du lieu et de l'instrument dans les *Topiques.*" In G. E. L. Owen, ed., *Aristotle on Dialectic: The Topics,* 164–88. Oxford: Clarendon Press, 1968.

———. *Les Topiques d'Aristote et la dialectique platonicienne.* Freiburg: Editions Saint-Paul, 1965.

Pearson, Lionel. "Characterization in Drama and Oratory." *Classical Quarterly* 18 (1968): 76–83.

Pelling, Christopher, ed. *Characterization and Individuality in Greek Literature.* Oxford: Clarendon Press, 1990.

Penner, Terry. "Desire and Power in Socrates: The Argument of *Gorgias* 466a–468e that Orators and Tyrants Have No Power in the City." *Apeiron* 24 (1991): 147–202.

———. "Socrates on the Impossibility of Belief-Relative Sciences." In John J.

Cleary, ed., *Proceedings of the Boston Area Colloquium in Ancient Philosophy*, vol. 3, 263–325. Lanham, Md.: University Press of America, 1988.

Perelman, Chaim, and L. Olbrecht-Tyteca. *The New Rhetoric: A Treatise on Argumentation.* Translated by John Wilkinson and Purcell Weaver. Notre Dame, Ind.: University of Notre Dame Press, 1969.

Posner, Richard. "The Homeric Version of the Minimal State." *Ethics* 90 (1979): 27–46.

———. "The Jurisprudence of Skepticism." *Michigan Law Review* 86 (1988): 827–91.

Price, H. H. "Belief 'In' and Belief 'That.'" *Religious Studies* 1 (1965): 5–28.

Putnam, Hilary. *Meaning and the Moral Sciences.* London: Routledge & Kegan Paul, 1976.

Raphael, Sally. "Rhetoric, Dialectic, and Syllogistic Argument: Aristotle's Position in *Rhetoric* I–II." *Phronesis* 19 (1974): 153–67.

Rees, B. R. "*Pathos* in the *Poetics* of Aristotle." *Greece and Rome* 19 (1972): 1–11.

Ricouer, Paul. *Conflict of Interpretations.* Edited by Don Ihde. Evanston, Ill.: Northwestern University Press, 1974.

———. "Mimesis and Representation." *Annals of Scholarship* 2 (1981): 15–32.

———. *The Rule of Metaphor.* University of Toronto Press, 1977.

Roberts, W. Rhys. "Reference to Plato in Aristotle's Rhetoric." *Classical Philology* 19 (1924): 324 ff.

Rorty, Amélie Oksenberg. "*Akrasia* and Conflict." *Inquiry* 23 (1980): 193–212.

———. "Akrasia and Pleasure: *Nicomachean Ethics* Book VII." In Amélie Rorty, ed., *Essays on Aristotle's Ethics*, 267–84. Berkeley: University of California Press, 1981.

———. "Aristotle on the Metaphysical Status of Pathē." *Review of Metaphysics* 38 (1984): 521–46.

———. *Explaining Emotions.* Berkeley: University of California Press, 1980.

———. *Mind in Action: Essays in the Philosophy of Mind.* Boston: Beacon Press, 1988.

———. "The Place of Contemplation in Aristotle's *Nicomachean Ethics.*" *Mind* (1978): 343–58.

———. "The Psychology of Aristotelian Tragedy." In Amélie Oksenberg Rorty, ed., *Essays on Aristotle's Poetics*, 1–22. Princeton University Press, 1992.

———. "The Two Faces of Courage." *Philosophy* 61 (1986): 151–71.

———. "Varieties of Rationality, Varieties of Emotion." *Social Science Information* 24 (1985): 343–53.

———, ed. *Essays on Aristotle's Ethics.* Berkeley: University of California Press, 1981.

———, ed. *Essays on Aristotle's Poetics.* Princeton University Press, 1992.

Ross, James R. "Justice Is Reasonableness: Aquinas on Human Law and Morality." *Monist* 58 (1974): 86–103.

Ross, W. D. *Aristotle.* London: Methuen, 1953.

Russell, D. A. "*Ethos* in Oratory and Rhetoric." Christopher Pelling, ed., *Characterization and Individuality in Greek Literature*, 197–212. Oxford: Clarendon Press, 1990.

Ryan, Eugene F. "Aristotle's *Rhetoric* and *Ethics* and the Ethos of Society." *Greek, Roman and Byzantine Studies* 13 (1972): 291–308.

————. *Aristotle's Theory of Rhetorical Argumentation.* Montreal: Bellarmin, Ryle, 1984.

Ryle, Gilbert. "Philosophical Arguments." In *Collected Papers,* vol. 2. New York: Barnes & Noble, 1971.

Salkever, Stephen G. "Aristotle's Social Science." *Political Theory* 9 (1981): 479–508.

————. *Finding the Mean: Theory and Practice in Aristotelian Political Philosophy.* Princeton University Press, 1990.

————. "Tragedy and the Education of the *Demos:* Aristotle's Response to Plato." In J. Peter Euben, -ed., *Greek Tragedy and Political Theory,* 274–304. Berkeley: University of California Press, 1986.

Saxonhouse, Arlene. "The Philosopher of the Particular and the Universality of the City." *Political Theory* 16 (1988): 281–99.

Schiappa, Edwin. *Protagoras and Logos: A Study in Greek Philosophy and Rhetoric.* Columbia, S.C.: University of South Carolina Press, 1991.

Seeskin, Kenneth. "Judaism and the Linguistic Interpretation of Jewish Faith." *Studies in Jewish Philosophy* 3 (1983): 71–81.

Sherman, Nancy. *The Fabric of Character: Aristotle's Theory of Virtue.* Oxford: Clarendon Press, 1989.

Sherwin, Richard K. "Law, Violence, and Illiberal Belief." *Georgetown Law Review* 78 (1990): 1785–1835.

Shiner, Roger. "Aristotle's Theory of Equity." In Spiro Panagiotou, ed., *Justice, Law, and Method in Plato and Aristotle,* 173–92. Edmonton: Academic Printing and Publishing, 1987.

Shklar, Judith. *The Faces of Injustice.* New Haven: Yale University Press, 1990.

Smith, Adam. *The Theory of Moral Sentiments.* Edited by D. D. Raphael and A. L. Mackie. Oxford: Clarendon Press, 1976.

Solmsen, Friedrich. "The Aristotelian Tradition in Ancient Rhetoric." *American Journal of Philology* 62 (1941): 35–50, 169–90.

————. *Intellectual Experiments of the Greek Enlightenment.* Princeton University Press, 1975.

————. "Leisure and Play in Aristotle's Ideal State." *Rheinisches Museum* 107 (1954): 193–220.

Sorabji, Richard. "Aristotle on the Role of Intellect in Virtue." In Amelie Rorty, ed., *Essays on Aristotle's Ethics,* 201–20. Berkeley: University of California Press, 1981.

Stigen, A. *The Structure of Aristotle's Thought.* Oslo: Universitetsforlaget, 1966.

Stocker, Michael. "Affectivity and Self-Concern: The Assumed Psychology of Aristotle's *Ethics.*" *Pacific Philosophical Quarterly* 64 (1983): 211–29.

————. "Akrasia and the Object of Desire." In Joel Marks, ed., *The Ways of Desire,* 197–216. Chicago: Precedent, 1986.

————. "Dirty Hands and Conflicts of Values and of Desires in Aristotle's *Ethics.*" *Pacific Philosophical Quarterly* 67 (1986): 36–61.

————. "Emotional Thoughts." *American Philosophical Quarterly* 24 (1987): 59–69.

————. *Plural and Conflicting Values.* Oxford: Clarendon Press, 1990.

————. "Psychic Feelings." *Australasian Journal of Philosophy* 61 (1983): 5–26.

————. "Some Problems with Counter-Examples in Ethics." *Synthèse* 72 (1987): 277–89.

Stone, Geoffrey R., Richard A. Epstein, and Cass R. Sunstein, eds. *The Bill of Rights in the Modern State*. University of Chicago Press, 1992.

Sullivan, Kathleen M. "Religion and Liberal Democracy." In Geoffrey R. Stone, Richard A. Epstein, and Cass R. Sunstein, eds., *The Bill of Rights in the Modern State*, 195–223. University of Chicago Press, 1992.

Sunstein, Cass R. "Free Speech Now." In *The Bill of Rights in the Modern State*, Geoffrey R. Stone, Richard A. Epstein, and Cass R. Sunstein, eds., 255–315. University of Chicago Press, 1992.

———. "Naked Preferences and the Constitution." *Columbia Law Review* 84 (1984): 1689–1732.

———. "Preferences and Politics." *Philosophy and Public Affairs* 20 (1991): 3–34.

Tanner, Michael. "Sentimentality." *Proceedings of the Aristotelian Society* 77 (1977): 127–47.

Taylor, Charles. "Explanation and Practical Reason." In Martha Nussbaum and Amartya Sen, eds., *The Quality of Life*, 208–31. Oxford: Clarendon Press, 1993.

———. "Rorty in the Epistemological Tradition." In Alan R. Malachowski, ed., *Reading Rorty*, 257–77. Oxford: Blackwell, 1989.

———. "Social Theory As Practice." In *Philosophy and the Human Sciences: Philosophical Papers*, vol. 2, 91–115. Cambridge University Press, 1985.

———. "What Is Human Agency?" In *Human Agency and Language: Philosophical Papers*, vol. 1, 15–44. Cambridge University Press, 1985.

Thomas, Laurence. "Rationality and Affectivity: The Metaphysics of the Moral Self." *Social Philosophy and Policy* 5 (1988): 154–72.

———. "Trust, Affirmation, and Moral Character: A Critique of Kantian Morality." In Owen J. Flanagan and Amélie Oksenberg Rorty, eds., *Identity, Character, and Morality: Essays in Moral Psychology*, 235–58. Cambridge: MIT Press, 1990.

———. "Trust and Survival: Securing a Vision of the Good Society." *Journal of Social Philosophy* 20 (1989): 34–41.

Thucydides. *History of the Peloponnesian War*. Translated by Thomas Hobbes and edited by Richard Schlatter. New Brunswick, N.J.: Rutgers University Press, 1975.

Trilling, Lionel. Introduction to *Homage to Catalonia*, by George Orwell. New York: Harcourt Brace Jovanovich, 1952.

Trimpi, Wesley. *Muses of One Mind: The Literary Analysis of Experience and Its Continuity*. Princeton University Press, 1983.

———. "The Quality of Fiction: The Rhetorical Transmission of Literary Theory." *Traditio* 30 (1974): 1–118.

Trivers, Robert. "The Evolution of Reciprocal Altruism." *Quarterly Review of Biology* 46 (1971): 35–57.

Vickers, Brian. *In Defence of Rhetoric*. New York and Oxford: Oxford University Press, 1988.

Vining, Joseph. *The Authoritative and the Authoritarian*. University of Chicago Press, 1986.

von Wright, George. *Varieties of Goodness*. London: Routledge & Kegan Paul, 1963.

Wallace, James D. *Moral Relevance and Moral Conflict*. Ithaca: Cornell University Press, 1988.

Wallace, William. "Aquinas on Dialectic and Rhetoric." In Ruth Link-Salinger, ed., *A Straight Path: Studies in Medieval Philosophy and Culture*, 244–54. Washington, D.C.: Catholic University of America Press, 1988.

Walton, Kendall. "Fearing Fictions." *Journal of Philosophy* 75 (1978): 5–27.

Ward, John O. "Magic and Rhetoric from Antiquity to the Renaissance: Some Ruminations." *Rhetorica* 6 (1988): 57–118.

Wellman, Vincent A. "Practical Reasoning and Judicial Justification: Toward an Adequate Theory." *University of Colorado Law Review* 57 (1987): 45–115.

White, James B. "The Ethics of Argument." *University of Chicago Law Review* 50 (1983): 849–95.

———. *Heracles' Bow: Essays on the Rhetoric and Poetics of the Law.* Madison: University of Wisconsin Press, 1985.

———. *Justice As Translation: An Essay in Cultural and Legal Criticism.* University of Chicago Press, 1990.

———. *The Legal Imagination.* Boston: Little, Brown, 1972.

———. "Translation, Interpretation, and the Law." In Bernard P. Dauenhauser, ed., *Textual Fidelity and Textual Disregard*, 17–37. New York: Peter Lang, 1990.

———. "What Can a Lawyer Learn from Literature?" *Harvard Law Review* 102 (1989): 2014–2047.

———. *When Words Lose Their Meaning.* University of Chicago Press, 1984.

Wiggins, David. "Weakness of Will, Commensurability, and the Objects of Deliberation and Desire." In Amélie Rorty, ed., *Essays on Aristotle's Ethics*, 241–65. Berkeley: University of California Press, 1981.

Wilkerson, T. E. "Uniqueness in Art and Morals." *Philosophy* 58 (1983): 303–14.

Williams, Bernard. "Conflicts of Values." In Alan Ryan, ed., *The Idea of Freedom: Essays in Honour of Isaiah Berlin.* New York and Oxford: Oxford University Press, 1979.

———. "Deciding to Believe." In *Problems of the Self: Philosophical Papers, 1956–1972*, 136–51. Cambridge University Press, 1973.

———. *Ethics and the Limits of Philosophy.* Cambridge: Harvard University Press, 1985.

———. "Political Philosophy and the Analytical Tradition." In Melvin Richter, ed., *Political Theory and Political Education*, 57–75. Princeton University Press, 1980.

Wisse, Jakob. *Ethos and Pathos from Aristotle to Cicero.* Amsterdam: Hakkert, 1989.

Wong, David B. "Three Kinds of Incommensurability." In Michael Krausz, ed., *Relativism: Interpretation and Confrontation*, 140–58. Notre Dame, Ind.: University of Notre Dame Press, 1989.

Woodruff, Paul. "Aristotle on *Mimesis.*" In Amélie Oksenberg Rorty, ed., *Essays on Aristotle's Poetics*, 72–96. Princeton University Press, 1992.

Young, Charles. "Aristotle on Justice." *Southern Journal of Philosophy* 27 (1988): 233–49.

———. "Aristotle on Temperance." *Philosophical Review* 97 (1988): 521–42.

Zyskind, Harold. "The New Rhetoric and Formalism." *Revue internationale de philosophie* 127–8 (1979): 18–32.

INDEX TO PASSAGES FROM ARISTOTLE

GENERAL INDEX

Adler, Jonathan, 282 n. 12
Aeschylus, 9, 105, 106, 111, 113, 148
Anger, 112, 124–25, 127–30
Arendt, Hannah, 5, 237, 251 n. 3,
    256 n. 22, 274 n. 10, 291 n. 24
Aretē. See Virtue, moral
Art
    as an intellectual virtue, 23, 34
    civic vs. professional, 7, 11, 12,
        18–21, 35, 39, 40, 45–51, 81, 89,
        139, 183, 186–87, 190, 206, 223,
        230, 245, 258 n. 35
    of rhetoric, 22, 25, 31, 32, 87, 121,
        139, 223, 227
        as indefinite art, 20–21, 40, 42,
            71, 84, 86–87, 251 n. 2
        limited to argument, 36–38, 40,
            53, 175
        practical art, 42–43, 47, 73, 237–
            39, 242
    of sophistic, 57, 183, 184, 187
    of delivery; *see* Delivery
    vs. chance, 31, 33, 39, 252 n. 6
    vs. moral virtue, 19, 20, 34, 43, 44,
        218
    vs. nature, 32–33, 61, 252 n. 6
    vs. *phronēsis,* 34, 212, 228, 233, 242

Bacon, Francis, 254 n. 11, 282 n. 11,
    290 n. 21, 293 n. 9
Baier, Annette, 293–94 n. 12
Bakhtin, Mikhail, 283 n. 16
Barker, Ernest, 50, 191

Barthes, Roland, 253 n. 9, 280–81
    n. 3, 283 n. 17
Beiner, Ronald, 267 n. 19
Belfiore, Elizabeth, 286 n. 4
Belief. *See Pistis*
Bernstein, Richard, 294–95 n. 2
Biagioli, Mario, 263 n. 17
Bialostosky, Don, 283 n. 16
Bird, Otto, 266 n. 12
Blundell, Mary Whitlock, 285–86
    n. 3
Bobbitt, Philip, 282 n. 14
Bolgar, Robert, 286 n. 6
Booth, Wayne C., 271 n. 33, 282
    n. 10, 291 n. 29
Bourdieu, Pierre, 288 n. 13
Brennan, William, 105, 115
Broadie, Sarah Waterlow, 252 n. 8,
    253–54 n. 10, 257 n. 31, 262 n. 16,
    270 n. 32, 288 n. 12, 292 n. 4, 294
    n. 15
Buber, Martin, 278 n. 30
Buchanan, Allen, 259 n. 37
Burke, Kenneth, 85, 265 n. 8, 286
    n. 6, 291 n. 28
Burnet, John, 9, 249 n. 4

Card, Claudia, 277 n. 29
Cause
    actual, identical with its effect, 35,
        36, 38, 40, 59, 60, 119, 120, 181,
        192, 237, 275 n. 17
    efficient, 159, 225

final, 141, 144, 155, 164–65, 193, 202

formal, 35, 141, 144, 155, 164, 165

material, 40, 124, 129

Cavell, Stanley, 295 n. 4

Chamberlain, Charles, 286 n. 4

Character; see also *Ēthos*
vs. precision, 50, 84, 152, 154, 183, 215, 293 n. 7

Cicero, 251 n. 2

Cleverness, 69, 121, 147, 149, 153, 158, 164, 166, 176, 184, 186, 204, 213, 233

Cohen, L. Jonathan, 281 n. 6

Cole, John O., 259 n. 38

Cole, Thomas, 87, 252 n. 5, 265 n. 11

Conley, Thomas, 250 n. 6, 261 n. 8, 278 n. 32

Consistency, as an ethical value, 80, 82, 92–93, 103, 135, 190, 209, 229, 266–76 n. 18

Cope, Gerald, 254–55 n. 14, 264 n. 2

Courage, 46, 47, 190–91, 213, 219–22, 242–43

Cowan, Joseph L., 266 n. 12

"Creation science," 57, 168, 187

Crook, Peter J., 259–60 n. 1

Dale, A. M., 286 n. 3

De Certeau, Michel, 257 n. 28

De Pater, W. A., 265 n. 6

De Romilly, Jacqueline, 273 n. 4

De Sousa, Ernest, 266 n. 18, 270 n. 33, 273 n. 5

Delivery, 41, 201, 208, 247

Dewey, John, 11, 154, 186, 232, 250 n. 9, 266 n. 14, 287 n. 11, 289 n. 16, 293 n. 10, 294 n. 1

Dialectic, compared to rhetoric, 22, 28, 29, 52, 53, 61, 72, 78–81, 84–88, 93, 100, 137, 154, 164, 166, 182, 188, 207–13, 217, 222–23, 226

Dover, K. J., 251 n. 3, 258 n. 35, 290–91 n. 24

Dynamis
rational vs. irrational, 26, 33, 50, 92, 187, 188, 203, 211, 212, 236
rhetoric as a, 25, 27, 100, 137, 139, 203, 211
trained incapacity, 178–85, 199, 202

Easterbrook, Frank, 269 n. 28

Else, Gerald, 3, 249 n. 2

Ends, internal vs. external, guiding vs. given, constitutive vs. posited, 24–44, 47–50, 51, 53, 60, 73, 76, 139, 140, 164–67, 169, 170, 176–80, 182, 185, 186, 191, 194, 196, 199–203, 208–11, 214, 217–19, 233–37, 242, 246–47, 253–54 n. 10, 254 n. 13, 255 n. 17

Energeia
first and second, 29, 32, 83, 141, 150, 185, 289 n. 15
rhetorical argument as, 28, 35–40, 47, 52, 61, 104, 119, 120, 144, 223
shared between speaker and hearer, 36–38, 104, 120, 192
vs. *kinesis; see kinesis*

Enthymeme, 162–71
apparent vs. real, 157, 162, 163–69, 183, 222, 290 n. 22
formal, 170
body of proof, 53, 63, 77, 141, 150, 151, 171, 173, 175, 177, 202, 285 n. 3
demonstrative, 162
refutative, 161
rhetorical syllogism, 32, 80, 102, 135, 149, 169
preferred method in judicial rhetoric, 67, 70, 95, 96, 117
vs. example, 54, 283 n. 17

Epstein, William, 259 n. 38

Equity, 100, 116, 117, 218, 268–69 n. 24, 269 nn. 28–29

Ēthos, 114, 136, 151, 183–91

Instrumental reason, 26, 40, 42, 51, 67, 69, 76, 145, 169, 184, 186, 243
Irony, 214–19, 221, 225–27, 229
Irwin, T. H., 214, 249, 274–75 n. 13, 293 n. 11, 296 n. 10

James, William, 289–90 n. 21
Jewish cooking and science, 149
Jonson, Albert R., 263 n. 19
Judgment
  as conclusion of rhetorical argument, 70, 106, 109, 114, 116–19
  ethical nature of practical, 99
  of particulars, need for, 58, 125, 129, 287–88 n. 11
Justice, 183, 218–26
  as subject for rhetorical argument, 58, 63–68, 97, 99
  as a moral virtue, 115, 130, 179, 217

Kant, Immanuel, 10, 55, 224, 250 n. 8
Kennedy, George, 86, 253 n. 9, 260 n. 1, 285 nn. 2, 3
Kenny, Anthony, 267–68 n. 21, 271 n. 34, 295 n. 3
Keyt, David, 261 n. 11
Kinesis, vs. *energeia,* 28, 33–40, 106, 116, 118, 144, 255 n. 15
Korsgaard, Christine, 261 n. 7, 281 nn. 4, 6
Kronman, Anthony, 290 n. 22

Ladd, John, 271 n. 34
Larmore, Charles, 270 n. 32
Lear, Jonathan, 249 n. 2, 250 n. 7, 256 n. 24, 260 n. 2, 263 n. 18
Leighton, Stephen R., 271 n. 1, 274 n. 8, 277 n. 28
Lennox, James, 261 n. 9
Levinson, Stephen, 291 n. 25
Lloyd, G. E. R., 249 n. 1
Logos, as source of proof, 36, 110, 114, 117, 145, 154, 159, 172, 185–91
Lomasky, Loren, 281 n. 6

Lord, Carnes, 251 n. 3, 258 n. 32, 273 n. 6, 279 n. 34
Lovibond, Sabina, 263 n. 19, 269–70 n. 30
Luban, David, 256 n. 22, 259 n. 38, 284 n. 20

MacIntyre, Alasdair, 5, 9, 33, 208, 249 n. 5, 253 n. 10, 255 n. 17, 256 n. 23, 259 n. 39, 281–82 n. 7, 292 n. 2, 293 n. 10
McConnell, Michael W., 264 n. 21, 266 n. 13, 266 n. 14
McKeon, Richard, 251 n. 4, 267 n. 21, 268 n. 22
Magnanimity, 226–27, 239
Maxim, 147, 152, 157, 159–60, 175, 197, 199, 200
Medicine, compared to rhetoric, 10, 25, 28, 29, 32, 33, 39–46, 186, 188, 216
Mill, John Stuart, 81, 257 n. 30
Modrak, Deborah, 274 n. 9
Moline, Jon, 265 n. 3
Moraux, Paul, 258 n. 32
Mourelatos, Alexander, 253 n. 9, 256 n. 25, 278 n. 30
Music, 48–50, 239–40, 290 n. 23

Nature, human; *see* Function, human
  internal principle of motion, 26, 32, 62
  vs. art, 32, 33, 228
  vs. convention, 56
  argument from, 66, 67, 69
  logical, 154
  vs. purpose, 27, 40, 120, 121, 227, 243, 245, 247
Nehemas, Alexander, 252 n. 7, 275 n. 15
Newman, John Henry, 142, 143, 177, 189, 280 n. 2, 281 n. 6, 289 n. 17
Nietzsche, Friedrich, 149, 188
Noble, subject for rhetorical argument, 64, 65, 68, 174